IN
TE

THE TERMINAL SPY

THE TERMINAL SPY

The life and death of Alexander Litvinenko

Alan Cowell

Doubleday

LONDON · TORONTO · SYDNEY · AUCKLAND · JOHANNESBURG

TRANSWORLD PUBLISHERS
61–63 Uxbridge Road, London W5 5SA
A Random House Group Company
www.rbooks.co.uk

First published in Great Britain
in 2008 by Doubleday
an imprint of Transworld Publishers

This book is a work of non-fiction based on the research of the author.
The author has stated to the publishers that the contents of this
book are true.

A CIP catalogue record for this book
is available from the British Library.

ISBN 9780385614153 (cased)
ISBN 9780385614160 (tpb)

Lines from 'The Second Coming' by W. B. Yeats are reproduced with the permission of
A. P. Watt Ltd on behalf of Gráinne Yeats.

Addresses for Random House Group Ltd companies outside the UK
can be found at: www.randomhouse.co.uk
The Random House Group Ltd Reg. No. 954009

The Random House Group Limited supports The Forest Stewardship
Council (FSC), the leading international forest-certification organization. All our
titles that are printed on Greenpeace-approved FSC-certified paper carry the FSC logo.
Our paper procurement policy can be found at
www.rbooks.co.uk/environment

Typeset in 11/14pt Sabon by
Falcon Oast Graphic Art Ltd.
Printed and bound in Great Britain by
CPI Mackays, Chatham, ME5 8TD

2 4 6 8 10 9 7 5 3 1

Mixed Sources
Product group from well-managed
forests and other controlled sources
www.fsc.org Cert no. TT-COC-2139
© 1996 Forest Stewardship Council
FSC

For Sue

CONTENTS

CONTENTS

AUTHOR'S NOTE

The reporting for this book began when, as head of the *New York Times* bureau in London, I covered the breaking news of the Litvinenko case in the days before and after his death. Over the subsequent weeks and months, my research expanded to include interviews and conversations with contacts and the key players in Austria, Britain, France, Germany, Israel, Italy, Russia and the United States. Throughout the book I have tried to identify by name the people I spoke to. But there were other sources who could not be so easily identified because of the nature of their work. In the case of informants able to speak only in return for anonymity, I have honoured their desire for confidentiality.

Alan S. Cowell
Paris, May 2008

DRAMATIS PERSONAE

The Victims
LITVINENKO, ALEXANDER: former officer in the KGB and FSB
POLITKOVSKAYA, ANNA: Russian journalist, murdered in Moscow,
October 2006

Visitors to London, November 2006
KOVTUN, DMITRI: former Soviet army officer, business associate of
Andrei Lugovoi
LUGOVOI, ANDREI: former KGB bodyguard, now owner of a private
security company and member of the Duma
SOKOLENKO, VYACHESLAV: former KGB bodyguard, business
associate of Andrei Lugovoi

Londongrad
ABRAMOVICH, ROMAN: wealthy Russian tycoon, owner of Chelsea
Football Club, former business associate of Boris Berezovsky
BEREZOVSKY, BORIS: wealthy Russian tycoon in self-exile in Britain,
bitter opponent of Vladimir Putin, one-time employer of Andrei
Lugovoi and Alexander Litvinenko
BUKOVSKY, VLADIMIR: Soviet-era dissident living in Cambridge
CLARKE, PETER: former head of British counterterrorism police
GORDIEVSKY, OLEG: former KGB double agent and defector to Britain
HYATT, BRENT: British detective investigating the murder of
Alexander Litvinenko
ZAKAYEV, AKHMED: exiled Chechen leader in London and neighbour
of Alexander Litvinenko

DRAMATIS PERSONAE

The Kremlin
MEDVEDEV, DMITRI: president of Russia nominated by Vladimir Putin
PUTIN, VLADIMIR: former KGB officer, ex-president, now prime minister, of Russia
YELTSIN, BORIS: former president of Russia

The Family
BELYAVSKAYA, NINA: mother of Alexander Litvinenko
LITVINENKO, MARINA: second wife of Alexander Litvinenko
LITVINENKO, MAXIM: half-brother of Alexander Litvinenko, living in Italy
LITVINENKO, NATALIA: first wife of Alexander Litvinenko
LITVINENKO, WALTER: father of Alexander and Maxim Litvinenko

The American Connection
FELSHTINSKY, YURI: Russian-American historian, sometime associate of Boris Berezovsky, living in Boston
GOLDFARB, ALEX: senior aide to Boris Berezovsky, living in New York
SHVETS, YURI: former KGB officer living in Washington, DC

The French Connection
LIMAREV, YEVGENY: Russian security consultant living in France

The Italian Connection
GUZZANTI, PAOLO: head of the Mitrokhin Commission investigating KGB activity in Europe
SCARAMELLA, MARIO: Italian researcher, consultant to the Mitrokhin Commission

The FSB Connection
GUSAK, ALEXANDER: former commander of Alexander Litvinenko in URPO unit of FSB
KHOKHOLKOV, YEVGENY: former commanding officer of URPO unit of FSB
PATRUSHEV, NIKOLAI: head of the FSB
PONKIN, ANDREI: former FSB colleague of Alexander Litvinenko in URPO unit

SHEBALIN, VIKTOR: former FSB colleague of Alexander Litvinenko in URPO unit
TREPASHKIN, MIKHAIL: FSB whistle-blower
TROFIMOV, ANATOLY: Moscow regional chief of FSB, murdered in Moscow, April 2005

Business Connections
GLUSHKOV, NIKOLAI: Berezovsky associate jailed in connection with Aeroflot embezzlement case
KHODORKOVSKY, MIKHAIL: former head of Yukos oil company, imprisoned on embezzlement and fraud charges

The KGB Connection
CHEMEZOV, SERGEI: contemporary of Putin in the Dresden station of the KGB, headed the state arms exporter
CHERKESOV, VIKTOR: former KGB officer in Leningrad, head of Russia's drug-control agency
IVANOV, SERGEI: former KGB spy, first deputy prime minister of Russia
IVANOV, VIKTOR: former KGB officer and senior aide to Vladimir Putin, chairman of Aeroflot
KHOKHLOV, NIKOLAI: KGB defector, poisoned in Frankfurt, 1957
SUDOPLATOV, PAVEL: former officer of Stalin's secret police

The History
CURIE, MARIE AND PIERRE: discoverers of polonium

THE TERMINAL SPY

PROLOGUE

The English autumn was unseasonably warm, and 1 November 2006 – the day Alexander Litvinenko began to die – was no exception.

A breeze from the northwest rustled leaves turned gold on the trees of Muswell Hill – a demure suburb of Edwardian terraced houses in north London. The temperature was in single digits on the Celsius scale but well above freezing. The red double-decker buses ran in their familiar not-quite-predictable way. Life unfolded with the unhurried complacency of far-flung neighbour-hoods when those abandoned to humdrum routines pause between the day's panicky bookends – the school run, the super-market, the dry cleaner, the post office, furtive affairs, perhaps, behind hastily drawn curtains.

The climate, not to mention the tranquillity, must have seemed incongruous to Litvinenko, a one-time secret agent turned whistle-blower, an exile and defector from his native Russia and bitter enemy of its regime. Raised for many years in the northern Caucasus, he had trained for a career in the KGB to spy on his comrades, to interrogate ragged child prisoners from Chechnya and to chase down the Russian mafia in Moscow. But Litvinenko had turned his back on all that, on everything he had been taught to do, as the Soviet Union dissolved into the new Russia. Brazenly, he defied his masters in Moscow, betraying what he insisted were their innermost secrets.

Now it was payback time, although, as so often in matters of deceit, the victim was the last to know.

On this day in late 2006 – the last when his life might pass for normal within the somewhat abnormal *émigré* circles he inhabited – Litvinenko bade farewell to his elegantly coiffed wife Marina and his gifted twelve-year-old son Anatoly, of whom he was exceptionally proud. He headed for the city centre – the capital of his own adoptive land. Just weeks earlier, on 13 October, Litvinenko and his family had been granted citizenship, and he boasted happily to friends that he was British. He brandished his pristine plum-coloured passport, proclaiming with an almost childish delight that it was his protector, the freshly burnished shield of this crusader against evil, this champion of the free (this tilter at windmills, some thought, this swashbuckling D'Artagnan).

To mark the family's new status, his son hung their new banner – the red-on-white cross of St George – from the first-floor balcony of the Litvinenkos' pale brick town house a mile north of the centre of Muswell Hill in Osier Crescent.

The three-storey house was one more unassuming home in a new-looking development in the commuter belt on a quiet street that filled with young children when the school day ended and with parked cars when the workday was over. But for Litvinenko it was his castle. Outlawed and outcast by the Kremlin, given refuge in London, he told his wife with tragic naivety that they were safe now.

In many ways the journey from his semi-gentrified suburb to Mayfair – London's swankiest square mile – offered a metaphor for his own life, caught between dream and reality, between modest circumstance and grand vision.

If, as Litvinenko had often done, you walk south from Osier Crescent and take the bus – the 134 – from the parade of shoe shops and off-licences and pubs on Muswell Hill Broadway, if you sit on the upper deck and peer out at the level of the lesser treetops, you will see a London the tourists never see, displaying its confused and conflicted soul – tawdry, vain, self-congratulatory, decaying.

After St James's Church, with its bright billboards and blunt entreaties to worship, the bus lurches and grumbles its way past the ivy-choked, ghostly trees of Highgate Wood, turning left on to the Archway Road, a north–south artery rushing with commuter cars and white-flanked delivery vans. If you want to spy, you peer into the first-floor bed-sitting-rooms of the houses along the route, but there is little to see beyond the greying net curtains and the weak glow of low-wattage lightbulbs. If you want imagined drama, you wait for the point where the road runs below the wrought-iron curve of the Hornsey Lane bridge, nick-named Suicide Bridge to honour those who leaped in despair and plunged a hundred feet into the traffic below.

But on this day, there is no despair for Litvinenko. He is spry of foot, nimble in his early forties. His thoughts are in a different London, in the London of five-star hotels and wealthy shopping streets, of discreet, whispering offices and plump consultancies, of contact with his erstwhile peers in the KGB, with people who, like him, inhabit an opaque world between illusion and reality, between conspiracy and riches.

In retrospect, it was easy to ask the question: why was this day, this Wednesday 1 November – not one day earlier, nor one day later – chosen to be his last in good health, and by whom? But then, on that day, there seemed to be nothing exceptional. There was no premonition of catastrophe.

'Sasha was absolutely normal,' his wife Marina recalled, using the affectionate form of her husband's first name by which his friends and associates knew him. 'Sasha was absolutely looking forward to life.'

Just a day earlier, he had bought expensive new boots – 'very high quality' – in a sale. He had plans, happy to be busy. 'Everything was just normal, as it was every time,' Marina told me during one of several encounters when she met me at rendezvous points of her choice – in offices and cafés and once on the steps of St Paul's Cathedral – to go backward and forward over her memories of their life together.

Most days when he headed into town, she would drive him to the Northern Line underground station at East Finchley to catch a southbound train on the High Barnet branch – a routine commuter ride through some of the city's oldest, deepest, grimiest tunnels. On that day, though, she had made promises to friends, she had other things to do, and he did not mind making his own way. He took a bus to start his journey, then the underground, using an Oyster card. For most Londoners, the cards were a commonplace, a device for discounted travel on public transport, linked to a central computer through terminals on buses and in underground stations. For Litvinenko, the card would offer a vital clue to the timing of a murder.

To look at him with his sandy hair and boyish mouth, perched on his seat, peering indifferently at the city luring him to his destiny, to its dark and glistening heart, you would not know that this is a man on such critical missions as Litvinenko has in mind.

His cover is intact. He does not stand out from the crowd. No one in his immediate circle – not even his wife – really knows what the day is supposed to bring or what it will, in fact, yield. No one would guess at this precise moment that the fate of Alexander Litvinenko will nudge East and West towards a revival of the Cold War.

The 134 bus route burrowed through the palimpsest of bleak and cosmopolitan modernity that time has spread over the Gothic frame of Victorian London – the kebab houses and betting shops, the McDonald's and Burger Kings and KFCs, the cold pubs, the angry, gridlocked traffic, the newsagents ('Shannon News – Irish and Continental Newspapers'), the unremitting gloom punctuated by Chinese takeaways and Balti houses, the Western Union money transfer shops, the ailing churches, the busy mosques. The stops along the route – Archway and Tufnell Park, Kentish Town and Camden – were places where life ground the people down, dealt them poor hands played out in council blocks and on benefits. By the looks of many of them, they seemed to be the walking wounded of cool Britannia, aged prematurely by alcohol and poverty, myopic from the failing light of shrinking horizons. On the street corners, on the bridge at Camden Lock, knots of peddlers hawked drugs. The young women with their hair pulled back from their pale faces wore tight jeans and spindly high heels, shaky as stilt walkers. The young men were hooded, inscrutable. Police officers ventured forth only in pairs.

On this day, among these people yet not of them, Litvinenko has higher goals. He rides the bus among the losers, but knows he belongs among the winners, a survivor of many adventures and near misses.

On 1 November 2006 Alexander Litvinenko was celebrating the anniversary of his flight from Russia to Britain. He had arrived by a circuitous route exactly six years earlier, on 1 November 2000. He had been given political asylum in 2001 as a precursor to citizenship. But, whatever the passport proclaimed him to be, Alexander Litvinenko, aged forty-three years and eleven months, never to reach forty-four, was still steeped in Russia, as his CV had moulded him to be: former counter-intelligence officer in the Dzerzhinsky Division of the Interior Ministry troops, former operative of the KGB (the Komitet Gosudarstvennoy Bezopasnosti, the Soviet Committee for State Security), and former lieutenant colonel in its domestic successor, the FSB (the Federalnaya Sluzhba Bezopasnosti, the Federal Security Service). In exile, he followed and fuelled Moscow's conspiracies, writing articles on dissident websites, publishing books, giving interviews to anyone offering a platform for his tirades against the Kremlin. He fed on news from the motherland, sought information assiduously, placing calls back to Moscow, exchanging e-mails across what had been the Iron Curtain. He sought friendships and information from those who visited from Russia. His grasp of English was imperfect, halting, and some of the people he met in London told him he should try harder. (His wife, by contrast, became fluent in the language, and his son Anatoly won academic acclaim in his English classes at an upmarket private school.) But he missed no opportunity to demonize the rulers of modern Russia, Vladimir Putin in particular.

Only days before his final commute, Alexander Litvinenko rose among an audience at the Frontline Club, a boozy journalists' haunt in the side streets near Paddington railway station, to denounce Putin in the murder in Moscow on 7 October 2006 of Anna Politkovskaya, a Russian investigative reporter of some renown, shot dead in the lobby of her apartment house co-incidentally on Putin's fifty-fourth birthday. 'My speech is difficult for me, can I use translator?' he enquired in accented English to preface his verbal assault on the Kremlin – one of many *J'accuse* moments in his *émigré* life.

Litvinenko lived among dislocated exiles, condemned to pine for a homeland that no longer existed in the way they recalled, and had not changed in the way they hoped. His passion was to expose the iniquities of his home country, to burrow under the Kremlin walls shielding the new elite. Among his friends and acquaintances, he counted former spymasters and Soviet-era dissidents, Chechen separatists, at least one self-exiled tycoon. He moved in a twilit, ambiguous world of rumour and riddles, populated by plotters and fantasists, hoodlums and propa-gandists. He cultivated people who, like himself in his final months, sought to turn KGB training into careers in private secur-ity, industrial espionage. He was big on ideas, short of cash.

After his death, the Kremlin went to great lengths to belittle Litvinenko as a thug, a lowlife, a former guard on military convoys, a man of no substance. But why, then, did someone spend so much money and time and flawed ingenuity to ensure that he would be launched unwittingly on to the trajectory of the most macabre and gruesome assassination of modern times? If he was a nobody, why snuff out the last flicker of his nonentity with such lurid drama? But if he was more than the Kremlin depicted him to be, what had he done to deserve a death that depended on such ingenuity and cruelty?

On 1 November 2006 Litvinenko's mental diary listed a series of critical meetings. All of them foreshadowed his murder, but one of them at least seemed improbable, melodramatic if not bathetic. He made a late start in Muswell Hill and headed into town. He bought a newspaper from a newsstand some time after noon at Piccadilly Circus, within sight of the statue of Eros, one of his landmark rendezvous points in central London. (He liked to ask people to meet him there so that he could observe them unseen, approach them without their knowing and startle them with a tap on the shoulder. Tradecraft, he called it.) That day he met with a man called Mario Scaramella, who walked west with him for a late lunch three hundred yards away in the itsu sushi bar on Piccadilly. Scaramella drank water. Litvinenko, an aficionado of Eastern food, took miso soup.

Scaramella was an Italian gadfly who had brought with him the printout of an e-mail warning that moves were under way among a sinister group of former KGB professionals called Dignity and Honour to harm Litvinenko, among many others. The e-mail offered hints about the murder of Anna Politkovskaya – a killing that fascinated Litvinenko and distracted him from considerations of his own security. The hit list was almost certainly a work of dubious value, a figment of some feverish or cynical imagination. Litvinenko was inclined to dismiss it as being without substance. But, in his case, it was curiously, improbably prophetic.

There is a lacuna in the publicly known reconstruction of Litvinenko's last day as a whole and healthy person – one or two hours that are not explained by the chronology offered subsequently for public consumption. The gap lies between Litvinenko's arrival in the city centre and his meeting with Scaramella. If he left Osier Crescent in the late morning, where did he go until his mid-afternoon meeting with Scaramella? Did he drift about town, knocking on his contacts' doors, filling time? Or did he leave home later, arriving in time to meet Scaramella and stroll past the clogged traffic on Piccadilly, past the bookstores and cafés, to the self-service haven of itsu? It was in that space that some sought the answer not to the question of why Litvinenko had to die but to an equally urgent question: how was he lured to this watershed, this *Wendepunkt*? And if the answer to 'how' can be found, perhaps the questions of 'who' and 'why' will become less mysterious.

From the itsu sushi bar, Litvinenko headed northwest towards Grosvenor Square and the Mayfair Millennium Hotel, close to the forbidding off-white rampart of the American Embassy beyond the Roosevelt Memorial in the square's gardens. From the front door of the hotel, on most workdays, you could see the lines of visa applicants outside the fortress-embassy, threading past armed British police officers through the concrete barriers designed to prevent truck bombings. (The building, constructed in easier times and opened in 1960, was seen as such an inviting target for Islamic militants that the wealthy people in the adjacent Georgian town houses complained noisily that their property values were deflated by the threat of collateral damage in what George W. Bush called the war on terrorism.) Grosvenor Square also hosted its own 11 September 2001 memorial gardens. Five years after those attacks in New York and Washington, the Litvinenko case was to offer the chilling possibility that terrorists might make his destiny a template for more insidious ways of spreading mayhem.

The revolving glass door at the Millennium gave on to a lobby in white stucco with gilded columns, a chandelier and banks of lifts with clock-like indicators to show which of the seven floors the lifts were on. There was a hint of faded glory, of pretension, about the place. It looked as if it ought to be a five-star hostelry; in fact it qualified for only four.

Litvinenko turned sharp left at street level, through the white double doors of the Pine Bar, where he met with at least three other Russians – Andrei Lugovoi, Dmitri Kovtun and, briefly, Vyacheslav Sokolenko. There was another man Litvinenko would describe as having cold, dark eyes. The bar was noisy, busy. He drank tea – green tea with honey and lemon – from a pot already on the table while his companions drank alcohol. At least four more Russians whose names were never publicly acknowledged sat in an arc surrounding the table where Litvinenko met his contacts. Were they players or bystanders, in place by accident or by design?

With one of the men at the table, Andrei Lugovoi, Litvinenko had business to talk about, a contact to be nurtured, a line to be kept open to events back home.

There were some who met him that day who would question whether the inexorable process of his demise had started earlier, in that mysterious gap between his commute and his appointment at the statue of Eros on Piccadilly with Mario Scaramella. But it was the Pine Bar that the British authorities identified as the place where Litvinenko's destiny took its final turn, on his adoptive home turf, on territory he knew well and reconnoitred often.

From the Millennium it was a two-minute walk to the offices of a private security company, Erinys, at 25 Grosvenor Street, where Litvinenko had, in the recent past, sought to learn the inside story of Russia's booming oil and gas business, to trade information on such corporate giants as the former Yukos and Gazprom – entities laden with secrets worth far more than one man's life. Grosvenor Square indeed provided a kind of centre of gravity for this downtown double life that Litvinenko led, away from his suburban home. At the end, Litvinenko's stock-in-trade had become what private security contractors call due diligence – the gossip and pay dirt on companies and individuals in Russia being sought out as business partners by Western entrepreneurs. It was a thriving business.

It may have cost Litvinenko his life.

From his hasty meeting at the Pine Bar he went on – not too far away – to the offices of his mentor, Boris Berezovsky, an exiled Russian oligarch with a reputation for ruthless and devious business dealings.* Berezovsky had made his money as an

---

*The use of the word 'oligarch' became widespread in Russia in the 1990s, initially to denote those people whose political influence in the inner circles of the Kremlin both derived from and yielded great wealth, acquired in the sell-off of state assets that marked the end of the Soviet Union. Later, it came to mean any wealthy tycoon. Berezovsky was one of the earliest examples of the term's original meaning.

entrepreneur-cum-politician in Moscow's freewheeling 1990s. In that era, his power was such that he was known as the grey cardinal of the Kremlin. (He sued *Forbes* magazine for calling him a godfather rather than a cleric.) In those days, like a snug inner layer of a Russian Matryoshka nesting doll, Berezovsky enjoyed the wraparound protection of President Boris Yeltsin, and then, in turn, folded his ambiguous embrace around his closest protégés and protectors – who, it turned out, included both Litvinenko and at least one of the men he met that afternoon in the Pine Bar. Berezovsky's influence and good fortune inside Russia did not endure; power turned to opprobrium and self-exile; and that wove another thick strand in the Litvinenko story.

Like Litvinenko, Berezovsky burned with a visceral hatred of Vladimir Putin, Yeltsin's successor, himself a former KGB officer, who had replaced Russia's chaos with a new nationalism – popular among Russians, menacing to outsiders.

On 1 November 2006, at Berezovsky's offices, Litvinenko xeroxed the papers he had received from Mario Scaramella. He handed them to Berezovsky, who said he was too busy to read them as he prepared to leave London for a brief business trip to South Africa. The two men were not as close as they had once been. But Litvinenko still had access to the rich man's office.

Finally, to complete a Russian's day in London, Litvinenko caught a ride home through the clogged traffic with a prominent Chechen separatist, Akhmed Zakayev, another exile sponsored by Berezovsky, another part of this modest galaxy of malcontents that orbited around the tycoon and his munificence. The Kremlin called Zakayev a terrorist and fugitive from justice. But his public persona in London was far more nuanced. A former actor who had performed Shakespeare, he impressed Westerners as courteous and elegant. He dressed neatly, favouring dark two-piece suits and colour-coordinated ties, tending carefully to his short silvery beard and quiffed hair. Among his allies he counted Vanessa Redgrave, the actor. Like Berezovsky and Litvinenko, he yearned for Putin's overthrow as his passport home to Chechnya. He was Litvinenko's neighbour, so they drove home through the traffic jams to Muswell Hill, where the day had started a few hours earlier with a bus ride.

At around 7.00 p.m., Zakayev dropped off his friend at the town house in Muswell Hill, then worth around £800,000, which Berezovsky had bought through a front company in the British Virgin Islands for around £350,000 in 2002 and placed at the Litvinenko family's disposal. (Berezovsky also paid Litvinenko around £5,000 a month to act as his agent and emissary – a stipend that had recently been severely reduced as the two men drifted apart.)

Litvinenko promised to call at Zakayev's nearby home later. But he never did. Instead, he stayed home with Marina and Anatoly and ate the chicken dinner – a favourite – that his wife had prepared for him, relishing, as she said often, the home-maker's role she had assumed in Britain. The recipe came from her mother, who had visited a week earlier: chicken diced small, mixed with herbs and sour cream, turned in a frying pan. Litvinenko liked it and had asked for it again on the anniversary of their arrival in London, so it was being prepared when he arrived home. There was no sign, at that precise moment when he entered the house, passing his homemade gymnasium on the way to the kitchen at the rear, that he had begun to die.

In Russia, Marina Litvinenko had studied the oil and gas industry at Moscow's Gubkin Institute. She had been on the professional ballroom dancing circuit and maintained a dancer's poise and power. She had taught aerobics and fitness classes. But now, with a smart new house and a son at school – as well as a husband prone to obsessions and crusades beyond the imagination of most Don Quixotes – she had adopted what she thought to be the ways of an English wife.

'I do everything for our son,' she told me. 'I am involved in everything he does, his activities, his trips.' She had tried to persuade her husband to be less of a serial conspirator, more of a father, and felt she was succeeding: Alexander Litvinenko had even started taking his son for swimming lessons. But Marina kept a close and not always approving eye on her husband's increasingly inflammatory writing in the articles he produced for Zakayev's ChechenPress website.

'I was a strong critic. I was very hard on him,' she said. But he was a different man from the one she had married in Moscow, more mellow perhaps, with fewer hard edges. 'I could see how he changed when he arrived,' she said. 'He was an officer of the FSB in England – but he changed into a different person.'

This small, tight-knit family seemed to find England to its liking, at least in Marina's account. 'I never had any second thoughts that I would like to leave England. We were very happy here. He was very proud of our boy. He said he was like a real English boy, and we had a lot of friends who supported us.'

But even on this special anniversary night, Litvinenko could not quite tear himself away from the parallel world of conspiracy. The following morning he had scheduled a meeting at a security company called RISC Management along with the men he had met at the Pine Bar, Lugovoi and Kovtun. He had e-mails to send, one of them to Vladimir Bukovsky, a Soviet-era dissident living in Cambridge and one of the leading lights in the émigré circle that had embraced the Litvinenko family.

Nothing in his behaviour suggested that he was in any way aware of the death sentence that had just been executed. He was a man preparing for life, not death. The family dinner in their unassuming suburban home was to mark the distance they had travelled together and the routes they planned for the future, certainly not the end of the road.

'On 1 November Sasha and I decided to have a family dinner in honour of the anniversary of our move to London,' Marina Litvinenko said. 'Sasha came home and didn't even stop by to see Akhmed Zakayev the way he usually does. He went upstairs, checked some information on the Internet and then we had dinner together.'

At 9.33 p.m. Litvinenko sent an e-mail to Bukovsky, attaching a photograph of himself twenty years earlier in camouflage uniform at the KGB's counterintelligence school, lying in a field of leaves in a forest aiming a sniper rifle on some kind of military training exercise. He seemed to be marvelling at the changes in his life that had brought him from a KGB academy to the suburbs of London. His caption, in English, read: '20th year ago! 1986'.

But then he began to vomit, uncontrollably, as if his entire body were in open revolt to expel some vicious, anonymous, irresistible intruder. He was racked with convulsions, bending over the lavatory to throw up. 'It's just like a horror movie, a mysterious coincidence,' his wife said. He became so ill that she made up a separate bed for him in the first-floor room that he had converted into a study where he kept his computer and his trove of files and videos.

No one in his immediate circle imagined that Alexander Litvinenko had fallen victim to what his father, Walter, would later describe as a 'tiny' nuclear attack. But the fact remained that on 1 November 2006, the sudden onset of an inexplicable, gut-wrenching nausea was the beginning of the end.

Twenty-two days later he was dead, poisoned in a manner that seemed to propel his native land and his adopted nation back towards the brink of the East–West confrontation. Nobody would, or could, answer the question, why? Those in high places who knew the answer were not talking. And those who did not know the answer could only guess. But the basic facts as they emerged were incontrovertible. Murder had been committed in broad daylight, near the American Embassy, in central London. The evidence pointed in one very clear direction – towards Moscow. Litvinenko's death was, in the words of one group of experts, 'likely [to be] the first provable act of radiological terror' in the Western world. But the unfolding of the Litvinenko story suggested that no killer would be brought to justice.

If you talk to people now and ask them what kind of man Alexander Litvinenko was, they will tell you – with varying degrees of forbearance or scorn – that he talked too much. He seized on ideas. He was undiscerning of the truth. He relished campaigns, reached wild conclusions. He was a zealot. He was flaky. He saw connections where no one else did. He was obsessive. But they will also say he was professional, an investigator, well practised in the dark arts of his business. He could get to the bottom of things, gather information, distil mysteries into actionable quantities. He had a great memory, phenomenal recall of dates, places, people, times. He loved his wife, his son, never smoked, never drank, never strayed.

Did that mean his hands were clean? Very unlikely: he had been trained in the counterintelligence branch of the KGB, where they did not breed gentleman spies. Were there stains on his record? Why not? He had interrogated Chechen prisoners for the FSB – the domestic successor to the KGB – and had worked for a secretive FSB unit in Moscow that he boasted openly was licensed to kill. So how could he be an innocent? Why would he not have used the terrible powers vested in him by his rank and calling, first in the KGB then in the FSB?

If you ask, people will reach for literary caricatures, not just D'Artagnan and Don Quixote but also Jekyll and Hyde – a dual person, sunny and open, naive, cruel, insecure; indifferent to money, desperate for riches; loyal, devious. 'Inside, Sasha always remained a child,' his father, Walter Litvinenko, a government physician who had worked in the Soviet penal colonies, said later. Perhaps, like a child, he fed an inner life with dreams and was uneasy with reality. Perhaps, his father meant to say, he was easily convinced of a righteous cause, undiscerning, lacking in judgement, too ready to trust those who meant him harm.

Yet people will also say that he made enemies, within his family, among his colleagues. He inspired violent reaction. He infuriated the Kremlin by publicly insulting Vladimir Putin, labelling him, among other things, a paedophile – a far cruder taunt than simply calling him a dictator, which might even bring some approval in his native land. Some of Litvinenko's former associates called him a 'scumbag', a Judas. He exasperated people, including his sponsor, Boris Berezovsky, and he used people as a sounding board for crazy ideas. He pestered them and attached himself to them, seeking benefit for himself and his causes. He tried to please, to help, to arrange other people's lives. But he quested for opportunity, advantage. If you ask those who met him, they will say he was physically fit, a model of abstemiousness. He could run – not jog – ten miles at a stretch. He pumped iron. He had a sense of humour that did not appeal to everyone: after his death the *Observer* newspaper got hold of a photograph showing him wearing a Scottish tam-o'-shanter and KGB-issue gauntlets, waving a double-handed Chechen sword. The eyes were cold, the face unshaven, the mouth tight, unsmiling, cruel. The portrait was taken by Pavel Stroilov, a friend of Vladimir Bukovsky's, to celebrate the family's naturalization as British citizens. The backdrop was a Union flag, and perhaps it showed just how many conflicting influences had coalesced in the man who began to die on 1 November 2006.

1

BROKEN HOMES, BROKEN EMPIRE

Alexander Valterovich Litvinenko was born on 4 December 1962, in a hospital in Voronezh, three hundred miles south of Moscow, a university town where his father was a medical student specializing in pediatrics. He arrived one month before term. He weighed 2.4 kilograms, around 6 pounds. His mother, Nina, remembered a difficult birth. She fretted he might not survive. Then a woman in another bed in her ward at the Soviet-era hospital told her that all eight-month babies became famous – an adage that no one would deny in Litvinenko's case, though not in the manner his mother would have forecast or preferred. Even so, who could have imagined that a child of the USSR would secure renown in such a bizarre manner, so far from home?

In 1962 Nikita Khrushchev was in power in Moscow, and the Soviet empire spanned half the globe, from central Asia to the Baltic and the Pacific, its satellite states patrolling the line that divided Europe. The Soviets had been the first to put a man in space – Yuri Gagarin – in 1961, a huge propaganda victory over the United States, challenging Americans with the shocking implication that Communism, progress and technology were not incompatible. This sprawling, secretive empire was not shy about confronting American power. Litvinenko was born in the year of the Cuban missile crisis that pushed the United States and the Soviet Union to the brink of nuclear war. True, Khrushchev had offered a kind of liberalization after the death of Joseph Stalin, permitting the publication of the works of Aleksandr Solzhenitsyn and famously decrying the Stalinist 'cult of personality'. But Khrushchev also led a muscular drive to cement Soviet influence. He approved the crushing of the Hungarian revolt in 1956, the building of the Berlin Wall in 1961. And at home, the state's writ ran unchallenged, its power exercised through the taut sinews of the KGB and other internal forces created to forestall dissent. Soviet troops occupied garrisons across Eastern Europe. Soviet spies tunnelled into the Western political establishment. When Alexander Litvinenko was born, the Cold War was decades away from any thaw, and the Soviet Union was years from collapse. None of that brought direct comfort to ordinary citizens struggling to get by, find an apartment, a telephone line, a car, a television set. The economy ran to order, according to the principles of scientific socialism. Save for the elite, and those with scarce American dollars or British pounds to finance themselves, there was no abundance. The output from the collectivized farms failed to keep pace with the growing population. The harvests were often poor. The shelves in the rubles-only food stores were never full, usually empty. Queues formed. In grim concrete apartment blocks, ordered up by Khrushchev himself to ease a dire shortage of dwellings in postwar Russia, communal heating sputtered and failed. The Russian winter had no mercy.

Litvinenko's life spanned his land's liberation and its emasculation – from oppressive superpower to something far less than that, yet something far more than an ordinary nation: a diminished land that dreamed of glory revived. He was a child of history.

'We lived in a small room in a hostel in Voronezh,' Nina Belyavskaya, Litvinenko's mother, recalled in an interview, sitting in the same two-bedroom apartment outside Moscow where her son spent some of his early years while his father moved on to the northern Caucasus and Russia's far east. 'We went hungry and cold because there was no food in the shops, no meat in Russia at the time. We used to buy bones.'

When she spoke in the summer of 2007, Nina Belyavskaya was sixty-seven years old, a frazzled, faded blonde living on the margins of Russian life, remote from the glitzy ostentation of downtown Moscow with its high-end imported cars and smart eateries. She tended a makeshift shrine to her lost son with a photograph and flowers and lived on a pension worth about £76 a month.

The early years were not so easy, either. Imagine a young woman in her early twenties, boiling bones for soup, prising open cans of cheap meat, suckling a child from reluctant breasts. 'There was no milk in the shops and I had very little milk. In the factory next to where I worked, they used to give workers special milk rations. I'd go there at 4.00 p.m. as people were leaving with their milk and would ask them to sell me a couple of bottles to feed my baby,' she said. 'Life was very hard.'

In the Soviet way, with the Russian Orthodox Church suppressed, his mother took the infant Litvinenko secretly to a priest for clandestine baptism – a common enough occurrence in those days.*

Through the rosy glow of maternal retrospect, Nina Belyavskaya recalled the early years of motherhood as a valiant single-parent struggle to make ends meet while tending an ailing but virtuous child.

'Sasha was a very good boy,' she said. He would come home from kindergarten – the kind of childcare the Soviet system offered to all so that all could work in their designated slots in the command economy – and balance on a stool at the kitchen sink to start washing the dishes she had left unwashed and tell her not to worry, he would 'do everything for you'. She gave him scarce kopecks to buy ice cream when he went for a day at the VDNK exhibition complex in northern Moscow. He returned with a cigarette lighter. 'I decided to buy you a lighter because you are

*In the very last days of his life, Litvinenko's adherence to his baptismal faith became something of an issue, but his family disputed the extent of its importance to him. His mother insisted that the young Sasha had no interest in religion at all.

always saying that by using matchsticks you are poisoning your-self,' he told her.

During his early school years, he made for her a wood burning – a pyrograph – depicting Snow White and the Seven Dwarfs, and she kept it throughout her life. He was a skinny, spindle-shanked boy, too eager to please, begging recognition, offering favours as a coded way of seeking love or at least attention. An early photo-graph of mother and son showed a wistful-looking woman with peroxide blonde hair, wearing a polka-dot dress, with the young Sasha in a white shirt and with combed fair hair, peering at the camera with a look that could be interpreted as reproachful or sulky. Neither of them smiled. In the young Sasha, there was an uncanny resemblance in the set of the mouth and the directness of the gaze to the iconic photograph of the dying Alexander Litvinenko that the world came to know in 2006. Then, as ear-lier, he sought attention.

'He was gentle and attentive and loving,' his mother said, but 'we didn't always have much time to spend together.

'Sometimes I'd come home and would do some work at home. "Mum, stop working," he'd say. "Let's spend some time together."' The loneliness of the latchkey kid would one day create a yearning for company, for a team, for a mentor. Sasha was never destined to be a loner. 'He was very sociable,' his mother said. When he was a young man and living away from her, 'I bought a lovely suit from Finland, and when he got back, I asked him where it was. He said he gave it to a friend who was going to Germany. He was one of those who would give anything to a friend.'

The precise calendar of those early years remained splintered through the rival memories of those close to him. Litvinenko's genealogy got caught up in a family whose lines bifurcated with divorces and liaisons of the kind that carried over into his own adulthood. Was he, thus, two or four years old when his parents split up? Perhaps it was enough to say that they did split up when he was a toddler, that Nina, his mother, met another man,

Vladimir Belyavska, and that this newly minted couple moved to Fryazino, just east of Moscow city limits, when Sasha was nine years old. His mother and stepfather produced a daughter of their own, Svetlana, a half-sister to Alexander Litvinenko, who went on to live in Germany. 'Sveta once asked me who I loved more – her or Sasha,' Nina Belyavskaya said, remembering a time when Litvinenko was in military training. 'I said: "Sasha, because you are always here with me and he is far away at the academy." Mothers always love their sons more.'

By his mother's account, the infant Sasha was sickly, prone to pneumonia and colds, but he grew into an open, gregarious child, shuttled between maternal homes in Voronezh and Fryazino and Nalchik, the capital of the Kabardino-Balkaria Republic in the northern Caucasus, where Alexander Litvinenko's grandparents still lived.

And then, on the other branch of his biological family, there was Walter, his father, who returned to Nalchik, his home town, in the northern Caucasus after graduating in Voronezh, abandoning a failed college marriage to build a second life with three more children – Tatiana, Vladimir and Maxim – and travel far away to Sakhalin Island on his business as a penal colony doctor.

In Walter Litvinenko's memory, his young son lived with his grandparents in Nalchik until he was five years old, then spent seven years with his mother before returning to the Caucasus. But the father and son never synchronized their lives. When Sasha returned to Nalchik, his father moved to Sakhalin. And when Walter returned from Sakhalin, Sasha went into the army.

The northern Caucasus, eight hundred miles southeast of Moscow, is known these days as an unstable area, perched uneasily on a fault line of faith and ethnicity. The string of cities that moulded so much of Litvinenko's life – places such as Nalchik and Vladikavkaz – were products of the advance of Russian imperialism in the late eighteenth and the nineteenth centuries, when tsarist armies built forts and sought with varying degrees of success and failure to subdue regions straddling access to the Caucasus and beyond. In these places, along a fissure of empire, Islam collided with Orthodox Christianity, and the Russian advance met fierce resistance for decades. Historians date the Caucasus War as lasting from 1817 to 1864 and argue that many of the modern conflicts that have seized the region, most notably in Chechnya and Dagestan, have their roots in those distant campaigns at the intersection of the same beliefs that moulded Alexander Litvinenko.

Yet when his mother sent her son to Nalchik as a child, her reasons had nothing to do with gods or conflict. The fresh air of the Caucasus foothills, 1,600 feet above sea level on the Nalchik River, was known for its restorative powers and its spas. 'I sent him for two reasons,' his mother said. 'Firstly, it was a healthier place but more importantly because I thought it would be easier for him to get into university there. He wasn't brilliant at school . . . It was hard to get into university then. You had to have an exam, but they took students in without an exam if you excelled at sports. In Nalchik there was a very good school for pentathlon. So I decided to send him there.'

Were there other reasons she chose not to recall? Possibly. In most broken families, memory is elastic, stretched between denial and half-truth – good training for spies and operatives at ease with ambiguity.

Decades later, with his own son on the cusp of his teens in London, secure in a family that had not divided, it is tempting to imagine Litvinenko thinking back to his own mixed-up childhood, his dislocations and resettlements, glad to be giving his own boy a modicum of security that was not, as it turned out, to endure.

In his early years, his mother said, he was drawn to collections of objects that could be ordered and controlled and catalogued – bright postage stamps and pins and toy soldiers and miniature tanks. She brought recruits for his small armies as gifts when she returned from trips to Moscow, she said, and there is something poignant about these platoons, these maternal brigades. Litvinenko's many critics said later he was no more than a toy soldier himself, a construct, an artifice created in a world outside reality. But he went on to witness the real wars that gnawed away his faith in Russia's political leaders as much as his belief in the Church of his secret baptism. When he was a child, his miniature heroes fell in tabletop battles. When he was a man, the games gave way to reality: a comrade died in his arms, he would recall for the benefit of interviewers, and others returned from the Chechen fray suicidal with despair, abandoned by the politicians who dispatched them to war. So maybe, after all, there was no room in a hardened heart for memories of a time when he played with toy soldiers.

If he compared his life with that of his own twelve-year-old son, perhaps Litvinenko's thoughts sometimes flipped back to his own age of pre-teen innocence and the first stirrings of love beyond his family. Alexander Litvinenko, too, was twelve years old when he attended a friend's birthday party in Fryazino and met an eleven-year-old girl called Natalia, who was to become his first love, his first wife. (He met his second wife at someone else's birthday party, too.) The way Natalia described those remote events, Litvinenko had struck up a close friendship with her cousins in Fryazino before she ever met him, but he became a regular caller at her family's dacha (her family was better off than his, Natalia said, and his mother thought her quite a catch).

'He was thin and modest, he did not stand out, but he was good-looking. He had big blue eyes and fair hair,' Natalia said. 'My two cousins were his closest friends. The three of them were always together. He was friendly. In the summer I and my cousins lived at the dacha, and Sasha would often come to visit. We'd spend the days running around the fields, swimming in lakes, and so on.'

How remote those memories seem from Litvinenko's destiny – the sunlit, endless summer days, the chill frisson of fresh, clean water on sunburned skin, the pollen in the air and the games of hide-and-seek and desultory, childish chatter in the heat of the day. It was a time when Soviet military and diplomatic power facing the United States was at its height, the time of Leonid Brezhnev's thaw in the Cold War that became known as détente between East and West. It must have seemed as if the world would never change.

'For both, it was our first love,' Natalia said. 'Once, we sat next to each other during a theatre performance, and for the first time we sensed this very strong feeling between us, a platonic love between two children which grew with every passing year.'

But, in those days as much as later, a dark shadow crossed the sun.

'Vadim, one of my cousins, even then told me that Sasha was not a good friend,' she recalled. 'He said he was tricky. He could betray you, he told me. I didn't ask why.'

One thing everyone seemed to agree on is that this young man, this future KGB operative whose death would unfold on a global stage, was no great achiever in class. His Russian grammar was poor. He liked maths and geography, but his grades were middling. He did better at sports. Walter, his father, said he cut classes to go shooting at tin cans, to nuzzle horses and ride them, to run. 'He was a bit like Forrest Gump,' his father said. He liked to play chess and to swim. He gravitated towards the modern pentathlon, which demands skills in pistol shooting, épée fencing, swimming, horseback riding and cross-country running. But he was never going to make it on to college without a bribe, a behind-the-scenes contact or an upsurge of academic excellence, and he had none of those.

Whatever he learned in class at No. 5 High School in Nalchik, or on the track, Alexander Litvinenko built routines with his grandfather, who had been an air force bombardier and had fought in the war against Japan. The Litvinenkos saw themselves as heirs to a proud military tradition. When I met Walter Litvinenko a year after his son died, he described how the young Sasha once declared to his grandfather that he did not wish to grow up to become 'a bloody soldier'. The old man responded by breaking a plate over his grandson's head. There were, of course, more benign moments.

Together grandfather and grandson visited the zoo and the

cinema. The grandfather gave the young Litvinenko a camera, and he enjoyed taking photographs. At the regional history museum, his grandfather showed him the Red Army banners from the Great Patriotic War, as the Second World War is known in Russia. In 1942 and 1943, Nazi forces briefly occupied Nalchik as their push to the eastern Caucasus faltered. The city had been devastated, and the memory of that destruction by outsiders infused a deep vein of patriotism. Russia, Alexander's grandfather told him, must always be defended against any future threat. The teenager took the message to heart. From his own perspective, whatever his critics said, Litvinenko was always a patriot, even if that meant saving the motherland from itself, from its own institutions and from its own leaders.

When his father Walter finally returned to his native Nalchik, he brought with him his newer family. Litvinenko was unsettled by their arrival, by the disruption of his routines, by the strangers sharing his father's time and affection.

So the picture emerges of a young Sasha, the latchkey kid, the nascent jock, a not-too-bright boy without a permanent family, moved from mother to grandparent, raised with a half-sister in the home of a stepfather, forever competing for attention with the children of his parents' other liaisons. When he was conscripted into the army at the age of eighteen, he was glad enough to go.

'In Fryazino his mother had a second husband and a daughter, and in Nalchik his father had a big family with many kids,' Natalia Litvinenko said during a long conversation in the summer of 2007 in the kitchen of her small wooden dacha outside Moscow – a modest place with no running water and an outhouse for a toilet.

'No one needed him,' she said. He 'didn't really have a proper family'.

In 1980 Alexander Litvinenko was drafted into the Interior Ministry forces, a unit totalling some 260,000 soldiers, responsible for an array of duties that included guarding strategic installations and, most importantly, quelling unrest and internal disorder that might threaten the iron grip of the Soviet Communist Party.

The force dated from 1919, when it was established as a uniformed wing of the NKVD – the forerunner to the KGB. Then the Interior Ministry took control, but by the time young Alexander pulled on his uniform for the first time, it had again been infiltrated by KGB counterintelligence operatives on the lookout for any signs of disloyalty. Litvinenko was to become one of these latter-day commissars.

For his mother, the choice of the Interior Ministry troops was a relief. In 1979, one year before Litvinenko was drafted, Soviet forces invaded Afghanistan, and the troops of the Interior Ministry were held back, out of harm's way, within the Soviet Union and its republics. But life as a conscript was not easy. When I talked with Litvinenko's father about his son's early life in the military, he became agitated, as much by the memory of the harsh conditions as by a sense of loss. 'We used to take him food, chicken,' he said. 'He was so hungry he would tear it apart with his bare hands and eat it.' The father told the story with appropriate gestures, mimicking the actions of a starving man. He leaped up to show how his son had grabbed the chicken. But his anger suddenly dissolved into a welling of tears, and he ceased his narrative, sitting down abruptly in his chair.

In his son's early days in the military, Walter Litvinenko recalled, the Communist system worked on individual networks of influence and contacts – people with debts to repay, obligations to redeem. And so, through various channels, Litvinenko secured a place at the Internal Forces military academy in what is now called Vladikavkaz, the capital of North Ossetia, a city of some 300,000 people only eighty miles from Nalchik. For much of the Soviet era, the city had been known as Ordzhonikidze, and in that period the military school had been named for S. M. Kirov, an associate of Joseph Stalin's assassinated in 1934. Some scholars perceive Kirov's murder as a pretext for unleashing a reign of terror that culminated in the murder of millions. Years later,

Litvinenko's friends raised similar questions about the Kremlin's pursuit and abuse of power. Would Russia's modern rulers resort to the same tactics of murder to cement their supremacy? Certainly Alexander Litvinenko believed so.

The academy – now called the North Caucasian Military Institute of Internal Forces of the Ministry of Interior of the Russian Federation – offered Litvinenko his first experience of life outside his extended family. He was an eighteen-year-old at the beginning of a four-year course that would mark him out as an officer – a career his parents welcomed. But he was also a young cadet in the throes of early manhood, casting about for love, for attachment, for passion. Adrift from his complicated family, he may well have been plain lonely, too.

Out of the blue, and after a silence of four years since his move to Nalchik, Natalia Litvinenko recalled, Alexander began writing to her to rekindle their childhood romance, although under different circumstances: she was on the rebound from a broken relationship with a boyfriend who left her; he was pining. Neither of them were children any more.

Alexander 'wrote many very affectionate letters. He was in the academy, felt lonely. I fell in love later. At first it was a way of getting over my boyfriend.' As an aside she also noted that his epistles were grammatically challenged. 'He couldn't write without making grammar mistakes. Later, when he used to write to me, I used to always correct his Russian and send him back his letter, covered in red marks.'

Whatever their literary flaws, the letters led to encounters, to trysts during the summer vacation in Moscow, to breathless phone calls and to yet more letters promising fidelity and undying love when the two were apart. The relationship blossomed. (Litvinenko's mother had always taught him to behave honourably with women: 'I used to say: "Don't run around after women, be sensitive and clear with them," ' she said.) But in the harsh light of jilted hindsight, Natalia recalled a stranger, darker side to him.

'At the academy, they had the equipment to listen in on phone calls,' she said. 'I was once chatting to a male friend of mine when suddenly Sasha's voice interrupted us, jokingly asking me who I was talking to. From Ordzhonikidze he had linked up and hooked into our phone call. It was a joke, but he was always checking on me. It was in his blood.'

In later life, Natalia recalled such moments to build a crescendo of enduring bitterness towards Litvinenko.

The wedding of Alexander and Natalia took place in Moscow on 25 August 1983. He was still at the military academy. She was studying optics at the Moscow Energy Institute and living at home with her parents in northeastern Moscow. The honeymoon lasted three days before he was obliged to return to his studies.

Alexander Litvinenko can no longer shape the debate about the nature of his childhood, this reconstruction of his growth to manhood. There are snippets and versions, captured on videotape, in notebooks, in memories. But ultimately, the picture that emerges is coloured by the judgements of those he left behind and their assessment of his nature, influenced as much by political as by personal considerations. There are flashes of insight, of tenderness, of treachery.

Consider, for instance, Natalia's memory of the birth of their first child, Alexander, on 5 January 1985, while the father was close to the end of his studies in Vladikavkaz and his young wife lived with her parents in northeastern Moscow, in the same apartment that Natalia lives in to this day. 'He was here on holiday at the birth, but then had to go back to finish his exams,' she recalled. When their son was just twenty-nine days old, he returned to Moscow. Natalia was still in the hospital after a difficult birth. This soldier from the Caucasus, this putative KGB operative accused later of so much cruelty and deceit, 'blushed at the sight of his son. He didn't know how to behave, was shy. His reunion with our son was a very beautiful and emotional moment.'

If he was uncertain around infants, he was less so in his career. Just as he had won a place at the military academy through family connections, Alexander Litvinenko pulled strings, courted the right people, networked. A friend's uncle had connections with the elite unit of the Interior Ministry troops – the Dzerzhinsky Division, named for Felix Dzerzhinsky, the head of the Cheka secret police, the wellspring of Soviet and Russian internal espionage. And that was the unit he joined after his four years in training school.

Its training manuals dwelled on crowd control, protection of the party leadership, keeping watch on sensitive cargoes – some of them human in the prison trains that rumbled across Russia's icy time zones. The Dzerzhinsky Division had fought outlaws in the 1930s and joined in the Battle of Finland in 1939. Its regiments guarded strategic locations such as the vaults holding the national gold and currency reserves and the perimeters of nuclear facilities. In the old days of the May Day military parade on Red Square before the assembled bosses of the Soviet Communist Party, soldiers from the division's Third Regiment would dress in police uniform, deployed in the huge, ornate GUM store across the way from the Kremlin, ready to put down any displays of dissatisfaction with the Central Committee.

The Dzerzhinsky Division was also known as ODON, the Separate Special Purpose Division, and it was garrisoned near Moscow. To be assigned to it was not just a smart career move, it was the kind of move an ambitious military wife like Natalia Litvinenko would approve – far more than being dispatched to some remote provincial garrison. But for Alexander Litvinenko it meant something else that would change his life: while still in the Dzerzhinsky Division, he joined the KGB, and from that point on his destiny was sealed, one way or another.

For, as countless former agents have testified, the KGB was a lifelong commitment: you might think you can quit, but you can never escape its long reach.

Little has been reported about the precise mechanism of Litvinenko's recruitment. Andrei Soldatov, a Russian journalist specializing in coverage of the intelligence world, told me that

Litvinenko's absorption into the KGB did not fit the normal pattern, largely because he did not have the usual college qualifications. Recruitment, Soldatov said, was 'normally from school or from technical university if you have technical skills in maths and so forth'.

But there was one account that drew little attention, and it came from Alexander Litvinenko himself in a remarkable four-and-a-half-hour interview in late 2001 with the British novelist Gerald Seymour. (The notes from the interview inspired the fictional character of a KGB interrogator called Yuri Bikov in Seymour's novel *Traitor's Kiss*.)

Seymour conducted the interview under unusual conditions. Apart from himself and Litvinenko, a third person was present who had arranged the encounter. Seymour promised to protect that person's identity, and he did. The circumstances of the interview, however, were such that Litvinenko would have found it difficult to mislead his interlocutors. He was speaking in the very early days of his time in Britain, and, Seymour indicated to me, the third person at the interview was a very knowledgeable invigilator indeed whom Litvinenko would have been reluctant – and probably unable – to deceive. Seymour handed me his notes from the interview only in return for a guarantee of anonymity for this mysterious 'third man'.

During his interview with the novelist, Litvinenko seemed to be on unfamiliar ground, not yet the noisy *émigré* he became and still feeling his way in a new life of exile.

'I had the impression that he had never done anything like this before,' Seymour told me when we met at his home in rural Somerset in early 2007. 'The idea that anyone would come and pick his mind was quite new to him. We spoke through an interpreter. The first thing that struck me was how young he was. He told me that he was a lieutenant colonel. I'm thinking: this is very much a high-flyer.'

But there was a hint of the sense of dislocation that would come later as Litvinenko hovered between his Russian roots and the uneasy transplanting to Britain.

'I felt very sad for this man,' Seymour said. 'I just thought he would be totally cut off.'

The very fact that Litvinenko had learned so little English in the period since his arrival 'is saying that this man has not accepted that he has to integrate and become English and get a job and do a couple of lectures a year. He's living the life of a refugee. It must be a sign – the failure to learn English, the failure to be employable.'

From Seymour's notes it emerged that Litvinenko's recruitment to the KGB was a slow and cautious process. When he first joined the Dzerzhinsky Division, his day job was hardly spectacular. As his enemies in the Kremlin recounted with scorn after his death, he was no James Bond. Along with others, he guarded trains carrying diamonds, gold bullion, currency printed in Russia for use in Cuba and Mongolia. The trains carried prisoners, sometimes women. ('They'd jump on a man, like animals, if they had a chance,' he told his wife.)

But within his unit Alexander Litvinenko was working towards a new goal – the cherished invitation to join the KGB, at that time considered a matter not just of patriotic pride but of advancement and benefit. Of all the military units, Litvinenko told Seymour, the Dzerzhinsky Division had the highest per capita proportion of KGB informers enlisted to snoop and report on their fellow soldiers.

Three officers from the KGB, or its successor, the FSB, were attached to every regiment, and each officer was required to recruit a minimum of twenty-five sources. 'Some would be the wives of officers or troops, some would be locals living close to the barracks. In addition, each officer must recruit a further thirty "confidential sources" – agents who are less important and do not have files maintained on them,' Litvinenko explained. 'Out of the 1,000 officers and men in the regiment there could be 170 sources and confidential sources.'

Russia at that time was moving, finally, towards liberalization. In 1985 – the year Alexander Litvinenko joined the Dzerzhinsky Division – Mikhail Gorbachev became general secretary of the

Communist Party and, later, the executive president until the coup of 1991 that deposed him and brought Boris Yeltsin to power.

Gorbachev's rallying cries were 'glasnost' and 'perestroika' – 'openness' and 'restructuring'. But the break with the old Soviet ways did not seem to extend to the KGB. By the account relayed to Gerald Seymour, Litvinenko was first recruited as a 'source, then is invited to join the KGB after two and a half years with the division. He becomes a cadre officer of the KGB, a first-year candidate. He has been a source for one year at that time. In his probation period he writes reports on many fellow officers that are scrutinized by the KGB for reliability.'

There was no hint here of opposition to the KGB or its function. Litvinenko emerged from this conversation with Seymour as an ardent agent in the making. When people protested much later at the use of the word 'spy' to describe him, they chose a narrow definition of the word relating to overseas espionage.

True, Alexander Litvinenko was not a KGB First Directorate agent sent to the West, or even a lesser spy like Vladimir Putin dispatched to East Germany, then a vassal state of the Soviet Union. But he was an officer in the Third Directorate – counterintelligence, which meant spying on his comrades to vet their loyalty and to seek out enemy agents. And his family was proud of him.

'Joining the KGB was an honour then,' Natalia, his first wife, said. 'There's a big difference between the Ministry of the Interior and the KGB. A different level. Much better people. This opened up all sorts of opportunities, a far cry from guarding prisoners all your life,' she said.

His father Walter said the popular image of the KGB was built on propaganda television programmes depicting valiant Soviet agents infiltrating Hitler's armies during the Second World War. 'I was very pleased when Sasha was asked to join the KGB,' he told me. 'It was very honourable.'

KGB agents interviewed both Alexander and Natalia to assess their loyalty and suitability. Natalia hoped her husband would one day become a general. But there were many delicate steps along the way for a young couple starting on what had all the makings of a good career.

With their infant son, they set up home for two years at the KGB Military Counterintelligence School in Novosibirsk in Siberia. The early days were not all free from difficulty, from challenges to be met, in part by pulling strings, calling in connections. As a newly commissioned KGB officer, Alexander Litvinenko was assigned to a dismal outpost in Novomoskovsk, six hours south of Moscow – an experience his wife did not enjoy and set about reversing.

'They gave us a derelict small house full of rats. To make things worse, we were close to a TB colony. I went to see one of Sasha's bosses and caused a big fuss: "We can't live here. My child is sickly." Eventually we started renting a small flat but didn't spend more than a year. We managed to get sent back to Moscow, thanks to influential contacts my family had.'

Litvinenko returned to the Dzerzhinsky Division, this time as an agent of the KGB, a commissar of sorts. The job commanded an unusual status, at least in the account he gave Gerald Seymour, since KGB officers could make or break the careers of the less exalted commanders of the Interior Ministry forces. No promotion was approved without the KGB's assent. To the highest level of the command structure, counterintelligence officers shadowed the division's own hierarchy. And the division itself occupied a special position on the outskirts of the capital, its garrison resembling a separate city with its own subway line to transport troops into Moscow to put down unrest if needed. The assignment was perfect for Natalia Litvinenko, determined to enhance her husband's career and keep him out of harm's way. When Sasha was dispatched to danger zones, she wasted no time in trying to bring him back.

One of the first of his trouble spots, in the late 1980s, was Nagorno-Karabakh, the object of dispute between Armenia and Azerbaijan. 'I was very scared. He used to call me on a special line, and I could hear shooting in the background,' she said.

It was not the life she sought for them. She had a clear sense of the way rank and power would bring them comfort and security throughout their lives, a place in Moscow, a job at the Lubyanka – the dread building in central Moscow that housed the KGB headquarters – a proper apartment, a car and driver and prestige.

'I always used to tell him that we didn't need much money,' Natalia said. 'As long as he was in the KGB-FSB, he had power, and that counts more than money. I used to tell him that money solves nothing unless you have power, and if you leave the Lubyanka, you'll have no power. Now you have power and a gun, we don't need much money. You'll become a general, a KGB general; you won't need anything else.'

Through her family, she said, the couple had access to high-level people who influenced his career and his deployments. That was not peculiar to the old Soviet Union or the modern Russia: many societies operate on hidden channels of influence and patronage. But Litvinenko's reliance on a patron, a mentor, seemed to be a recurring pattern of behaviour: a Russian saying has it that everyone needs a *krisha*, a 'roof', for protection.

'After a while, thanks to recommendations people in the KGB gave, he was transferred to Moscow. We had a good family, I had good parents, a good education. I always pushed him because I wanted him to become a general,' Natalia said.

At times he took the networking too far.

'He came home from work, and instead of spending time with his son, he'd get on the phone and start making calls. First one KGB general, then another, to wind them up against one another. I worried and told him to stop lying to these people, to stop plotting. He wouldn't listen. He loved intrigue, muckraking. He did it to further his career. It was his hobby.'

And there was one incident later, close to a turning point in Litvinenko's life, that showed his first wife how he defined his loyalties, and the extremes to which he was prepared to go to pursue them. It happened soon after Litvinenko moved on from the Dzherzinsky Division in 1991 to join the KGB at its Moscow headquarters, just as Russia was teetering on the cusp of the chaotic era dominated by Boris Yeltsin. Natalia explained:

I remember once, at night, we were chatting in bed. I told him that at work some women had come up to me to ask me to add my signature to a petition in favour of Yeltsin, who at that stage was in opposition to Gorbachev. I was against Yeltsin and refused. They started putting pressure on me. I didn't like the way they sought to force me. I told Sasha about it that night and complained that they had put so much pressure on me. The next day as soon as I arrived at work – a plant which developed military equipment – I was summoned to a huge office. We had KGB officers at the plant since it was linked to the military and developed sensitive equipment.

I was met by three men. Our local KGB officer and two from the Lubyanka. And they started to question me. They wanted to know who had been putting pressure on me to sign in favour of Yeltsin. I refused to give them any names and was amazed. Sasha – that morning – after I had told him about it in bed, had gone to work and reported the incident. He snitched. I was very upset and scared. He saw it as his duty to report it because he had to support whoever was in power, in this case Gorbachev, and therefore to report anything he'd picked up which could be seen as being against Gorbachev. I was shocked and felt betrayed. I confronted him that night. 'Why the hell did you report something so trivial which I told you in a private conversation?' He didn't care and barely listened. I saw it as an act of treason. It was a small incident, but looking back at it now, it was very telling. He was inclined to betraying.

The history of Soviet control in Russia and across Eastern Europe was studded with instances of families divided by informers, and so perhaps this episode was not exceptional in the culture of the times. Perhaps, too, it displayed the evolving nature of the patriotism that Litvinenko claimed to embrace in different ways throughout his life.*

---

* I offer the anecdote with a note of caution since it may be coloured by the harsh judgements of a former spouse, or it may in a perverse way show the extent to which he sought to protect her in the complex political shoals of his calling.

*

When you asked people after his death what kind of person Litvinenko was, there was no uniform answer. As with most families – broken or whole – the Litvinenkos built their own memory, their own narratives. Litvinenko was different things to different people, and their perceptions of him cancelled each other out to the end – hero and villain, Judas and martyr, man of courage and coward.

In the months after his death, there was a snatch of poetry that, as much as anything, revealed something of Litvinenko's questioning about his identity. The poem surfaced in a state-sponsored and very negative television documentary about him in which mother and ex-wife both referred to lines he was said to have penned in London, his only poem, perhaps concocted – who knows? – as he mulled over life from the grimy window of the 134 bus. The documentary evoked the anguished musings of a man wondering whether, after death, his soul would migrate to become 'the soul of a scumbag, and an executioner'.

Each version of this same personality provides a point of departure to see the man who began to die on 1 November 2006. At the simplest level, Litvinenko was a symbol, a cardboard cut-out, a pawn in a bigger game played by people who did not seek his consent. But the accounts provided by his family and parents and colleagues suggest a much more complex figure.

Asking that question – who was Alexander Litvinenko? – I was tempted to ponder whether opposites could be contained within the same entity without one dominating the other, whether conflicting personalities could coexist in the same person.

In Litvinenko's case it might be more accurate to say that he revealed himself to different people in different guises depending on his requirements of them – hardly an exclusive characteristic. For such people, good and evil, light and shade fight a perpetual battle for dominance. But some of those Litvinenko left in his wake had much less sympathetic words to describe him.

With the cruelty of the abandoned, his first wife ascribed his behaviour to clinical schizophrenia: 'I think that Sasha was ill . . .

I think that even when he was still with me, he behaved strangely at times.'

Towards the end of the conversation at her dacha, the condemnation moved into strident high gear. 'I think he was a traitor because he betrayed his family, the FSB, his country, his religion. By nature he was very slippery. He was not transparent. He loved intrigue and plotting and all that. You'd look him in the eyes, and I'd feel sorry for him and think he's honest and open and so on, when in fact behind his eyes was a mess. He was messed up. He was a terrible person, a traitor, someone who could do anything.'

From her point of view, the biggest betrayals began when two new people entered the life of Alexander Litvinenko, setting him on a course that would wrench him far from his provincial roots and loyalties.

One was a ballroom dancer of modest means called Marina Shtoda. The other was a very rich man called Boris Berezovsky.

2

POOR MAN, RICH MAN

Boris Berezovsky's tastes ran to big cars, very expensive wines and political intrigue for the highest stakes. Slight of build, he had a manner that seemed somehow larger than life. He lived on a 215-acre estate at Wentworth, in Surrey, in a home that, he said, he bought for £14 million in 2001 after a marathon bout of wine drinking and deal making to persuade the property's owner, who had only just acquired it, to sell it. When Berezovsky commuted into town, it was usually in a convoy that included a $600,000 Maybach sedan – the very top of the Mercedes range – and a dark-windowed SUV (also Mercedes) laden with French body-guards.

In his offices at 7 Down Street in Mayfair, the curtains were permanently closed to thwart snipers and snoopers. He had sur-vived assassination attempts in the past and took elaborate precautions to avoid them in the future.

In many ways, Berezovsky was the most public of Vladimir Putin's enemies – a self-exiled, self-appointed advocate of regime change in the Kremlin whose campaign became all the more strident after he fled Moscow in 2000 to escape certain imprison-ment on fraud charges.

In other ways, he was the most elusive.

One moment he seemed to be everywhere, giving interviews and holding news conferences, offering himself up to scrutiny at places like the Frontline Club, the journalists' haunt where Alexander Litvinenko made one of his last public appearances in October 2006. In mid-2007 Berezovsky appeared on a late-evening political talk show. He wore smartly tailored dark suits and expensive white shirts without a tie, his balding pate ringed by a tonsure of dark hair. As a former owner of television stations, he enjoyed the attention of the cameras, even in settings he could not control with the same facility that he once enjoyed among Russia's most powerful media tycoons. When he summoned reporters to press conferences, usually at short notice to keep his opponents off guard, he liked to charter a colonnaded auditorium at the Royal United Services Institute, a venerable private policy research institute in Whitehall at the heart of ministerial London. Other considerations apart, the choice of venue projected a sober respectability, suggesting a direct line to the inner sanctum of British policy-making.

When he dropped out of sight, he was nowhere. An aide answered his cell phone. Requests for access went unanswered. He might be in Britain or Israel, or anywhere – except Russia, of course, or any of a growing number of places, such as Brazil, where Russian prosecutors pursued him with legal suits demanding extradition to Moscow. Wherever it was, he was incommunicado. His political life was public; his business dealings were not.

His exits and entrances always smacked of melodrama, as if designed to be theatrical in their impact. Berezovsky generated the impression that his destiny, as much as his view of the world, was framed in absolutes: life and death, good and evil, freedom and tyranny.

On one occasion in the summer of 2007, for instance, he disappeared and reappeared weeks later to say he had travelled to an undisclosed hideout on the advice of Scotland Yard after receiving word from confidential sources in Moscow that a hit man – travelling with a child as cover – had been dispatched to shoot him dead in the five-star Park Lane Hilton close to his office. Coming from anyone else, the story might seem preposterous. But

Scotland Yard did indeed confirm that a Russian man had been arrested and deported. The episode revived memories of the gun-slinging 1990s in Moscow, where Berezovsky made his fortune, moving from threadbare obscurity to high-octane celebrity and riches with bewildering speed and determination. History offered Boris Berezovsky the chance to seize a great fortune; and he took it with both hands.

When the Litvinenko story broke in late 2006, it introduced the world to a cast of idiosyncratic, complicated and sometimes sinister characters, many of them clustered around Berezovsky.

Among them, he ranked as the wealthiest, most influential and most compelling, a man who had moulded Russia's fortunes in the 1990s, manoeuvring with presidents and billionaires, only to be cast aside in a new century. His résumé generated myriad questions about his tactics, his ruthlessness, his morality. People who studied his life labelled him menacing as frequently as they evoked a certain roguish charm. A fellow billionaire, George Soros, called him an evil genius. People like Marina Litvinenko called him caring and supportive, spontaneous in his generosity towards those he trusted. But all the assessments had one common strand: the labels attached to Boris Berezovsky were never bland or uncomplicated.

Since he was the man who bankrolled many of those drawn into the drama of Alexander Litvinenko, it was not surprising that people turned to him for answers when they asked why Litvinenko had to die. Sometimes he responded. Other times he did not.

Boris Abramovich Berezovsky was born on 23 January 1946. The Second World War was over, Nazi Germany had been defeated and the Cold War was beginning. Joseph Stalin ruled the Kremlin and spread Soviet Russia's tentacles across great swathes of Eastern Europe.

The intimate details of Berezovsky's childhood remained unchronicled for much of his life, but he seemed happy enough to fête his early years during a conversation one blustery evening at his London offices a year after Litvinenko died – one of several interviews with him, dating back to 2003. He was about to leave for a visit to Israel and was wearing a black crewneck sweater and blue jeans. We had spoken before in the inner sanctum of his office, where he presented me with a set of *The Art of the Impossible* – a three-volume, 1,800-page compilation of news reports about him and transcripts of interviews with him dating from the 1990s and including some references to his early years. (The weight of the volumes offered ample testimony to Berezovsky's determination to make his case.) This time, we met in the boardroom of his offices and spoke across a long, gleaming conference table. In a hallway outside, the walls were covered in artfully printed black-and-white photographs of Russian leaders from Tsar Nicholas and Lenin to Khrushchev and even including an image of Vladimir Putin. I wondered whether Berezovsky still saw himself as a claimant to inclusion in this pantheon. As we sat down to talk, he offered me a copy of *Verdict*, a newly published tome containing the full transcripts of a successful libel suit brought by Berezovsky in a British court against adversaries in Russia who had accused him of threatening them. We began with his earliest memories.

'I felt absolutely happy. My childhood was absolutely fantastic,' he said with obvious enthusiasm. To keep the conversation focused, I presented him with a list of written questions, which he had not seen in advance but which he answered assiduously.

'I really was an only child,' he said. 'My mother, she is still alive. She had her eighty-fourth birthday. Now living in France. She was a nurse at the Institute of Pediatrics in Moscow. My father died in 1979. He was an engineer in a factory producing bricks.'

His father, he said, worked in several plants outside Moscow so that 'my first six years I spent in the countryside.' In those days of postwar hardship, Berezovsky said, 'we were not wealthy but we were not poor.'

I asked him about his own personal experience of being raised as a Jew in Soviet Russia, and as at other times, in other interviews, he seemed to prefer to refute any suggestion that he had suffered in his childhood from anti-Semitism.

'My father was Jewish, my mother semi-Jewish – Italian, Ukrainian, Russian, Polish – many bloods,' he said. 'Until ten or eleven, I did not know anything about my identity – Jewish or Russian. My family was very, very cosmopolitan. I didn't feel anything at school. When I became eleven, I started to feel that people say that I'm Jewish: it was not any special pressure.'

He did acknowledge, though, that his family suffered more than others in the final years of Stalin's rule. 'My father had a complicated time. There was an anti-Semitic campaign by Stalin. At that time we were poor. Didn't have enough food.'

Elsewhere, Berezovsky had spoken of an earlier incident that made him aware of his Jewishness when he was around eight.

'We had a fight with other boys at the skating rink, and one of our opponents said: "You are Abram." I was surprised that he knew my patronymic.' But it was only much later, he told me, when he was sitting entrance examinations at Moscow State University, that he sensed that being a Jew might close doors open to non-Jewish Russians.

In the Soviet Communist era, religion was officially suppressed, and Berezovsky dismissed any suggestion of zealotry in his family or upbringing. He grew up, he said on several occasions, as a Soviet boy, keen to join the Young Pioneers and the Komsomol youth movement, never seeking to emigrate to Israel, as other Soviet Jews did.

'I never heard in my home that Jews were good and Russians were bad. I wouldn't say this theme was taboo; there were just lots of other topics for discussion. I don't know if it is good or bad, but I never received a Jewish impulse in my life.'

That was a way of saying that Berezovsky's attitude to faith was never dogmatic, always flexible. 'I was never under pressure to be religious,' he said. In 1994, he formally adopted Christianity, even though, at the time, he had acquired Israeli citizenship alongside his native Russian nationality. Later, he stuck by his decision. 'As long as I am on this way' of Christianity, he said, 'the more I believe that I made absolutely the correct decision.'

Some reports spoke of Berezovsky's parents listening in late at night to the foreign radio broadcasts that brought uncensored – or at least pro-Western – news into Soviet Russia.

But he was at pains to insist that there was nothing about the Berezovskys that threatened the Soviet state. 'They were never dissidents. They were very loyal to the system,' he said. He had a happy childhood, he said, because his parents 'loved me very much.

'We were an absolutely typical Soviet family,' he said. 'Not VIP.'

Compared with his life as a tycoon – the country mansion, the big cars, the Château Latour – his early ambitions were modest, like those of most Soviet citizens, centred on acquiring life's basics: an apartment, a car and a television set, objectives that seem laughable in light of Berezovsky's later opulence. For a career, he chose science and mathematics – not likely to earn him great riches – following a traditional route through Soviet academia.

He studied at the computer technology department of the Moscow Forestry Engineering Institute – a curious location for work that related to the Soviet space programme. After his graduation there in 1967, he moved to the mechanics and mathematics department of Moscow State University and the prestigious Academy of Sciences. His postgraduate qualifications included the equivalent of an American Ph.D. and the more stringent Russian doctorate. (His official biography noted that he wrote 'more than a hundred scientific articles' and 'two monographs on the theory of optimization'.) 'I married when I was very young, when I was twenty-three, and almost in two or three years had two children,' he said in late 2007 as an aide brought him a china cup with tea and a saucer of honey on the side. 'I looked after my family for myself: my parents weren't able to help.' Science brought few material benefits beyond the rare and cherished ability to travel abroad. Real privilege, he said, was reserved for high Communist Party and KGB officials. To illustrate the point, he told the story of how he shared a car with a friend.

'To have a car in the Soviet Union was exclusivity. It was not like today. Definitely not many people had that. I had a friend who got his car from his stepfather – a second-hand car . . . I was using it one week and him the next.' While the Mercedes and the Maybach came later, the first, shared car was a Soviet Zhiguli – the most basic of vehicles produced in conjunction with Fiat of Italy and exported under the brand name Lada.

Berezovsky said he joined the Soviet Communist Party in the late 1970s, but claimed not to have used his affiliation to advance, as some others did. Rather, it was in academic life that the seeds of his first fortune were sown. At the academy's Management Research Institute, he specialized in computer and automation systems for state-run businesses, including the car industry. His contacts with Soviet car-manufacturers were to prove central to his meteoric rise to riches as seven decades of Communism collapsed in the late 1980s, opening floodgates of rapacious, pre-capitalist asset-grabbing. But the impetus to desert academe in favour of business came from simple expediency. In 1989, state institutions stopped paying wages as the reform programme instituted by Mikhail Gorbachev began to falter. In response to the withdrawal of his salary, Berezovsky went into business, and when his friends asked if he was crazy to do so, he asked them which was crazier: to continue working for no salary or to try something different?

His generation was well placed for the kind of Wild West, new frontier, robber baron capitalism for which Moscow became famous in the 1990s. Russia was a nation navigating economic and political *terra incognita* in one of the greatest peacetime upheavals of the twentieth century. There were no precedents to cite and few laws to set limits on or regulate the behaviour of those who chose to make their fortunes. Berezovsky had been a scientist, but his past no longer interested him. Now he wanted wealth, not simply for its own sake but as a passport to political power.

He bought a used Mercedes in West Germany for 5,000 marks and sold it in Russia for four or five times as much. 'Then I took friends' on the next Mercedes-buying trip, he said with a punch-line grin. 'Ten of them.

'And it's the point where I understand business: people want and I deliver,' he told a packed, paying audience at the Frontline Club in June 2007.

The reminiscences sounded a little rehearsed, and many of his listeners remained sceptical of his subsequent record. At the time he was growing rich, many Russians were struggling to get by. One scheme of his to produce a 'people's car' financed with shares bought by ordinary people led nowhere and offered no return to its investors. But he deflected any suggestions of impropriety, saying the opportunities he seized were there for anyone to seize: few did.

Wealth empowered him, liberated him, but made him restless for new ventures. For most people, the attainment of an ambition might be an end in itself, but in Berezovsky's case success almost seemed to devalue itself. 'My previous goals had been achieved and thus destroyed, and I had to formulate my goals anew,' Berezovsky said.

So, his audience at the Frontline Club wanted to know, was he a crook in those crazy days when fortunes could be made as the planned economy disintegrated far from the purview of any form of economic oversight or financial regulation? After all, as Honoré de Balzac, the French novelist, wrote, every great fortune hides a great crime.

'As far as morality is concerned, I did not feel that I was immoral at that time. I used just my personal knowledge, my personal understanding,' he said.

'Everyone who recognize it's time of changing becomes successful,' Berezovsky insisted in his accented, rapid-fire, not-quite-grammatical English, whose flaws did not discourage him from making his points with speed and vigour.

'It's a different story how they operate. Some people just make million or two and go to islands and forget everything. Some people continue their way. I never accept that I have done something criminal.'

It was, he insisted, a time when the bold and the brave would succeed. But even by that simplistic yardstick, not everyone had the same driving urge for success, or the right connections to turn an idea into wealth. And not everyone acquired the same reputation as Berezovsky for ruthlessness even beyond the conventions of capitalist acquisitiveness.

In his time he owned or controlled television stations, newspapers, oil and aluminium companies, car dealerships, real estate and the Aeroflot airline. He acquired and manoeuvred, amassing billions. His fortune was matched only by a reputation for manipulative dealings. When people looked for historical comparisons to define Berezovsky, they reached for names like Machiavelli or Rasputin. His nicknames were not flattering.

In some photographs he bore a passing resemblance to a brooding Napoleon, also repulsed at the gates of Moscow. But no one's opinion was neutral. No one depicted him as anything less than an unscrupulous wheeler-dealer, or a charming rogue, or a misunderstood genius, or possibly all three in one.

When he first crossed paths with an unknown investigator called Alexander Litvinenko, Berezovsky was already rich and on his way to billionairehood, part of a coterie of fortune hunters who emerged from obscurity to translate the age-old alchemy of business and politics into massive wealth.

As a state-employed scientist, he had lived a modest life. But there was something disingenuous about Berezovsky's caricature of himself as an itinerant maths Ph.D. who happened to buy a used Mercedes in Germany, rather as if Henry Ford had depicted himself as a simple car mechanic. Berezovsky's deals were much more complex, and the era in which he made his money was unparalleled, too – a frenetic dash, in the name of a new capitalism, to privatize the old Soviet Union and its resources of gas and oil and minerals at bargain-basement prices.

If it was capitalism, then it was the kind of crony capitalism that depended more on connections than on free markets. George Soros, the Hungarian-born financier who had dealings with Berezovsky in the 1990s and later fell out with him, called it 'robber capitalism'.

Russia had no exclusive hold on the combination of patronage and profit, but Moscow's new moguls seemed to go about it in a much more obvious, cavalier and menacing way than the more discreet manoeuvres devised by the barons and baronesses of Western private enterprise to cloak their own equally rapacious accumulation of wealth.

The cornerstone of Berezovsky's empire was a company called LogoVAZ, formed in May 1989 – months before the fall of the Berlin Wall heralded the end of Communism. Technically, the company was a joint venture with a Turin-based firm called Logo System, a specialist in factory automation that had long worked with AvtoVAZ – the massive and inefficient motor manufacturer that produced the primitive Zhiguli and Lada sedans and unadorned, jeep-like Nivas.

Under Soviet law, the joint enterprise qualified for tax breaks and was able to park some profits in foreign bank accounts. But there was a more important twist. Berezovsky's key partners were the top managers of AvtoVAZ – including the chairman, Vladimir Kadannikov – who were to become his allies not in enhanced software design but in buying and selling AvtoVAZ's cars at a time when the demand for private automobiles was about to skyrocket.

Berezovsky broke ground by importing brand-new foreign cars – his favoured Mercedes among them. 'No one had sold foreign cars in Russia before,' he said later. He and his partners borrowed $7 million to import 886 new Fiats from Italy, defying forecasts that the cars would not find a market or would be sabotaged as they were being delivered. 'All the oligarchs, including me, did things no one believed in,' Berezovsky boasted.

In the studies of that era, most experts traced clear and close links between the new class of free-market predators, with access to cash and patronage, and the old-style Soviet management with the keys to the sweet shop.

In the case of the LogoVAZ–AvtoVAZ deal, fortunes were made in a variety of ways, such as buying new cars from the factory at knockdown export prices and then reselling them within the Russian market at a massive mark-up that benefited the dealers but not the increasingly indebted motor manufacturer.

The new elite found ways of arbitraging discrepancies between controlled domestic prices and free-market prices of commodities – not simply cars but oil, gas and metals. They operated through complex financial front organizations, located in Switzerland and in tax havens around the world. They founded their own banks, rewarded their own consultancies, stripped profits from the one-time behemoths of a superpower's state industries.

Berezovsky made no secret of his belief that in Russia's nascent free market, the first element to be privatized was the stream of profits coming from state industries: building viable businesses could come later. In the time of the oligarchs, the impoverishment of the state would contribute to the financial collapse of 1998 that spread chaos across world markets. It was left to future generations to ponder whether Russia in the 1990s simply confused privatization of profit with the personalization of wealth.

As George Soros recalled much later, one particular deal in 1997, involving bids for Russia's Svyazinvest telephone holding company, initially made him think that the oligarchs were about to change. That proved to be 'the biggest mistake of my career', he said. 'I thought that this was the transition from robber capitalism to legitimate capitalism and then owning the telephone system would have been a good investment.

'Instead of being a transition, it was the falling-out of the oligarchs with each other. There were two groups. They then got involved in a drag-out fight, almost like a gangster war between the two groups of oligarchs . . . They were more or less drawing guns on each other instead of beginning the transition to legitimate capitalism.'

Some accounts, such as Paul Klebnikov's *Godfather of the*

Kremlin, laid much stress on the links in the early 1990s between organized crime bosses and businesses, including car dealerships. Klebnikov, an American of Russian descent, was a crusading journalist at *Forbes* magazine who became the first editor of its Russian-language version. The subtitle of his book was *Boris Berezovsky and the Looting of Russia.* The two men tangled head-on when the litigious Berezovsky sued *Forbes* in a London court. At issue was not the book, published in 2000, but an article in *Forbes* in 1996 entitled 'Godfather of the Kremlin?' which portrayed Berezovsky as a Mafia boss whose deals coincided with a string of murders. Berezovsky settled the case, and *Forbes* retracted its allegations. Berezovsky did not challenge the book when it appeared.

Klebnikov himself was assassinated in Moscow in 2004, and his murder remains unsolved.

Before he died, Klebnikov insisted in his book that 'Berezovsky's success was due in part to his relationship with some of Russia's strongest gangsters.' But he also described Berezovsky as 'a man of big ideas, drawing up a grand strategy and leaving his subordinates and intermediaries to deal with the execution'.

In her study of the era, Chrystia Freeland, a *Financial Times* journalist, likened Berezovsky to a nomadic wanderer, moving on from one deal to the next. Both studies concluded that Berezovsky's capitalism diverted wealth to his own pocket rather than creating it for stockholders and stakeholders.

Some experts argued that Berezovsky was skilled not just in formulating his own ideas but also in spotting the good ideas of others – particularly his arch-rival and occasional ally Vladimir Gusinsky – and then emulating them.

But no one among his business peers seems to have been quite so adept at insinuating himself into the coterie of relatives and advisers – resembling a mediaeval court – that came to surround and insulate Boris Yeltsin after he assumed power in June 1991.

At that time, Berezovsky was already a very wealthy car tycoon, but he was also a student of human weakness, understanding the twin pulls of vanity and wealth and their ability to sway decisions. In the early 1990s, he was among those who grasped that the path to real riches lay through the Kremlin and its ability to dispense largesse to those Yeltsin chose to favour.

Berezovsky cast around for ways to project himself into the charmed circle, and he hit upon the deceptively simple idea of offering to publish Yeltsin's second volume of memoirs, *Notes of a President*, in 1994.

He resolved to make the book a classy production and chose a high-quality printer in Finland to bring out a volume that would appeal to Yeltsin's *amour propre*.

Berezovsky claimed the venture cost him $250,000, with his business partners contributing the same amount. But it was a golden, once-in-a-lifetime investment, and the payoff was beyond calculation.

Yeltsin permitted Berezovsky to join the President's Club, one of Moscow's most exclusive and elite venues, where the closest Kremlin advisers played tennis, the president's favourite game. Having gained a toehold at Yeltsin's court, Berezovsky set about using it to clamber ever higher into the presidential entourage. At the club, the players (in every sense) included Alexander Korzhakov, the president's bodyguard, amanuensis and closest drinking buddy, who controlled access to him. Berezovsky resolved to get alongside this key Kremlin doorkeeper, quite literally as it turned out, with a display of chutzpah and cunning that said a lot about his skills in finding the right person to turn opportunity to advantage.

Soon after joining the club, as Korzhakov lathered up after a triumphant tennis game, Berezovsky appeared in an adjacent shower stall, shouting over the din of the water to open a conversation. The ploy worked, but in later years it produced a retrospective bitterness towards Berezovsky among those who felt exploited by him. (One critic, an anti-corruption Russian police agent called Valery Streletsky quoted by Klebnikov in *Godfather of the Kremlin*, depicted Berezovsky as perceiving people as falling into two categories: 'a condom in its packaging and a condom that has been used'.)

'He uses every person to the maximum. That is his principle of life,' Korzhakov told Freeland after breaking with both Yeltsin and Berezovsky.

Berezovsky's eyes were on the real prize – access to the president's family via the friendship and support of Yeltsin's favourite daughter, Tatyana Dyachenko.

'He figured her out quickly,' Korzhakov said. 'Tanya worships gifts. So first Berezovsky gave her a Niva, then he gave her a Chevrolet.' As the president's publisher, moreover, Berezovsky had also opened a channel for payments into Yeltsin's bank account as royalties on Russian and foreign sales.

Within months, he was family.

The change in his prospects was enormous. Once a former mathematician struggling to buy his children's winter clothing, Berezovsky now had a place at the very top table: Yeltsin's court was the epicentre of the deal-making that came to be associated with the corruption of the 1990s – a symbiotic bond between political power and money, a self-perpetuating exchange of favours in which the oligarchs obtained state assets at knockdown prices in return for political support of Yeltsin, which in turn led to even greater riches as oil, minerals, gas and metals companies fell into private ownership.

As a direct result of his presence in the inner circle, Berezovsky persuaded Yeltsin to look favourably on his acquiring control of such businesses as ORT, the biggest state television broadcaster, and Sibneft, an oil company set up purely for the purpose of being sold off to Berezovsky and a youthful entrepreneur called Roman Abramovich. At that time Abramovich was Berezovsky's protégé. Later, he became a mortal foe.

The investments were derisory in relation to real value.

In 1995 Berezovsky acquired control of ORT for an initial stake of $320,000, though its advertising franchise alone was worth over $100 million and possibly much more.

He and Abramovich paid just over $100 million for Sibneft,

which, two years later, was valued at $5 billion on the Moscow stock market. By the time Abramovich came to sell it in 2005, Sibneft was Russia's fifth largest oil company, valued at $18 billion: after investing an initial stake of $50 million, Abramovich cashed out for $13 billion.

Most of the big state assets were sold in auctions where the winnings were parcelled out in advance among the tycoons and their partners in the Kremlin. By controlling the processes of privatization, the oligarchs determined the outcome. In return, the state gained infusions of badly needed cash. But the loss of future income from gas, oil, nickel and other commodities – and taxes, too – merely hastened the meltdown of August 1998, when Russia defaulted on billions in debt.

There was a third partner in the looting of the Russian state – American-backed economic zealots whose belief in privatization as the magical alchemy of a new Russia left them blind to the perils of selling the family jewels for a fraction of their value in return for cheap loans. As Freeland wrote in 2000, 'Russia was robbed in broad daylight, by businessmen who broke no laws, assisted by the West's best friends in the Kremlin – the young reformers.'

Berezovsky's talents lay not only in the structuring of deals to lessen their cost. He also placed loyal allies in management, both to reward them and as guarantors of his interests. By the mid-1990s, *Forbes* ranked him the ninth most influential magnate in the world and one of Russia's richest men.

Everything Berezovsky achieved became a stepping-stone to something else. There was a swagger to his self-enrichment. Klebnikov recounted one example of the impression Berezovsky made on some of those who dealt with him: he 'is not satisfied with stealing – he wants everybody to see that he is stealing with complete impunity,' said Alexander Lebed, the gravel-voiced paratroop general who played a brief but significant political role in Russia's turmoil of the mid-1990s.

The remark suggested that Berezovsky craved public

acknowledgement of his success and influence, but he also seemed to covet power, not simply over his businesses, his associates and his rivals, but also in affairs of state that would make him more than just a very wealthy man.

'I went into politics not only because my business interests pushed me to that. I was really worried about what was going on in the country. I felt personal responsibility for what was happening in Russia,' he once said. Maybe, as for other very wealthy men – media moguls such as Italy's Silvio Berlusconi and Berezovsky's role model, Rupert Murdoch – the nature of the game blurred formal distinctions between the twin goals of amassing wealth and shaping the course of events to suit the requirements of business.

Wealth, of itself, imparted great power – the rich always hold sway over those who covet their riches – but Berezovsky wanted more. After he acquired the ORT television broadcaster in 1995, he told Klebnikov: 'I did not intend to make money. I regarded it as an important source of political influence.'

In 1996, the extent of that influence became glaringly clear.

The Swiss village of Davos was an unlikely theatre for a great Russian drama.

True, the World Economic Forum – the global schmoozing venue for much of the world's moneyed and political elite – held its annual gathering there and was a reliable barometer of the world's fortunes, Russia's included. But Davos was no Gstaad or St Moritz or Courchevel. The stores were modest places, sticking pretty much to an offering of ski gear and multibladed Swiss Army penknives rather than the designer lingerie and furs of the fancier resorts. For most of the winter, the village's largely family-run hotels played host to skiers who had not come to see and be seen but to ski the pristine runs such as the Parsenn and Pischa that rise above the valley on the flanks of the Weissfluhjoch and other summits. The restaurants were far more likely to offer *raclette* (melted cheese), *rösti* (fried potatoes), and *Geschnetzeltes* (sliced veal) than foie gras or Cristal champagne or caviar. Before

Klaus Schwab, a German-born economist, founded the European Management Forum in 1971 (it took its present name in 1987), Davos's main claim to fame among outsiders was as the location of a sanatorium in Thomas Mann's novel *Der Zauberberg* – *The Magic Mountain.*

Davos had neither the hectic sprawl and disorder of Moscow nor the lure of the nightlife that would draw newly rich Russians to the French Riviera or London. Switzerland, after all, was a place for business with discreet investment bankers such as those Boris Berezovsky cultivated in Lausanne. Switzerland offered order and security, not glitz and gambles.

As a resort, Davos was downright boring.

But in January 1996 this same Alpine settlement provided the arena for events that changed Russian history.

A thousand miles to the east in Moscow, the prospect of scheduled presidential elections raised the dread possibility of a Communist revival, threatening everything that oligarchs like Berezovsky stood for.

Defeat for Yeltsin seemed inevitable, but the effort to save him – and the oligarchs' fortunes – began not in Moscow, or in Russian ballot boxes or newspapers, but in Davos.

Most years, some two thousand power brokers – chief executives, hedge fund bosses, presidents and prime ministers – attended the World Economic Forum, and many of the participants were journalists. Such was the preening and self-congratulation in Davos that a panellist once called the forum 'the temple of capitalist narcissism'.

Most of its advertised sessions were open to all the accredited delegates who had either been invited or paid registration, membership and 'partnership' fees, which accounted for most of the organization's almost $100 million annual income. Some debates were completely on the record. In other words, a lot of what was said in this public arena was quoted and reported around the world. Businesspeople gave self-serving interviews. Television stations set up live coverage as the snowflakes tumbled to provide a picture-postcard backdrop. The great gurus of international finance and economics such as George Soros, Joseph Stiglitz and Stanley Fischer offered cryptic comments that could shift perceptions of the world's well-being, or lack of it. In later years, blogs charted every available wrinkle and twist of the five-day gathering. Sometimes, Davos drew a flock of movie and rock-star celebrities, keen to burnish their credentials as eco-warriors, world savers, anti-hunger crusaders. In 2005 Sharon Stone rose to solicit bids for a fund to buy mosquito nets to save Tanzanians from malaria; within minutes she had received pledges in excess of $1 million. In the space of a couple of hours, a reporter might interview Angelina Jolie and Richard Gere, then watch politicans such as Bill Clinton and Gordon Brown and billionaires, including Bill Gates, mingle with the modern arbiters of global justice – Bono and Bob Geldof.

Klaus Schwab, the founder of the forum, presided over all this with the skills of P. T. Barnum, running a five-ring circus that made his name as something of a conjurer: if there was magic in the Magic Mountain these days, it was to be found in the remarkable spells cast by Professor Schwab, convincing some of the world's wealthiest and most powerful players that the annual pilgrimage up the narrow, snowbound, twisting road to Davos led to something more than just a talking-shop and media merry-go-round.

But there was another, far less visible Davos.

Here, in the smarter hotels, the Seehof and the Belvedere, business magnates who might never encounter one another under normal circumstances met in total confidentiality. Mining magnates, oil barons and computer tycoons who competed against one another for advantage all year round met to swap notes. Little if any of this was reported, despite the heavy media presence. And in 1996, the big secret that would change the world emerged from largely unchronicled contacts between a cabal of Russians that came to call itself the Big Seven.

Publicly, the dominant face of Russia at the 1996 forum was that of the Russian Communist Party leader, Gennadi A.

Zyuganov, who mounted a powerful and effective campaign to persuade the Western business community in the Swiss resort that it had nothing to fear from a Communist victory in the forthcoming elections back home. 'What we are going to do is create a climate of confidence,' he said, and people began to believe him.

The very plausibility of his campaign rang alarm bells among the Russian oligarchs who had also gathered in Davos, and their concerns crystallized in a brief, acrid conversation between Berezovsky and Soros.

There are various accounts of the precise wording of the exchange, but they all centre on a warning by Soros to Berezovsky that his days were numbered. One version had Soros telling Berezovsky: 'Your game is over. My advice to you is to take your family, sell what you still can and get out of the country before it is too late.' But in late 2007, both men acknowledged that the language had been far less restrained. Characteristically, both men – potential business partners who had ended up as harsh rivals – claimed to have had the better of the exchange.

'I told Boris Berezovsky that Zyuganov is being well received,' Soros recalled, and he warned him that if the Communists won the 1996 election, 'you are going to hang from a lamppost and nobody is going to reproach him for it. It made an impression on him.'

Berezovsky had a slightly different interpretation. 'Soros really told me that, Boris, you don't have any chance to win. You should get your money; you are not a poor man; you have millions already. And, yes, he really told me that you will be hanged from a lamppost. He was wrong, as you know.'

One person who overheard the exchange was Mikhail Khodorkovsky, then a youthful entrepreneur poised to become Russia's richest man with vast oil holdings. Soros's remark persuaded him that if the oligarchs were to preserve their fortunes, they would have to intervene directly to avert a Communist victory. And thus, while Zyuganov, the Communist leader, gave his interviews and charmed the capitalist elite, some of his own country's wealthiest men buried their fierce antagonisms and rivalries to group together in what was called the Davos Pact, although Faustian Pact might have been a more accurate description.

The oligarchs – led initially by Berezovsky, Khodorkovsky and Gusinsky – resolved first of all to persuade Boris Yeltsin to let them run his re-election campaign and to ignore the hard-liners in his entourage who were urging him to cancel the 1996 vote altogether. Then the oligarchs agreed to pay $3 million to Anatoly Chubais, one of the key economic reformers who had overseen the privatizations of the mid-1990s, to front their campaign. And, most important for media barons such as Berezovsky and Gusinsky, they pledged to throw the full weight of their television networks behind the ailing and unpopular Yeltsin, whose approval ratings had slumped to a staggeringly low 5 per cent. Rival politicians made accusations later that campaign financing rules had been ignored and that massive amounts were spent from secret funds.

The imperative was to rescue Yeltsin and preserve his commitment to free markets, guaranteeing the oligarchs' access to great riches. Once Yeltsin was re-elected, the oligarchs would again circle around the remaining state assets still up for grabs.

For Berezovsky, it was his finest hour, the headiest distillation yet of raw state power and bare-knuckle business, expressed later in his insistence to a reporter that 'the connection of business and state power is an absolutely normal event. Power that reflects the interest of capital is good.'

But the Davos Pact may also, with hindsight, have been the turning point.

Boris Yeltsin did, of course, win re-election in July 1996, with 53 per cent of the second-round ballot. Boris Berezovsky did, of course, cement his power in the Kremlin entourage, emerging more than ever before as a public figure – first as deputy secretary of Russia's Security Council. So keen was his desire for public office that in 1996 he formally gave up the Israeli passport he acquired in 1994 in order to meet the qualifications for appointment as a government official. The job involved trying to negotiate a settlement, free hostages and secure oil transit arrangements in Chechnya. Then, when he lost that job after a year, he became head of the Commonwealth of Independent States, the largely toothless body that bound Russia to eleven of the former Soviet republics.

In late 1999, Berezovsky went so far as to run successfully for election to the Duma, the Russian parliament, emerging victorious as the legislative representative of Karachay-Cherkessia, a tiny backwater and ethnic jumble of some 300,000 souls in the restive northern Caucasus. But of all his political gambits, none was so momentous as his reluctant decision in 1999 to support the rise to power of a one-time KGB officer called Vladimir Putin, then head of the FSB.

Putin was not Berezovsky's first choice as a candidate for the job of prime minister. Indeed, one year earlier, the two men had tangled in a dispute involving a man whose name would come to be closely tied to both of them – Alexander Litvinenko.

In 1999, according to one insider from that era, Berezovsky had his own candidate for the job of prime minister. But he was overruled by Yeltsin's own daughter, who saw in Putin a guarantor of the family's fortunes and immunity from any legal prosecution.

When Berezovsky realized that this unknown figure from St Petersburg had the backing of the Yeltsin family, he swung his support behind him, calculating that, as in the past, he would be rewarded handsomely for the support of his media outlets. Berezovsky turned his familiar charm on this grey and undemonstrative former spy. He invited him on skiing vacations and to his villa at the Cap d'Antibes in southern France, supporting his election campaign with some of the same media tactics he had used to ensure Yeltsin's re-election in 1996.

It was probably the biggest mistake he ever made.

As soon as he was elected, Putin rounded on those of the oligarchs who failed to fall in with his new regime and those, like Berezovsky, who might have resisted his rise to power. He delivered a blunt message: pay your taxes and keep out of politics.

At a meeting with some of the oligarchs in July 2000, he laid the blame for Russia's skewed economic situation squarely at their feet and told them they could not continue as before.

'I want to draw your attention to the fact that you built this state yourself, to a great degree through the political or semi-political structures under your control,' he said. 'So there is no point in blaming the reflection in the mirror. So let us get down to the point and be open and do what is necessary to do to make our relationship in this field civilized and transparent.'

Some of the tycoons, most notably Roman Abramovich, accepted the new order and went on to become ever richer. But Berezovsky and his sometime ally Gusinsky refused to accept Putin's writ, apparently believing that they had bought the Kremlin for him and he should now repay the debt. Their attitude left Putin harbouring a deep and abiding sense of betrayal by people whom he expected to support him unequivocally. And that deep schism provided the mood music, the context and possibly much more in the drama that began to unfold six years later when Alexander Litvinenko set out from Muswell Hill to Mayfair.

Less noticed beyond the big names and the broad canvas of the late 1990s, beyond the Kremlin elite and the oligarchs' conspiracies, a more modest list of dramatis personae coalesced around Berezovsky, one whose members would also be intimately involved, as foot soldiers, chroniclers, spin doctors and suspects, in the events of November 2006.

Many were people drawn like moths to the bright, magnetic light of wealth and power, the kinds of people who might provide a service or carry a message or provide the security required by the times or – in Shakespeare's language – 'To swell a progress, start a scene or two'. In the 1990s, they were offered bit parts in a constantly evolving, multidimensional chess game, dwarfed by the mighty icons of politics and business arrayed on Berezovsky's board.

But the story of Alexander Litvinenko was one in which events were not always shaped by grand designs. And if the lesser players were pawns at the time Berezovsky first assembled them, they later emerged as far more significant pieces in the game he continued to play against the Kremlin from his self-imposed exile.

Among them, almost certainly, were some who could answer the question of why Litvinenko, of all people, should pay the supreme price.

Russia in the early 1990s was a turbulent place, and it must have seemed that way to the Litvinenkos as they returned to Moscow after long spells in the provinces of Novosibirsk and Novomoskovsk. The city was in the throes of the power struggle that would deliver the Kremlin to Boris Yeltsin. Litvinenko's own unit was among those ordered to stand by to move into the capital in the heady days of August 1991, when Yeltsin led the resistance to a Communist plot to overthrow Mikhail Gorbachev, the last Soviet president. The certainties were falling away: the Soviet Union was dissolved in late 1991.

Cited in the opening pages of Klebnikov's *Godfather of the Kremlin*, W. B. Yeats's poem 'The Second Coming' might almost have been written in advance for the occasion:

> Things fall apart; the centre cannot hold;
> Mere anarchy is loosed upon the world,
> The blood-dimmed tide is loosed, and everywhere
> The ceremony of innocence is drowned.

The KGB had been the driving force of Litvinenko's career and adult life, the custodian of his dreams and ambitions. But its leaders were blamed for backing the attempted coup. Like hundreds of thousands of others, Litvinenko found himself adrift in a series of reorganizations that gave the old KGB a bewildering succession of different titles and missions. In the messy and time-consuming reforms that stripped the old KGB of its overseas intelligence responsibilities, there was another, equally major shift in the way Russia's security services related to the political leadership. The old KGB reported directly to the Central Committee of the Soviet Communist Party as its 'sword and shield'.

Control of the new FSB was up for grabs.

Almost in tandem with the uncertainty of the times, Litvinenko's personal life was heading for upheaval, too.

By the early 1990s he had been married to Natalia for a decade. The humble conscript had been promoted first to captain, then to major, on his way to becoming a lieutenant colonel. Both husband and wife were in their early thirties, and the world around them had become unrecognizable. The bedrock promises of their Soviet childhood lay shattered by a chaotic, new economic order. The sense of immutable empire imposed by the Kremlin of their childhood evaporated. Millions of ordinary Russians saw their savings wiped out overnight by rampant hyperinflation: in 1992 the price of milk shot up by 4,300 per cent; bread went up by 3,600 per cent. The Russian mafia took over great swathes of the economy. In early 1993 Yeltsin said organized crime had infiltrated two-thirds of all businesses in Russia. In 1994 the United Nations estimated the number of organized criminal gangs at 5,700 with three million members. The great new economic experiment following the fall of Communism had collapsed into banditry for some and penury for most ordinary Russians.

As an officer of the newly created FSB in Moscow, Litvinenko had been assigned to investigate economic and organized crime – the growth industry of the moment – running informers and moles in the crime gangs, probing the frequent excesses of extortion and bloodshed that marked the era.

Then came 7 June 1994.

On that day, at 5.07 p.m., Boris Berezovsky clambered into his Mercedes 600 at the headquarters of his LogoVAZ company on Novokuznetsk Street. His bodyguard sat beside him, and his chauffeur was alone in the front of the car. The car was heading toward the Paveletsky station in south-central Moscow when a bomb planted in a parked Opel exploded as the heavy Mercedes rolled by. The blast decapitated Mikhail Kiryanov, the driver, and left Berezovsky burned and shaken. The bodyguard, Dmitri Vasilyev, lost an eye. A fruit stand nearby was destroyed, and the windows of an eight-storey building across the way were shattered. Investigators concluded later that the explosion had been set off by a remotely detonated anti-tank mine.

'It's impossible to programme your behaviour for an extreme situation until you're in it,' Berezovsky said in an interview published in 1999. 'I don't list myself among the particularly brave, but I wasn't afraid at that moment . . . I can remember everything in precise detail, except for the sound of the blast. I didn't hear it. I just saw it – a flash, a burst of flame, breaking glass, and the blaze spreading over the passenger seat and my clothes . . . At first I wondered why Dima Vasilyev, my bodyguard, was doing nothing. Then, when I saw him, I immediately understood. I could feel my hair burning and my clothes smouldering, and I thought: Should I get out of the car, will they shoot at me? I didn't have time to get frightened; I simply had to survive.' Berezovsky's reaction – a blend of fast thinking and a fierce desire for survival – said a lot about the way he conducted himself in less fraught circumstances, too.

In the immediate aftermath of the bombing, Berezovsky left Russia temporarily, travelling for medical treatment to Switzerland and on to Israel to claim citizenship. Far less noticed at the time was the identity of the FSB officer assigned to the case: Alexander Litvinenko.

'I met Alexander Litvinenko for the first time in June 1994, the day after an attempt to kill me, which until now is unsolved,' Berezovsky told me. 'He was presented as an officer of the FSB.'

The brief meeting brought together two men of vastly disparate backgrounds, but a relationship formed, cemented by subsequent events in which Berezovsky cast Litvinenko as a guardian and protector. 'Really, Alexander several times saved my life . . . Definitely he became very close and became my friend,' Berezovsky avowed in late 2007.

From that moment on, Litvinenko's destiny was bound to that of Berezovsky, his mentor and benefactor, first in Russia and again in London after both of them fled Moscow in 2000, sharing a belief that they had no place in the land of their birth.

3

ACOLYTES

I first heard of the 1994 encounter between Litvinenko and Berezovsky in late 2006 from Alex Goldfarb, another of the people who gravitated to Berezovsky's court in the 1990s.

Goldfarb flitted through the Litvinenko chronicles like a doppelgänger, a man always to be found somewhere between the sidelines and centre stage at moments of crisis, sometimes expediter, sometimes praise singer, sometimes mythmaker.

He was a man who seemed to thrive on mystery, offering information in carefully calibrated doses: when I first interviewed him near the *New York Times* office in London shortly after Litvinenko's death, he insisted on meeting in the back seat of a dark blue Mercedes driven by a burly and uncommunicative man. He juggled a laptop, a cell phone and a BlackBerry, switching in his communications between Russian and English with ease. At Litvinenko's funeral, Goldfarb was at the side of Marina Litvinenko, abruptly widowed at age forty-four, at London's Highgate West Cemetery, just across the way from the East Cemetery, where Karl Marx was buried. With her, Goldfarb co-authored a book about her husband – *Death of a Dissident* – just as he had provided a preface for an earlier book by Litvinenko, *Lubyanka Criminal Group,* and facilitated the distribution of a Russian-language version of *Blowing Up Russia* by Litvinenko and a Russian-American historian, Yuri Felshtinsky.

In truth, the link between Litvinenko and Goldfarb ran directly through the discreet and expensive offices of Boris Berezovsky.

Goldfarb was the executive director of Berezovsky's New York-based International Foundation for Civil Liberties, which helped finance Litvinenko's self-exile. But he had also been on hand whenever Berezovsky needed him for duties other than those of the foundation, even predating its creation.

In November 2006, as Alexander Litvinenko lay dying, Alex Goldfarb suddenly materialized to offer reporters an account of his associate's decline; he was usually quoted as a spokesman for the family, but it soon emerged that Goldfarb was very close indeed to Berezovsky – one more cross-tie in the tangle of relationships surrounding Alexander Litvinenko. Goldfarb's own story had its moments, too.

He was born in Moscow in 1947, the son of Cecilia and David Goldfarb. His father was a molecular geneticist and Communist Party member who maintained occasional ties with Western correspondents and who would later become a refusenik – a Soviet Jew refused permission to emigrate. Alex Goldfarb grew up, he told me as he sipped a beer over lunch in June 2007, 'in a privileged, educated family in central Moscow, half a mile from the Kremlin'. He began learning English at the age of five and by thirteen was reading Agatha Christie – perhaps a foretaste of his penchant for the mysterious.

'I grew up during Khrushchev's thaw,' he said, referring to a brief period following the death of Stalin when the Kremlin loosened some modest control over Soviet citizens. 'Foreign radio stations were not jammed, and Solzhenitsyn was published.'

After graduating from Moscow State University, he worked as a biologist at the Kurchatov nuclear research institute (where he would most likely have been warned of the perils and symptoms of radiation sickness). Unlike his father, Alex Goldfarb was permitted to emigrate and did so in 1975, studying for a doctorate at the Weizmann Institute in Tel Aviv. He spent a year in Munich before leaving for the United States in 1982 to become a microbiologist in New York at Columbia University.

Four years later, his father was finally able to join him. By that time, David Goldfarb, who had fought for the Red Army and lost a leg at the Battle of Stalingrad in 1942, was sixty-seven years old and a very sick man, suffering from diabetes and failing eyesight. His Soviet doctors had told him it might be necessary to amputate his remaining leg because a wound on his foot was not healing properly.

'A seriously ill man who had been in critical condition twice in the last year, I did not expect to live long,' David Goldfarb wrote in the *New York Times Magazine* in 1986.

Finally, he was permitted to emigrate in a remarkable unfolding of synchronized events that involved Armand Hammer, the chairman of Occidental Petroleum Corporation, an American tycoon who maintained unusually close ties to the Soviet leadership.

At the time, Moscow and Washington were in the throes of a complicated exchange of spies, refuseniks and an American journalist, Nicholas S. Daniloff. But even by the Cold War standards of the time, the sudden emigration of David Goldfarb and his wife ranked among the more dramatic.

After eight years of rejected applications for permission to emigrate, the Goldfarbs' exit visa came so quickly that American Embassy officials in Moscow had no time to issue US entry visas for them. Within hours of the Soviet decision, Hammer rushed the couple to his corporate Boeing 727 jet in Moscow and flew them into Newark, New Jersey, where the plane landed at 6.15 p.m. on 16 October 1986. Alex Goldfarb, credited with intense lobbying to secure his parents' emigration, was on hand to meet them with a thick bouquet of pink roses. The family had not been united for eleven years.

The collapse of the Soviet Union, of course, rewrote the possibilities open to people like Alex Goldfarb, untainted by association with the old regime, fluent in Russian and English and boasting a solid scientific record.

In 1992 Alex Goldfarb went to work directly for George Soros, who had established a foundation dedicated to the promotion of science in Russia. In the turbulent 1990s, Goldfarb said, he supervised the disbursement of some $130 million to Russian science and health projects funded by his boss. By most accounts, other Soros employees did not find him an easy person to deal with.

'Alex is a stubborn, suspicious, and prickly man,' Michael T. Kaufman of the *New York Times* said in a biography of Soros published in 2002. 'He has scored his most important victories by standing up to bureaucrats, by demanding things, by refusing to compromise, and he has seldom shown gratitude. Few people within the Soros empire have nice things to say about him, and many describe him as "arrogant", "rude" and "cunning".'

Once back in Moscow as a visitor on Soros's business, Goldfarb became a regular at Berezovsky's Logovaz Club – a nineteenth-century mansion in central Moscow named after the tycoon's car company. The house had once been owned by the Smirnoff family, and it is hard to resist the idea that Berezovsky saw it not just as a validation of his status and wealth but also as a power centre and bolt-hole, a secure and private environment in which he could play out his manoeuvres with impunity. He had restored the building in a lavish Empire style – a personal salon where supplicants queued for audience and oligarchs mulled over the future.

'The Club was a famous and mysterious place. A visit there was proof of one's status. The quality of wine and the artistry of the chef were legendary,' Goldfarb wrote in 2007. 'In the wake of the assassination attempt on Boris in 1994, the security was impressive, including metal detectors, closed-circuit television monitors, an ID registry, and the presence of many attentive young men with the demeanor and habits of the old KGB Kremlin guard.'

Goldfarb in those days seemed to perform a high-wire act balancing between Soros and Berezovsky, two Promethean figures determined in their own ways to shape the future of Russia. But there was no evidence of real cordiality between Soros and Berezovsky, and in 1997 the two billionaires split openly over the massive Svyazinvest phone company privatization deal, when

Soros invested almost $1 billion to back Berezovsky's rival, Vladimir Potanin. In the same year, Soros told me, he met Berezovsky alone in the Logovaz Club to discuss a business dispute, in which Berezovsky felt Soros had gone behind his back. Berezovsky was annoyed, and 'I felt he could kill me,' Soros said in 2007.

He had recounted the same episode in an article in the *New York Review of Books* on 13 April 2000. 'His anger gave me the chills. I literally felt he could kill me. He did not say so but he made me feel that I had betrayed him. It was a turning point in our relationship.'

In late 2007, in a conversation in the boardroom of his offices in London, Berezovsky was asked about the incident, and he fell briefly silent. 'Soros is a person who never likes to lose, even in the argument,' he said. 'In 1995, I put $1.5 million into the Soros Foundation for a special programme for Russian students. And at the time he never said I was a robber baron. He took my money.'

As ever, there was a subplot.

Goldfarb had been an intermediary in the business relationship between the two billionaires, so much so, according to Goldfarb, that Soros once asked him directly whether he was in Berezovsky's pay in the run-up to the Svyazinvest deal.

When the deal went sour, 'looking back, this was the point where my disagreement with George Soros took root. I was squarely on Boris's side,' Goldfarb wrote in 2007. (People in the Soros camp said the break between Goldfarb and Soros was rooted in a dispute over the treatment of TB patients in a Soros-funded prison health project.) The final rift between Goldfarb and Soros came three years later, and an outsider might well have pondered how difficult – and perilous – it was for Goldfarb in the intervening period to go about Soros's business while dealing with the mercurial Berezovsky.

In all of these manoeuvrings, there was one constant venue: the Logovaz Club, the place to be – and not just for Alex Goldfarb.

There was a high-definition television set over the bar – the first in Moscow – and a white grand piano 'played occasionally by one of Boris's old friends, an elderly Jew in a white suit,' Goldfarb recalled in 2007. 'In the corner stood a stuffed crocodile, for reasons unknown. Boris was always behind schedule, so his visitors usually had to wait.

'On any given day at the club you could rub elbows with ministers and TV personalities, deputies of the Duma and top journalists, provincial governors and Western fund managers, as well as people no one knew, such as an unremarkable young man in a jeans suit who often sat in a corner: Sasha Litvinenko.'

And in that era, there were other 'people no one knew' in Berezovsky's entourage.

One of them would later be accused of Litvinenko's murder.

When Boris Berezovsky took over the ORT television station in the mid-1990s, he won a prize of enormous value – the only station capable of broadcasting throughout Russia and the linear descendant of the state broadcaster most Soviet citizens had relied on for 'official' news.

The prize needed protection, and Berezovsky's aides chose a man as head of security whose qualifications seemed impeccable – the scion of a prominent and respected Red Army family, a former member of the KGB's 40,000-strong Ninth Directorate in charge of guarding some of the highest members of the Kremlin elite.

His name was Andrei K. Lugovoi.

Lugovoi was born in 1966 in Azerbaijan, the son of an itinerant army family that moved between assignments and boasted a long military tradition. He told visitors that his grandfather fought and was decorated for his courage in the Russo-Japanese War of 1904–5. His father, Konstantin, had risen within the missile corps of the Soviet army to become its ranking officer in charge of 'political education'. Andrei had an elder brother, too, serving in a Special Forces dive unit. He spent his childhood in military schools as his father moved between bases in the Soviet Union and the satellite countries of the Warsaw Pact, such as the former

Czechoslovakia (now divided into the Czech Republic and Slovakia).

When it came time for college, Lugovoi won a place at the Supreme Soviet Higher Military Command School – the Soviet equivalent of West Point in the United States or Sandhurst in Britain. Among his earliest childhood friends, he counted another man whose name would emerge much later as one of the last people to meet with Alexander Litvinenko before he began to sicken – Dmitri Kovtun. Both their fathers were commanders in the Moscow garrison of the Red Army.

Lugovoi's first contact with the KGB came in 1986, a year before he graduated and joined the Ninth Directorate's elite Kremlin Regiment. One of his colleagues there was Vyacheslav G. Sokolenko, also present as a guest in the Millennium Hotel near the American Embassy in London on 1 November 2006 – the day Alexander Litvinenko began to die.

Like Kovtun and Lugovoi himself, Sokolenko denied all knowledge of the events leading to Litvinenko's death, and, like Kovtun, he was not formally accused by the British police. But these serendipitous encounters seemed to underline one of the peculiarities of Litvinenko's story: alliances and connections forged many years earlier revived and coalesced mysteriously in the days leading to his death, almost as if those who planned for him to die had sought to surround him with people he would trust instinctively.

By 2006 Lugovoi had become everything that Litvinenko's first wife said her husband wished to be: he had made the transition from state to private business; he had turned his training as an official bodyguard for the Kremlin elite and his KGB connections into the credentials to set up his own security company. He had diversified into a separate drinks business. He was rich.

In public appearances, Lugovoi's manner was supremely self-confident, almost cocksure, an exemplar of the New Russian man that Putin sought to midwife from the ruins of the 1990s. Physically he was in good shape, neatly turned out with close-trimmed hair and a dandyish penchant for loud pin-striped suits. He showed no hesitation posing for TV cameras on the firing range of his security firm, pictured in a Clint Eastwood stance with legs apart, blasting away with a 9-mm pistol, the standard KGB issue. Neither was there any hint of doubt or uncertainty about his denials of involvement in Litvinenko's killing. But then, his upbringing had not prepared him to waver.

When the KGB was dissolved in 1991, he transferred automatically to the General Guard Department of the Russian Federation, acting as a bodyguard for such high-ranking figures as Yegor Gaidar, a deputy prime minister, and Andrei Kozyrev, the foreign minister. Three times, he travelled with senior officials to the United States, and claimed to have stood alongside President Clinton on one of those visits.

Later, his responsibilities came to include the personal protection of Boris Berezovsky during the tycoon's spell as deputy secretary of the Russian Security Council in 1996.

It was no coincidence that after Lugovoi worked in an official capacity for Berezovsky, the tycoon sought to bring him into the charmed circle of the Logovaz Club, appointing him head of security at the ORT television station.

Berezovsky maintained that he was not directly in charge of ORT security: he had delegated that responsibility to his long-time close business associate Badri Patarkatsishvili. But Lugovoi came with a strong recommendation from Gaidar as what Berezovsky called a 'brave and open man'.

'Berezovsky's HQ at the time was in the Logovaz business club,' Lugovoi said in early 2007. 'This is where the shareholders' meetings, board of directors' meetings, took place. I visited this place frequently.'

Indeed it was at the Logovaz Club that two men who would later be cast as victim and perpetrator first met, a decade before their final meeting on 1 November 2006.

'Litvinenko also worked for Berezovsky,' Lugovoi said. 'Though I did not work for Berezovsky, I worked for the company. Litvinenko frequented this place, too, and once somebody introduced us. It was just an introduction – Alexander, Andrei – not anything in connection with some future business deals.'

Litvinenko 'was considered to be a member of Berezovsky's close circle. We had no business or personal contacts, we never called each other on the phone, we never met. At the moment he was still in the service, though I had resigned by that time,' Lugovoi said.

Litvinenko 'was with the FSB, but worked for Berezovsky,' Lugovoi said.

'Well, then, in mid-1990s . . . it was a transition period, the oligarchic system of social control. Officials appointed or paid by oligarchs, this is what Russia was in the 1990s. In my view it was much further from democracy than today's Russia. Because anything could be bought or paid for quite openly. Believe me. I am a well-informed person; for five years I was in charge of the security of the top officials. Later I worked in the structures of one of the most famous oligarchs. That is why I know how decisions were formed and made at the highest level. What was happening in the mass media was nothing but a cover-up for tearing up anything they could lay their hands on.'

He and Litvinenko were not close to each other, Lugovoi said, 'but we met occasionally.'

Perhaps, though, history will depict that chance encounter as the start of a chain of events that bound the two men together under the most bizarre and improbable circumstances at the very end of Litvinenko's life.

Lugovoi's crossover from public to private employer was not unusual in a decade when thousands of trained bodyguards, thugs and investigators from the KGB or its successor agencies suddenly found themselves jobless or subsisting on salaries cut to shreds by inflation.

Neither, for that matter, was it unusual for state security officials to moonlight for private employers ranging from businessmen to gangsters – job descriptions that sometimes blurred all too easily with each other. By 2007, according to Igor

A. Goloschapov, a former KGB counterintelligence agent who headed a lobby group for private security firms, there were 4,200 licensed private security agencies in Moscow alone, in addition to unlicensed outfits operating more or less openly and hiring themselves out to the highest bidder for all kinds of nefarious activities. Would that include contract killings?

'I do not exclude that this could happen when something needs to be done,' Goloschapov told a *New York Times* reporter in Moscow. 'Where this kind of business starts, the truth ends.'

Another visitor at the Logovaz Club was Yuri A. Felshtinsky, a historian who would later emerge as a co-author with Litvinenko and the editor of Berezovsky's *Art of the Impossible* – which took its title from an adage ascribed in the book to Machiavelli: 'Politics is the art of the possible.' (In fact, the phrase is usually attributed to Prince Otto von Bismarck.) Felshtinsky also edited *Verdict,* the collection of courtroom transcripts published by Berezovsky in 2007.

Goldfarb likened Felshtinsky's role to his own as 'a peripheral planet in Boris's solar system, orbiting once every few months, advising him on various matters'. But, as with some of Berezovsky's other collaborators and advisers, Felshtinsky would be called upon to play more dramatic roles.

Indeed, looking back at Berezovsky's career, it is abundantly clear that those who worked with him were sometimes required to take unexpected risks for their boss.

For Lugovoi, the test came in a court case in 2001 when he was accused of trying to help a Berezovsky aide, Nikolai A. Glushkov, escape justice. The allegation – denied as much by Berezovsky as by Lugovoi – was that Lugovoi organized a failed conspiracy to free Glushkov from a prison hospital at a time when he was accused of massive fraud at Aeroflot, the airline controlled by Berezovsky. The case assumed great significance for Berezovsky because, he maintained later, the Kremlin used Glushkov as a hostage to pressure him into selling Russian assets in return for his aide's freedom. Caught up in this battle, Lugovoi said he was jailed for fourteen months. For his part, Berezovsky depicted Lugovoi's jail term as a token of loyalty worthy of reward.

After his release from prison, Lugovoi prospered, although it is not clear who staked this former KGB man with a high-profile criminal record in his security and drinks businesses. But, to the very moment of Litvinenko's death, Berezovsky remained friendly towards Lugovoi and acknowledged a debt of gratitude to him. While Glushkov 'all the time said Lugovoi was a provocateur, I still trusted Lugovoi', Berezovsky told me.

In early 2006 Berezovsky even invited Lugovoi to his glittery sixtieth birthday party, where he shared a table with none other than Alexander Litvinenko and his second wife, Marina. 'At that time I calculated that Lugovoi was my friend,' Berezovsky said.

The party was held at Blenheim Palace, a magnificent pile built between 1705 and 1722 that ranks as one of Britain's biggest country houses, the home of successive dukes of Marlborough and the birthplace of Winston Churchill. 'It was a typical British-organized party when you sit at a table and you don't know who you will sit with but you know where your name is,' Marina Litvinenko told me. 'Generally speaking, it was a Russian-speaking table.'

At the time of the party, Goldfarb wrote, he dismissed Lugovoi as 'a shadow from the Russian past'. But Lugovoi's invitation to the party also offered Litvinenko a chance to talk business, sounding him out on likely arrangements to be made as advisers and consultants to British risk assessment and private security companies.

'I knew about him since our time in Russia,' Marina Litvinenko said. 'Sasha talked about how he was head of security at the ORT television channel. He wasn't unpleasant about it. Sasha just said he's a KGB man from unit 9, and because it is all just bodyguards and Sasha was from a more active unit, it was like a real job, and unit number 9 was just people who open the door and tell people where to sit.'

When she met him at the Berezovsky party for the first time in

2006, Marina recalled, 'Sasha says: "This is Lugovoi." We have some conversation about nothing – how are things in Moscow? He was absolutely unemotional. He was like a fish.'

In the Russia of the 1990s, Boris Berezovsky was not alone in becoming immensely rich or wielding disproportionate political power. But he was unique among Russia's super-wealthy in the strident public campaign against the Kremlin that he mounted after fleeing Moscow in 2000 to embrace a life of self-exile in Britain.

Far from home, he balanced between assailing Vladimir Putin and nurturing the British tolerance that enabled him to mount his pulpit in London in the first place.

Sometimes, his criticism of Putin overstepped what Britain viewed as the permissible limits of political discourse. On those occasions the Foreign Office took umbrage, reluctant to permit Berezovsky to jeopardize British trade and diplomatic ties to Moscow. In early 2007, the *Guardian* newspaper quoted Berezovsky in an interview as calling for the violent overthrow of the Putin government. Within hours, the Foreign Office press office formulated a public rebuke deploring 'anyone who uses their residence in the UK as a platform to call for the violent overthrow of a sovereign government'. Berezovsky qualified his remarks to insist he had been calling not for bloodshed but for a 'soft' revolution similar to those he had backed in Ukraine and Georgia.

For the tycoon, as for other asylum seekers, Britain was a particularly prized haven. Successive governments refused to comply with Russian demands to hand him over, and Berezovsky frequently acknowledged his gratitude to the British for granting him political asylum in 2003. As often as Russia demanded his return to Moscow, the British refused to comply.

The British argument was that sanctuary could be denied only by the courts, not by political fiat. Russia never accepted the British refrain, which became a mantra in contacts between London and Moscow.

According to one diplomat, a sentence the British ambassador in Moscow could pronounce in Russian 'without engaging mental gears' was to say that only the judiciary could rule on Berezovsky's extradition, not the executive. The Kremlin kept a team of lawyers on retainer in London to pounce on any prospect of securing Berezovsky's deportation. In their dealings with Britain, nothing galled the Russians quite so much as the vision of Berezovsky taunting the Kremlin from the stockade of British asylum while British diplomats recited some kind of legalistic formula to shield him from extradition. The law was not Berezovsky's only defence. Acutely aware of the importance of his public image in Britain as a shield against the Kremlin, Berezovsky sought out one of London's premier PR masterminds, Lord Tim Bell of Belgravia.

Soon after fleeing to Britain in 2000, Berezovsky met Bell over tea in the refined and ornate public rooms of the Dorchester, Park Lane's poshest hotel – a fugitive Russian tycoon and a chain-smoking, pin-striped British entrepreneur with a coveted place on the red benches of the House of Lords and an impressive list of contacts across British society and the British media, including Rupert Murdoch, a shared contact whose photograph Berezovsky kept on his desk in London.*

Berezovsky was in the process of seeking political asylum and wanted Bell's contacts and skills to shift British opinion away from the belief, encouraged by the British government, that Vladimir Putin was a worthy interlocutor and a man to do business with. The Russian oligarch also wanted an introduction into the influential set in London to offset the unsavoury image attached to him by his adversaries in Russia as an unscrupulous and unpopular baron of the new capitalism. And, as the Bell

---

*Berezovsky was one of eighty-two guests at Murdoch's wedding to Wendi Deng in June 1999 aboard Murdoch's yacht *Morning Glory* in New York harbour, according to an Associated Press report in the *New York Times* on 27 June 1999. The yacht sailed from Chelsea Piers 'as a string ensemble played Mozart'.

camp told it, he wanted to win his asylum openly through the courts, not by some sleight of hand.

To some extent this enormously public Berezovsky was an incomplete image, a mirage, a facade. His friends said that with Boris, what you see is what you get – outspoken, devious, charming, dangerous; a restless nomad questing constantly for personal advantage. So the question that always baffled outsiders was where his true motives lay.

It could be argued that Berezovsky's carefully nurtured reputation in the early years of the twenty-first century as the highest-profile exiled crusader against Vladimir Putin was simply part of a broader campaign to remove the single biggest obstacle to a renewed career back in business or politics – or both – in Russia.

After years in self-exile, the pressures were certainly mounting.

In relative terms, his fortune was dwindling, down from something on the order of £800 million to £500 million, according to the widely followed Rich List published in the *Sunday Times*.

A few years earlier, Berezovsky had calculated his own wealth at $3 billion, though, of course, there was always a certain reluctance on his part to be pinned down too closely.

'Are we selling or buying?' he asked an interviewer in 2002. 'If we are selling – it is $3 billion, if we are buying it is $2 billion.'

By late 2007 Berezovsky put the figure at somewhere between $2 billion and $3 billion following the sale of his companies to his Georgian business partner Badri Patarkatsishvili.* As to the exact amount, Berezovsky said, 'I don't know.'

In the meantime, though, his one-time fellow oligarchs had pushed the definitions of real money into the stratosphere: Roman Abramovich was reckoned to be worth in excess of $20 billion, and he was not alone in that super-rich category of Russians. Berezovsky, by contrast, had spent millions of dollars supporting Putin's opponents in Russia, Georgia and Ukraine, not

---

* Patarkatsishvili died at his mansion outside London in February 2008. After an autopsy, the authorities ascribed his death to heart failure. He was fifty-two.

to mention London and New York. It was an uneven battle. As head of the Kremlin elite that controlled Russia's oil, gas and mineral reserves, Putin had virtually limitless resources. Berezovsky's fighting fund was shrinking. So who was winning?

4

RENEGADE

At times of risk and upheaval, people are called upon to make choices that will affect their lives in ways they cannot begin to divine, deciding their future when there is no clear promise of safety or benefit, when the outcomes are obscure.

For officers like Alexander Litvinenko, the early 1990s in Moscow presented one of those challenges, and his responses set the coordinates for a life that was to end cruelly and prematurely in London.

Sometimes, of course, people delude themselves into thinking that they make decisions on their own exclusive account, but circumstances, chance encounters and coincidences play a big part, too. So it was with Litvinenko.

In the space of a few short years he befriended a billionaire, broke with his comrades in the Russian security services and encountered the man who was to become his obsession – Vladimir Putin. Along the way, he roamed the fringes of Russia's brutal campaign in Chechnya, lost faith in his superiors and swapped one family, one woman, for another.

In the early years of the decade, the issue confronting a person like Litvinenko was simple and baffling at the same time: where should his loyalties lie – with the system that nurtured him (and paid him) or with the new privateers who turned their training to advantage in the free-for-all of robber baron capitalism? Would it be a modest life on a devalued government salary or a slice of the fabled riches accruing to the few? The skills of officers like Litvinenko – or Lugovoi, or Sokolenko, for that matter – were much in demand among the new elite in business and the organized crime gangs that emerged brazenly from the crumbling of Soviet power. The KGB had trained its operatives as spies, informers, agents, investigators, bodyguards and killers. So did they maintain their oaths of duty, or did they embrace the get-rich-quick ethos of the era? The decisions were hard because the future offered no clear guides or markers about the way society would turn out. And the choices were momentous because they were made by instinct alone: as if crossing a personal Rubicon, one could not turn back.

This was the world in which Litvinenko – a young officer raised to loyalty, now serving in an agency awash with corruption – contemplated his options. State security operatives moonlighted as bodyguards, extortionists, contract killers. Law enforcement officers spied on one another – colonel on colonel, general on general. Agents and prosecutors developed expensive appetites for gambling and loose women. Organized crime gangs – Chechens, Slavs – fed not just on the suddenly freed economy but also on its supposed guardians, infiltrating police units and buying off senior commanders. Tycoons rode around town with security details equivalent to private militias, drawn from the ranks of the police and the KGB-FSB. In a normal society, Litvinenko's promotion to the rank of lieutenant colonel by his early thirties should have offered a prospect of high office, a promise of responsibility and respect. But this was not a normal society. And his career was not the only thing on Litvinenko's mind.

On 15 June 1993, at a birthday party in honour of a ballroom dancer called Marina Shtoda, née Tsybina, Alexander Litvinenko came up short against a choice of a different kind that would upend his life in much the same way that the end of Communism had upturned his country: he fell in love.

Somewhat improbably, Litvinenko's supporters said he attended the birthday gathering because of his job: he was keeping an eye on two of Marina's friends caught up in an extortion racket, and they had invited him along to the party. He was not the kind of guest the hostess expected: a casually dressed outsider with the mysterious aura of his trade; a secret agent, an *operativnik* in the argot of the FSB, one whose mission was to cull 'operational data', not provide evidence strong enough for a hearing in court. He was married with two children, one a toddler. He inhabited a twilit milieu Marina knew only from the pages of thrillers. And he saw in her something rare, a glamour that was missing from his world. She had competed in ballroom dancing contests and had the poise of her profession. She was trim, elegant, divorced. She taught aerobics and dance and had bright grey-green eyes that somehow combined passion and mystery as he gazed into them.

The mutual magnetism was irresistible.

Soon after the birthday party, his marriage failed. By August 1993, the new couple had begun to live together in the apartment Marina shared with her parents in south-central Moscow – one of the massive residential complexes that constituted the principal architectural legacy of much of the Soviet era. By October, Marina had become pregnant, despite previous medical advice that she would need fertility treatment if she wished to bear children. They were married a year later, four months after the birth of a son, Anatoly.

Those were the bare facts, almost banal: boy met girl, boy left wife, boy and new girl wed. But to those embroiled in such break-ups and re-bondings, there is never anything banal: events progress with the force of an earthquake, wreaking damage far beyond the fury of the epicentre.

The easy parts of a story of new love, of passion magnified by novelty and secrecy, are told by people who have just met, have just recognized the mutual signals of availability and have been drawn by intuitions of compatibility. New lovers are Teflon-coated, immunized from the pain of the others left behind. They look to a future filled with hope and aim for it resolutely, self-absorbed. The losers look back to better times when they were the happy ones, now left to feed bitterness on a diet of lost memories that poisons their own future. Versions and counter-versions of true love's course sprout like malignant growths from the dark loam of marital distress.

In some ways, Litvinenko's break-up and remarriage echoed the turmoil of his own land. But it is hard to say which interpretation of events provided the truer parallel for his own country's divorce from its past: did the collapse of Litvinenko's first marriage mirror Russia's painful departure from a tortured history? Or did Russia's dash into a new era provide the metaphor for a love triangle that mercilessly blessed the new bond at the expense of those who could not keep pace?

Like his parents before him, Litvinenko had embarked on a first marriage that would not endure, leaving children to reap the harvest of bitterness and confusion. By 1993, when he met Marina, he had a son, Alexander, a young daughter, Sonya, twenty-one months old, and a wife, Natalia, who had stood by him through his years as a cadet and trainee agent, a woman who had endured the years in the provinces and who hoped her reward would be to become the wife of a general.

He had been in the military or the KGB or the FSB since he was eighteen. He was used to structures and conspiracy. He had been promoted, and he lived a life of danger – tracking down organized crime figures in Moscow and the northern Caucasus. He boasted of secret missions that took him far from home. His adrenalin stemmed from probing the world of gangsters, hoodlums, thugs – hardly a breeding ground for the kind of family man Natalia wanted, the kind of man who would play with the children and spend evenings at home. Their marriage, moreover, had reached the stage where bonds fray and partners stray.

But later, after he died, when those he knew pored over his history to look for clues to his character, the break-up of his marriage provoked questions about the nature of the man. Was there something in him – a pattern of deceit, a propensity for making enemies – that made a bad end inevitable? Was there a certain nobility to him – as he wanted the world to believe – or was there a more sordid side to his nature: an aptitude for treachery, as his former wife and some of his former colleagues would come to assert? And if his adversaries were correct in their assessment of him, who or what might Litvinenko have betrayed to provoke the excruciating death that befell him?

The family album photographs of Alexander and Marina Litvinenko show a remarkably clean-cut couple. In their wedding photo taken on 14 October 1994, both had their eyes cast downward as Alexander slid a ring on to Marina's right hand in the Russian Orthodox manner. Unusually, he wore a suit and tie. The way Marina recalled it, they married in a civil office in Chertanovo, south of Moscow. The couple initially wore casual clothes, planning to simply sign the official record and go, but the registrar suggested that for the sake of their already-born son they put on their best clothes, invite guests, take photographs to preserve the moment for posterity. That explained the unfamiliar suit and tie. In the wedding photographs, Litvinenko's clothes hang smoothly from a slender, athletic frame. He looks clean-cut, trim, a regular guy, his hair short and neat. Marina wore a dark dress, bought at the last moment, and has high Slavic cheekbones, full lips. Later she would laugh at this reversal of the colours for bride and groom – he in light clothing, she more sombre. They made a handsome couple. When they met at her thirty-first birthday party, Marina said, he was 'light somehow, radiant, and as emotional as a child'.

But the divergent accounts of their early days began at that precise moment.

From the start, he acknowledged quite freely that he was a married man, already spoken for, Marina said, but he seemed 'uncared for, unanchored somehow'. She felt that all was not well between him and his wife, but had a rule against dating married men. To her surprise, when they next met a week later, he told her his wife had thrown him out and piled his goods outside the apartment he and his family shared with Natalia's parents. The cause of her anger – in his account – was his decision to delay a family vacation to work on the extortion case relating to Marina's friends. Three weeks later, he told Marina he had asked his wife for a divorce. It was the beginning of a rapid courtship, as if fate had thrust together two people meant for each other. 'I found a wife and a friend in one person,' Litvinenko said many years later.

But that sequence of events bore no relation whatsoever to the memories of Natalia, the jilted first wife, which she broadcast on Russian television and in interviews with foreign reporters. The only point not at issue was that Litvinenko was investigating a case relating to extortion and involving a couple Marina knew from the professional dance business. The rest, for Natalia, was a story of clandestine encounters and betrayal.

'He started to work at night,' Natalia recalled in the summer of 2007 at her dacha outside Moscow. 'He'd tell me he was staking people out. It was hard. I wanted more attention. Then one morning he came home covered in another woman's perfume – French perfume, which, at the time, was very expensive and rare. I confronted him.'

In this version, it was Litvinenko himself who bundled his clothes together in the apartment where they had lived thanks to the generosity of his parents-in-law; he called a service car from the FSB pool; he left. Natalia had been trying to save money in a small box so that one day the couple might purchase their own apartment.

'He gathered all his clothes and took the money I had been saving for the flat, around $7,000. He then picked up my handbag and took out all the money I had in my purse. I couldn't believe it. He took everything, down to the last kopeck.' In the chronicles of his adversaries seeking to discredit him, that pecuniary detail was possibly the most damning – and the least provable.

But Natalia had not given up altogether. She thought Litvinenko had moved in with his mother, and she caught sight of him once in a limousine – 'he was showing off.' He took Natalia and the children to McDonald's in the Old Arbat district of central Moscow. 'I thought he would come back to us, but he didn't,' she said. 'I didn't know he was with another woman. I thought, it's a moment of crisis and he'll be back. He loved Sonya and Alexander. There were no warning signs.'

She tracked him down to the forbidding Lubyanka building that had been the headquarters of the KGB – the cliché image of the spurned wife demanding access to the lost husband at his place of work when all else fails to draw him back to the marital hearth. 'He came out and we went for a walk. I told him he was wrong, that he couldn't leave the kids. He didn't try to explain anything. All he said was that we wouldn't live together any more, that's for sure, he said. I was in a state of shock and was nearly run over by a car as I crossed the street. I told him, "You are a bastard," and he replied, "Yes, I am." '

It was five years before she saw him again – and then under very different circumstances indeed. But the twin perceptions of Litvinenko haunted him to the end: was he a mercenary-minded double-dealer or a hero; a Judas or a naif – someone his own mother described as 'a person who became lost in life'?

Perhaps no one's personality can be analysed in such simple categories. Perhaps the reality fell inconveniently somewhere between the two. And perhaps morality reserves a special category for affairs of passion, beyond the common categorization of good and evil. There are no greater tests – so frequently set, so often failed – than those of the heart.

'In 1993 I met my husband, Sasha,' Marina Litvinenko said in December 2006, a few days after she had buried him. When she pronounced his name, she paused. She was wearing a beige turtle-neck sweater. The venue for the interview was a conference room at the headquarters on Curzon Street of Bell Pottinger, Lord Tim Bell's PR company. Alex Goldfarb joined in halfway through, offering occasional translation but no other advice. Marina gave the impression of someone struggling to keep a lid on powerful emotions, reaching for a sense of control that she could not quite guarantee. Her outfit, her coiffed brown hair, her grey-green eyes, spoke to me of a kind of strength. Her skin was pale, with that washed-out look of immense grief slowly giving way to resignation. Struck by her apparent serenity in the early stages of our interview, I wrote the word 'composed' in my notebook. At the last moment, just as I went to switch off the tape recorder, I made another note that she had reached for a small packet of tissues that she had brought with her, as a precaution against this very moment. Then there was a scribbled annotation: 'tears'.

'I blamed myself that I did not do more for Sasha,' she said. 'I kept blaming myself for not saving him. It is still unbearable that he is not here. Just everybody who knew Sasha could describe him: he just loved life too much.'

Despite questions concerning her life, her thoughts, her feelings, the conversation kept on veering back to Litvinenko. She called him her birthday present in 1993 because of the meeting at her party.

'At this time Russia was like the Wild West because anybody who wanted to take money from other people could do it,' she said. 'I could see Sasha worked hard, but he could not explain everything to me. He spends not normal time. He would start early morning. If he started to do something, he could not sleep for two, three nights. You could describe him as workaholic. I just knew he was an unusual person. He looked so absolutely . . . he did not look tall, strong, big. He did not like to wear suits, ties. For him it was better to be invisible.'

But there was another comment on the times. 'We could see how corruption started. People did not like to work without extra money. A salary was worth nothing,' Marina told me. 'Because Sasha worked for the police, it was quite good money compared to others.'

Even Litvinenko's associates found that assertion improbable. Yuri Felshtinsky, the historian, who first met Litvinenko in the late 1990s at the Logovaz Club in Moscow along with some of his FSB colleagues, insisted that the 'official' salary could never have sufficed alone. 'The FSB salary is a delusion,' he said. 'Nobody ever lived on this salary since 1991. All of them were involved in different levels of commercial activity. Money was there. There was no problem.'

The money theme recurred, even as Litvinenko lay dying and his adversaries sought to discredit him. His first wife, Natalia, depicted her husband as almost obsessed with self-enrichment. But if wealth was his ambition, he never seemed to achieve it. One thing both wives agreed on was that Litvinenko was no Midas. He had no sense of how money was to be accumulated and nurtured. His financial problems, indeed, left him vulnerable in the end – overdependent on his mentor, Boris Berezovsky, over-anxious to make deals with people he mistakenly believed he could trust.

'In the early 1990s, when many KGB officers started leaving the Lubyanka to work for private companies, Sasha used to complain because he wanted to earn more money,' Natalia Litvinenko said. 'He always loved money, counted every single penny.'

His second wife offered a different, more generous impression: he was simply not equipped for life in the treacherous shoals of private enterprise; he needed a sponsor, a guide.

Like Natalia, Marina depicted money as a preoccupation for Litvinenko, but not so much because of greed as because of naivety, bewilderment about how to make it in the first place.

'Sasha did not know how to handle money,' Marina said in 2007. 'I mean, we always had enough, but we did not live luxuriously. We finally did buy an apartment, but it was small, just a one-bedroom. Our car was an ordinary Zhiguli. When his friends began driving foreign cars and buying fancy apartments, it became obvious that Sasha did not know how to do what they were doing to make money.'

Alex Goldfarb said that when Litvinenko was assigned to investigate the attempt on Berezovsky's life, the *operativnik* and the oligarch 'became friends'.

But how must that have seemed at the time?

Most successful businessmen had their contacts, their people, within the state structures, as informants or as officials able to block investigations or provide compromising information – *kompromat* – on opponents and rivals. If Litvinenko was Berezovsky's friend, how far did the friendship go? What were the terms? If there were gifts, what was expected in return? At that time, Berezovsky was playing a high-stakes game for influence in the innermost sanctum of the Kremlin. As friendships go, in other words, it was fairly uneven. Berezovsky was in the process of amassing a $3 billion fortune; Litvinenko was one year into his new relationship with Marina and struggling with a government salary shredded by inflation.

Berezovsky ran the Logovaz Club and had a magnificent dacha on the outskirts of Moscow. Alexander and Marina, with a child on the way, shared a two-room apartment with her parents. The tycoon sipped Château Latour. The investigator drank water. And yet he had a friend and sponsor called Boris Berezovsky – at least until just before he began to die.

Berezovsky maintained that Litvinenko had not been on his private payroll when the two men were in Moscow. At one point, Litvinenko 'came to me when I became executive secretary of the Commonwealth of Independent States,' Berezovsky said, but suggested that his protégé was still an employee of the state.

'Until he moved to London, he was just an employee of the FSB. I never had any business relations with him,' Berezovsky said. In London, Litvinenko was on the payroll. Berezovsky paid him a monthly £5,000. But, the tycoon told me, 'Half a year before he was poisoned, he left me. He took another job. One day he said: "Boris, I got another job – what do you think?" And I said: "I like that because it's better to be independent."'

According to Berezovsky, Litvinenko did not say what the job was, beyond the assertion that it was 'confidential'.

There is no doubt that on 1 November 2006, as he boarded the bus that trundled south to the glittery heart of London, Litvinenko was casting around with increasing desperation for some new way of making money. Even though he had quit his job with Berezovsky, Marina Litvinenko recalled, her husband secretly hoped that Berezovsky would try to keep him on and was somewhat bewildered when he did not.

'Maybe he expected Boris to say: "No, please stay with me." But Boris said: "OK – it is your decision." But it wasn't any broken words. Of course Sasha was just a little bit upset about it because he thought Boris maybe did not need him any more.'

For the first time in more than a decade, Litvinenko had no patron to offer him an all-embracing safety net, although Berezovsky paid the tuition for Anatoly Litvinenko at an upmarket private school in London. The increasing financial problems could well explain why the former agent's guard was down, why he cultivated people such as Andrei Lugovoi in quest of new business ventures, a new beginning.

Litvinenko's death has been described as a murder foretold, but his life did not always seem locked on such grisly coordinates. After his association with Berezovsky began in 1994 – one of many strands in the tycoon's web of contacts – the relationship looked set to proceed with a kind of mutual assistance that would benefit both men and help both survive in the Wild West free-for-all of Moscow.

Litvinenko had a new bride, a new son, a new sponsor.

He was soon obliged to demonstrate where his loyalty lay.

On 1 March 1995, one of Russia's best-regarded television talk-show hosts and managers, Vlad Listyev, was gunned down in the lobby of his apartment block in Moscow after announcing a moratorium on advertising at ORT, the television station that Berezovsky had come to control under a deal with Boris Yeltsin. Listyev was its director general.

The Listyev murder came to fascinate the writer Paul Klebnikov, particularly Berezovsky's frantic efforts to avoid arrest after the killing when police came to the Logovaz Club, demanding to interrogate him and search the premises.

Berezovsky refused point-blank and began to call on his

contacts. One of them was Alexander Litvinenko, whose pager started to buzz with an urgent message to call his 'friend' Boris.

As Alex Goldfarb later told it, Litvinenko, then holding the rank of major, first called a senior FSB commander with whom he had good relations – General Anatoly Trofimov, the head of the Moscow division of the FSB. Trofimov urged him to get in touch with Berezovsky and do what he could to resolve the crisis.

Litvinenko sped to the Logovaz Club to face down Berezovsky's tormentors. Confronting a Moscow police unit he believed to be corrupt, Litvinenko drew his service pistol and brandished his FSB credentials to pull rank, thwarting their efforts to search the Logovaz Club and take away Berezovsky for questioning about the Listyev murder.

If Berezovsky had agreed to accompany the officers, he would almost certainly have been jailed. In the worst scenario, he might never be seen alive again. At the very least, his ability to talk his way out of the crisis and distance himself from the murder would be severely constrained.

As a result of Litvinenko's intervention – and some behind-the-scenes manoeuvring – the police agreed to take Berezovsky's statement at the Logovaz Club, and then left. Denied the opportunity to search the building, police officers complained later, they were never able to complete their investigation, and no one was ever charged. Whoever murdered Listyev was never found.

Litvinenko had played a central part in this drama of a tycoon's political and physical survival – a fraught moment that could have cost Berezovsky his friendship with Yeltsin and thus his livelihood as a Kremlin insider. It remained a moot point whether Litvinenko frustrated judicial processes or prevented an abuse of them. But the crisis shifted his friendship with the tycoon on to a different level.

From then on, Berezovsky began referring to Litvinenko as a man who had saved his life. Rather than risk offending Litvinenko with the offer of a cash reward for his loyalty, Goldfarb recounted, Berezovsky took his new protector with him on a trip to Switzerland – a rare foreign excursion for the Russian *operativnik*. Not for the last time, Litvinenko travelled on false papers identifying him as Alexander Volkov, a diplomat at the Russian Embassy in Bern. When he called home to Marina, Litvinenko marvelled at life in Switzerland – his first and somewhat misleading impression of the West. 'You won't believe it; they don't lock the doors in the hotel, and the cops are as polite as your academics,' he said.

The events at the Logovaz Club that day in March 1995 are worth a second look because they show just how easily competing versions of events take root and begin to cross-pollinate in the annals of Litvinenko's adventures. In the versions recounted by Alexander Litvinenko and his friends, he did indeed draw his loaded service pistol. But in a newspaper interview in 1999, Berezovsky himself said, 'He did not have a weapon, as the provocateurs claim.' If that is the case, then the account of an armed FSB officer facing down a police unit is clearly one example among many of self-aggrandizement. Even if he did not draw a weapon, though, the episode was dramatic enough. Translated into a British context, the incident was the equivalent of a lone MI5 officer facing down men from Scotland Yard because he believed they were in the pay of the Mafia in a conspiracy to spirit away a British tycoon and frame him for the murder of Trevor McDonald.

If that sounds improbable, then it was a token of how far Russia in the 1990s had slipped away from Soviet controls and from any Western standard of normality. Of course, Litvinenko did have a service pistol. His first wife accused him of carelessly leaving it lying around at home where the children could find it. And he did have an FSB ID – a powerful totem in a world conditioned to omnipotent security services from the days of the Cheka, the forerunner of the KGB.

But perhaps the incident tells us more about the assumptions of those days.

If Litvinenko did draw a gun, then it was nothing unusual. If he believed he was facing down a police unit infiltrated by an organized crime gang, then that was nothing out of the ordinary either. And if he was acting, as he said, on the orders of a senior FSB commander to defend a businessman wanted in a high-profile murder case, then that, too, was nothing special. These were the times he lived in. These were the moments when his work led him to the belief that Russia's security services were honeycombed with corruption that he had a duty to eradicate – a conclusion that moulded his destiny.

5

WAR STORIES

At the time Berezovsky was becoming ever richer, Litvinenko embarked on a transformation of his own that had nothing to do with his wealthy mentor and would colour his views of his native land up to the very moment of his death.

In December 1994 Russian troops invaded Chechnya, a restive, mainly Muslim region in the northern Caucasus, close to the areas where Litvinenko had spent part of his childhood and undergone his basic military training. As an FSB officer, Litvinenko was deployed to interrogate prisoners and, by his own account, to ensure the loyalty of the ground troops involved in the fighting.

In his own case, however, this brief return to the northern Caucasus seemed to achieve precisely the opposite, accelerating Litvinenko's transformation from loyal operative to whistle-blower. (In later years, it was always assumed that Litvinenko was deployed in Chechnya itself, although the anecdotes that survive from that era suggest he operated in his home town of Nalchik and in the restive republic of Dagestan rather than in Chechnya.) A photograph from the era showed Litvinenko atop what looked like a T-80 tank, with its distinctive slabs of ceramic armour on its hull and turret. He was wearing bulky, cold-weather camouflage fatigues and a knitted black cap. Both he and an FSB colleague in the same uniform –

Alexander Gusak – carried AK-47 assault rifles with spare thirty-round clips taped to the magazine so that they could be switched quickly in combat, a common ploy among people who expect to be expending large amounts of ammunition. There was a hint of snow on the ground, and behind the tank other troops could be seen in ramshackle buses. Gusak and Litvinenko – friends then, later to become enemies – smiled at the camera. There was nothing in this picture to suggest that it showed more than two swaggering Russian buddies, city boys, embroiled in Moscow's unpleasant and frequently unsuccessful effort to subdue the unruly Muslim warlords of the northern Caucasus. They were out in the open, not taking cover from any enemy within range. Compared with the ragged state of some Russian soldiers in the Chechen campaign, the two FSB men looked well clothed and well fed: this was not a photograph showing the muck and blood of frontline fighting.

The campaign in the mid-1990s was only the latest of many attempts to pacify the Chechens, dating back some three hundred years. Indeed, in 1944, Stalin ordered the deportation of the entire Chechen nation to Kazakhstan and Siberia. Up to one-third of the deportees died in the process – a memory imprinted on the Chechen soul. This time, in late 1994, Boris Yeltsin ordered his troops to quash an independence movement under Dzhokhar Dudayev, a former Soviet air force general who proclaimed the region free from Moscow's control in 1991. It ended badly for Russia in May 1996, after the deaths of an estimated forty thousand people – most of them civilians.

As an FSB officer, Litvinenko was involved in both the recruitment and running of agents and the interrogation of prisoners. Using the same cover name that he had in Switzerland – Alexander Volkov – he worked out of the FSB headquarters in Nalchik, according to Akhmed Zakayev, a Chechen leader now exiled in London and supported by Boris Berezovsky.

Unknown to the FSB, the Chechen separatists had their own mole in the Russian security services, and 'Volkov' was soon identified by local people who knew him from his younger days in the town and from his father's family. Indeed, a half-sister, Tatiana, worked for the FSB handling secret cables between Nalchik and Moscow.

According to Zakayev, Litvinenko did succeed in 'turning' Chechen captives and sending them back to Chechnya as his agents. But, in the rose-glow of hindsight, the Chechen war exposed another aspect of Litvinenko as a sensitive and effective interrogator. That image was woven deeply into the portrayals that emerged before and after Litvinenko's death.

Zakayev believed that Litvinenko enhanced his reputation greatly when he questioned Alla Dudayeva, the widow of Dzhokhar Dudayev, assassinated by a sophisticated guided missile homing in on his cell phone close to the end of the war in April 1996. The Russians captured his widow as she attempted to flee the region, but they could not persuade her to confirm the fact of his death or identify his place of burial.

Litvinenko was among the FSB contingent assigned to guard her and, after a conversation with her, came to the conclusion that Dudayev had indeed perished in the missile attack. The widow was freed at the end of the war just five weeks after her husband died, and she returned to Chechnya. 'When she arrived back, she told me that a young officer of the FSB who interrogated her was Alexander Litvinenko and she had a very high opinion of him,' Zakayev said. Litvinenko had shown sympathy for her bereavement, and his questioning had been gentle and considerate. 'She called him "an accidental officer of the KGB structure" who did not belong there,' Zakayev said.

Not everyone agreed with that portrait of a touchy-feely Litvinenko, certainly not under the strain of battle: if there was one moment that tested Litvinenko, it came earlier in the small border village of Pervomayskoye in the bitter chill of a northern Caucasus winter.

At that time – January 1996 – Russian troops under FSB overall command had surrounded some two hundred Chechen fighters holding 140 hostages taken when they overran a hospital in nearby Kizlyar. Now they were struggling to return home, keeping the hostages as human shields. They had half a mile to go to the Chechen border.

Russia was not prepared to simply let them go.

The war had been raging for thirteen months. Around thirty thousand people had died, and the Russian military had been humiliated, held up for all to see as a hollow shell of the colossus that had repulsed Napoleon and Hitler. Now the fugitive Chechens were holed up in an unassuming settlement of a few score homes built around a mosque on a crisscross pattern of narrow streets. With their enemies apparently cornered, Russian commanders called in Special Forces backed by helicopter gunships and batteries of ferocious Grad missile launchers. The Russians also called in FSB men to interrogate Chechen fighters. That contingent included Alexander Litvinenko and Alexander Gusak, his companion in the tank photograph.

An initial Russian ground campaign to take the village of Pervomayskoye went badly. For two days, Russian troops, spear-headed by the supposedly elite Alfa and Vympel counterterrorism forces, sought to advance across snowy open ground, far too few in number to overrun the fortified, dug-in positions taken up by the Chechens. Some of the Russian units, drawn from the Interior Ministry forces that Litvinenko had once been part of, were unprepared for close combat. Wounded soldiers complained to reporters that they did not even have enough bullets to load into their AK-47s.

Reporting from the nearby village of Sovetskoye, Michael Specter, a correspondent for the *New York Times,* wrote as follows on 15 January: 'From a hill in this village, which borders Pervomayskoye, houses could be seen bursting into brilliant orange flames this morning as helicopter gunships, tanks, rocket-propelled grenades, and thousands of soldiers with machine guns tried to turn the hamlet's 100 buildings into ashes. One of the buildings in flames was the school where the rebels had confined their hostages, although some reports suggested that the captives had been moved.'

The longer the siege continued, the more Russia was put to shame by a handful of Chechen irregulars.

To highlight the impasse and to bring pressure on the Russians, moreover, Chechen separatists staged two more hostage dramas – one aboard a ferry packed with Russians on the Black Sea, the other in Chechnya itself. Russian patience at this humiliation grew thin and finally snapped on 17 January 1996, when Aleksandr Mikhailov, a Russian security services spokesman, announced that the Chechens had killed their hostages – an assertion that turned out to be completely untrue.

'Now we will destroy the bandits,' he said.

Within minutes, the Russians set about their attack, using heavy mortars and Grad multiple launchers firing volleys of 122-mm rockets designed to carpet-bomb battlefields and known more for massive destructiveness than for accuracy. One salvo from the truck-launched missiles could rain death and destruction on to an area the size of a football field. As the snow fell, Mi-24 helicopter gunships raked the flaming village with rocket fire. Journalists covering the siege were penned by the Russians in a nearby town, but even at that range the ferocity of the onslaught was clear.

'The Grads fell with monstrous concussive force throughout the day,' Specter wrote from the town of Kemsi-Yurt on 17 January. 'In this town, about four miles away, where journalists have been herded by Russian forces, windows cracked at the force of the repeated blasts.'

The attack ran on into the night with flares dropped from planes to illuminate the field of carnage. When it was all over, witnesses described the village as a ruin, the homes no more than skeletons of blackened roof timbers and the streets littered with dead cows and sheep, bloated under an icy shroud of snow. Valery Yakov, a Russian correspondent trapped in the village for four days, said: 'It was hell.' Miraculously, though, many of the Chechen militants and their hostages fled unscathed.

Litvinenko went into some detail about the siege of Pervomayskoye when he spoke in 2001 with Gerald Seymour, offering a lengthy account of his tactics as an interrogator and, in particular, an encounter with a young Chechen captive.

Seymour's notes concerning the episode are particularly illuminating, not simply because of the way Litvinenko described his own role but because they seemed to foreshadow a more refined version of a moment that came to be depicted as a Pauline conversion, when the FSB officer's eyes were opened to a reality that contradicted everything his KGB training had taught him about those who wielded power in Russia.

'In a military situation,' he told Seymour, 'the job of the FSB counterintelligence officer is to rate the men and officers – who is a coward, who is using drugs, who is selling weapons, who may defect to the Chechen bandits, who might be in touch with the independent media.'

There was no suggestion that Litvinenko went to Dagestan with anything other than patriotic duty on his mind. But then the interrogation of prisoners began and, with it, his own questioning of the entire Chechen campaign.

'The captured Chechens are interrogated. They are body-searched because many of them wear Western clothes and their dress is examined . . . and a search for military items, documents. Polaroid photos are taken of them for circulation among the hostages – did this man shoot/kill? The immediate objective is to separate hostages from Chechens.'

Seymour's notes suggested that Litvinenko cast himself as a subtle inquisitor, more good cop than bad.

'Interrogation technique . . . want to make the prisoner very relaxed because he is very stressed – give him a cigarette, imagine what he has been through in the last ten days and finally the terror of the battle and capture – he is isolated in a room, terrified that he will be tortured. Some of them are wounded. Nothing will be learned unless the interrogator can make a personal contact.'

As in Zakayev's account of the questioning of Alla Dudayeva, the suggestion was of a sensitive interlocutor, offering dialogue and sympathy, drawing the captive into a debate, using threats sparingly. Litvinenko dwelled, according to the notes, on one particular prisoner, a seventeen-year-old whom he called Sayed. He described him as a tough guy who challenged the interrogator to torture him and refused to give his real name.

The interrogator deployed 'the soft counterattack', exerting indirect psychological pressure, not physical duress.

Litvinenko told the seventeen-year-old that his photograph would be shown to surviving hostages to establish whether he was a killer likely to face murder charges. The interrogator hinted that the FSB would put out the word in his home village that Sayed had 'turned' to become an informer, exposing his parents to retribution. Litvinenko 'gets him to start talking about the Chechen cause after Alexander has apologized for what Russia has done to Chechnya. That's good – starts a political debate and the FSB officer can wrap the seventeen-year-old round his little finger.'

Within this narrative, one anecdote became a cameo that re-surfaced later in different forms as Litvinenko and others used his memories to build his myth.

'He learns everything about the boy, and then gives him water and food,' Seymour noted. The teenager told Litvinenko that a 'whole class of seventeen-year-old Chechen kids from a village had gone to war'.

In this account, the detail was recounted almost as an aside.

Three years later, however, in an interview for a Dutch film-maker, Jos de Putter, that same encounter with a teenage fighter moved to centre stage to explain the impact on Litvinenko of his exposure to the Chechen campaign. The boy was younger, but the episode was essentially the same except that it now seemed to have been embellished, spun.

'Once he told me a story about prisoners of war,' Zakayev, the exiled Chechen leader, told De Putter in 2004. 'One was a boy of fifteen. Sasha interrogated him: "Why are you one of those gangsters? Isn't school the best place for you? Why are you here?" And so forth. The boy said: "I'm not the only one. My whole class went to the front." Well, that incident touched Sasha deeply. "I now know for sure," he said, "that Russia will never win this war. Whatever the ideology may be, if a whole class joins in a fight, something else is going on." He then realized what the war means to Chechens. He told me that for him it was a radical turning point in the way he thought about this war.'

The same 'turning point' recurred in different forms among the episodes recounted by Litvinenko's friends after his death as they pieced together the hagiography of their lost crusader.

In Moscow and London, Litvinenko's critics came forward with their own rather different recollections.

Consider for a moment the account of the Pervomayskoye siege offered by Alexander Gusak, Litvinenko's comrade atop the tank, after the two men fell out bitterly.

'We had captured several militants that day,' Gusak said in one of several Russian newspaper interviews in November 2006. 'I spotted Litvinenko and instructed him to take one of the militants to the filtration point. That evening when I wanted to question the Chechen, they told me that Litvinenko had apparently tortured him to death. Litvinenko liked to make the prisoners scream. The young prisoner did not scream. So Litvinenko stuck a finger in his wound.'

So much for the 'soft counterattack'.

As for Litvinenko's courage, Gusak said that during the fighting for Pervomayskoye, 'I turned round and saw that Litvinenko was lying down. At first I thought he had been wounded. But when I came up to him, I saw that he was clearly scared out of his wits. This was the reason he was subsequently withdrawn from frontline operations to staff work.'

But how did that accusation of cowardice fit with the bravery Litvinenko later displayed in standing firm against the full might of the Kremlin as a whistle-blower within the FSB? If Litvinenko showed a yellow streak in Chechnya, why was he then chosen to join the same secret and elite unit as Gusak when the war was over?

For an outsider seeking unambiguous truths, the story of Alexander Litvinenko created much the same impression as a hall of mirrors at a fairground: somewhere in there was a straight and balanced image. The trick was simply to find it; to discount the extremes, the exaggerations; to draw a finer, less distorted picture. Litvinenko was a man who wielded the power of life and death over his prisoners but considered himself the custodian of a military tradition. He sought victory in Chechnya for Russia, but not at the expense of Russia's soul. But he was a man who had trained for the darker sides of soldiering and counterintelligence work, to track down organized crime gangs, to deal with tough people in tough ways.

War zones force people to acknowledge their true selves, and there is no harsher crucible of comradely knowledge than a shared foxhole: the battlefield creates its own ratings of courage and cowardice, and no one can hide from themselves for long. So why should Litvinenko's experience at Pervomayskoye have been somehow exempt from the brutality of a conflict that ranked among the most heartless, pointless and destructive of all those fought since the Second World War? Why should he have been a hero when few others were?

Perhaps, in the propagandists' rush for black-and-white definitions – coward or crusader – the finer shadings got lost. Maybe the true picture was of a man whose record was mixed and whose memories had been moulded retroactively – a man like others, prey to fears and rage yet seeing himself forged of nobler stuff than his fellows.

Vladimir Bukovsky came to know Litvinenko well and had his own views on the nature of the work he undertook for the FSB in the northern Caucasus.

Bukovsky was among the most prominent of the former Soviet dissidents, a hero among human rights activists, who had spent twelve years in the Gulag after disclosing the abuses of Soviet psychiatric institutions. He lived in a ramshackle detached home in a suburb of Cambridge. The front door, approached via a narrow path overgrown with prickly thorns, looked as if it needed a coat of paint. Bukovsky, a neurobiologist, had been in England for twenty-four years when Litvinenko arrived to begin his exile, and he received the newcomer over a battered table in his living room.

In the Russian way, Bukovsky drank dark tea diluted with hot water and smoked incessantly. In his study, the curtains were closed, and the ashtrays on his cluttered desk overflowed.

Bukovsky had been a father figure to Litvinenko, a guru, a role model in the annals of dissent against the prevailing power in Moscow. If Litvinenko had a father confessor about events in Dagestan, Bukovsky seemed a likely candidate.

'Of course, he was involved in all that,' Bukovsky said. It was, after all, a war, and Litvinenko was part of it.

But he went on: 'I can say only one thing for Sasha, I'm convinced that he never did anything dishonourable. That I'm sure of. He might have done something just as stupidity, as a mistake. That could be, but an intensely dishonourable thing, he couldn't do.'

Another Russian who spent time with Litvinenko in London was Andrei Nekrasov, a filmmaker who made several generally favourable documentaries about the fugitive agent's life in exile. 'He had fought in the mud, in the cold and the rain, as he himself said,' Nekrasov recalled. Perhaps there had been excesses of some kind, he went on, but they stopped short of the extremes men like Gusak accused him of.

'He was probably no angel,' Nekrasov said. 'People who are involved in things like that had to make a lot of compromises. But there was one boundary he could not cross.'

However it came about, something changed in Litvinenko after his experiences in the mid-1990s, as if Russia's – or his own personal – behaviour in that dirty, distant war had planted some shame or guilt in him.

Litvinenko himself railed against the Russian political leadership that had committed poorly equipped and badly trained soldiers to the disastrous war and then abandoned them. 'Soldiers have died in my arms,' he said. 'I was there when a boy of eighteen was hit by a bullet. He was gone in a second. All that time, not a leader, not a politician, told us why we were there, whom we were protecting, whom we were fighting.'

De Putter, the Dutch filmmaker, told me he sensed something

beyond anger – something more akin to guilt – in Litvinenko's memory of who he had been and what he had done in the mid-1990s.

'He must have been a tough character: you don't want to witness interrogation in Chechnya. They are always tortured,' De Putter said in May 2007.

Reminiscing about a three-hour interview he filmed with Litvinenko over the kitchen table at Osier Crescent on a dark February night in 2004, De Putter said he had been left with the impression that Litvinenko felt a profound urge to atone for his own actions in the mid-1990s – a tangle of personal and national guilt that would accompany him to his grave.

'I think he takes the blame for what happened. He went across some line he could not reverse,' De Putter said.

People seeking to explain Alexander Litvinenko's death said he made enemies, lots of them. It was also clear that, by accident or design or a combination of both, there was barely a moment in Litvinenko's career that could be classified as normal or routine. He met or mingled with the elite – including Berezovsky and Putin. He consorted with the man who would be accused of his own murder. He spied on his superiors, yet revered generals who attracted his loyalty. As an operative supposed to work in secrecy, he abandoned anonymity and thrust himself into the public eye, then sought to flee it. His death became even more unusual – bizarre, even – than his life: a man of humble roots achieved posthumous celebrity across the globe. His name, once unheard, became synonymous with Russian perfidy.

In his own narrative, Litvinenko always cast himself as the crusader, the champion of probity and cleanliness. At the same time, though, he moved in a dark world, assigned after the northern Caucasus to a unit with the initials URPO – the Department of Countermeasures Against and Prevention of the Activities of Organized Criminal Formations. As a body of men, it seemed bound by betrayals of one kind or another.

His immediate superior was Alexander Gusak, Litvinenko's

brother in arms from Pervomayskoye. The commander of the directorate was Yevgeny Khokholkov.

URPO, Litvinenko maintained, had been set up as what he called a 'fully autonomous, super-secret unit to carry out occasional "special tasks"' – in other words, extrajudicial killings, the kinds of operations the KGB called 'wet work'. As before in his career, however, there was a subplot. Litvinenko described his mission as going beyond simply working for the unit: within it, he was to act as a spy, a secret agent working on behalf of one FSB general against another. His former commander in the FSB's counterterrorism unit, Vyacheslav Volokh, bore a deep and abiding mistrust of the new URPO commander, suspecting him of diverting $1 million from the operational budget allocated to the Dudayev killing.

'Volokh was upset that there would be a rival operational division with greater powers than his own. So he gave me a secret assignment,' Litvinenko wrote of his transfer to URPO, 'to dig out all the dirt I could find on Khokholkov,' his commander.

Litvinenko seemed all too ready to imbue a drama with conspiratorial elements, amplifying his own part in the proceedings.

'I ended up in a division that worked for "the court",' he told De Putter in 2004. 'And I saw how . . . the brass lived. Then I realized that these people were just robbing my nation. Some FSB officers became richer and richer. They had expensive cars, dachas, houses, bank accounts. They also ran banks. They did that clandestinely. With help from criminals. Nineteen ninety-six was the key year. Around 1996 the leadership of the FSB fell into the hands of those who had been fighting dissidents all their lives, former officers of the KGB's Fifth Division, and now we see that the secret services have grabbed power.'

The assignment to this new unit, he said, seemed to be propelling him inexorably towards becoming precisely the kind of hit man he had been trained to root out and bring to justice. He knew that whatever choice he made would set the coordinates for the rest of his life. Within URPO he cast himself as a moral leader, albeit under the formal command of Alexander Gusak.

'When I was ordered to kill people, I refused,' he said later. 'At first I just didn't do it, and no one made a fuss. But when they kept insisting, I openly refused to do it.'

As he told his subordinates, they faced three choices.

'We can start killing, but there's no way back. We'll be rich, of course. We'll murder for our bosses, who will let us kill in our own interest. We'll earn a lot of money. In Moscow, hit men easily make $20,000 a month. But if we start doing that, there's no way back.

'The second possibility is that we just don't do it and risk being demoted.

'The third possibility is that we go public, which means standing in front of a camera.'

He was fully aware of the stakes. 'Opposing this system is suicide,' he said – not the only time in his life that melodramatic words turned out to be eerily prescient.

One order in particular brought Litvinenko up short against a test of loyalties – to his FSB comrades or to the tycoon who called him a friend.

On 27 December 1997, Captain Alexander Kamyshnikov, Khokholkov's deputy, called Litvinenko and members of his unit to his office and issued an order to kill. The target was Boris Berezovsky, and there was a warped logic to the command.

Litvinenko's superiors evidently calculated that he was the man for the job because his relationship with Berezovsky would enable him to get close.

Instead, Litvinenko told Berezovsky about the order. Berezovsky told the newspapers and the president himself.

There is a riddle here within the broader mystery. At this time, Berezovsky was a man of enormous wealth and influence. He had played a central part in manoeuvring Yeltsin back into power. Berezovsky was known to be a Kremlin insider. So who would dare order his murder? And who would dare pull the trigger?

Yet on 5 November 1997 – seven weeks before the order – Yeltsin had unceremoniously sacked Berezovsky from his influential government job as deputy secretary of the Russian Security Council.

The move was taken as the dramatic outcome of a power play between Berezovsky and his supporters among the oligarchs and economic reformers in the Kremlin, led by the deputy prime minister Anatoly Chubais.

Chubais had been a central figure in the Davos Pact, but had since favoured a Berezovsky rival, Vladimir Potanin, within the ranks of Russia's politically connected tycoons. Berezovsky's dismissal was seen as a sign that he was losing the fight. So was there a hint of weakness in Berezovsky's position?

If Litvinenko subsequently depicted himself as the crusader for justice, he also took his time to weigh the options. As he recalled later, he told his URPO colleagues: ' "I don't know what will happen to me," I said, "but each of us must decide for themselves what to do." We thought about it for a few months, then we publicly defied our superiors. We told the public prosecutor that we had been given criminal orders.' That led to an internal inquiry, during which Litvinenko and some of his comrades were suspended from duties.

The chronology of the time suggests that it was indeed at least two months later, in February or March 1998, that Litvinenko and his comrades passed on the news of the assassination order to Berezovsky himself. When they did, however, they handed Berezovsky a powerful weapon.

With Berezovsky's active support, the dissident officers also took out a kind of insurance policy, secretly taping a video recording of themselves late one night in April 1998 in the presence of a television journalist, Sergei Dorenko, the leading anchor at Berezovsky's ORT station.

Their reasoning was simple: they believed they were at risk of being killed themselves, and so they wished to place on record their allegation that they had been issued with unlawful orders; the tape's existence just might protect them from assassination. For Berezovsky, too, the tape provided potent ammunition in his joust with the FSB leadership of the times.

There was never any doubt about what the dissidents claimed they had been ordered to do. 'For me it was like an order, because first came one assignment, then another, and then: "You should be ready to kill Berezovsky",' Litvinenko told the camera.

He also denounced Kamyshnikov as the source of the order. 'He was sitting at his desk, then he stood up and said: "You should kill Berezovsky." First he asked: "Are you ready?" And then: "You should kill." That was in the presence of three other officers.'*

The video-recording session began just before midnight at Berezovsky's luxurious dacha outside Moscow and showed Gusak, the section commander, Litvinenko and a third member of their team, Andrei Ponkin, who acted as Litvinenko's second-in-command. Marina Litvinenko, present at the dacha, witnessed the whole confession of the dirty tricks her husband and his colleagues were involved in – the first time he had exposed her to the dark side of his work. But the dissident officers were not the only people who took out insurance that night: Berezovsky kept a copy of the tape to broadcast at a time that suited him best.

The outcry concerning URPO prompted a purge within the FSB. Its director, a Berezovsky adversary called Nikolai Kovalyov, was dismissed in July 1998, and Khokholkov was shunted sideways into a job with the tax authorities. But the manoeuvring had one momentous side-effect, underlining the law of unintended consequences.

As head of the FSB, Kovalyov was replaced by an obscure Kremlin administrator called Vladimir Vladimirovich Putin – an

---

* The time gap between this purported order to kill and the whistle-blowing it inspired has led some to suggest that the order was never given, that it was simply invented by Berezovsky as part of a plot to persuade President Yeltsin to purge the FSB of his enemies. Many years later, however, Alexander Gusak did say that the order had been given – but not in any seriousness, and not in writing.

appointment at the time seen as so lacking in significance that it merited only a five-paragraph news agency story in the *New York Times*.

The power play had begun.

Berezovsky was determined to press his advantage and purge the FSB of opponents, using the new and untested director as his tool. One of his first ploys was to arrange for Litvinenko to meet with Putin soon after Putin assumed his new responsibilities.

Much later, when Litvinenko lay dying in London, the fact that he had met personally with Putin was not widely known outside the narrow circle of Berezovsky's entourage and Litvinenko's supporters. But Litvinenko himself had in fact written about the encounter in *Lubyanka Criminal Group* – a tirade against corruption in the FSB that had been published in Russian in 2002.

In hindsight, it made interesting reading. For all Putin's later efforts to belittle Litvinenko and for all his denials that he knew much about him, the book showed that Litvinenko had in fact met the future president at a time when Putin's career was beginning its meteoric rise.

It seemed improbable that a former KGB officer such as Putin, with antennae quivering to detect disloyalty, would have forgotten a man who confronted him with a far-reaching choice: to purge the FSB or to maintain the loyalty of his chosen allies.

It was equally clear that, at this time, Litvinenko saw his chance to make a dramatic step forward, ingratiating himself with a new director apparently indebted to his mentor, Boris Berezovsky. For an ambitious FSB colonel, the possibilities must have seemed immense.

The night before the meeting with Putin, Litvinenko barely slept, spending his time drawing up an operational chart for the new boss of the FSB. 'It contained all I knew about organized crime and corruption, the principal mob groups, with their areas of activity. Each had arrows leading to their connections in the government, the FSB, the Interior Ministry, the Tax Service.'

Litvinenko arrived at Putin's office in the Lubyanka 'with two colleagues, but Putin wanted to see me alone.

'It must be incredibly tough for him, I thought. We were of the same rank, and I imagined myself in his shoes – a mid-level *operativnik* suddenly put in charge of some hundred seasoned generals with all their vested interests, connections and dirty secrets. I did not know how to salute him without causing embarrassment. Should I say "Comrade Colonel", as was required by the code? But he pre-empted me and got up from his desk, shook my hand. He seemed even shorter than on TV.

'From the very first moment I felt that he was not sincere. He avoided eye contact and behaved as if he were not the director but an actor playing the director's role.'

Putin showed no interest in Litvinenko's charts and arrows, or even in a list Litvinenko presented with the names of reliable officers. 'These officers are clean,' Litvinenko told him. 'I know for sure that you can rely on them in the war on corruption.' The name at the head of the list was that of General Anatoly Trofimov, who, long after his retirement as a state security officer, was gunned down in mysterious circumstances on a street in Moscow in April 2005 along with his young wife and in front of his four-year-old daughter.

Vladimir Putin never pursued the contact with Litvinenko – not directly at least. 'He never called,' Litvinenko wrote. 'Many months later I got the chance to study my own file, and I learned that he had ordered a case against me right after that meeting.' Indeed, according to Litvinenko, when he handed Putin his phone number for further contacts, Putin immediately ordered a tap on the line.

Berezovsky, though, seemed determined to maintain pressure on the new director of the FSB.

On 11 November 1998 he sent an open letter to Putin, published in his own newspaper, *Kommersant*.

'Dear Vladimir Vladimirovich,' Berezovsky wrote, using the respectful patronymic, 'I am astonished that no due assessment was given to the URPO bosses' activity after your appointment as FSB director.

'Criminal terror is gaining pace in the country,' the letter said, asking Putin to 'use your powers to restore constitutional order'.

Then, by no coincidence at all, on 17 November 1998, Litvinenko led several other URPO officers at an extraordinary news conference to restate their insistence that they had been ordered to murder Boris Berezovsky.

If Litvinenko had not secured the enduring opprobrium of Vladimir Putin at their meeting in July, he certainly succeeded in doing so at the news conference in November.

More than any single event in Litvinenko's career as an ally of Boris Berezovsky in the Moscow of the 1990s, the news conference sealed his reputation as a turncoat who had forfeited any claim on the protection of the FSB hierarchy. That seemed to be the exact opposite of what he was trying to achieve, at least in his own eyes. For him, the event represented a chance to advocate a new order in the security services. Instead, he marked himself for all time as an adversary of those Putin regarded as his allies.

The press conference took place at an auditorium in the Interfax news agency headquarters in central Moscow. The night before, Yuri Felshtinsky met Litvinenko for the first time at Berezovsky's Logovaz Club as he and his comrades drafted their statement. 'It was clear that Alexander was the leader,' Felshtinsky said. 'He was the person writing the statement, reading the statement.' The fact that the preparations were made at the Logovaz Club showed clearly that Berezovsky was manoeuvring for advantage, as he had in the secret taping session with Sergei Dorenko.

The whistle-blowers accompanying Litvinenko at the news conference that day included Andrei Ponkin – one of the three dissidents who recorded the video back in April 1998 – Colonel Viktor Shebalin, Lieutenant German Shcheglov and Senior Lieutenant Konstantin Latyshonok. The veteran operative Alexander Gusak, sensing that a chill wind had begun to blow on the entire whistle-blowing venture, did not participate.

The mavericks' appearance, to say the least, was unusual.

One of them, Shebalin, wore a full-face ski mask to hide his identity. Others wore large dark glasses, as if that would offer some disguise. Litvinenko showed his face completely. There was another FSB man there – Mikhail Trepashkin, an FSB officer and lawyer – but he was not an URPO operative: rather, he wished to testify that Litvinenko and his URPO comrades had indeed carried out an illegal order by beating him up.

On another occasion, the dissident officers said, they had been ordered to arrange a hostage-taking to ransom a prominent hotelier and businessman, Umar Dzhabrailov.

Bizarrely enough, Putin was the man the whistle-blowers most wanted as an audience, the man they were appealing to as the potential scourge of FSB corruption.

'We would like to emphasize right off that we are not the enemies of the FSB and its present chief, Vladimir Putin, as our opponents would have the public believe,' Litvinenko said in a joint statement he read aloud on behalf of the maverick opera-tives. 'We do not seek to compromise the Federal Security Service, but to purify and strengthen it.'

Litvinenko's complaint at the news conference was simple, the beginning of a refrain that would accompany him to his death: the FSB, supposed to be the very guarantor of Russian security and probity, was corrupt, eroded from within by officers linked to the very criminal activities they were supposed to guard against. Far from protecting the nascent post-Soviet state, FSB agents and high-ranking officers were offering themselves as hired guns 'to settle accounts with undesirable persons, to carry out private political and criminal orders for a fee and sometimes simply as an instrument to earn money.' The maverick agents went so far as to accuse the highest-ranking FSB officers of 'abusing their offices, issuing illegal orders to commit terrorist acts and assassinations, to seize hostages, to extort large sums of money from commercial structures, and other illegal actions.

'We are not opponents of the system of state security,' Litvinenko insisted. 'On the contrary, we want it to be strength-ened. But how can state security bodies be strengthened if they have in their employment individuals who are actually violating the constitution and our legislation?'

There was a counter-theme, too, that would be revisited often by critics after Litvinenko's death, suggesting that, far from exposing the corrupt ways of the FSB, he had been an exponent of its worst excesses.

From the very moment Litvinenko began to speak out, he attracted smears. Russian newspapers, he told the news conference, had 'claimed that together with my colleagues and comrades I had committed eleven assaults, that I was implicated in ten murders and that I extorted $70,000, resorting to torture and violence with regard to a merchant.' Those allegations would return in the days after his death, when it became pressingly important for the Kremlin to denigrate him.

The news conference was unusual in other ways.

'I have a question to the man wearing a mask,' a Russian television reporter said. 'You are hiding your face and your comrades wear dark glasses. Are you afraid of something?'

The masked man, Shebalin, replied: 'Because I have often worked in various trouble spots and carried out such assignments as infiltrating the criminal world, I have to work to this day. So I have to wear a mask.'

'And your comrades wear dark glasses,' the reporter persisted.

'I have worked for a longer period than they,' the masked man replied, somewhat ambiguously.

At that point Litvinenko broke in to say that the reason he was not masked was simply that he had been identified by a Russian newspaper six months earlier. As at other points in the news conference, he seemed almost petulant, observing that he had lodged countless official complaints about harassment but his superiors had done nothing to support him.

Perhaps it did not occur to him that whistle-blowers rarely receive the protection of the institutions they accuse of gross malpractice. It was not the first time that he seemed naive or just plain stubborn.

For months before the news conference, Litvinenko disclosed, he and his superiors had been at loggerheads not only over his refusal to murder Berezovsky but also over his refusal to keep quiet about it. Fellow agents, he said, accused him of 'not allowing patriots of the country to kill a Jew who plundered half of the country'.

The news conference was a turning point in many ways. The event left Putin embarrassed. His service was being openly challenged by a manipulative tycoon and an upstart FSB officer whose rank reminded him of his own career ceiling as a lieutenant colonel.

It is unlikely, to say the least, that by 2006 Putin would have forgotten the secret agent who went public to denounce the service he was heading and demand that it be cleansed of corruption and treachery.

It is equally unlikely that Litvinenko's death would cause too many tears to flow either at the Lubyanka or in the Kremlin. 'What's probably important to understand is that you would not find too many people in the FSB who would not think that he should be killed,' Felshtinsky said during a telephone conversation in early 2007.

At the time, the news conference drew little attention outside Russia. With hindsight, it may well have begun to trace the outlines of the power play that would cost Berezovsky his access to the Kremlin and his tenure in Russia, placing him on the wrong side of the manoeuvring centred on Putin's FSB.

Less than one year later, in August 1999, President Boris Yeltsin appointed Vladimir Putin as his prime minister – against Berezovsky's wishes. Within months, the former FSB director was elected president of the Russian Federation, and Berezovsky, once the new leader's sponsor and supporter, would be preparing for life in exile.

The looming showdown was perhaps foreshadowed in the tone of a public statement by Putin issued on the same day as Litvinenko's press conference in response to Berezovsky's open letter to him.

It left no room for doubt that the whistle-blowers' campaign was doomed – and Berezovsky's career, too, if he continued siding with them. It was a warning that Berezovsky ignored at his peril.

'In the first place,' Putin said of Berezovsky's complaints, 'the letter puts the new Russian security service, which is defending the interests of the entire nation, in the same category as extremist forces and quasi-criminal elements. We find this sort of comparison insulting.

'Our service is acting strictly within the framework of the law. It defends the constitutional system and security of an individual, society and the state against threats, wherever they may come from. I believe any person who cares about the country's interests will support this principled stance.'

Putin was serving notice that, as a former KGB officer himself, he would build its successor agency into the central bulwark of his power base. He criticized the whistle-blowers, threatening them with legal action if their case was not proven. Although Berezovsky later helped fund Putin's presidential election campaign in 2000, just as he had sponsored Yeltsin in 1996, the rift between the two men – by no means simply related to the Litvinenko affair – was far too deep for bridging. Even a country the size of Russia, it seemed, was not big enough for both of them.

By way of a response to Putin's rebuke, Berezovsky aired excerpts from the tape recorded by Litvinenko, Gusak and Shebalin seven months earlier – thumbing his nose at the new head of the FSB.

The events surrounding the news conference set the stage for the subsequent clash of wills pitting Putin's assertive new economic and political nationalism against oligarchs like Berezovsky, whom he saw as little more than looters, scavengers on the Soviet carcass. The lesson for Berezovsky and his lowly protégé was the same, as many others have since discovered: Vladimir Putin did not brook challenge. Within months, Alexander Litvinenko had been jailed on charges of abusing his office and had been suspended from the FSB along with his fellow whistle-blowers.

'I was sacked on 10 January 1999,' Litvinenko said later. 'It was his personal signature. Personal. My order of dismissal was signed personally by Putin.'

Clearly, Litvinenko could expect no mercy or protection from Vladimir Putin – a factor that his widow and others would cite as evidence of the Kremlin's complicity in his death.

Not only that, but in tilting at the FSB establishment, Litvinenko earned the abiding hatred of some of his former colleagues and fellow whistle-blowers who later found it only too easy to return to the FSB and denounce him as the author of their own betrayals and downfalls.

Viktor Shebalin, for instance, warned him in 2000: 'Litvinenko, you had better come back and give yourself up. You have no other way out . . . Let me make it clear: we do not forgive traitors.'

Alexander Gusak also accused him of betraying his comrades, setting himself up for vengeance. 'I tell you honestly,' he said in 2007, 'I didn't advise any of them to go and kill Litvinenko, though one of them did say: "Listen, he's done you so much wrong. Shall I bring you his head?" '

Gusak left no doubt as to how he believed Litvinenko should be treated. 'I consider him a direct traitor, because he betrayed what's most sacred for any operative – his operational sources.'

Gusak's accusation, made long after Litvinenko fled Russia, was never proven, but it foreshadowed similar allegations after his death linking him to British intelligence.

'For that – and I speak as a lawyer – what Litvinenko did comes under Article 275 of the Criminal Code,' Gusak said. 'It's called treason. And there are sanctions – prescribed punishments. Up to twenty years in prison.

'But that's in accordance with the law. I was brought up on Soviet law. That provides for the death penalty for treason – Article 64. I think if in Soviet times he had come back to the USSR, he would have been sentenced to death.'

The bitterness was deep and abiding.

When I met Maxim, Litvinenko's half-brother, on the Italian

coast in the summer of 2007, he told me that the news conference and the accusations against Litvinenko 'worried me a lot. Our brother would never have been part of any dirty political games.' In 1998, Maxim was a seventeen-year-old high school student, and as a result of the press conference, he said, he was accused of drug offences and suspended for two months. His father was beaten up on his way to work. His older sister, Tatiana, an FSB cipher clerk in Nalchik, learned that the agency had launched a smear campaign against Alexander Litvinenko. 'They went to friends, neighbours, to say he was a traitor. But the family could not abandon our brother, so we had to go against the whole system,' Maxim said.

By January 1999 Litvinenko was facing the first of several trials, accused on five counts of torturing witnesses, tampering with evidence and abuse of office. The charges included beating up the driver of an organized crime suspect – and leaving a tiny bruise. He spent seven months in the FSB's Lefortovo prison in Moscow, thirty-six days of it in solitary confinement. The prison was still notorious as the facility used by the KGB to detain and 'disappear' its suspects.

'Lefortovo crushes you spiritually,' Litvinenko recalled. 'There is some negative energy coming from those walls. They say that birds avoid flying over it. Perhaps it's the legacy of the old days when Lefortovo was a place of mass executions and torture.'

On 26 November 1999 a judge found Litvinenko not guilty on all counts. But the minute he was acquitted, masked and armed officers wearing camouflage fatigues rearrested him in the courtroom. He returned to a different prison – Butyrka, the biggest criminal jail in Moscow. Again he was accused of beating and extortion, only to be freed several weeks later, on 16 December 1999.

It is unlikely that either Putin or Berezovsky was focusing particularly closely on the case: Russia went to the polls to elect a new parliament on 19 December 1999; Berezovsky joined the Duma as the deputy for Karachay-Cherkessia, the small region in the northern Caucasus where he had campaigned for election; the

Second Chechen War was under way and Putin, by then prime minister, cemented his position as the most favoured candidate to become president of Russia.

When Litvinenko was released in December, his passport was confiscated, and the authorities ordered him not to leave Moscow. But his exit plans went far beyond the city limits.

6

FROM RUSSIA WITH STEALTH

After so many court appearances, so much notoriety, Litvinenko was a man marked for retribution. The career that had consumed his working life was in ruins. The Russian security service, his master for two decades, had repulsed him as a turncoat; he would not be forgiven. At the very least, his trials on unfounded charges would continue.

Scanning his uncertain prospects as a new century dawned, Litvinenko knew it was only a matter of time before he was re-arrested to face a different catalogue of accusations, this time that he had stolen explosives from an FSB depot and used them as a plant to frame a suspect.

With every new set of charges, the hearings would be set in ever more remote courtrooms far from the relative judicial scrutiny of Moscow. His protestations of innocence would carry no weight.

Additionally, Litvinenko no longer believed that his former employers in the FSB would leave his family out of his feud with them, and he feared that his wife, Marina, and young son, Anatoly, would be harmed if he continued his uneven campaign against the system that had rejected him so comprehensively. Former associates made clear that the judicial process against him had to do with punishment, not justice. It was not inconceivable that, once convicted, he would disappear for good. Yuri

Felshtinsky, the historian, counselled him to flee. But that advice, too, raised an acute dilemma: if staying in Moscow seemed impossible, escape was fraught with hazard.

He had surrendered his passport for foreign travel to the authorities, so any journey beyond Russia's frontiers would require a degree of tradecraft in subterfuge and the acquisition of false papers. That might not be an insuperable problem for a man with his background – and his connections. But this was 2000: the Cold War had been over for a decade. Defections, always treated with suspicion by Western intelligence agencies, were no longer in vogue. Unlike some of the big names in the annals of East–West espionage such as Oleg Gordievsky, Litvinenko had no big-time handler in the CIA or MI6 to pluck him to safety. He may have been a whistle-blower, but he was not a prized double agent; the secrets he had learned in the line of duty were of uncertain value outside Russia. There was no record of anyone owing him a debt for services rendered to a foreign intelligence agency (even if such debts were acknowledged in that murky world of compromise, ambiguity and betrayal).

And even if he managed to leave Russia, how could he ensure the safety of his family?

In practical terms, Litvinenko's problems divided neatly into two questions, neither of which offered easy answers: how to get out of Russia, and how to find some place in the West to offer sanctuary.

Initially, Litvinenko turned for advice to General Anatoly Trofimov, the high-ranking officer in the FSB whose counsel he had sought in the Listyev murder case in 1995. But when he spoke to the general, he was in for another surprise. As much as parts of Russia were unsafe for Litvinenko, the general warned him to regard large parts of Western Europe as off limits, too.

'Trofimov said don't go to Italy, France, or Germany,' Litvinenko recalled. 'He advised me to go to two countries: Britain or the United States.' But neither of those countries could be reached without two things Litvinenko could not simply conjure out of thin air: a valid passport and a visa. Even if he miraculously acquired authentic papers, it was inconceivable that he would simply walk through the departure controls at Moscow's Domodedovo or Sheremetyevo airport without unwelcome attention from his former comrades in the FSB.

If he was to flee, the itinerary would be roundabout, risky and illegal – no way to travel with a family in tow. But if he left his family behind – an option he was loath to consider – his wife and son would surely be punished for his actions, held hostage to force his return from self-exile.

Of course, a successful flight into exile would place him beyond the reach of prosecutors preparing a new dossier to bring him back to court. But if his escape failed, if he were apprehended at some far-flung border crossing carrying false papers, the list of charges against him could only increase. He would be breaking a court order to remain in Moscow while seeking the blessings of a foreign power. The prosecutors, and the Kremlin propaganda machine, would have no difficulties at all in punishing and vilifying him, not just as a rogue agent and a whistle-blower but as a traitor and a fugitive from justice too.

Litvinenko's quandary showed just how much Russia – and his place in it – had shifted since the days when he had been a regular at the Logovaz Club, rubbing shoulders with the power elite.

Putin, whom he initially perceived as a potential ally, had turned against him, accumulating ever greater power as prime minister and then as president. And Berezovsky, Litvinenko's mentor, was in trouble himself. His days of power-broking and self-enrichment were over. If the tycoon stayed in Russia, he would almost certainly face punitive legal action, the kind the Kremlin reserved for those among the oligarchs – such as himself and Mikhail Khodorkovsky, head of the Yukos oil giant – who earned Putin's disfavour. Putin had chosen those he would allow to be rich – such as Roman Abramovich, once Berezovsky's protégé – and those he would bring to heel, along with their acolytes. Berezovsky was Litvinenko's 'roof', but his protection was fraying rapidly.

Berezovsky was already spending increasing amounts of his

time out of the country. Prosecutors were investigating his stewardship of the Aeroflot airline. The tide of history had turned against both the oligarch and his operative.

It was time to escape.

It may have crossed Litvinenko's mind that self-exile was no foolproof guarantee of security, as the events of 1 November 2006 would confirm all too finally. But defection certainly seemed the only choice left open to him.

'I'm not sure that Sasha wanted to leave the country,' his half-brother Maxim told me. 'It was only at the moment that he believed his son was in danger. People said he was a traitor, but he was a patriot. Right up to the end, anything he did, he did for Russia.'

In the autumn of 2000, an uneasy-looking family group gathered in the sun-struck resort of Antalya on Turkey's Mediterranean coastline, offering an unusual addition to the last of the season's package tourists. There was a slender man – with light brown hair and dubious travel documents – who had arrived on a circuitous route from Moscow via a clandestine ferry crossing and a mysterious third country. His wife, a former ballroom dancer, and six-year-old son had flown in to join him from a different destination in Marbella, Spain. Finally, there was Alex Goldfarb, who would emerge much later as the family spokesman in yet more difficult times. And, standing by to meet them farther on in their journey, a New York immigration lawyer called Joe had flown in from a job in Eastern Europe.

When the members of the Litvinenko family group met in Antalya, one thing was abundantly clear: Turkey could offer no more than a brief halt in transit. If their status became known to the authorities in Ankara, the Russians would most likely be slung into detention and then sent back, willy-nilly, to Moscow. The local newspapers were full of stories about a massive official campaign to repatriate Russians residing illegally in Turkey.

Litvinenko was heading west, but Turkey was an ambiguous

way station, caught between Europe and Asia, spanning a landmass that stretched from the western border with Greece and Bulgaria to, in the east, the mountainous redoubts abutting Iraq and Iran along with lands of the former Soviet Union – Azerbaijan, Armenia and Georgia.

Since the days of Mustafa Kemal Atatürk, the soldier who founded the modern Turkish state in 1923, Turkey's secular ideologues had looked for inspiration to the West, but its soul could not escape the pull of Islam or the memory of the great realm of the Ottoman Empire stretching to Mesopotamia, Palestine, the Nile and beyond.

Turkey was a member of the NATO alliance but a land whose MIT security services had a reputation for being as pervasive and brutal as the KGB.

Moreover, Turkey had a centuries-long history of wars with Russia – an epic clash of empires and cultures – and was in no hurry to open another chapter of hostilities, certainly not with a new and untested president in power in the Kremlin.

As the immigration lawyer was to remark, Turkey was far less a place of sanctuary than a place that some of its own citizens preferred to flee.

There was no way back to Moscow, but it was not at all certain which country they would go to next.

Unlike most people in Antalya, content to soak up the last rays of the season's sun, the Litvinenkos could barely wait to leave. Their difficulty lay not so much in locating loungers on the beach or choosing a restaurant for dinner as in finding a place to be safe for the rest of their lives.

The escape from Moscow fell into two parts: Litvinenko's solo flight beyond Russia's borders and the subsequent journey of Marina and Anatoly to join him for the final, fraught voyage to sanctuary.

Litvinenko had already shown a grasp of complex logistics and artifice to get to Antalya, and he had one ace to play: while the authorities in Moscow had stripped him of his passport for foreign travel, they had not taken away his 'internal' passport, according to Yuri Felshtinsky. Like Alex Goldfarb, Felshtinsky claimed a significant part in the escape.

In the autumn of 2000, Litvinenko told his wife that he was heading out of town to visit his father Walter in the northern Caucasus town of Nalchik. The trip was no more than a cover story, a fiction.

Instead of visiting Nalchik, Litvinenko took an internal flight and then a bus trip to the Black Sea port of Sochi in southern Russia. His plan was to take one of the frequent ferries plying the 170 miles of water to Batumi, in Georgia, close to the border with Turkey.

But there was a problem to be resolved. Russia's border guards were supposed to keep close watch on the ports to ensure that neither criminals nor 'terrorists' fled the country. The rules required travellers to check in several hours before their ferry's departure so that their identities could be verified. Litvinenko could not run the risk of being detected so early in his escape, while his wife and son were still in Moscow. If his identity was exposed at the ferry port, the entire escape plan would collapse, with disastrous consequences for himself, his family and his backers.

Litvinenko delayed his arrival at the ferry terminal until just a few minutes before the vessel was due to sail. The border guards remonstrated against his late arrival, but, according to Felshtinsky, Litvinenko talked his way on to a ship with a combination of bluster and a $10 bribe.

At that time, citizens of Georgia and Russia – once bound together in the Soviet Union – did not require foreign travel pass-ports to visit each other. The 'internal' passport was enough to permit him to travel, Felshtinsky recalled.

As the ferry pulled out from Sochi, Litvinenko breathed a sigh of relief: phase one – the escape from Russia – was over.

Now all he needed was a destination to offer him sanctuary, and he still hoped that would be the United States of America.

*

As a transit stop, Georgia was a natural choice. Since the collapse of the Soviet Union, it was a sovereign nation, with its own airport and, most important of all, an American Embassy. It had the added distinction that it was home to Berezovsky's close associate, Badri Patarkatsishvili.

Like Berezovsky, Patarkatsishvili had fallen foul of Vladimir Putin and was wanted in Russia, along with Berezovsky and another executive, Yuli Dubov, accused of embezzling funds from the AutoVAZ company in 1994–95, when the ascent of the oligarchs was well under way. By 2000, Patarkatsishvili's Georgia had become a refuge. For Litvinenko, it also offered a bridge to neighbouring Turkey, and thence a route to the West. It is hard to imagine that the financial outlays for the escape did not come from the coffers of Boris Berezovsky, himself planning to formalize his departure from Russia in late 2000 as Vladimir Putin's net closed around him.

Back in Moscow, Marina Litvinenko was in an anguish of uncertainty. Her husband had simply dropped out of sight. She suspected something was afoot but had no sense of the audacity and scope of Litvinenko's plan. She did not even know how to contact him until Litvinenko got word to her through a mutual friend to obtain a new cell phone whose number would not be known to the authorities.

In Tbilisi, the Georgian capital, Litvinenko met up with Felshtinsky, a resident of Boston and a historian whose career had been divided between Russia and the United States. Felshtinsky had flown in from the United States at the behest of Boris Berezovsky.

Publicly, Felshtinsky was an academic who would emerge as an editor and author of various projects linked to Boris Berezovsky and Alexander Litvinenko. But he was not a covert operative: helping a fugitive FSB officer escape Russia could hardly have been in his comfort zone.

As Felshtinsky explained later, as soon as Litvinenko arrived in Georgia, the signal went out to Marina to take the first available package tour she could find to a destination in Western Europe.

She reserved places for her and Anatoly on a trip to the Spanish resort of Marbella, flying from Moscow to Málaga on their 'external' passports. Those documents, Felshtinsky said, still had valid visas to visit the Schengen group of European Union countries, including Spain, which did not require passports for travel between them.

Felshtinsky's logistics were rather more upmarket than those of a simple package tour. He told me he was travelling by private jet, paid for by Berezovsky, which he used to fly to Málaga to meet Litvinenko's wife and son to explain to them what was happening. There is every suggestion that Marina was not immediately aware of the enormity of the step she had just taken as she settled in to await developments in a hotel in Marbella. Felshtinsky then flew back to Georgia. He was travelling with several cell phones, but the only one that worked in Georgia used a Russian SIM card, easily penetrated by the FSB.

In Tbilisi, meanwhile, Litvinenko had tapped high-level business and government sources to secure a false Georgian passport. But the alarm bells were beginning to ring. Georgia was too close to Russia. The long arm of the FSB might easily stretch across the Caucasus into this former Soviet republic on the Black Sea. Litvinenko was not even supposed to have left Moscow, let alone Russia. If his whereabouts were betrayed to Russian agents in Georgia, one telephone call from Vladimir Putin, or from his new commander in the FSB, Nikolai Patrushev, would have brought the two fugitives under immediate threat. Even the most cursory examination of Litvinenko's papers would have provoked suspicion: he was carrying a Georgian passport as well as Russian ID, both using the same photograph.

Felshtinsky and Litvinenko, staying at a private apartment hotel in Tbilisi, had another good reason to worry: once they reached Georgia, Felshtinsky's Russian cell phone suddenly burst back into life.

He began receiving calls, he said, from Andrei Ponkin, one of the FSB officers who shared a platform with Litvinenko and who now seemed to want a friendly chat, including an enquiry about Felshtinsky's whereabouts.

'It became clear that the FSB knew something was happening,' Felshtinsky said. 'They knew that something was going on.'

At this stage in the escape, Litvinenko and his supporters still harboured the dream of an American visa.

'We started talking to the Americans in Tbilisi,' Felshtinsky said, recounting how he tried to persuade contacts in Washington to arrange sanctuary for Litvinenko, offering what must have seemed a most unlikely bargain so long after the end of the Cold War: asylum in the West in return for a defector's secrets.

There were meetings in Tbilisi, Felshtinsky said, some late at night in secretly arranged locations. Litvinenko himself met with American officials, but 'in the end they didn't give him a visa'.

That left the two of them sitting in a remote Black Sea capital worried that the FSB was on their tail, even as the CIA blocked off their hoped-for escape route. Onward travel was no simple matter.

With the documents he had, Litvinenko could not simply fly to Spain from Georgia to join up with his family, because he did not have a visa and his papers were, at best, questionable. 'It was too risky to stay in Georgia,' Felshtinsky said. 'And Turkey was the only country we could go without a visa.'

By now, events had come to resemble the kind of Cold War extraction that provided the grist of spy thrillers. But this time there were no complex swaps of agents and captives on the misty sweep of the Glienicke Bridge in divided Berlin. In late October 2000, there was just one edgy FSB operative running for his life ever farther from home while his wife thought he had gone to see his father. In a way it was a blue-chip, almost ostentatious defection: in Felshtinsky's account, he and Litvinenko travelled to Antalya by private jet. Felshtinsky booked Litvinenko into a five-star hotel, before flying on alone to Marbella to collect Marina and Anatoly for the family reunion in Turkey.

At Berezovsky's behest, Goldfarb, too, was on his way to Antalya as Litvinenko's guide through the thickets of his onward escape, his minder. But the way forward was still unclear: Litvinenko's fake passport was good only for the places he least wanted to go – to Georgia or back to Russia.

In all this, Marina Litvinenko depicted herself as the innocent, ignorant of the game in which she had been called upon to play an unwitting part. In Moscow, she had become used to the notion that her husband was a pariah. He had been imprisoned for months, first in Lefortovo, the FSB prison, then in Butyrka, a prison for common criminals. His former colleagues had turned their backs on him. Some of those who had joined him at the news conference in 1998 were under strong pressure to recant or had already denounced him. Their protector, Berezovsky, was himself in disgrace in Moscow, under investigation by the agents of a new regime he had helped bring to power.

But to Marina Litvinenko exile still seemed a remote, impossible notion. Only when she was in Spain, waiting to be reunited with her husband, did she begin to grasp that she would never see her homeland again. Throughout her days visiting him at Lefortovo or standing at his side as he lost his job and his prospects, he had not suggested to her that the future might lie somewhere far to the west, least of all in a suburb of London called Muswell Hill – least of all, of course, in a hospital bed, racked with poison.

'Sasha called me and told me I have to go to Turkey and meet him,' Marina told me, recalling the days she spent in Spain awaiting his call. 'It was the first time he told me: "Marina, prepare yourself not to go back to Russia." It was very devastating for me. I just could not believe it.'

Berezovsky said later he had urged Litvinenko to flee and had told Marina that her family would never be safe or whole again if she stayed behind in Moscow. But she had her doubts about the entire project: the family would be moving to a place where they did not speak the language and did not even have a bank account, far less a home, or prospects of work. For all she knew, it could be the start of a life as itinerant fugitives, forever looking over their shoulders.

'It was very important for me not to stay on the road, not to live a life like a gypsy,' she recalled. She was worried about her son, his schooling, the family's future. 'It was very important for me to have a guarantee, and it was Boris Berezovsky who gave it to me,' she said. Whatever else might be said of Berezovsky, his guarantee of financial security proved to be a generous gesture towards the family of a man he had no pressing need to rescue. His motive, he maintained, was that Litvinenko had saved his life and become a friend. Cynics suggested he wanted Litvinenko's flight to test the waters for his own imminent self-exile.

Whatever those considerations, Litvinenko and his family still had to reach the West, and it was very unclear how that would happen.

With the exception of a brief foray to Switzerland, nothing in Litvinenko's biography suggested that he had ventured far beyond Russia or into lands where his own language was not the lingua franca. True, he had served with the FSB, deployed in some of Russia's crisis zones. But that was in the formal, structured world of the seurity services. True, he had worked undercover, but on his own home turf in Moscow, surrounded by people eating the same food, familiar with the same rhythms and seasons of life.

Nothing had prepared him for the loneliness of a scared defector, caught between his point of departure and an uncertain point of arrival, marooned at a midway station that might turn out to be as hostile as the environment he was fleeing.

He had been trained as part of a vast state institution. In Turkey Litvinenko had no protection of rank, or office, to rely on, no sidearm, no credential to wave. His papers were of dubious value if scrutinized closely.

'We were very scared, really,' Marina said.

Goldfarb flew in at a moment of crisis, as he did in different circumstances in 2006. Clearly, the small group of Russian speakers on Turkey's southern coast could not simply stay in

Antalya. There was no means of knowing whether the hunt was on for Litvinenko, whether his escape had become known, whether, even now, the FSB was on his trail. Certainly, the Russian secret services, like their American and British counterparts, would have operatives in place in Turkey – declared or undeclared – able to raise a posse of agents to capture, repatriate or simply dispose of their fugitive ex-comrade.

In Moscow, there were plenty of high-level FSB agents who would be only too glad to choreograph his capture, or even perhaps arrange an 'accident' on the twisting mountain roads or azure seas of southern Turkey. But the group had to break cover if the Litvinenkos were to find a haven to run to, and history was against them.

In the Cold War, a defector might have had a certain value to Western intelligence agencies. But in the early days of Vladimir Putin's rule, Western leaders were looking for ways of doing business with this new and unknown Russian supremo, and would certainly not wish to antagonize him for the sake of a rogue FSB officer. The timing was not propitious for the Americans, either. In the United States, the 2000 elections were looming, a matter of days away. Potential international incidents with Cold War overtones were unwelcome. So great was Washington's desire to disavow all knowledge of Litvinenko that six years later, the State Department and the American Embassy in Ankara both denied that Litvinenko ever sought their protection. Yet Goldfarb, Berezovsky and Litvinenko himself before his death all insisted that an approach to the Americans did indeed take place, with the outcome they subsequently recounted.

The most direct route from Antalya to Ankara, the Turkish capital, lay along the winding roads heading north from the Mediterranean coast. The road clambered abruptly over a high pass, reaching almost five thousand feet as it headed towards the Anatolian plateau and the town of Konya, where the thirteenth-century poet and mystic Jalal ad-Din ar-Rumi founded the order known to outsiders as the Whirling Dervishes. It is unlikely that the intrepid party of Russians saw their journey as a touristic excursion or an exploration of the roots of mediaeval Sufism. Their goal was the clunky, low building on Ankara's Atatürk Boulevard that housed the American Embassy and, they hoped, their passports to freedom. But after the five-hour drive from the coast, they were destined to be disappointed.

First, Goldfarb's wife, Svetlana, went ahead to the consular section of the embassy to get a sense of the lie of the land. Then Litvinenko recorded a video telling his life story, his reasons for seeking refuge in the United States and, as a potential sweetener to the American authorities, his knowledge of the circumstances surrounding the murder in Moscow of Paul Tatum, an American businessman who, in 1996, had been killed in a dispute over the ownership of a five-star Radisson hotel in Moscow. (The theory was that knowledge of a crime involving an American would help secure refugee status.) The tape was then to be sent to the CBS News headquarters in New York.

From the beginning, the results of Litvinenko's overtures seemed discouraging. Svetlana Goldfarb reported back that American officials seemed to have foreknowledge of Litvinenko's quest for sanctuary, according to an account of the proceedings Goldfarb produced as the foreword to *Lubyanka Criminal Group*, Litvinenko's memoir.

'They are waiting for you at the consulate at one,' she told Litvinenko and his advisers. 'I explained everything, and, strangely, they understood everything too quickly. I had a feeling they knew about you.'

Now it was Litvinenko's turn to present himself for inspection.

According to Goldfarb, Litvinenko was interviewed by two Americans at the embassy on Atatürk Boulevard. One of them said he was a consular official. The older of the two, aged around forty, was identified to the Russians as Mark, a second secretary from the Political Section – a ridiculously low rank for a man of that age.

The bad news came quickly.

'Embassies do not provide asylum,' the supposed consular official said. Mark, the older man, had a conversation in private with Litvinenko, speaking without Goldfarb's translation from Russian. A knowledge of the Russian language, of course, would only have been required of a low-ranking American official in Turkey if his mission included responsibilities for monitoring developments on what had once been NATO's southeasternmost flank with the Soviet Union. During the Cold War, Turkey had been a crucial buffer, its 500,000-man standing army deployed as cannon fodder to meet any, albeit unlikely, conventional advance by the Red Army across Anatolia.

When he returned to his travel companions, Litvinenko seemed shaken.

'This man knows everything' about Russia's secret life, he said of his mysterious American interlocutor. 'He asked if I know this one, that one. I don't know the majority of those he asked about, but I heard about them. He asked if I have anything that could interest them. I said no. He asked if I am going to sit quietly or speak publicly. I said that I would speak, want to write a book . . . He said: "Wish you success. This is beyond us." '

If Goldfarb's account is correct, Litvinenko may well have damned himself from the beginning, simply by playing an honest game. Other fugitives might have put some spin on what they knew or did not know, teasing the Americans into an offer of asylum. Litvinenko said he knew nothing and, on top of that, planned to become a speaker and writer – a rabble-rouser, a troublesome exile. Western intelligence agencies prefer their defectors to maintain a discreet silence – except, of course, in the presence of those to whom they tell their stories in the CIA or MI6.

'It wasn't successful. We were very upset,' Marina said. 'What we hoped is just lost. We were almost paralysed.'

In the account he co-authored with Marina Litvinenko in 2007, Goldfarb said Litvinenko did in fact offer the Americans a nugget of information – identifying his one-time nemesis General Yevgeny Khokholkov as a player in the acquisition of the

American technology used in the assassination of the Chechen leader Dzhokhar Dudayev in 1996. But that was not enough to buy sanctuary.

In fact, the Americans were not alone in their seeming reluctance to provide a refuge for Alexander Litvinenko. When I spoke to Vladimir Bukovsky in Cambridge, in early 2007, he told me of his little-chronicled part in the entire escapade – an intervention that, if anything, made the immediate future seem even more bleak for Litvinenko and his family.

After the Americans rejected Litvinenko, 'then they went to the British,' Bukovsky said.

By this account, a fellow Soviet exile – a former KGB man – spoke to MI6 on Litvinenko's behalf and said, 'Look, a very important defector is sitting in Turkey. You better go and retrieve him,' Bukovsky said.

But the plan to spirit Litvinenko to Britain foundered at the very highest level, according to Bukovsky's understanding from his contacts. And Sasha and his family were still stuck in Turkey. Goldfarb was going mad.

In Ankara, Litvinenko was growing increasingly restless at the Sheraton and began to believe that the group was being followed. The antennae from his training picked up a tail from the American Embassy, half a mile away, back to the hotel. Again, a sense of insecurity overcame the group, and once more their options had narrowed.

Later, the United States would embrace such former KGB luminaries as Oleg Kalugin, who became an American citizen in 2003 after serving during the Cold War as one of the most senior Soviet agents in the United States. But there was no such welcome for an errant FSB lieutenant colonel with his wife and son in tow in Ankara in October 2000.

As soon as the Americans turned him down, Litvinenko's position became even more precarious. His cover was frail, and his illicit presence in Turkey was known. It could not remain secret for long. Again, they sensed, it was time to flee.

The Russians packed and loaded their bags into the trunk of a rental car in the hotel's underground garage. Fearing that hostile agents were closing on them, they sped off into the chill October night at 1.30 a.m.

From Ankara, the highway to Istanbul first ran north then turned west at Gerede, a ribbon of four-lane asphalt unfolding across the bald Anatolian uplands, climbing to 3,000 feet on the Fakilar pass before narrowing at Bolu on the lip of an escarpment facing west. There the road began to fill with truck and car traffic as it approached Istanbul through the struggling towns of Duzce and Adapazari and Kocaeli, skirting finally along the Sea of Marmara. For years Istanbul's urban sprawl had spread with liquid ease, spilling eastwards from the Bosporus strait just as the proliferation of apartment blocks and highways had transformed the landscape on the western shore into a tangle of concrete.

For the Russians, the journey was fraught with worry. The fog closed in on them. They got lost on the approaches to the city and its soaring bridges over the waters of the Bosporus – the natural geographic frontier between East and West, Asia and Europe.

For those who visited the city on vacation by plane or cruise ship, old Istanbul was one of the world's most exotic destinations, its roots stretching deep into Byzantium before the Muslim conquest by the Ottoman Turks in 1453. It was a place caught up in its own history of commerce and empire. Here the traveller might locate the leftovers of the city's past as its soul changed with the centuries – residual minorities of Jews and Armenian Christians; the patriarchate of the Orthodox Church; the Basilica of Saint Sophia, once the largest cathedral in Christendom and later Istanbul's principal mosque until it became a museum in 1935. Now the city's countless minarets stitched the sky to the tumble of alleyways and balconied villas around the gold sellers and carpet vendors of the Grand Bazaar and the stately gardens of the Blue Mosque. The Golden Horn waterway divided the really old section of the former Ottoman capital from the newer areas around Istiklal Caddesi, where travellers on the Orient Express once paused on their eastward journeys in the luxury of the Pera Palas hotel. That was the Istanbul the tourists came to see.

For the small group of Russians, however, the only part that counted was the airport. As they worked on an escape plan, they took rooms at the Hilton – an upscale watering hole by any standards, presumably paid for by Berezovsky – where their papers would almost certainly be examined and registered at the check-in desk for subsequent, routine scrutiny by the police and immigration authorities.

As they cast about for ideas of where to go next, Berezovsky came up with a notion that might have seemed enticing had their plight been less dire. With the flair of a billionaire used to big spending and elegant environments, Berezovsky suggested to Goldfarb that the fugitives charter a yacht and 'spend some time in neutral waters'.

Goldfarb dismissed this idea as somewhat fanciful, arguing that sooner or later they would have to come ashore and would again face the issue of securing refuge. In the meantime, Goldfarb discovered that Barbados and the Dominican Republic did not require visas for Russians. But that idea had a major drawback that made it impractical: there were no direct flights to either place from Istanbul. To reach the Caribbean, the group would need to cross US territory while changing flights and would therefore require a transit visa to board any America-bound plane. Even in the days before 9/11 the United States sought to protect its frontiers from casual interlopers or illegal immigrants by requiring some travellers to secure permission to transit in advance. And after the episode at the American Embassy in Ankara, help from the United States was out of the question.

The inspiration for the final ploy – a simple stroke of genius under the circumstances – was subsequently claimed by both Bukovsky and Goldfarb. Britain, they both realized, did not require transit visas at Heathrow, and so travellers with onward tickets to a country they were entitled to visit could fly into London's airports, provided that they planned to continue their journey elsewhere. Once inside the airport, however, it was a simple matter – as many asylum seekers have discovered – to go no farther. Most of all, though, the ploy required a degree of chutzpah to persuade the Turkish airport authorities that the group planned no more than a transit stop in London.

The Russians bought tickets from Istanbul to Moscow with a Heathrow stopover. There was still the issue of the passports as they navigated the hurdles of check-in and immigration, where they might all too easily face detection. Goldfarb and Litvinenko's family had valid passports, but Litvinenko did not. As an American, Goldfarb did not need a British visa. But Marina's Russian passport was good only for the Schengen group of countries, which does not include Britain. And Litvinenko's Georgian papers also required a visa for travel to London. Adding to their worries, the group's presence in Turkey was known to American agents, and who could guess what kind of observation they might maintain at the country's points of exit in tandem with their counterparts in the Turkish intelligence services?

Again, the Russians believed they were followed at the Istanbul airport, this time by two Turks who tailed them from the check-in and seemed to make no attempt either to disguise their own presence or to arrest those they were following. The Litvinenko party secured boarding passes with no undue difficulties. But at the boarding gate, perilously close to the scheduled take-off time, the booking clerk from Turkish Airlines realized that Alexander and Marina had no British visas in their passports. Neither did they yet have London–Moscow boarding passes to reinforce the myth that they planned only a transit stop in London. And indeed, as this very observant boarding clerk seems to have noticed, they were taking a pretty peculiar route to reach Moscow when there were much shorter and more convenient direct flights from Istanbul.

'We always go through London to shop duty-free at Heathrow,' Goldfarb said quickly.

The airline clerk was not convinced by this flimsy explanation. Departure time was only minutes away. The Turkish agents had followed them through the airport, breaking into a trot as the

Russians hurried to make their flight. The clerk insisted on checking with her boss. Even at this late stage, with freedom only a short walk away down the tunnel of a boarding pier, the venture could be frustrated.

As the moments ticked by, Litvinenko must have considered the appalling alternative to escape: deportation in disgrace to Russia, arrest at the airport, prison at least and possibly much worse. He would be paraded as a fugitive from justice; those who had stood with him in the 1998 press conference would line up to denounce him; the list of alleged offences would lengthen and, with it, the likely spell he would face in prison. His punishment might be much worse – summary justice was a feature of the times, and by late 2000 he could no longer rely on Boris Berezovsky's influence. In Russia, his alliance with the oligarch had become a liability and, if sent back to Moscow, he would be no more than a pawn in the game as Putin and Berezovsky squared off in their showdown.

Litvinenko understood the vindictiveness and cruelty of those he had betrayed – after all, he had been one of them – so he must have known this was truly the roll of the dice that would determine his destiny, as a free man in Britain or as a prisoner and target for brutal vengeance in Moscow.

'Sasha was deadly pale,' Goldfarb's account continued, describing the moments as the airline boarding clerk disappeared with their travel documents. 'One of our followers followed the girl, the other kept watching us. Ten minutes later, the girl and one of the Turks showed up. "Everything is OK," she said. "Have a good trip." '

As they pieced the events together, Litvinenko and Goldfarb concluded that the Americans in Ankara had tipped off the Turkish secret service about Litvinenko's true identity. The Russians had been followed not to be apprehended but to be seen safely off the premises. Neither the Turks nor the Americans wanted the inconvenience and paperwork of a Russian defector in Turkey. Better, they seemed to calculate, to pass the problem on to the British.

Once the Russians landed in London, Litvinenko asked for political asylum, and, no matter how Prime Minister Blair felt about it, British law required that the request be heard.

It was 1 November 2000, six years to the day before Alexander Litvinenko began to die.

By 16 May 2001 Litvinenko's request for asylum had been granted. Physically, Russia was behind him, but he would not or could not let go. His relationship with Boris Berezovsky bound him to the *émigré* world of ever more virulent opposition to Vladimir Putin, and somewhere in the half-light of his adopted universe Litvinenko played out the Faustian pact that brought him celebrity of the most macabre kind. He had found a new 'roof', a new sanctuary, but also a new notoriety, a new cause for vilification among those he had left behind.

The decisions leading up to the family's flight from Moscow set Litvinenko on course for a life that bore the seeds of his downfall. He had made political enemies and planned to make a lot more; he had played in the stratospheric world of the oligarchs and would do so again; he had dabbled in the nefarious under-world of the FSB, at the dark crossroads between state intelligence and organized crime. Any one of those activities could have foreshadowed his death, as Scotland Yard came to puzzle out years later.

Had he stayed in Moscow, retribution would have come sooner rather than later, possibly with the same outcome. So there had been no option but to seek safety for himself and his family. But as the events of November 2006 proved with grim finality, his defection merely postponed the reckoning. True, he gave his wife and son a new life in suburban London, new prospects of security in a tiny, mostly tidy island off the coast of continental Europe – so utterly different from the vast, brash, ramshackle reaches and multiple time zones of Russia. But he never abandoned the image of himself as a player in the events that shaped his native land. He never accepted the role of the quiet defector.

The saga of Litvinenko's flight had a strange footnote. After initially rejecting his request for asylum at the embassy in Ankara,

Goldfarb said later, the American authorities changed their mind and were prepared to do a deal, if they could locate Litvinenko to tell him so.

They tried to reach Alex Goldfarb – but, by his own account, in his exhaustion after the abrupt departure from Ankara and the long drive to Istanbul, he had switched off his cell phone. By the time the American intelligence officers spoke to Goldfarb to tell him the good news, Litvinenko and his family and friends had already reached Istanbul, and the American offer was withdrawn.

It is tempting to ponder how Litvinenko's life would have unfolded in the United States if Alex Goldfarb had not switched off his mobile telephone. Almost certainly, Litvinenko would have been physically remote from the *émigré* circles in London dominated by Boris Berezovsky. Almost certainly, those who wished him ill would have found it much more difficult to conspire against him in the United States.

Litvinenko's escape had other effects. After Goldfarb's high-profile role in the defection, George Soros, his boss, finally told him it was time to leave his employment. Goldfarb became the chief executive of a new human rights foundation Berezovsky had decided to create in New York, the International Foundation for Civil Liberties – a body that would promote dissent against the Kremlin in Russia and the former Soviet satellite countries. The foundation also offered a vehicle for Berezovsky to provide financial support for Litvinenko, sponsoring his book-writing projects in the early years of his time in London.

But those events were overshadowed by other decisions that would set the markers for subsequent years. The year 2000 was a turning point in the way politics was played in Russia. Putin came to power as president with his own loyalists and chosen associates to replace the oligarchs and courtiers who had clustered around his predecessor. And a significant source of opposition to the Kremlin moved offshore: just two weeks after Litvinenko arrived in London, Boris Berezovsky himself announced from his French château that he would not be returning to Moscow. The stage was set for the battle between *émigrés* and Kremlin insiders that would consume the years leading to Litvinenko's death.

For months, Berezovsky had been nervous about spending too much time in Russia, and by mid-November 2000 he had holed up at his ornate villa, the Château de la Garoupe, on the Cap d'Antibes overlooking the Bay of Nice in southern France – a luxurious retreat from the growing pressure of Russian investigations into his business dealings.

Back in Moscow, the authorities ordered Berezovsky to report to the Prosecutor General's Office on 15 November 2000, to face questioning about $700 million in Aeroflot funds said to have gone missing in Swiss accounts. According to Goldfarb, the tycoon's initial instinct was to return and face his accusers, but his allies talked him out of it. From that moment on, Berezovsky embarked on a new life, far from the arena of his greatest triumphs. Like Litvinenko, he traded the life he had known in Moscow for an alien's status in London. Unlike Litvinenko, he had a fortune at his disposal to soften the blow and continue his campaign of vitriol against Putin – even though, as events would indicate, he left Russia in something of a hurry, without the time to liquidate some of his biggest media, minerals and oil assets on the most favourable terms.

'Today I have made a difficult decision – not to return to Moscow for interrogation,' Berezovsky said in a press statement transmitted to the Russian capital at 7.00 p.m. on 14 November – hours before the deadline set by the public prosecutor. 'I am taking this step because I have found myself under increasingly strong pressure from the authorities, and from President Putin in person.' For their part, the Russian authorities depicted the issue as a criminal case of fraud and embezzlement, as they continued to do for many years. But Berezovsky was already looking ahead to his likely reception in the West, honing his arguments for sanctuary outside Russia as a victim of political persecution. 'I have been compelled to choose between becoming a political prisoner or a political emigrant,' he said.

One question that recurred after November 2006 was whether the feud between Berezovsky and Putin claimed Litvinenko as its victim. Could this murder in London have been a surrogate killing with a message for Berezovsky, or a cruel ploy to discredit the Kremlin? But who would have foretold the events that began to unfold six years after that small family group of Russians gathered fearfully on Turkey's Mediterranean coastline?

7

SILOVIKI

Early in 2007, in the snowy retreat of Davos, the familiar crowd of political and business leaders settled in for the annual gathering of the World Economic Forum in the Swiss Alps. Some arrived by helicopter, others in chauffeured cars, still more by train or chartered bus from Zurich Airport, winding their way up a deep, twisting tree-lined valley easily sealed against anti-globalization protesters and any other unwelcome guests. For all the volume of participants had grown over the years, the Davos organizers still quested anxiously for exclusivity and buzz to lure corporate bigwigs into paying thousands of dollars each to attend. And among the key players this time were some of the most powerful people in Russia, the barons of state capitalism.

It was eleven years since a different, edgier cast had assembled, troubled by events back home, where Boris Yeltsin seemed likely to fall to an electoral threat from resurgent Communists opposed to everything the oligarchs represented and wished to retain.

This time the characters from a newer generation were confident, boastful and controlled, reciting economic data and comparative statistics to show how the Russian economy had blossomed out of all recognition under new management since the dark days of the financial collapse in 1998. These were Putin's people, some of those he had chosen to run enormous companies and powerful portfolios in the Kremlin – often both at the same time.

They were led by Dmitri Medvedev, the first deputy prime minister and chairman of the Gazprom energy giant, who, even at that time, was tipped to succeed Putin as president in the 2008 elections. Later, Medvedev seemed to slip from pole position, overtaken by a man close to Putin's heart – a former KGB active-service spy, Sergei Ivanov. Then, with characteristic inscrutability, Putin changed the line-up yet again, endorsing Medvedev in December 2007 to become Russia's next president.

Medvedev ranked as a leader of a 'liberal' group of loyal tech-nocrats within the Kremlin, drawn from a different background from the so-called *siloviki* – the men of power with their roots in the KGB who clustered most closely around Putin and controlled the state's businesses and security services. Medvedev had been chosen to represent his country at the forum because, with his boyish looks, confident manner and relative informality, he seemed best able to offer a non-threatening face of Russia's future. With his deadpan expression and sartorial neatness, he sometimes looked like a junior version of Putin, a favoured son.

Medvedev had a twin message to purvey. One part of it was that Russia was open for business, pragmatic and reliable, despite growing doubts in the West about its commitment to democracy and genuinely free markets. The second part was tougher.

'We are not trying to push anyone to love Russia,' he said. 'But we will not allow anyone to hurt Russia.' The remarks epitomized the Kremlin's depiction of Russia as a land besieged by hostile forces, defended by stern patriots who would not countenance disrespect.

The high point of the Russian performance in Davos that year was a formal dinner for around two hundred people in one of the bigger conference rooms in the bunker-like Congress Centre used by the World Economic Forum. Its theme was 'Russia's more muscular diplomacy'.

Medvedev was at the centre table, and grouped around were other seating arrangements including prominent figures, many of them Russians, orbiting and offering tribute to the focus of power and attention. Not all the guests were pushovers for Russia's 'muscular diplomacy'. At one table was David Miliband, a British politician who would become foreign secretary as relations between Russia and Britain spiralled sharply downwards later that year as a result of the Litvinenko investigation. But the evening was curiously flat, as if the contributors from many of the satellite tables were far too concerned about giving offence to the Kremlin to speak their minds openly. The days when Russians at Davos were known for crazy, vodka-fuelled parties, flashy women and hair-raising conspiracies were over; buccaneering businessmen could no longer tell the politicians what to do. As Medvedev pointed out, 'Russia today is a different country.'

As the dinner progressed, a handful of speakers from the outlying tables did offer something close to a dissident voice, an alternate vision to Moscow's prevailing orthodoxy. Predominantly, they were Westerners who chose to dwell on precisely those issues that the officials from Moscow chose to ignore: authoritarianism and the abuse of power.

Joseph S. Nye Jr, a professor at the John F. Kennedy School of Government at Harvard University, compared Russia to a pendulum. 'Under Yeltsin it swung too far toward chaos, and it may have swung too much the other way.'

Timothy Garton Ash, a British historian from Oxford University, sent a small frisson through the gathering by reminding the assembled guests that only months before, Anna Politkovskaya, the investigative journalist, had been murdered in Moscow, one of a slew of unsolved killings of reporters, editors and others during the Putin era. Clearly, Garton Ash was not expecting this particular assembly of dignitaries to take up the cudgels on her behalf. But, he insisted somewhat frostily, 'the name of Anna Politkovskaya should be mentioned at least once this evening.'

Even those Westerners in Davos prepared to offer Russia the benefit of the doubt in its protestations of change acknowledged that Moscow's message had not come across particularly clearly.

'People do not understand how fundamentally changed Russia is,' E. Neville Isdell, the chairman and chief executive of Coca-Cola, said at one point. But, he added, the Russians 'have not always put the right face to the world'.

Anyone coming to Davos from London, where the British police believed they had identified Litvinenko's killer as a former KGB officer, and where the newspapers were full of stories about a Putin-inspired conspiracy to commit murder in broad daylight on the streets of the British capital, would have found it hard to disagree.

But perhaps the most telling moment was not related to anything said publicly, or even in the quieter conversations around the tables as phalanxes of waiters and waitresses arrived with successive courses and their corresponding wines. Rather, it came as the evening was drawing to a subdued close. No one had heard anything new or unexpected in this choreographed Kremlin event, and I wanted to swap impressions with a Russian businessman I had met in earlier years. I remembered him as a talkative observer of the political scene, not afraid to criticize the regime. As a colleague and I approached him, however, he took one look at us and drew his forefinger and thumb together across his lips in a zipping motion to make clear he was not about to say anything. Then he walked quickly away, losing himself in the crowd.

Vladimir Putin was inaugurated as Russia's president on 7 May 2000, the designated and now elected leader of a nation desperate for renewal and self-respect.

His predecessor, Boris Yeltsin, had announced his planned departure from office on New Year's Eve 1999, as if the timing might draw a symbolic line under a turbulent decade. It also upstaged the millennium celebrations unfolding across the globe: most capitals relied on pyrotechnic displays to mark the event; Moscow got a political bombshell, too.

As part of the deal that propelled him upward, Putin's first public act was to guarantee Yeltsin and his family immunity from prosecution for any transgressions in the corrupt 1990s. But the

West, too, was keen for signals from Yeltsin's anointed successor in the Kremlin, and, generally, Western leaders liked what they saw.

Tony Blair, then the British prime minister and a close ally of the United States, travelled to Russia at Putin's invitation in March 2000, even before the elections that same month sealed the former KGB operative's ascent to the presidency. Blair was the first Western visitor of any stature to size up the new Russian leader after Yeltsin's departure, and the encounter was heavy with symbols, bringing together two men who, in their different ways, saw themselves as global architects.

In those heady days, it seemed the two leaders shared almost regal ambitions for geopolitical change that placed them on the same side – an illusion that did not endure.

With tsar-like panache, Putin received Blair in St Petersburg, the Russian leader's home town, and they took their places beside each other in the royal box of the celebrated Mariinsky Theatre, known in Soviet days as the Kirov, to watch a performance of Sergei Prokofiev's opera *War and Peace*.

Of the two options in the opera's title, it was clear that Putin was suing for the latter – at least while he accustomed himself to the trappings of power.

'Tony Blair and I belong to the same generation,' he said. 'I think that he is a very serious and honest partner.' Blair reciprocated, inviting Putin back to London in April for a visit that included tea with the Queen. Despite Western concerns about Russia's bloody campaign in Chechnya – the Second Chechen War had been launched just a few months earlier as Putin sought to enhance his standing among Russians – Blair announced that the new Russian leader was 'impressive'.

'The relationship between Britain and Russia is immensely important for the future. Russia is a major power, a major country with whom we want good relations,' Blair said. The signal, clearly, was that the West could do business with Russia despite human rights abuses in Chechnya or anywhere else. 'His vision of the future is one that we would feel comfortable with,' Blair added.

When George W. Bush met Putin for the first time as president in June 2001 in Slovenia, the mood of modern-day *détente* deepened even further. Famously, Bush said that he 'looked the man in the eye. I found him to be very straightforward and trustworthy. We had a very good dialogue. I was able to get a sense of his soul.'

Less than three months later, Vladimir Putin became the first world leader to call President Bush to offer his support after the 9/11 attacks.

With the American president shaken and reeling from the onslaught, Putin's call represented fancy diplomatic footwork. But it was also part of a shrewd effort to align and equate Russia's campaign against Muslim separatists in Chechnya with the broader fight against Islamic terrorism that was about to be launched from the White House. Putin depicted Russia and America as allies in the same war against different manifestations of the same enemy – Islamic terrorism steered by Al Qaeda. And he had prepared the ground well.

'No government can stand idly by when terrorism strikes . . . Terrorism today knows no boundaries. Its purveyors collaborate with each other over vast distances,' Putin said in an article on the opinion page of the *New York Times* in November 1999 as he sent Russian troops once again into Chechnya. His analysis was indistinguishable from the mantra that became commonplace in the United States and Britain after 9/11. In the early days of Putin's and Bush's tenures, thus, it seemed as if both men were reading from the same script, even though Washington was promoting policies in Eastern Europe that Moscow would come to view as hostile.

In November 2001, Bush welcomed the Russian leader to his ranch at Crawford, Texas, sharing with him a barbecue and pecan pie and fêting the former KGB operative as 'a new-style leader, a reformer, a man who loves his country as much as I love mine, a man who loves his wife as much as I love mine, a man who loves his daughters as much as I love my daughters, and a man who's going to make a huge difference in making the world more peaceful by working closely with the United States.

'When I was in high school, Russia was an enemy,' Bush went on to say. 'Now Russia is a friend.'

In those early days, there was much talk in Washington, Brussels and Moscow of Russia becoming closer to NATO, the military alliance whose *raison d'être* in the Cold War was to bind Western nations together under US leadership against the Soviet-led Warsaw Pact. But the honeymoon was short-lived: no amount of cordial talk could overcome the divergent perceptions in Washington and Moscow of the post-Cold War world and how it should be organized. Those distinctions widened exponentially as America and Britain invaded Iraq, against Russian and other objections, in 2003 and went on to pressure Iran over its nuclear ambitions.

The biggest difference between Putin and his Western inter-locutors, which Western leaders seemed reluctant to acknowledge, lay in their most basic views of global power. After the defeat of Communism, Washington's hawkish neo-conservatives flaunted American power as the sole repository of military, economic and political authority. But Russia hankered for a return to the old days when a broader set of managers ran the globe. In the past, the Kremlin believed, the United States and the USSR squared off as equals. After the chaos of the 1990s, Putin wanted Russia's importance to be acknowledged anew.

The diplomacy of combating terrorism offered both sides a common goal – but not much more.

Western powers seemed to expect a pliant Russia to move towards a European type of democracy, offering outsiders un-fettered access to its vast energy and mineral resources. But Putin was a Russian nationalist. The 1990s had been a decade in which many Russians believed the West seemed only to exploit their weaknesses and dismiss their giant nation and one-time nuclear superpower as a spent force. Putin was acutely aware of the assessment that had become the received wisdom from Berlin to Washington in the closing years of the Yeltsin era: Eastern Europe had swung to the West; the Russian economy was a shambles; and energy prices were low and likely to remain so. With China rising as the new economic power to be courted, and the United States dominating the technological revolution sweeping the world, Russia no longer counted as a major player.

Nothing summed up that dismissive view as succinctly as an article written in 2000 by Thomas E. Graham Jr, a former American diplomat at the Carnegie Endowment for International Peace in Washington, DC, who had served at the American Embassy in Moscow in the 1990s.

In the United States, he wrote, 'the image of Russia as an aspiring democracy has given way to an image of a hapless land mired in deep pervasive corruption, where organized crime operates unrestrained. The American political establishment is suffering from a severe case of Russia fatigue, and the "Forget Russia" school is gaining adherents in the Congress. This school would not gratuitously harm Russia, but it is not prepared to spend much time, energy, or money to nurture good relations with Russia. It simply believes that Russia does not matter much any longer in the world.' That view, or variants of it, had emboldened the West in countless ways to encroach on what had been the Soviet Union's 'near abroad' – the ring of satellite states that once formed the Soviet Union and its protective circle of vassal states in Eastern Europe.

The European Union, and, more significantly in Russian eyes, NATO, had taken advantage of Russia's weakness to expand to its very frontiers, even courting lands such as Georgia and Ukraine, not to mention the Baltic states that Russia had long seen as its bailiwick. The former Warsaw Pact nations, once contained by the Iron Curtain, were now vying publicly for membership in the Western camp.

Putin's theme, by contrast, was that Russia had been great and would be great again. And he felt quite simply, as one British diplomat put it, that 'people shouldn't be telling Russia what to do.'

From that perspective, confrontation was inevitable from the beginning, but it took a while for the West to realize that the Russian soul into which President Bush had peered so deeply was far darker than he imagined.

Bush, Blair and Putin were from similar postwar generations. They kept themselves in shape, dressed well and prided themselves on family values. On the international stage in the early days of their relationship, they projected a sense of men in their political prime, seeking a new way of running the world. But as they contemplated one another across the gleaming conference tables of international diplomacy, or in the less formal setting of the Bush ranch in Texas, the gulf between them must have been evident. They had been raised in opposing camps on either side of a great ideological divide that split the world for decades; and their disparate roots in their respective societies seemed almost a classic illustration of what revolutionary theory called class warfare.

Putin differed from Bush and Blair in many ways, not just those drawn from the land that formed him, with its icy winters and authoritarian history, or even from the fact that he had been a KGB operative. After all, Bush's own father, ex-President George H. W. Bush, had been director of the CIA from 1976 to 1977, so there was a precedent for the transition from espionage to politics.

But Putin's upbringing offered him none of the affluence of Texas oil money or the British professional classes, or of the culture that underpinned Western prosperity. He had no real experience of politics in the sense of an open, public competition. His background was in a conspiratorial security service and in a world where political patronage counted for a lot more than votes. Bush and Blair grew up protected by the shield of comfort and support offered by well-heeled parents. Blair attended Fettes College, one of Scotland's top public schools, and went on from there to Oxford University. Bush hailed from a family deeply embedded in the Ivy League American establishment – the kind of background that bred self-assurance, a sense that whatever befell others, life would always deal a trump card when it really mattered.

Putin started out with no such advantages.

Born in Leningrad on 7 October 1952, diminutive in stature, a street fighter at school, this new Russian leader with pale blue eyes below thinning hair projected himself as an icon of the underclass, an emissary from the disadvantaged Soviet poor. In his childhood, his family lived in a fifth-floor one-room apartment with shared kitchen and toilet facilities – but no shower or hot water – in a communal apartment building in what is now St Petersburg. The family went to the public bathhouse to wash. The city was still battered from German bombardment during the siege of Leningrad, and their apartment building was infested with rats. Putin made no effort to hide his proletarian roots; if anything, he magnified them as a display of his political credentials.

In *First Person,* a series of interviews with him in 2000 conducted by three Russian journalists, Putin relished telling an anecdote about being pursued by a monstrous rat that turned on him after he drove it into a corner. He was the only child after the early death of two brothers, who died in the hunger and penury of the Second World War. The conflict came close to claiming the life of his mother, Maria Ivanovna Putina, who worked as a cleaner. Vladimir Spiridonovich Putin, his stern and uncommunicative father, was a toolmaker in a railway carriage factory and Communist Party stalwart. In the Second World War, he had been a frontline demolitions expert serving with a military unit of the NKVD, Stalin's forerunner to the KGB. Putin's father had a tough war – a familiar experience for many Russians – and he limped for the rest of his life because of shrapnel wounds to his legs. But the family did lay claim to a modest link to Soviet power: Putin's grandfather Spiridon had been a personal chef to Lenin and Stalin, a position that implied a significant degree of confidence in his reliability at the Kremlin at a time of obsessive paranoia about the leadership's security. When he came to join the KGB, Putin's proletarian lineage must have helped establish his suitability for the job.

Looking back on his youth, Putin liked to describe himself as a hooligan, saved from delinquency by a teacher, Vera Gurevich, who persuaded him to learn German. With his intellectual energies absorbed in language studies, he channelled his physical aggression into martial arts – first boxing and finally judo. The accounts of his childhood, though, came with a caveat: much of what was said about Putin's early years was moulded by him in the interviews recorded in *First Person* – as good an example as any of a KGB operative writing his own legend. One of the journalists who spoke with him for those interviews, Natalia Gevorkyan, spent a total of thirty hours in conversation with Putin and said later that the Russian leader seemed to be 'a big zero at the personal level. He is a man who, given the circumstances of his life, has a lot of complexes which dominate his behaviour. He's the small man, the man from the poor family. He has a lot of devils inside him. He doesn't control them.'

Yet, she said, the ascent to the Kremlin had moulded him as a leader. 'He's very self-assured. He absolutely enjoys power.'

Putin presented many faces to the West and to his own people – the business-suited statesman at formal summit meetings with the Group of Eight industrialized nations, of which Russia became a late and, some would argue, flawed member in light of its human rights record, economic illiberalism and authoritarian reflexes. He offered himself to the public as a soldier or pilot or sailor, wearing the uniform of the commander in chief. He approved photographs showing him in his black-belt judo outfit, hurling an opponent to the floor. Once he was filmed lifting the T-shirt of a young boy and kissing his stomach in what he insisted was a perfectly normal show of affection.

In 2007 the Kremlin's spin doctors allowed the release of a photograph of Putin, ostensibly on a fishing expedition, stripped to the waist to reveal a hairless and well-muscled torso with an Orthodox Christian baptismal cross on a chain nestling between sculpted pectorals. Like Litvinenko, Putin had been baptized clandestinely – an act of faith arranged by his mother without the knowledge of his father. Before he embarked on an official visit to

Jerusalem in 1993 as a representative of St Petersburg, Putin said later, his mother gave him the cross 'to get it blessed at the Lord's Tomb. I did as she said and then put the cross around my neck. I have never taken it off since,' he said.

In the photograph of his fishing expedition, the Russian leader wore a bush hat, jungle camouflage trousers, lace-up desert boots and narrow designer sunglasses, with a bone-handled hunting knife hanging from his belt. The fishing rod looked like an un-familiar prop and showed little sign of real use. If it was an attempt to look macho, it was not entirely successful. One British newspaper, the *Sunday Times,* jokingly took issue with the idea of men waxing away their chest hair and lampooned Putin's poses as camp. But in Russia his popularity blossomed. He had come a long way from the slums of Leningrad.

From his teenage years, Putin yearned for a job in the KGB, fascinated by the thought that one smart spy could achieve as much to undermine an enemy as a whole division of troops.

As a schoolboy, Putin said, he had gone along to the agency's offices to volunteer, only to be told the KGB did not take walk-ins off the street. Like the Litvinenkos, he had been inspired by propaganda films such as *The Shield and the Sword*, which showed gallant Soviet agents behind the Nazi lines.

For outsiders, the KGB represented the ever-taut sinews of oppression, the outfit that bugged homes, stifled opposition, murdered at will, dispatched dissidents to the Gulag, declared sane people mad. The Soviet KGB was synonymous with thickset men in parked cars on icy street corners awaiting victims to be beaten – torturers, poisoners, assassins who traced their roots to the original Cheka founded by Felix Dzerzhinsky supposedly to protect the October Revolution. They were the officers who culled secrets under physical and psychological duress, turned children into informers on their parents, held the keys to the locked cage of the Soviet Union. The KGB was the protector and guardian of the Communist Party of the Soviet Union, deployed to eradicate all opposition to the regime. Its weapons were coercion, blackmail and state-sponsored extrajudicial killings.

It was, indeed, all those things.

Yet the KGB seemed to have a different reputation among some Russians – perhaps those willing to look the other way and divert their gaze from the true nature of the Soviet state. Even Litvinenko insisted that he did not understand the role and functions of the KGB until after he joined it.

'What was wrong with the KGB?' Walter Litvinenko, Alexander's father, once said. 'Every country needs to have an intelligence service, right? We had been brought up to be patriotic and know our heroes. So why not? My son was in the KGB. We were proud of it.'

Indeed, as the Cold War unfolded, pitting East against West in the great ideological battle that ended with the collapse of the Soviet Union in 1991, the KGB secured significant victories in its shadowy conflict with adversaries such as the CIA, MI6 and West Germany's federal intelligence service, the Bundesnachrichtendienst. Each side, of course, sought to infiltrate, undermine and spy on the other's intelligence, political and military establishments. Western agencies recruited Soviet spies such as Oleg Gordievsky and Viktor Suvorov. Even in the post-Communist era, British intelligence gave sanctuary in 1992 to Vasili Mitrokhin, a former archivist for the KGB whose massive trove of stolen Soviet files was to have a significant bearing on the Litvinenko case and the theories surrounding his death. (Like Litvinenko, Mitrokhin went first to the Americans, in Tallinn, Estonia, but was rejected as a possible fraudster.)

But the KGB launched its own secret operations that deeply undermined Western intelligence-gathering. As a former MI6 insider pointed out somewhat ruefully, it was the KGB that managed to close down America's network in Russia by recruiting Aldrich Ames as its super-mole in the CIA.

Ames worked for the Russians from 1985 to 1994, when he was arrested and jailed, long after the fall of the Soviet Union and the formal demise of the KGB. As head of the CIA's Soviet desk, he was the highest-ranking official of the agency ever to be exposed as a spy. The KGB recognized his value, paying him $2.5 million for a catalogue of treachery that enabled him to buy a fancy home and a Jaguar car – emblems of affluence that he could never have afforded on a CIA salary alone. In the same era, the KGB recruited the FBI's Robert Hanssen, accused of spying for Moscow for fifteen years. Well before those coups, the Russians had tunnelled into British intelligence at the highest level, recruiting Kim Philby and four other agents from Cambridge University in the 1930s and nurturing them as they progressed higher into the top ranks of British espionage. It was Russian intelligence, too, that stole the crucial nuclear technology from the West after the Second World War. Klaus Fuchs, who had worked on the Los Alamos project to build the atom bomb, was unmasked as a Russian agent in 1950.

'There are many glorious pages, bright examples of true heroism and courage in the history of national state security organizations,' Putin told intelligence veterans in 2007 – as clear a statement as any of his abiding commitment to and reliance on Russia's undercover operatives. 'This profession employs those who love our motherland and who are selflessly devoted to their people,' he proclaimed.

The KGB, in other words, was an elite, the equivalent in career terms of studying at the Ivy League or Oxbridge universities that shaped Western leaders-in-waiting like the young George W. Bush or Tony Blair. But it was no monolith, and it is perhaps worth considering Putin's career as a spy not so much in the broad context of the KGB as in his particular division of it.

The KGB was divided into directorates with a variety of specialities. The First Directorate, now reformed as the SVR (Sluzhba Vneshney Ravzedki, or Foreign Intelligence Service), busied itself with spying on foreign countries, while the Fifth was preoccupied with maintaining the ideological purity of the Soviet Union – in other words, repressing all dissent. Then there was the Ninth Directorate, which employed people like Andrei Lugovoi and Vyacheslav Sokolenko to guard the Kremlin elite. Litvinenko told Gerald Seymour he had been an officer in the Third

Directorate, which focused on military counterintelligence – the department that maintained informers and agents in all units of the armed forces to report on the loyalty and morale of the Red Army.

There seems to have been some crisscrossing between these different directorates: several former KGB men have indicated that Putin, like his ally Sergei Ivanov, did some time in the notorious Fifth Directorate in Leningrad before moving on, although neither of these two men acknowledges that role in his official biography, both preferring to cast themselves as rising stars who quickly secured plum assignments outside Russia.

Whatever directorate KGB operatives worked for, however, they shared the common characteristics of obscuring their true goals, operating in conspiratorial and secretive ways and, above all, cherishing the belief that the end justified the means, the end meaning control of all the levers of power – judicial, economic and political. Their philosophy was built on the self-fulfilling belief that Russia faced malign forces that wished the nation only harm. 'A few years ago, we succumbed to the illusion that we don't have enemies,' Putin told the FSB in 1999, 'and we have paid dearly for that.'

Indeed, by April 2005, Putin seemed almost wistful for the stern certainties of the past – and pugnacious in asserting Russia's right to mould its own future.

'The collapse of the Soviet Union was the greatest geopolitical catastrophe of the century,' he said in his annual state-of-the-nation address to parliament. 'Russia is a country that, at the will of its own people, chose democracy for itself. It set out on this course itself and, observing all generally accepted political norms, will decide for itself how it will ensure that the principles of freedom and democracy are implemented, taking into account its historical, geopolitical and other characteristics.'

In pursuit of his dream, Putin studied law at Leningrad State University because he believed it would qualify him to become a spy, and he quickly fulfilled that overriding ambition.

The question of whether he spied on fellow students remains murky. While he became a Communist Party member at the university, his official recruitment to the KGB came only after he graduated in 1975 at the age of twenty-three and embarked on the series of training courses that would qualify him as a fully fledged spy. He spent much of his first decade with the KGB in Leningrad, with spells in Moscow. His official record listed his speciality as 'foreign intelligence', drawing on his knowledge of the German language.

Like Litvinenko, he reached the rank of lieutenant colonel, and the zenith of his career was a five-year posting to Dresden from 1985 to 1990, under somewhat obvious cover as an official of the Soviet–German Friendship Society, working with the feared East German secret police, the Stasi. There were accounts suggesting that his presence in Germany was part of a wider conspiracy within the KGB to reform the Soviet economy through the clandestine acquisition of advanced Western technology, helping the Communist system overcome the rapidly widening gap with the West. But his own version of the assignment in East Germany was far more humdrum.

Aficionados of James Bond movies or le Carré novels might still cherish an image of sinister KGB agents crisscrossing the Iron Curtain, receiving coded orders from perilous dead-letter drops in the shadows of divided Berlin. The Putins – and maybe this was disinformation, too – liked to give the impression that they spent their time in Dresden in more domesticated mode.

The KGB agents came home for lunch each day, regular as clockwork, according to Lyudmila Putin, and, on weekends, headed out into the hills of Saxony, eating German sausage and drinking German beer. At the office they recruited agents and sent reports on the political situation back to Moscow, hardly heavy lifting in a client state whose leaders were slavishly loyal to the Soviet Union and were happy to assume the role of national oppressors. Nonetheless, the KGB residents spent long hours at their desks; Putin complained that, unable to work out, he gained twenty-five pounds during his stint in the German Democratic

Republic. Indeed, his entire career path, bringing him back to Leningrad after his time at a modest provincial outpost in Dresden, does not suggest the trajectory of a high-flyer in the KGB hierarchy.

'He was zero in intelligence, a medium-level KGB colonel,' according to Natalia Gevorkyan of the *Kommersant* newspaper. 'If you are at least somebody, you go to Dresden, then you move to a capitalist country, West Germany, for instance, then back to Moscow.'

Putin, by contrast, had no formal experience in the West – unlike the KGB officer Sergei Ivanov – and returned to Leningrad, joining the city administration under the tutelage of Anatoly Sobchak, the reformist anti-Communist mayor who had been among Putin's teachers when he studied law at Leningrad State University.

The appointment surprised some in St Petersburg since the two men seemed to be on opposite sides of Russia's looming transformation after the glasnost and perestroika of Mikhail Gorbachev. But to others it seemed plausible that Putin, still in the KGB's 'active reserve', may have been useful to his new boss as a conduit to the security services, while the security services would certainly benefit from any information passed along by a member of the active reserve.

Formally, Putin left the KGB in 1991, although old KGB hands like to say you never really quit. Putin himself was widely quoted as saying, 'There is no such thing as a former Chekist.'

The timing of this resignation was a calculated risk, but the odds were pretty clear. By that time, the architecture of the Soviet Union was crumbling fast, and the KGB's influence was disappearing. In backing the failed anti-Gorbachev coup of August 1991, moreover, senior KGB officers – betting on a different outcome – ensured the demise of an organization of some 500,000 people that had wielded enormous power in supporting the Kremlin.

Putin maintained that he resigned twice – the first time before the coup and the second time as it unfolded. 'As soon as the coup began, I immediately decided whose side I was on,' he said later.

The real legacy of his years in the Russian secret services was arguably the anonymity that cloaked his rise to power in the 1990s. Putin was not the only KGB operative to take pride in his ability to pass unnoticed: his friend and ally Sergei Ivanov made much the same boast as he rose to high rank within the Kremlin. 'I am not able to tell you everything that gets taught in intelligence officers' training establishments, but I was definitely taught not to stand out from the crowd,' Ivanov once said. 'And I now consider a lack of distinguishing characteristics to be a sign of professionalism. I have never liked cliques, and have no desire to shine in front of cameras or frequent high society.'

Indeed, while displays of naked ambition might be lauded in the West, the collective orthodoxy of the Soviet Union frowned on ostentatious desires for advancement – careerism – and Putin always took care not to tip his hand. 'I can't say he was a careerist,' said Mikhail Frolov, a retired instructor at the Andropov Red Banner KGB school in Moscow who wrote an assessment of Putin as an intelligence service officer. 'I do remember that I wrote about several negative characteristics in his evaluation. It seemed to me that he was somewhat withdrawn and uncommunicative.'

Another, unidentified KGB trainee who displayed great technical aptitude for the intelligence job, Frolov noted, never made it as a spy. 'Unfortunately, his personal qualities – his careerism and his lack of sincerity towards his comrades – disqualified him immediately.'

Putin's bland looks, by contrast, might well have equipped him to tail a suspect through a crowd without being detected, or travel on the underground without drawing attention. When she first met him, his wife, Lyudmila, said, 'I would even say he was poorly dressed. He looked very unprepossessing. I wouldn't have paid any attention to him on the street.'

His gift for anonymity served him well. Putin drew suspiciously little public attention as he progressed rapidly from the St Petersburg administration to the inner circles of the Kremlin, then on to the Lubyanka as head of the FSB before Boris Yeltsin made him prime minister and president-in-waiting in 1999.

Perhaps that kind of progress was only possible in an era of chaos and transformation presided over by the capricious and increasingly erratic Yeltsin. Perhaps, indeed, Putin was an accidental tsar, thrust by default into positions of high office as an increasingly desperate Yeltsin looked for reliable lieutenants to whom he could entrust the ramshackle remnants of Russia and who would, above all, not betray the family secrets. In the three years since the 1996 elections, the Russian president had chosen and then discarded four prime ministers before he settled on Putin, and had given no indication that the relatively unknown bureaucrat from St Petersburg would become his political heir.

'Yeltsin had been through everybody else, and they had tried and failed,' a seasoned Russia expert in London told me. Putin was 'ostensibly the caretaker. He had no charisma, no political feel.' But perhaps that was merely the legend he created. Certainly, he arrived at the gates of power with a very clear sense of who his friends and enemies were.

From the very moment he began his rise from obscurity in 1998, Putin advanced the fortunes of people he had met in the KGB and in Leningrad. Behind the inscrutable facade, he built a power base from a remarkably narrow cohort of loyalists.

Sergei Ivanov, a former First Directorate spy with operational experience in Scandinavia, Africa and London (whence he was expelled in 1983), was an early beneficiary of Putin's largesse, rising quickly to become head of the Russian Security Council, then minister of defence, before Putin made him first deputy prime minister in 2007.

Nikolai Patrushev was another, replacing Putin himself as head of the FSB in 1999.

Putin's men had a mission that went far beyond occupying the offices of state. Some of them boasted formal titles that suggested little of their true goal in restoring the Kremlin's direct control over Russia's huge state-owned companies and the billions in their coffers. If the 1990s had been about privatization à la Berezovsky, then the opening years of a new century were devoted to reversing that process.

Igor Sechin, a graduate of Leningrad State University, veteran of the St Petersburg administration and an aide to Putin since the late 1990s, was appointed chairman of Rosneft, the big state oil producer. While his official CV did not list him as a former KGB operative, other accounts of his career as a Portuguese speaker said that in the 1980s he acted as a 'military translator' in Angola and Mozambique, both run at the time by pro-Soviet former liberation movements. Sechin was close to Putin in different ways: when Putin's wife Lyudmila and daughter Katya were injured in a car accident in 1994, it was Sechin who was delegated to pick up Putin's daughter from the hospital; Putin, by his own account, was escorting Ted Turner and Jane Fonda around St Petersburg as part of negotiations for the forthcoming Goodwill Games.

But Putin did ensure that his wife was transferred from a dingy civilian hospital – 'there were stretchers in the hallway with dead bodies on them,' Putin's wife recalled – to the leading military clinic in the city. Its director was Yuri Shevchenko, later to become Putin's health minister.

Viktor Ivanov, another close Kremlin aide who spent time in the KGB during the Soviet occupation of Afghanistan and later rose to high office in Putin's FSB, became chairman of Aeroflot, the Russian airline once controlled by Boris Berezovsky, and of Almaz-Antei, which produced air-defence missiles. Alrosa, the state diamond monopoly, was headed by Alexei L. Kudrin, the Russian finance minister, a veteran of the same St Petersburg city administration as Putin, and an alumnus of Leningrad State University. There was evidence, too, of a dynasty taking root.

A son of Sergei Ivanov's became a vice-president, at the age of twenty-six, of Gazprombank, Gazprom's in-house bank. A son of the FSB director, Patrushev, became an adviser to Sechin at Rosneft. Putin's web embraced the highest echelons of Russian public life, creating what has been described as a corporate state. The Kremlin press secretary, Alexei Gromov, had a seat on the board of the main television station, Channel One, once controlled by Berezovsky. Sergei Chemezov, a contemporary of Putin's in the Dresden station of the KGB, headed Rosoboronexport, the state arms exporter. The FSB Academy in Moscow became the Ivy League of elite schools, grooming a new generation of interconnected *siloviki*.

'I have a lot of friends, but only a few people who are really close to me,' Putin said in one of his long interviews in 2000. 'They have never gone away. They have never betrayed me, and I haven't betrayed them, either. In my view that is what counts most.' Putin's insistence on loyalty did not waver. Even in 2000, in the *First Person* conversations, Putin listed Sergei Ivanov, Nikolai Patrushev, Dmitri Medvedev, Alexei Kudrin and Igor Sechin among the leading players on the ruling team he would take with him to the Kremlin. But the reverse side of the coin was Putin's abhorrence of betrayal: if he reserved great rewards and high office for loyalists, he despised treachery.

One of Litvinenko's many errors was to break Putin's code by going public in 1998 at the press conference. Putin took the act as a betrayal of the intelligence services that had formed so many of his reflexes.

Even as a child, Putin's teacher Vera Gurevich recalled, 'he never forgives people who betray him or are mean to him.'

Once the former KGB men had seized power in the Kremlin under Putin's rule, they lost no time in formulating a messianic justification for this creeping *coup d'état*.

'We must understand that we are one whole,' Viktor Cherkesov, the former Fifth Directorate boss in Leningrad, wrote in a celebrated article, referring to the bonds cementing the *siloviki*. 'History ruled that the weight of supporting the Russian state should fall on our shoulders. I believe in our ability, when we feel danger, to put aside everything petty and remain faithful to our oath.'

Even Putin liked to hint that the rise of the former KGB men was no accident. 'A group of FSB operatives, dispatched undercover to work in the government of the Russian Federation, is successfully fulfilling its task,' Putin told his former intelligence comrades shortly before assuming the presidency.

It might have been meant as a joke, but it was no idle boast either.

According to Olga V. Kryshtanovskaya, the head of the Centre for the Study of Elites at Moscow's Institute of Sociology, a full quarter of the top one thousand people in Russia's presidential administration, government ministries, parliament and regional authorities had a formal and acknowledged background in the intelligence services or the military. If the calculation was expanded to include people defined as having been affiliated in some way with those agencies, then the number rose to a staggering 78 per cent – almost eight hundred people with secret service backgrounds running a land that wanted to change the world.

The average age was fifty-two – the Putin generation.

There were some finer shadings within his entourage.

Looking at the Russians fronting for Putin in Davos, it was clear that alongside – or possibly just below – his reliance on former KGB officials, there was a tribal link to St Petersburg, his home town, and its university – his alma mater – which produced technocrats such as Dmitri Medvedev and economists such as German Gref, the relatively liberal minister of economic development and trade. Perhaps they were intended merely to be the acceptable face of Russian capitalism, while true political power over the supreme leadership of the country was left to the former KGB men surrounding Putin. When Putin finally chose Medvedev as his anointed successor, he selected a man seen until then as the most pliant of loyalists and the most open to Putin's continued influence.

For many years, the Kremlin, under both Yeltsin and Gorbachev, sought to reform (but not completely dismantle) the KGB, chopping and slicing it into new divisions and formations, even as many of its members, like Andrei Lugovoi, abandoned state employment to set up their own security businesses. The KGB was formally dissolved by Boris Yeltsin after the attempted coup of August 1991. A short-lived Ministry of Security was created partly in its place as the forerunner to the FSK (Federalnaya Sluzhba Kontrrazvedki, Federal Counterintelligence Service), formed in 1993, before the birth of the FSB in 1995. Initially, the reforms seemed to weaken Russia's security services. Western intelligence specialists gloated that, such was the disarray, potential agents keen to turn against their one-time bosses in the Lubyanka were ten a penny.

In the early days of the reforms, at least eleven thousand security personnel left government employment to work for private security firms, or the in-house security divisions of big companies (some little less than private armies), or organized crime gangs. Some of the most senior KGB officers went into private business, running security details for the richest oligarchs.

Certainly, as a centralized organization with a web of disparate arms of oppression and espionage, the old KGB was not replicated directly in modern Russia. Too many of its operatives went into private business. Too many freedoms – to travel abroad, to do business, to surf the web, to make money on the fringes of legality – took root to be snuffed out by a revived Fifth Directorate. But something else happened. In spirit, Putin's critics maintained, the KGB never died altogether, it simply hibernated for a period, and when it reawoke as the FSB in the Putin era, its reflexes revived at the highest levels in the Kremlin.

It was hard to argue, for instance, that the old habits had all died out when people like the former oil tycoon Mikhail Khodorkovsky or the former FSB agent (and Litvinenko ally) Mikhail Trepashkin were held in remote penal settlements far beyond the Urals on criminal charges derived from their opposition to the system. Political protest meetings may have taken place in Moscow and St Petersburg in 2007, but the protesters were often outnumbered four or five to one by riot police doing the same job as the old Fifth Directorate. The old-style KGB – holding foreign and domestic security services in its fierce embrace – was replaced by a culture of centralized power whose tentacles spread across Russia from Moscow to the distant fiefdoms of regional governors.

In the past, Russians like Olga Kryshtanovskaya at the Institute of Sociology liked to say, the KGB was at least formally under the control of the Politburo of the Communist Party. 'In earlier times you had the Communist Party and the Politburo, and the KGB had only one seat on the Politburo,' she said. 'Now Putin's Politburo consists entirely of ex-KGB. In Soviet times there were forces that could say no to the KGB. Now there's no one to say no.'

'Putin has no independent source of information,' the journalist and intelligence specialist Andrei Soldatov said. 'He has only the FSB.'

The perils of reliance on the *siloviki* became apparent in October 2007, when reports began to trickle out of Moscow that these powerful men put in place by Vladimir Putin had become jealous of one another's share of the patronage and profit accruing to the Kremlin insiders. The feuding was seen as part of the power struggle preceding the end of Putin's second term in 2008, when, according to the constitution, he was required to step down as president. (He intimated well before that time that he would simply continue as prime minister with enhanced, quasi-presidential powers.) One of the combatants in the power struggle was Viktor Cherkesov, the former Fifth Directorate heavyweight in Leningrad, whom Putin appointed as head of Russia's drug-control agency. Increasingly, he clashed with Sechin and the FSB's Patrushev. The rivalries became so intense that armed units from the drug-control agency and the FSB confronted each other at a Moscow airport and almost became embroiled in a gunfight over the arrest of General Alexander Bulbov, Cherkesov's right-hand man.

'They stood together as long as they were robbing others of their assets,' a political analyst wrote in an online journal called

Yezhednevny Zhurnal. 'But after dividing the spoils, they realized that they can only expand their wealth by robbing one another.'

Cherkesov himself tried to defuse the dispute in a remarkably public way. 'There can be no winners in this war,' he wrote in the business newspaper *Kommersant*. 'There is too much at stake.'

But there was an ominous element to this battle among the clans Putin had promoted within the Kremlin from the ranks of his long-time supporters – one that seemed particularly unsettling considering the earlier events of November 2006.

Almost one year after Litvinenko's poisoning, two officers from Cherkesov's Drug Control Service, Konstantin Druzenko and Sergei Lomako, were found dead in a ditch in St Petersburg. Initially, investigators concluded the two men were drunks who had died in their cups of hypothermia, but subsequent inquiries established that the men had been poisoned after a drinking bout with a contact among the St Petersburg city authorities. The fatalities rekindled debate in Russia over the infighting within the Kremlin, some of it linked to business arrangements dominated by one clan or another.

In this case, Bulbov maintained he had been singled out by his enemies within the FSB because his organization had investigated a large furniture company called Tri Kita, whose executives were accused of bribing FSB officers to smuggle imports without paying duty. (To translate the allegations into British terms, imagine that Scotland Yard ordered the arrest of a senior narcotics cop to punish him for uncovering a protection racket run by other officers from the Met.) The link to the Tri Kita company dated to an earlier investigation in 2003 by a legislator and journalist, Yuri Shchekochikhin, whose name was to recur in the analyses of the Litvinenko case; Shchekochikhin was poisoned, too.

Putin, however, remained aloof, perhaps content to permit his subordinates to weaken themselves through internecine squabbles. What counted most for him, in any event, was their loyalty.

Referring to the death of his father, Konstantin Shchekochikhin said: 'No investigator will get to the bottom of this unless there is a political will.'

After November 2006, many of Putin's adversaries saw Litvinenko's destiny as all too familiar in the culture of vengeance shrouding the long and brutal history of the Russian intelligence services.

Litvinenko had chosen a foe that regarded itself as omnipotent and would have no compunction or difficulty in removing a troublesome enemy.

He was not, like some Don Quixote, tilting at windmills. He was taunting people and institutions wielding absolute power.

'A secret service is designed to fight another secret service,' Litvinenko told a reporter from the *New York Times* in a telephone interview in 2004 during the inquiry into the poisoning of Viktor A. Yushchenko, then a Ukrainian presidential candidate. 'When a secret service goes after an individual, they have no chance.'

Putin's compact with broader Russian society was tough, brutal and – if opinion surveys mean anything – popular with 60 or 70 per cent of his people. His party, United Russia, won 64 per cent of the vote in parliamentary elections in December 2007, although the scale of his victory was contested by Russian opposition groups and some outsiders. Whatever else, his supporters argued, he brought a sense of calm, order and direction after the Yeltsin roller-coaster of rags and riches. He restored Russians' self-respect. He raised wages and pensions by 10 per cent a year. And he reintroduced the old Russian social bargain of deference towards the ruler in return for predictability.

'Yes, stability has come to Russia,' the investigative journalist Anna Politkovskaya wrote in 2004. 'It is a monstrous stability under which nobody seeks justice in law courts, which flaunt their subservience and partisanship. Nobody in his or her right mind seeks protection from the institutions entrusted with maintaining law and order because they are totally corrupt. Lynch law is the order of the day, both in people's minds and in their actions. An eye for an eye, a tooth for a tooth.'

A little over two years later, on 7 October 2006, she was dead with three bullets in her upper torso and the fourth – known among Russian hit men as the 'control shot' – in her head.

Politkovskaya had returned to her seventh-floor apartment with part of her food shopping and then taken the lift back down to collect the remaining bags. As the lift door opened on the ground floor, an assassin stepped forward with a 9-mm Makarov pistol.

Twelve days later in London, Alexander Litvinenko took the microphone at a memorial gathering at the Frontline Club and, speaking in Russian, declared through a translator: 'It is Mr Putin, the president of the Russian Federation, who has killed her. I am totally confident that only one person in Russia can kill someone with her standing and fame, and that's Putin.'

Within weeks, he had begun to die himself.

It was easy for Putin's critics to blame the Kremlin for both killings and just as easy for Putin to deny them. But the more complicated question was whether the Putin era, with its roots in the KGB, had produced a culture in Russia that made such killings not only conceivable but probable. 'Even if Putin wasn't directly responsible,' a former American diplomat told me, 'he has created an environment in which it is plausible that high officials were.'

In 2006 the New York-based Committee to Protect Journalists estimated that, in six years, thirteen journalists had died in contract killings in Russia connected unambiguously to their profession. Some estimates of this grisly tally were even higher.

After Politkovskaya's death, newspapers outside Russia published montages of photographs showing at least twenty journalists who died in Russia in mysterious and bloody circumstances and whose murders had gone unsolved.

There was, for instance, Ivan Safronov, found dead after ostensibly falling from a window while investigating a Middle East arms deal; and there was Paul Klebnikov, an American citizen of Russian descent and the editor of the Russian-language version of *Forbes*, shot dead in Moscow on 9 July 2004. There was a common theme to many of the deaths: the reporters had died while probing shady business deals and high-level corruption.

According to the International News Safety Institute, a non-governmental body in London focusing on journalists' security, Russia came second only to Iraq in a bloodstained league table based on the number of reporters killed on its territory. Not all the Russians died in Moscow. In the car-making town of Togliatti (named for an Italian Communist leader and the location of the first Fiat car-making subsidiary in the Soviet Union) three journalists investigating corruption in the motor industry were killed, one of them, Aleksei Sidorov, stabbed in the chest with a sharp object resembling an ice-pick – the weapon chosen for the murder of Trotsky in exile in Mexico in 1940. Dmitri Shvets, a senior executive at a local television station in Murmansk, was shot dead outside his station's offices. Natalya Skryl, a business reporter in Rostov-on-Don, died after being beaten with a heavy object. In ten years to 2007, the International News Safety Institute said, 88 media personnel died in Russia compared with 138 in Iraq and 72 in Colombia – the top three. In Russia, the methods included torture, suffocation, stabbing, beating, poisoning and attacks with weapons, including a hammer and an axe.

'What we can say is that the Russian authorities, in their failure to properly investigate and prosecute crime against journalists, have fostered a climate of impunity, in which reporters are afraid to cover sensitive subjects and enemies of the press are encouraged to continue killing journalists,' said Nina Ognianova, the Committee to Protect Journalists' coordinator for developments in Russia. Under 'this cycle of impunity', she said, 'the roster of dead journalists will continue growing, with terrible consequences for Russia's press corps and the public.'

Ognianova was speaking days before Litvinenko died. By then the tally of sinister killings in Russia had expanded to other spheres of society, not just reporters. In September 2006 Andrei Kozlov, the forty-one-year-old deputy chairman of the Russian Central Bank, was gunned down as he was leaving the Spartak football ground, where he had been playing for an in-house corporate team. Kozlov had been entrusted with cleaning up Russia's corrupt banking system. No one doubted that his killing was an assassination. But the question people began to ask in November 2006 was whether, as in the past, the list of targets had again been expanded to include adversaries overseas.

In July 2004 a court in the gas-rich Persian Gulf state of Qatar convicted two Russian secret agents, Anatoly V. Belashkov and Vasily A. Bogachyov, of murdering an exiled former president of Chechnya, Zelimkhan Yandarbiyev.

With his camouflage fatigues, black beard and tall astrakhan hat, Yandarbiyev had been one of the most distinctive Chechen figures to negotiate a cease-fire agreement with Boris Yeltsin after the First Chechen War ended with Russia's humiliation in 1996. But he fled Chechnya after the start of the Second Chechen War in 1999 and settled in Qatar in 2001, using his self-exile to raise cash for Chechen separatists fighting Russian forces. Fifty-one years old at the time of his death, and known in the West variously as a poet, nationalist and suspected terrorist, he died in February 2004 when a bomb planted underneath his Land Cruiser exploded as he drove away from a mosque in Doha, the Qatari capital, where he had been at prayer with his thirteen-year-old son, Daud.

While the Russians accused of the bombing insisted on their innocence and claimed they had been brutally tortured into making confessions, the Qatari judge in the case, Ibrahim Saleh al-Nisf, laid the blame bluntly at the Kremlin's door. 'The Russian leadership issued an order to assassinate the former Chechen leader Yandarbiyev,' the judge said. He did not mention Vladimir Putin but said 'Russian intelligence headquarters in Moscow' had begun plotting the assassination months earlier.

A third Russian arrested with the two agents was identified as Alexander Fetisov, an intelligence officer working under diplomatic cover at the Russian Embassy in Doha, who was released under the rules of diplomatic immunity. At the time, some Russian officials acknowledged that all three men had ties to Russian intelligence but explained their presence in Qatar by saying they were working to counter Islamic terrorism – a term that,

Russia believed, included Chechen separatists held responsible for a string of atrocities on Russian soil. Russia had earlier sought Yandarbiyev's extradition on many occasions, and he figured on lists compiled by the United States and the United Nations of people suspected of being linked to Al Qaeda. The trial of the Russian agents was held in camera at the request of defence lawyers, but at the sentencing one of the people in the courtroom was Akhmed Zakayev, the Chechen separatist official living in London who gave Litvinenko his last ride home on the day he began to die.

'If the international community does not give proper attention to what happened in Qatar,' Zakayev said after the Russians were convicted, 'I am absolutely sure that these methods may be tried again in other countries, including Western countries.'

Whatever happened to troublesome journalists at home or Chechen dissidents abroad, it was hard to fault Putin's long-term strategic view: if Russia no longer had the military clout to frighten the West with its nuclear arsenal and its badly demoralized armed forces, there was one weapon it could deploy: energy. Russia's oil and gas reserves were among the biggest in the world and would give it the power to demand respect from those Western countries, oligarchs and companies that had tended to write off the Kremlin in the 1990s as weakened and irrelevant.

At the top of his list of people to be brought to heel were those among the oligarchs who failed to heed the ground rules of a new era, particularly Berezovsky, Gusinsky and the oil baron Mikhail Khodorkovsky. But the catalogue soon widened to include the relatively free media, particularly television stations, human rights organizations, political opposition, foreign oil companies, former Warsaw Pact nations now deemed too close to the NATO alliance, and, ultimately, the United States or at least the Bush administration's plan to station an anti-missile shield in Poland and the Czech Republic – both parts of what Putin saw as Russia's historical sphere of influence. To fight those battles, Putin would not tolerate any dissent or power plays from remote regional governments or troublesome legislators in the Duma – let alone from exiled dissidents like Litvinenko railing against the Kremlin from the safety of London. Putin restored what Russians call the 'vertical' power structure, whose apex is the Kremlin.

But he began by reversing the power of the oligarchs in two specific areas – media, which held the key to domestic control, and energy, the basis of a new international power.

'The legacy of Putin will be the reassertion of state control and the primacy of the state,' a British Kremlinologist said.

In July 2000 Putin offered the oligarchs a deal, holding out the chance to keep their enormous riches from the privatizations of the 1990s in return for staying out of politics, paying their taxes and aligning strategic industries with the aims of the Kremlin. In that month, Putin summoned his country's billionaires to a two-and-a-half-hour meeting that left no doubt in his interlocutors' minds about his intentions. The deal was clear enough: wealth accrued in the 1990s could be retained, but only if businesses changed their ways of operating.

'The president said that the authorities would not review the outcome of the privatizations,' the Kremlin said afterwards. 'At the same time, it was unacceptable for competing companies to use state structures and law enforcement agencies to achieve their goals.'

The time of the oligarchs manipulating the authorities to their own ends was over. In the future, the reverse would obtain: the writ of the state would be paramount.

The new edict seemed designed to strip some oligarchs in particular of power and wealth, and that was evident from the list of participants: Gusinsky and Berezovsky were not present at the encounter with Putin. Gusinsky had already fled after being imprisoned, forcing him to sell his Media-Most company to Gazprom. Under investigation in the Aeroflot case, Berezovsky was about to follow him into self-exile. But they did not go without a last, scornful display of their influence over public opinion. As one British expert on Anglo-Russian relations put it, Gusinsky and Berezovsky 'had the swagger to say: "Who are you? I just bought you the Kremlin." '

*

On 12 August 2000 an explosion aboard the *Kursk* nuclear submarine in the Barents Sea sent it sinking through hundreds of feet of water with 118 men on board. What followed was a public relations disaster for Vladimir Putin, always hypersensitive to criticism but particularly so in the opening months of his tenure as he charted the unfamiliar corridors of power: one year earlier, he had been a functionary in charge of the FSB; now he was the supreme leader of a vast land whose assets ranged from nuclear weapons to oil and gas fields and whose army he had again sent into Chechnya.

It is perhaps a fallacy to view the Kremlin's takeover of the Russian broadcast media as a simple suppression of the free flow of information. In the Soviet era, the media had been tools of propaganda. And as television stations fell into the hands of the oligarchs in the 1990s, they became mouthpieces for the competing business and political interests of their proprietors – hardly a Russian monopoly.

In 1996 and in 2000, Berezovsky's own television outlets supported the oligarchs' choice for president and greatly influenced the outcome. It was no coincidence that Berezovsky's role model as a media mogul was Rupert Murdoch, who acquired TV channels and some of the world's most prestigious newspapers such as *The Times* and, in 2007, the *Wall Street Journal*. Indeed, Russia's lurch into relative press freedom in the 1990s offered proprietors like Berezovsky political powers akin to those of Citizen Kane.

In August 2000 Gusinsky and Berezovsky showed that their control of the media was a double-edged sword, using their privately owned television channels to air embarrassing public criticism of Putin's handling of the *Kursk* tragedy. In the process they underscored the appearance of callousness and indifference to human loss that Putin would seem to display throughout his presidency, not least in his responses to the deaths of Politkovskaya and Litvinenko.

At the time, Putin was on leave in the Black Sea resort of Sochi.

Television footage showed him barbecuing and vacationing, displaying little inclination to break off his summer leave for the sake of dead submariners. At the same time, the wives and mothers of the lost submariners were shown in all their pain demanding action to save their menfolk or at least attempt to raise the *Kursk*. The newspapers, too, seized on the government's inaction.

It emerged later that twenty-three of the Russian sailors survived the initial blast aboard the submarine and spent their final days trapped in the stricken vessel and awaiting a rescue that never came.

Only belatedly did Putin make a statement, and when he did, he diverged from his prepared text to launch a bitter and hardly veiled attack on Gusinsky and Berezovsky in their 'villas on the Mediterranean coast of France and Spain'.

The last thing Putin wanted from his one-time sponsors was a catalogue of his failings, and he resented their refusal to accept his rise to power in the same pliant manner that other oligarchs had. The interpretation was that he would not permit anyone to belittle his judgement and standing by suggesting inadequacy. 'There's nothing the boy done good hates more than being reminded of his shortcomings,' one Putin watcher said.

After the imbroglio of the *Kursk*, there was no way back for Berezovsky, and no way Putin would show mercy. But the new Russian leader had learned a crucial lesson: no one would control Russia without controlling television.

With Gusinsky and Berezovsky out of the way, two of the biggest obstacles to a state takeover of Russia's principal broadcast channels had been removed. True, small newspapers like the *Novaya Gazeta*, which published Politkovskaya's articles, were permitted to continue publishing, albeit in the scornful belief of the Kremlin's spin doctors that no one read them. But pro-Kremlin businesspeople were encouraged to take over the ownership of bigger newspapers, as Berezovsky had done in the 1990s.

The consequences of the new order were clear enough to some

of the oligarchs, such as Roman Abramovich, who made a public show of fighting poverty in Russia's far east even as he augmented his fortunes at the Sibneft oil company he had purchased for a modest $100 million with Berezovsky in 1995. Many of the leading players from the 1990s made the transition to the new rules, seeing them – as Mikhail Khodorkovsky once told me – as the guarantor of their new fortunes. After making billions in the Yeltsin era, the oligarchs stood to cement their enormous wealth with at least the appearance of respect for regulation and the law. Suddenly it became the vogue to talk of corporate governance and transparency – mechanisms that might shield the oligarchs' dubious acquisitions from the attentions of a new generation of predators. But, ironically enough, it was the law – or rather the judicial system supported by an array of state agencies – that Putin planned to use against those oligarchs who infringed the new compact.

Most prominent among them was Khodorkovsky himself, at the time Russia's richest man, with a fortune of $8 billion and a high-handed sense of his own importance and prospects. Had he played the game differently, bowing to the Kremlin, Khodorkovsky might have escaped the fate that befell him. But, pointedly, he did not bend to Putin. His company, Yukos, was Russia's biggest oil producer – a status that placed it right in the crosshairs of Putin's plans for the reassertion of state control of the economy.

In later years Yukos became an object of fascination for Alexander Litvinenko, who sought to make himself useful to those among the company's leaders who escaped its destruction. Once again, Litvinenko placed himself in opposition to the Kremlin on a matter that was close to Putin's project for a new Russia.

On 25 October 2003 an executive jet landed to refuel at Novosibirsk airport in Siberia. It was 5.00 a.m. On board were Mikhail Khodorkovsky and his retinue. Far from heeding the doctrine laid down by Vladimir Putin in July 2000,

173

Khodorkovsky had embarked on what seemed an increasingly reckless and undisguised challenge to the might of the Kremlin. Aged just forty at the time, the oil tycoon dropped heavy hints that he might sell a chunk of his company to an American oil major and that, by the time he was forty-five, he would be going into politics – just in time for the 2008 presidential elections. He openly supported movements opposed to Putin. He took to consorting with an international elite, including Henry Kissinger, Jacob Rothschild and George Soros. His oil company, Yukos, had agreed to a merger with its smaller rival Sibneft to become the world's fourth biggest. (The merger was never completed.) In the 1990s free-for-all, Khodorkovsky had been a brash and merciless bare-knuckle player in the scramble for state assets; when I interviewed him in Davos in early 2003, I remember thinking that I had rarely met anyone with such hard and unforgiving eyes. With his penchant for high-end designer casual clothes and his intolerance of those he considered fools, he had earned a reputation for ruthlessness and arrogance, at once sleek and intimidating in the manner of a leopard. Even in 2003 he had begun to argue in terms of a new era of moneymaking – no longer quite as rapacious as in the 1990s and reflecting a new notion of corporate responsibility. Most dangerously, he had begun to seek a role beyond business, partly in philanthropy and partly in politics, possibly as prime minister.

As he pursued his eyeball-to-eyeball confrontation with Putin, he must have known the stakes and the enormous perils.

Months before his plane landed at Novosibirsk to refuel, prosecutors had raided Yukos's offices. Two of his major business partners were charged with offences including stealing state assets and tax evasion. On 25 October 2003 he had been summoned to appear before investigators but, with characteristic insouciance, told them he was travelling that day and could not make the appointment. Yet for all his wealth and power, Khodorkovsky could barely have anticipated the speed and finality of the trap slamming shut on that chill Siberian morning.

Armed FSB agents stormed his executive jet, shouting, 'Weapons on the floor or we'll shoot,' according to a Yukos spokesman at the time. By evening he had been flown to Moscow, taken before a court, charged with fraud and tax evasion and jailed. His lawyer Anton Drel quoted Khodorkovsky as saying he was not sorry about anything he had done. 'Nor am I sorry about what's happened today.' But it was quite probable that Khodorkovsky simply did not understand that he had lost control of events, that even his fabled wealth and power could no longer protect him from the former KGB officer in the Kremlin who had grown up as a street fighter and had not forgotten the rules of the game. Khodorkovsky was 'a kind of romantic', another oligarch, Mikhail Fridman, said later. 'He thought that it's impossible that the richest, most well-known person would go to jail ... Khodorkovsky must have believed that he is an exception, a messiah, a kind of person that things will be forgiven.'

His arrest climaxed months of brinkmanship between himself and Putin. Years later, experts believed that neither man calculated their duel would go as far as it did, but neither was prepared to blink first. The arrest, however, was the beginning of a protracted exercise in corporate evisceration. Russia watchers became used to seeing Khodorkovsky photographed behind bars in a courtroom, impotent and humiliated. After an eleven-month trial, a panel of judges sitting without a jury found Khodorkovsky and his long-time business associate, Platon Lebedev, guilty on six of seven charges, including fraud, embezzlement, and corporate and personal tax evasion. In May 2005 they were sentenced to nine years in prison. The two men had already spent months in jail, and, theoretically, they would qualify for parole in early 2008 – just in time for the presidential election. Then, in February 2007, prosecutors brought fresh charges against the two men, accusing them of money laundering and embezzlement of $20 billion. The new accusations effectively forestalled the anyhow-slim prospect of parole.

The authorities made it as tough as they could for Khodorkovsky's lawyers. To face – and deny – the new charges,

Khodorkovsky and Lebedev appeared at a courthouse guarded by masked police in the Siberian city of Chita, on the Chinese border 3,700 miles east of Moscow. Their legal team complained that the location would place huge burdens on defence lawyers – far from scrutiny and probably ignored by the Kremlin's captive media. The defendants were given only days to read thousands of pages of evidence. Human rights organizations began describing Khodorkovsky as a prisoner of conscience – a title with some resonance in a society that produced such renowned dissidents as Andrei Sakharov, Vladimir Bukovsky and Aleksandr Solzhenitsyn. The change in his description mirrored the transformation in his destiny: from oligarch to jailbird, from tycoon to martyr.

While Khodorkovsky faced trial and imprisonment, his company suffered an even more terminal fate that seemed to bring Putin's plans full circle. The Russian tax authorities demanded billions in corporate back taxes. Yukos – once Russia's dominant oil company – was forced into bankruptcy, and its assets were sold off, mostly to Rosneft, the state oil giant whose chairman was Igor Sechin, one of Putin's closest aides. A planned Yukos merger with Sibneft fell through, and Sibneft, owned by Roman Abramovich, was bought in 2005 by Gazprom, whose chairman was Dmitri Medvedev, Putin's first deputy prime minister. Gazprom expanded its massive tentacles. Abramovich benefited to the tune of $13 billion from the sale – to the immense annoyance of Boris Berezovsky, who had choreographed the acquisition of Sibneft for a paltry $100 million in 1995.

At the same time, the Russian authorities pursued two major foreign investors – BP and a consortium comprising Royal Dutch Shell and two Japanese companies, Mitsui and Mitsubishi – pressuring them to relinquish majority control of oil and gas fields in which they had invested billions.

The beneficiary? Gazprom.

'Under Mr. Putin,' Andrew Kramer of the *New York Times* wrote in July 2007, 'the Russian government is establishing vast, state-owned holding companies in automobile and aircraft manufacturing, shipbuilding, nuclear power, diamonds, titanium, and other industries. His economic model is sometimes compared with the "national champion" industries in France under Charles de Gaulle in the 1950s. The policy of forcing owners of strategic assets to sell their holdings has also been compared to recent nationalizations in Venezuela and other Latin American nations.'

Or, as Olga Kryshtanovskaya put it, 'Private business exists only by the grace of the state.'

By the time energy and commodity prices soared midway through Putin's second term, the Kremlin was not only sitting on a gold mine but reaping its rewards. Stanislav Belkovsky, a Russian political scientist, claimed in a newspaper article that Putin had amassed a secret personal fortune of some $40 billion, making him Europe's richest man – a charge that drew a brusque 'no comment' from the Kremlin.

But that was still not enough. If Russia's strongmen controlled the bulk of Russia's natural resources, they also insisted on dominating the means of delivering oil and gas to the Western markets that provided their principal source of riches.

Pipeline policy became the new Great Game.

By the end of Putin's second term, Russia seemed to have wrested its energy reserves back into state control while maintaining its grip on the Soviet-era web of pipelines stretching from Siberia and central Asia to the well-heeled consumers of Western Europe. The Russian stranglehold worried the Europeans in particular: by 2006, a quarter of their gas imports came from Russia, and the proportion was set to rise to 50 per cent by 2020 as alternative supplies dwindled. Yet the Europeans were divided in how they should react to the encroaching influence of the Kremlin over their future energy supplies.

In 2006 and 2007 Russia briefly suspended supplies to smaller neighbours such as Belarus and Ukraine to forcibly wean them off subsidized prices and let them know how easily their central heating pipes and stoves could go cold. (Both suspensions, coincidentally, came about in the depths of winter.) In the late summer of 2007, German refinery managers also began to notice a drop-off in the supplies of Russian crude.

'Some have painted Gazprom as a monster,' Alexander Medvedev, Gazprom's deputy chairman, said in early 2007. 'But in truth we are as dependent on European customers as they are on us. Two-thirds of our sales are to Europe, and most of our investment programmes are also aimed at European customers.' That calculation of interests dated to the Cold War. Even as armies massed on either side of the Iron Curtain in the long decades of nuclear standoff, the Soviet Union proved a reliable supplier of gas to Western nations, showing that hard cash meant more than ideology. 'We have been a supplier of gas to Europe for over thirty years, and there hasn't been a single occasion when we didn't fulfil our contractual obligations,' Medvedev said.

But despite the schmoozing at Davos in 2007, Russia offered the West little cause for comfort: East and West seemed once again to be on a collision course.

'Russia is just behaving in character, and what Russia hates is to be disregarded,' one former British intelligence official said. 'And it has been disregarded by the US, and it's making damn sure that it is taken seriously in the future through energy.' But, the former official acknowledged, 'we are entering a new phase. The Russians are going to be extremely angular and awkward to deal with.'

During the Cold War, Russia's global power derived from its massive arsenal of missiles, submarines, nuclear warheads and conventional weapons. Oil and gas were simply the means of financing the arms race. But in the Putin era, energy supplies both supplanted Russia's dilapidated military machine as the prime source of its global influence and, as oil prices soared beyond $100 a barrel, provided a munificent income to begin to address the decay of its armies.

In May 2007 Russia said it had successfully tested a new

intercontinental ballistic missile, the RS-24, with a range of 3,400 miles and the claimed capability to carry up to six warheads designed to evade missile-defence systems.

The sabre-rattling was inspired in part by the Bush administration's determination to install parts of a missile defence system in the Czech Republic and Poland. Ostensibly, the American plan was designed to counter any future missile threat from Iran, but the idea was taken in Moscow as a deep affront, not only threatening Russia but using its former Warsaw Pact allies to do so. From a Russian hard-liner's point of view, America's actions seemed comparable to those of the Soviet Union in the Cuban missile crisis of 1962 – a parallel drawn by Putin himself.

'If part of the strategic nuclear potential of the United States finds itself in Europe and, according to our military experts, threatens us, then we will have to take corresponding retaliatory steps,' Putin told a group of reporters from the G8 countries. 'What are these steps? Of course we will have to have new targets in Europe.'

In August 2007, Putin revived Moscow's Cold War practice of sending Russian long-range nuclear bombers out on patrol far from Russia's frontiers for the first time since the collapse of the Soviet Union. Putin promised an increase in defence spending to rehabilitate Russia's tattered armed forces. And he dispatched Russian submarines deep below the ice-cap to plant a Russian flag engraved on titanium on the seabed, laying claim to the planet's last known major reserves of oil and gas underneath the Arctic Circle.

The manoeuvres offered a distraction from some of Russia's deeper internal woes. Not everyone benefited from the surge of oil wealth, and the gap between super-rich and dirt-poor was widening. Military morale was bad, destroyed by bullying and years of neglect. Not only that, the country faced an intractable demographic problem: the population was shrinking by hundreds of thousands, possibly one million, citizens a year. Poor health services, ingrained alcoholism and the unacknowledged spread of

AIDS created human tragedies that no amount of oil money could redress overnight.

As the strongmen around Putin saw it through the prism of their KGB training, it was time for Moscow to set its marker as a rallying point of opposition to the United States.

Internationally, the Kremlin offered itself as the leader of an alternative pole to Washington in world affairs, befriending the kinds of states America loved to hate, such as Iran, Syria and Venezuela. Far from the friendly overtures to Washington of Putin's early days, when George W. Bush called him 'a new style of leader', the Russian president launched a verbal barrage against America, likening US foreign policy in Iraq and elsewhere to that of Hitler's Germany.

America's 'hyper-use of force in international relations – military force' had brought the world 'to the abyss of permanent conflicts. Political solutions are becoming impossible,' Putin complained in February 2007 at a closely watched global security conclave in Munich.

The United States had 'overstepped its national borders, and in every area,' he said. The tone – and the Russian leader's readiness to revert to the language of the past – raised a terrifying prospect: could it really be that Russia was taking a step back towards the Cold War?

When asked that question in mid-2007, Putin replied simply: 'We are, of course, returning to those times.'

8

GILDED EXILES

The London that adopted Alexander Litvinenko after his flight from Russia in 2000 was a place of great riches, and he was only one of many compatriots drawn to it, albeit for a variety of different reasons.

For some, like Litvinenko, it was a place of refuge and political sanctuary. For others it was a city where money made in Russia could be spent, invested and protected. So many affluent Russians arrived in London seeking a luxurious bolt-hole that the British capital earned the sobriquets Moscow-on-Thames and Londongrad.

In the six years Litvinenko lived there, the city challenged, if not overtook, Wall Street as the global financial capital and drew vast Russian wealth into the discreet offices of private bankers, estate agents and the kinds of car dealers who sold the latest Bentley coupé, Aston Martin Vantage or S-Class Mercedes without needing to offer discounts.

Less than a four-hour flight from Moscow, and with far fewer immigration and regulatory hassles than the United States, London and its thriving financial markets offered a warm welcome to the billions generated by Russia's staggering wealth in oil, gas and minerals. British investors indeed proved eager to buy into Russia's newest offerings. In 2006 alone, corporations from the former Soviet Union sold stock worth some $26 billion in London.*

Historically, Russia's turbulence had always propelled some of its citizens to seek their fortunes far from the Kremlin, but in the first decade of the twenty-first century the British capital achieved a special status – remote enough from the Kremlin for safety, close enough for comfort, and so much more convenient than far-flung New York or Los Angeles for those who had not quite decided where they would finally hang their hat.

As Berezovsky noted in an interview with Anna Politkovskaya in 2003, London was for exiles who 'wish to return to Russia. America is a ten-hour flight away; it's too far, communication is difficult, but here one lives within the Russian informational space. America is for immigrants who don't want to return.'

By 2006 a third of Russia's thirty-three newly minted billionaires had established residences in London – tycoons and magnates who, sometimes with the Kremlin's assent and connivance, held a lock on some of Russia's vast reserves of natural resources. Among the influx of Russians, the number of mere millionaires was put at around one thousand. For Moscow's elite, a London home was becoming almost *de rigueur*: the British capital was safe, chic, booming. The government and the city authorities competed to put the past behind them, insisting that London had shed the kind of Cold War hostility that Vladimir Putin seemed only too ready to rekindle.

When the mayor, Ken Livingstone, staged a third Russian New Year's party in Trafalgar Square on 13 January 2007, some seventy thousand people attended.

'Thirty years ago it would have been inconceivable that we would celebrate the Russian New Year with tens of thousands of people in London,' Livingstone declared. 'London welcomes Russia.'

---

* One transaction – an initial public offering – raised over $10 billion for the oil company Rosneft, built on the expropriated assets of Yukos. Some market watchers in London regarded the Rosneft flotation on the London Stock Exchange as tantamount to laundering stolen assets. But they invested anyway.

To reinforce his point, a satellite link set up for the occasion permitted chess grandmasters in London and Moscow to play each other simultaneously in Trafalgar Square and Pushkin Square, moving pieces carved from ice. The result was a diplomatic draw. 'In the spirit of thawing Anglo-Russian relations we accepted their offer of a draw,' said Nigel Short, the head of the London team. 'Besides, some of the pieces were melting and a couple were sliding out of position.'

The Russians had plenty of good reasons for clustering in London, shielded from the nightmares of their own country's corruption and the Kremlin's increasing encroachment on private property rights. A personal tax regime – smiled on by the British authorities – offered great advantage to foreign-born people who could prove they were domiciled elsewhere even if they maintained residences in the United Kingdom. Most ordinary resident Britons were obliged to pay income tax of up to 40 per cent on their entire global earnings. But for the non-domiciled, the so-called nondoms, the British fiscal regime permitted them to pay taxes only on money brought into Britain – not that these were insignificant amounts – leaving the bulk of their wealth untaxed in offshore accounts. For the cash that did arrive, London offered the shops of Bond Street, with their multimillion-pound diamond necklaces and designer names from Ferragamo to Gucci to Bulgari. Rich Russians bought homes in the elegant white-stuccoed terraces of Belgravia, art from the galleries of Mayfair, amusement at the theatres of the West End and meals in celebrity restaurants, like Nobu on Park Lane and Gordon Ramsay at Claridge's. Upmarket stores such as Harrods hired Russian-speaking staff. The clothes and shoes, for those who could afford them, represented the very height of fashion.* And, on the streets, London offered the relative security of a Western capital, even if some tycoons found it impossible to kick the habit of moving

---

* One British podiatrist told me he made a substantial part of his living by beautifying the feet of Russian women to grace the latest footwear from Manolo Blahnik and Jimmy Choo.

with a retinue of bodyguards. For those who could afford to take advantage of it – not simply Russians – London offered much the same conditions as a Caribbean tax haven, albeit without the sunshine and beaches, but nonetheless handy for Moscow as a glittery gateway to the West.

In 2007 the Russian Embassy reckoned that between 250,000 and 300,000 Russians lived in London – and some other estimates put the figure higher. If tsarist Russian exiles tended to congregate in Paris after the October Revolution of 1917, then modern Russians gathered in London, writing the latest chapter in a long history of sanctuary. Since the time of Karl Marx in the mid-nineteenth century and Vladimir Ilyich Lenin in the early twentieth, London was accustomed to receiving illustrious outsiders.

In 1907 revolutionary stalwarts such as Stalin, Lenin and Trotsky gathered in London to attend the Fifth Congress of the Russian Social-Democratic Workers' Party. Stalin's true intention, according to the author and historian Simon Sebag Montefiore, was to secure Lenin's approval for a spectacular bank robbery in Georgia to fund the struggle against the tsars. But even then some Russians could not resist the lure of comforts that were not available to all. 'Lenin and his wife, Krupskaya, took rooms in Kensington Square – he had a private income – while the penniless Stalin started off in a fleapit,' Montefiore wrote.

A century later, it was safe to say, none of the new Russians arriving in the British capital were prepared to settle for anything less than the best accommodation – certainly not fleapits – and their readiness to pay top dollar warped property prices, endearing them to estate agents but raising some British eyebrows.

In 2006 almost a quarter of London homes sold for over £8 million went to Russians. And almost two-thirds of houses costing more than £10 million were bought by Russians prepared to bid up the price tag. By one estimate, Russian property purchases in 2006 totalled over £800 million – almost nine times as much as in 2000, when house prices were admittedly significantly lower. The Russians' spending on London homes and apartments put them ahead of the Saudis as the capital's new font of estate agents' profits – a role that had been occupied in turn by oil-rich Arabs, Japanese business tycoons and high-rolling American investment bankers. An informal survey of Russian ownership published in the *Evening Standard* showed Boris Berezovsky high on the list of property owners, with apartments and houses in Kensington, Chelsea, Belgravia and Surrey, where he maintained his vast country estate. Then there were his discreet offices at 7 Down Street in Mayfair – one of Litvinenko's last ports of call on the day he began to die.

Much of the Russian property portfolio was held by family members or through front companies registered offshore in places like the British Virgin Islands (such as Landry Estates, the official owner of Litvinenko's modest accommodation at Osier Crescent in Muswell Hill).

One reason the Russian *émigrés*, like other wealthy people, favoured such remote ownership was to avoid Britain's punitive inheritance taxes levied on all estates totalling more than £300,000 – a pittance by Russian standards. Another was that property purchase taxes were lower for houses and apartments owned by offshore corporations. Specialist advisers in the Channel Islands and the Isle of Man proved well versed in the art of establishing trusts that took the rich one step further away from paying the taxes levied on the not so rich.

The Russians were quick to snap up some of the huge and elegant villas and town houses that dated from the Georgian and Victorian eras. In those times, British class distinctions were much more obvious than they were in the early years of the twenty-first century, and the rich and aristocratic lived in a splendour unknown to ordinary citizens, as did the pre-revolutionary Russian aristocracy of Moscow and St Petersburg. Now it was the turn of a cosmopolitan Russian elite to occupy the heights of luxurious living and splendour unknown to the hoi polloi. The price tags may have seemed extreme, but this particular market moved upwards with such dizzying speed that a multimillion-pound investment was likely to provide double-digit returns, sometimes within months. The shipping magnate Igor Izmestiev bought in South Kensington for around £13 million. The Chernoi brothers, rich from the aluminium industry, purchased one of the luxurious penthouses at 199 Knightsbridge. The complex of apartments was designed to meet the requirements – security and convenience – of those boasting substantial wealth; Russians owned four-fifths of them. The penthouse cost an estimated £5 million, but was soon worth much more: just between June and July 2007, the price of properties costing more than £2.5 million increased by almost 4 per cent, or 1 per cent per week. And, calculated over a year, the prices leaped by 36 per cent – the highest increase since 1989, just before the British housing market crashed.

The pressure-cooker deals reflected the simple economics of supply and demand: such was the influx of foreign buyers (along with British bankers clutching huge annual bonuses) that the number of available properties costing over £2.5 million had fallen by a quarter since 2005. The surging prices merely seemed to encourage buyers. In Belgravia, according to the *Evening Standard*'s survey, the aluminium magnate Oleg Deripaska – one of Russia's truly rich men at the age of thirty-nine – owned a stuccoed Regency home, which he bought for some £25 million in 2003: small beer for a man whose assets totalled in excess of £10 billion. Leonard Blavatnik, an American energy billionaire of Ukrainian descent, spent £40 million on mansions in Kensington Palace Gardens, one of the most sought-after addresses in the capital, to use as home and office. Even that price tag did not look excessive for long: in 2006, according to the *Sunday Times*, two Indian brothers paid £60 million for a sixty-room home on the Mall. Almost two-thirds of properties sold for £4 million – roughly twenty times the average British house price – were bought by foreigners.

Some Russian men set up their wives and families in London houses and schools and spent the weekdays at work in Moscow before returning home for the weekend. In the skies between London and Moscow, scheduled flights on Aeroflot or British

Airways no longer sufficed: air charter operators reported brisk business in executive jets offering Japanese sushi as the in-flight snack. 'There are a massive number of Russians coming into London,' said Olga Sirenko, an adviser at Russian London, a firm set up to guide Russians through the process of moving to the British capital. 'It's very trendy right now to have an education in the UK, or buy property in the UK.'

London galleries specializing in Russian art boomed. 'The first thing a new businessman does is buy a house, and the second thing they do is stare at the walls and think they should get some art,' said William MacDougall, the co-owner of an auction house set up in 2003 to cater to Russians buying art by Russian artists.

As top-end property prices went up, they dragged the market with them, stirring a degree of discomfort among middle-class Britons suddenly nudged off the property ladder by the influx of Russians and other foreigners. Some of Britain's private educational institutions, moreover, began to show an unseemly preference for Russian candidates whose parents offered significant contributions to the school coffers.

'Fear and loathing of London's "superclass" of wealthy inter-national residents is a staple of the new urban myths,' the columnist Anne McElvoy wrote in the *Evening Standard*. 'But the impact of vast inflows of foreign wealth and a benign tax regime offering tax-haven status is real enough.

'It isn't just envy or resentment at work here,' she said. 'It is a sense that fair play is being disregarded.'

Fair play, of course, was not a distinguishing feature of the oligarchs' acquisition of enormous wealth, or indeed of the British housing market. But there was no doubt that a backlash was building against London's super-rich interlopers. Even Geordie Greig, the editor of the society magazine *Tatler,* who had close friends among the wealthy Russian set, warned his readers: 'The superclass is overtaking you in the race for the best schools, over-paying for the house you presumed was yours.

'They are leaving the central core of middle Britain feeling very left out,' Greig wrote in his magazine. 'That old sense of living in a country where fair play and an honest day's work led people to feel they could get what they strove for has been destroyed by dizzying extremes in wealth.' That view, of course, ignored a history in which Britain's *Tatler*-reading classes showed no compunction in pushing ahead of the lower orders deprived of access to upper-echelon schools and homes. So there was a degree of *Schadenfreude* among the less advantaged about this sudden onset of bourgeois blues.

Perhaps the best known of all the Londongrad Russians was Roman Abramovich, an ally of Vladimir Putin and a former associate of Boris Berezovsky who contrived to combine the greatest ostentation in his spending with the most obsessive privacy in his lifestyle.

When Abramovich spent fortunes on property in London's Chester Square, some people started calling it Red Square. Abramovich ranked as one of Russia's and England's richest people, with a fortune estimated at over $20 billion. He owned three huge yachts and commissioned a fourth, the *Eclipse,* as the world's longest private luxury vessel. His portfolio covered properties in London, Saint-Tropez and the remote Russian region of Chukotka, nine time zones and almost five thousand miles east of Moscow, where he became a philanthropic, though not always resident, governor.

Perhaps to impress Vladimir Putin with his commitment to goals other than self-enrichment, Abramovich spent hundreds of millions of dollars to revive Chukotka, a stricken area of tundra where reindeer outnumbered the 50,000 people by around four to one. The benefits were mutual: Abramovich registered Chukotka as the corporate headquarters of the Sibneft oil company, with significant tax breaks.

With so many homes to go to, he was cautious about saying where he really preferred to live.

'I live on a plane,' he once remarked. 'I like to visit London. If I had to think where I could live if not Moscow, London would be my first choice, and second would be New York. In Moscow I feel most comfortable. I'm used to four different seasons; it's difficult for people to understand. People brought up in Russia like my kids want to play in the snow.'

Among football-loving Britons, Abramovich achieved instant renown by purchasing Chelsea Football Club in June 2003 for £140 million. He went on to spend £500 million wiping out its debt and paying large amounts of money for a galaxy of world-class talent. The club's payroll reportedly surpassed that of the New York Yankees, and the tabloids soon nicknamed it Chelski. The purchase of the club did not imply a shift of patriotic loyalty. When the England national football team (including some Chelsea players) travelled to Moscow in October 2007 to play Russia, Abramovich was observed cheering gleefully when Russia beat England by two goals to one.

His purchase of Chelsea started something of a fashion. Alexandre Gaydamak, a French national of Russian descent, invested about £22 million in the premier-league team Portsmouth. Farther north, Vladimir Romanov gained control of the Scottish team Heart of Midlothian in 2006. In 2007 Alisher Usmanov, a Russian billionaire of Uzbek descent, whose holdings in iron, steel, media and sports were said to be worth £5 billion, bought a 23 per cent stake in Arsenal for roughly £120 million to become its second biggest shareholder. (A lesser investor was Boris Berezovsky, who maintained a hospitality box at the same club.)

Usmanov, the owner of *Kommersant* – among many other companies – was reckoned to be Russia's eighteenth richest man and was no stranger to grand gestures. When the world-famous cellist Mstislav Rostropovich died in 2007, Usmanov stepped in to prevent his art collection from being auctioned and split up among non-Russian buyers, paying more than £20 million to keep it intact. Usmanov put in his bid for the collection on the very eve of a public auction at Sotheby's. But his reputation was by no means solely as a patron of the arts. His business record emerged as a potential obstacle to his investment in Arsenal. 'People talk about me as an Uzbek businessman involved in narcotics and in a shady regime,' he told a news conference in Moscow. 'It is beyond my dignity to respond to all these allegations.'

Abramovich, a former oil trader raised as an orphan, owed his fortune in part to his fast footwork in recognizing useful allies and in knowing when, and how, to cut his losses.

When he broke up with his wife Irina, a former Aeroflot hostess, after a nineteen-year marriage in 2006, for instance, much attention focused on the divorce settlement. Under English law, British tabloids pointed out gleefully, his ex-wife could have been entitled to as much as half his fortune. In the end, the couple made their divorce settlement in Russia under laws that permitted Abramovich to keep most of his money while awarding his wife and four children a comfortable fortune of their own in perpetuity. There was, to say the least, enough to go around.

Abramovich's break-up with Berezovsky proved a more tangled proposition altogether. In the 1990s the two men had been partners, but that changed when Berezovsky fell foul of the Kremlin.

Berezovsky maintained that Abramovich played a central role in the manoeuvres forcing him to shed prized assets as he fled Russia for self-exile in London in 2000. The claims soured his relationship with Abramovich for years, and in October 2007 the rivalry between them flared into an embarrassingly public confrontation: Berezovsky resolved to serve a writ on Abramovich to claim damages from their joint business dealings.

Appropriately enough for such wealthy antagonists, the showdown – the OK Corral moment – came on Sloane Street, a thoroughfare lined with designer stores selling fine leather goods, elegant clothes and smart Italian shoes. At the northern end of the street, the well-heeled traveller would find luxury hotels and the Harvey Nichols department store, whose fifth-floor restaurant is known as the preserve of ladies who lunch. To the south lay Sloane Square, leading on to Chelsea's King's Road – a neighbourhood favoured by millionaires, rock stars and Sloane

Rangers. Chelsea, too, was the home of Abramovich's football club. And it was between these two beacons of luxurious living at either end of Sloane Street that the two tycoons chose their battlefield. Well, not really chose.

'Boris was in Dolce and Gabbana, Abramovich was in Hermès,' a Berezovsky insider said. (Abramovich's team declined to comment.) Both men were accompanied by their broad-shouldered minders – Abramovich reportedly favoured former members of Britain's SAS Special Forces, while Berezovsky relied on ex-members of the French Foreign Legion.

One of Berezovsky's bodyguards spotted the rival oligarch and tipped off his boss, who sent an aide to his car to retrieve a copy of the legal writ he wished to serve on Abramovich alleging damages of some $10 billion in lost assets and earnings. Abramovich's bodyguards were on the alert and blocked the doorway to Hermès as two of Berezovsky's heavyweights moved to escort their boss towards his rival. In the standoff between the bodyguards, so the story went in the Berezovsky camp, he side-stepped his rival's bodyguards like a fleet-footed fly-half, approached Abramovich and thrust the papers towards him. Abramovich refused to accept the documents, and they fell to the ground. Berezovsky believed his writ had been served, spun round and called off his bodyguards. The moment was observed by bewildered shoppers and store staff.

The episode showed how much Berezovsky resented his ignominious defeat in the high-stakes game for a place in Putin's Russia that Abramovich had played so deftly. And it received some publicity in the British newspapers as an example of the kinds of games oligarchs chose to play on British soil. The case came before the High Court in April 2008, when a lawyer for Abramovich dismissed Berezovsky's arguments as based 'wholly on oral conversations which are not documented'.

There were some attempts to spread a more cultivated veneer over this brash new wealth.

In the summer of 2006, Alexander Lebedev, a former KGB spy

in London who went on to become a billionaire banker, investor and crusader against corruption, joined Mikhail Gorbachev, the former Soviet president, to host a spectacular white-tie party at Althorp, Earl Spencer's estate in Northamptonshire, the childhood home of his sister Diana, Princess of Wales. The house, set in a walled park spreading over 550 acres of woodland and tended lawns, was the jewel in a bigger, 14,000-acre estate across three counties. Its history dated from 1508, and it stood as a preeminent symbol of the titled, moneyed classes that once dominated Britain. Diana's brother, the ninth Earl Spencer, liked to say it had been in the family for five centuries and was still a family home. But he also advertised it on the Internet as a visitor attraction used sometimes for corporate hospitality, or for events like the party thrown by Alexander Lebedev.*

The Althorp bash was designed to launch the Raisa Gorbachev Foundation – named for Mikhail Gorbachev's late wife, who died of leukaemia in 1999 – to combat cancer among children. Lebedev and his son Evgeny brought in performers such as the Black Eyed Peas to play for a crowd of entertainment industry stars, socialites and hedge-fund tycoons. According to Greig, the *Tatler* editor, who helped organize the function, 'The party reinvented the way British society looked at Russians in the UK.

'It was stylish, philanthropic, and generous-spirited on a new scale. There is a stereotype of the champagne-swilling, "See you at Cipriani," "I'm going to buy a football club" mentality,' Greig told a *New York Times* reporter, Sarah Lyall, who attended the Althorp party. 'But there are also people here like the Lebedevs who are an extraordinarily good example of what to do with your money.'

As Lyall recalled, the Althorp party was 'full of British and some American celebrities . . . the meal was sumptuous; a

---

* Given his background as a KGB officer in London, some British newspapers dubbed Lebedev 'the spy who came in for the gold'. But he also needled his former employers, or at least their successors: his portfolio included *Novaya Gazeta*, which published Politkovskaya's articles.

classical pianist played; the Black Eyed Peas performed; several Russian women demonstrated the art of pole-dancing.'

One year later, Lebedev repeated the event with similar splendour at Hampton Court Palace – once home to Henry VIII – offering tickets at £1,000 each. This time the performers included Sir Elton John and the Scissor Sisters. News reports made no mention of pole-dancing.

Then there were the malcontents, those who sought refuge in London for reasons of safety and politics.

'There are Russians and Russians' in London, Alex Goldfarb said. 'And the non-political ones do not touch the political ones with a ten-foot pole.'

This Londongrad, this web of dissidents and conspiracy theorists, was the city that welcomed Litvinenko.

In May 2001 the British authorities granted Litvinenko and his family political asylum after his lawyer argued that the former FSB officer had a 'well-founded fear of persecution' in Russia. The British authorities even offered him a cover identity for his travels outside the country on British documents: Edwin Redwald Carter, a name that remained a family secret until his death. (The surname came from an address in Carter Lane, where Litvinenko's lawyer had offices.) Londongrad had a new player.

After first living in an apartment in South Kensington, Litvinenko and his family took up residence at their house in Muswell Hill in February 2003. The following year Akhmed Zakayev, the leading spokesman in exile for the Chechen separatists, moved in on the same street. He, too, secured asylum in Britain.

Zakayev left Chechnya after he was wounded in the Second Chechen War. He had taken refuge briefly in Istanbul until the Turkish authorities ordered him out. The Russians pursued him with arrest warrants and lawsuits. He attended a conference on Chechnya in Copenhagen, and he was detained by Danish authorities on a Russian extradition warrant accusing him on thirteen counts, including murder and kidnapping. But the Danes refused to extradite him.

Zakayev's quest for sanctuary was more star-studded than most: when he flew to London to seek refuge in Britain in 2002, his case was supported by Vanessa Redgrave. Her public backing guaranteed a good measure of attention for Zakayev's argument that his return to Moscow would place him in peril.

In November 2003 Timothy Workman, a British judge who presided over many politically sensitive extradition hearings, declared: 'I have come to the inevitable conclusion that if the authorities are prepared to resort to torturing witnesses, there is a substantial risk that Mr Zakayev himself would be subject to torture.

'It would be unjust and oppressive to return Mr Zakayev to stand his trial in Russia,' the judge said. For Russia's leaders, Zakayev remained a terrorist, pure and simple. The Kremlin regarded his status as a political refugee in London with much the same outrage as London would display if Osama bin Laden were given asylum in Moscow.

Given their personal histories, Litvinenko and Zakayev seemed improbable neighbours. But they shared a passion for the over-throw of the Putin administration, forging a remarkable bond that endured to the very final hours of Litvinenko's life. For Litvinenko, Zakayev became a mentor, a spiritual and moral guide.

Earlier in 2003, Judge Workman had also considered a Russian legal attempt to extradite Berezovsky on fraud charges. But, characteristically, the case against Berezovsky had not proceeded without bizarre twists: during the hearings a mysterious figure emerged to assert that he had been recruited by the Russian secret services to assassinate Berezovsky with a poisonous fountain pen. The Russian authorities dismissed the entire episode as a fabrication designed by Berezovsky to project himself as a man under threat from Moscow. In the end, Berezovsky secured refugee status through an administrative decree in September 2003. The

British action brought the Russian extradition hearings to an abrupt close.

Like Litvinenko, Berezovsky was able to choose a new *nom de guerre*, and he became known on his official British travel documents as Platon Elenin – a curious mixture drawn from a movie character inspired by his example and the name of his wife.

The Kremlin's allegation of foul play in the extradition process lingered. After Litvinenko's death a man identified by Berezovsky as Vladimir Teplyuk appeared on state-owned Russian television to revive the accusation that Berezovsky had recruited him to give false testimony in the extradition process.

Berezovsky denied the accusation and threatened to sue.

Yet some questions lingered around Berezovsky's decision to seek refuge in Britain. Why had he chosen London over other places such as Israel that gave refuge to fugitive tycoons such as Vladimir Gusinsky and Leonid Nevzlin? 'These characters all have rich histories,' a former American official said cryptically. 'Berezovsky is not just some businessman sitting in London.'

As the ranks of *émigré* opponents protected by British asylum swelled, it was little wonder that the Kremlin railed publicly against the nest of dissidents in London. Much to the annoyance of British security officials, Russian spies from the SVR, working undercover in Britain, were ordered to keep close tabs on this world of conspirators and exiles.

'Since the end of the Cold War we have seen no decrease in the numbers of undeclared Russian intelligence officers in the UK – at the Russian Embassy and associated organizations – conducting covert activity in this country,' Jonathan Evans, the head of MI5, said on 5 November 2007, in his first major speech after he took over in April 2007 from Dame Eliza Manningham-Buller.

'It is a matter of some disappointment to me that I still have to devote significant amounts of equipment, money and staff to countering this threat. They are resources which I would far rather devote to countering the threat from international terrorism – a threat to the whole international community, not just the UK,' he said.

*

For many years, Soviet intelligence operations against Britain were conducted from Moscow's embassy at 13 Kensington Palace Gardens and from two locations in Highgate, north London – the military attaché's office at 44 Millfield Lane and the trade representative's office at 33 Highgate West Hill.

The Highgate outposts were chosen because they were well placed for electronic eavesdropping on the city below, according to intelligence experts. By the time Litvinenko began to die, British intelligence had become convinced that Russia had up to thirty agents operating from the embassy and trade mission and others under deeper cover in other institutions. 'Russian intelligence is well funded, very active, and is going to be pretty well represented in a city like London,' one former British intelligence official told me.

In the early days of the Putin presidency, when he and Tony Blair seemed to have struck up a friendship and a personal rapport, the British and Russian intelligence agencies felt able to collaborate with each other, particularly in areas where the two countries shared common diplomatic goals and in the campaign against Islamic terrorism. Towards the end of Putin's first term in 2004, however, partly under the influence of the ex-KGB coterie surrounding the Russian president in the Kremlin, the mood soured. The decisions by British courts to grant asylum status to Berezovsky and Zakayev became 'real tension issues', the former intelligence official told me. 'The atmosphere was pretty damn frosty.' The chill slowed the flow of information between Moscow and London, and the SVR – Russia's overseas intelligence agency – had no qualms about destabilizing the increasingly hostile community of émigrés. Even when the relationship between Britain and Russia was supposed to be on a relatively even keel in the early years of the twenty-first century, allies of Litvinenko insisted that an agent in place at the Russian Embassy had been ordered to keep him under surveillance.

It was not as if the Russian spies had an exclusive hold on misbehaviour.

In early 2006 Russian authorities uncovered what they claimed was a British espionage operation in Moscow using communications equipment hidden in a fake rock. The furore in Russia over the purported British activities stoked accusations that foreign intelligence services were funding non-governmental organizations that the Kremlin found objectionable.

Putin himself pitched into the debate. 'I think that nobody has the right, in the given situation, to claim that money has no smell,' he said.

Even business contacts between the two countries felt the chill.

In April 2007 the organizers of the Russian Economic Forum – a respected annual business gathering in London – began to receive a series of mysterious last-minute cancellations from high-profile Russian business leaders. With no plausible explanation, executives from banks and energy companies such as Rosneft and Gazprom along with senior officials from government ministries simply pulled out from the meeting – once seen as a high point on the Russian business calendar. I had been seeking an interview with a top Russian telecommunications executive, but even as we were fixing the date and agenda, his PR handlers in Washington e-mailed to say he would not be coming after all. They did not explain why.

Suspicion immediately fell on what *The Times* called 'Vladimir Putin's heavy hand'.

Putin had already signalled that he would prefer Russia's elite to attend a rival gathering, the St Petersburg Economic Forum, later in the year – a conference that had the twin distinctions of being located in his home town and being far easier to control than the London event. But the sudden rash of cancellations by high-ranking Russians came suspiciously soon after a barrage of criticism of Putin by Berezovsky and his allies, as if the Kremlin had simply chosen to send a signal to London, reminding the British authorities of the stakes at play in their relationship – far beyond the death of a former KGB officer.

In 2006 British exports to Russia had reached a record £2 billion, and Britain ranked as the biggest foreign investor in

Russia, with some four hundred companies doing business there, ranging from clothing outlets to glass factories to tobacco companies. Joint ventures between Russian energy companies and British companies such as Shell and BP totalled over £8 billion. According to the Russian federal statistics service, British investments in Russia in the first half of 2007 rose to £7.5 billion. And then there was the prospect of Russia becoming Europe's biggest supplier of natural gas.

By undermining the Russian Economic Forum in London, the Kremlin may also have been simply sending Moscow's business elite a reminder of who, ultimately, controlled its access to riches. But if Russia was sending such blunt messages, was London really listening?

Since the end of the Cold War, the focus of the British intelligence establishment had shifted in two key areas. The enemy without – the Warsaw Pact forces, the Soviet nuclear arsenal – had been neutralized by the collapse of Communism. Northern Ireland, whose brutal sectarian strife over thirty years had been the focus of so much British intelligence-gathering, was virtually at peace.

But the adversaries of the Cold War and Belfast had been replaced by the enemy within: the fiery hatreds and fervours that boiled in the hearts of young Muslims who might have been anyone's neighbour or workmate on the streets of an increasingly ethnically diverse Britain.

On 7 July 2005 four suicide bombers killed fifty-two travellers on the London transport system during the morning rush hour, attacking three underground trains and a bus. Exactly two weeks later, another group of terrorists tried and narrowly failed to do the same. The alarms and attacks recurred with stunning frequency. In August 2006 the police rounded up twenty-four suspects accused of planning to use liquid chemicals high over the Atlantic to blow up planes flying out of Heathrow to destinations in the United States. The suspects were Muslims born in Britain or immigrants to Britain, and it was a sign of Britain's increasing edginess about terrorist intentions that the arrests were made long before an attack seemed imminent.

In February 2007 British counterterrorist police were again beating on doors in the early hours of the morning, using ever more draconian counterterrorism laws to detain and question their suspects. This time the accusation was that a terrorist group planned to capture a Muslim soldier in the British army, on leave from duty in Afghanistan, and behead him in front of a video camera for footage to be displayed – Iraq style – on the Internet.

In late June and early July 2007, the nation shuddered anew as conspirators first tried to blow up two Mercedes sedans laden with gas canisters outside central London nightspots. Having failed in London, the bombers went on to smash a blazing Jeep Cherokee also laden with gas cylinders into a departure area of Glasgow Airport teeming with holidaymakers, including many schoolchildren.

In the perception of American counterterrorism specialists, Britain's minority of 1.6 million Muslims, many of them descended from Pakistani immigrants, had become the point of vulnerability – radicalized, susceptible to the call to jihad and, worst of all from an American point of view, armed with British passports that required no visa for entry into the United States. As Peter Clarke, a deputy assistant commissioner at Scotland Yard and Britain's counterterrorism supremo, put it in April 2007, 'The fact is that there are in the United Kingdom many young men who are vulnerable to being drawn into extremism and violence.

'The influence of the so-called preachers of hate and their fellow travellers is pernicious,' Clarke said. 'Of all the things I have seen over the past few years, one of the most worrying has been the speed and apparent ease with which young men can be turned into suicidal terrorists, prepared to kill themselves and hundreds of others – indoctrinated to believe that there are no such things as innocent victims.'

And, like a dark undertow, there was one fear that bore the authorities' edginess along: how soon would it be before terrorists got their hands on the raw materials for a more sophisticated attack than the homemade bombs used on 7 July and 21 July?

'Tomorrow's threat may include the use of chemicals, bacteriological agents, radioactive materials and even nuclear technology,' Manningham-Buller, then head of MI5, proclaimed in a speech in early November 2006, a few months before her retirement. Within days, that remark would be borne out by events, though not in the way she most likely envisaged.

Before London became known as Moscow-on-Thames, it had earned the sardonic nickname Londonistan, largely because of its tolerance of firebrand Islamic preachers who, the authorities belatedly acknowledged, had done their best to groom a generation of young British Muslims for jihad.

Even before the 9/11 attacks in New York and Washington, a young British Muslim of Indian descent, Dhiren Barot, reconnoitred potential targets in New York and Washington. Video footage he made showed the twin towers of the World Trade Center, and he had tilted the camera to one side to mimic a collapse, making a boom-like sound into the microphone as he did so to suggest an explosion. In 2003, two young Britons travelled to Tel Aviv to carry out a botched suicide attack on an Israeli nightclub. Incensed by Britain's participation in the invasion of Iraq, young Britons volunteered to travel secretly to Baghdad as suicide bombers. And with Britain's post-colonial links to Pakistan, there was no shortage of opportunities for potential bombers to visit training camps there to learn the art of bomb making. In one case, British undercover operatives even tracked a group of purported Islamic militants to what seemed a makeshift camp in the green fields of the English Lake District. Between 2006 and 2007, MI5's estimate of the number of people threatening 'national security and public safety because of their support for terrorism' grew from 1,600 to 'at least 2,000', according to MI5.

By way of response, Britain expanded the ranks of its domestic security services from 1,800 people to 3,000 and planned to increase the number to 4,000 by 2011. The emphasis now, however, was not on Russian-speakers but on ethnic diversity and the recruitment of agents with the skills to listen in at mosques or penetrate radical groups and their websites. The police, too, had expanded their counterterrorism forces, creating a special command, SO15, under Peter Clarke.

When the players in the Litvinenko saga assembled for the final act in London, the British security services were thus largely scanning the horizons from different coordinates. At that time, nine out of ten MI5 officers were assigned to tracking Al Qaeda sympathizers and supporters. Only a few of the rest were charged with keeping tabs on Russia's SVR network in Britain. And there was a further twist in the list of priorities. For MI5, the real threat to Britain's national security came from the SVR operatives themselves, not from the band of Russian *émigrés* they spied on. For the watchers of Britain's security services, the malcontents of Londongrad were a low priority indeed.

On 1 November 2006 it is reasonable to assume that Peter Clarke had barely heard the name of the former FSB agent whose story was about to explode across the headlines and redefine London's relationship with Moscow. But it was Clarke who would assume overall command of the operation to unravel the mysteries of the Litvinenko case.

Clarke was something of an incongruous figure. He gave every appearance of being mild-mannered, more in the slightly bumbling way of John le Carré's George Smiley than James Bond. He did not seem enthusiastic about the limelight of television and rarely, if ever, granted interviews. When he spoke in public, his delivery was deadpan, almost soporific: the glib soundbite, the throwaway wisecrack, were not his style. He followed his text closely and did not extemporize. Asked tough questions, he sidestepped. But Clarke chose his words with great caution, and his public utterances repaid close examination.

For his chosen sport, he favoured cricket, the quintessential English game that combined the appearance of teamwork with subtle and sometimes underhand individual tactics to put opposing players off guard. He was regarded by fellow officers as dogged and painstaking, not given to oratorical flourish or anything but the most measured tones in his public manner. When he was displeased, the eyes hardened and the tone sharpened. But, equally, when there was a joke – even against himself – his gap-toothed grin was almost boyish.

In April 2007, at London's conservative Policy Exchange research institute, within the sound of Big Ben chiming the hours at Westminster, I watched him deliver a major résumé of his time in charge of the SO15 counterterrorism unit, tracing the growing realization that a new kind of terrorism threatened Britain from within. In his dark double-breasted suit and Windsor-knotted tie, he was understated in his manner, but his message was chilling: 'The only sensible assumption is that we shall be attacked again.' His forecast was vindicated within months.

Remarkably, when he left the institute's offices, Clarke strolled down the street with his wife, unaccompanied by the retinue of bodyguards that might have attended someone in his position anywhere else.

Clarke was the product of reforms that brought a wave of college graduates into the force in the 1970s as the Metropolitan Police emerged from a deeply embarrassing and damaging series of corruption scandals. The college graduates were not especially liked by old-guard beat officers, who saw promotions going the way of politically savvy and university-educated rivals. But over time those distinctions blurred as ever more college graduates joined the force.

Like his boss, the Metropolitan Police Commissioner, Sir Ian Blair, Clarke was viewed by some police officers as too much of a bureaucrat and overly reluctant to share information. His unit did not mix easily with the rest of the force and was seen as elitist. He was not what they called a 'copper's copper'. For the media age, though, he was a competent if reluctant performer in front of television cameras – though his appearances were infrequent – and he became known on the international conference circuit attended by American and European security professionals.

By education Clarke was a lawyer, an alumnus of the University of Bristol who spent most of his policing days in London boroughs such as Tottenham, Hackney and Brixton known for high crime rates and strained relationships between the police and ethnic minorities. But, displaying an ambition that belied his mild appearance, he pursued a highly successful, fast-track career at New Scotland Yard. Clarke understood the ruthless politics of an institution where a patron could make or break a junior officer's career. In the 1990s, he began a steady advance as a staff officer to the former police commissioner Lord Condon, and later as head of the Royalty and Diplomatic Protection Department, in charge of providing close security for foreign dignitaries and members of the royal family. The job required discretion and diplomacy. Clarke was head of the unit when Diana, Princess of Wales died in 1997 in a car crash in Paris. Police insiders suspected that he knew far more than was ever said in public about her final moments.

After 11 September 2001 Clarke's counterterrorism department evolved rapidly as Britain's sense of threat shifted. Britons became subject to far greater surveillance than any other Europeans. Closed-circuit television cameras scanned public places in shopping malls, on main streets, in stores, on trains, and in stations, airports and bars. Investigations began with a scouring of thousands of hours of video footage, the kind that showed in terrible detail the 7 July 2005 bombers with their backpacks boarding a southbound commuter train at Luton station – their final journey before they spread out to launch their attacks. It was a concept of policing that relied on the most meticulous search of crime scenes and environments; the first the public knew of a major British investigation was usually the erection of a tent and screens around suspect locations and the arrival of officers in white protective suits.

The campaign against Islamic terrorism created another legacy. Scotland Yard in general – and Clarke in particular – became ever more annoyed about leaks tipping off reporters to their investigations, and their mistakes.

Twice in less than two years before the Litvinenko case, the Metropolitan Police had been embroiled in deeply embarrassing incidents that suggested its officers not only acted on poor intelligence but also shot first and asked questions later. On 22 July 2005 – one day after would-be suicide bombers tried unsuccessfully to emulate the 7 July attackers – armed officers pumped seven bullets at point-blank range into the skull of a Brazilian electrician, Jean Charles de Menezes, aboard a stationary underground train. At first, the police sought to justify the killing by saying de Menezes behaved like a potential suicide bomber, wearing bulky clothes and vaulting a ticket turnstile to enter Stockwell station in south London. Only much later did the police acknowledge that de Menezes, aged twenty-seven, had been wearing a light jacket, had used a standard electronic travel card to pass through the station and had been sitting quietly on the train, reading a free newspaper, when he was shot to death.

Throughout 22 July, though, Sir Ian Blair, the Metropolitan Police Commissioner, sustained the argument that de Menezes's death was, in his words, 'directly linked to the ongoing and expanding anti-terrorist operation'. Blair argued later that he was unaware of suspicions among his own officers on the day of the killing that the police might have shot the wrong man.

Within a year of the de Menezes shooting, the police faced fresh criticism when 250 officers raided a modest terraced house in Forest Gate, east London, in June 2006 and arrested two brothers at 3.00 a.m., shooting and wounding one of them in what was later described as an accident. Seven days after the raid, the brothers – Mohammed Abdul Kahar, who was shot, and Abul Koyair – were released without charge, and another high-ranking officer, Andy Hayman, was forced to make a public apology for arresting the men, both Muslims, without being able to indict them on any charges.

Not surprisingly, then, British police officers acted with a degree of caution when confronted with the public relations aspects of high-profile, politically sensitive and potentially explosive cases. The Litvinenko story certainly fitted that category.

Clarke bridled at the suggestion that a preoccupation with Islamic terrorism had distracted the British authorities from other threats. But, given the regularity of attacks by homegrown militants, and the enormous amount of police time it took to bring suspects to trial, it is no surprise that a handful of Russian *émigrés* in a city known as Londongrad might have seemed a less pressing priority.

9

CROWN PROTECTION?

In the six years and twenty-three days Litvinenko lived in London, he encountered and cultivated a remarkable cast of characters with whom he did business of one kind or another. Among them were former operatives – including one who would later be accused of his murder – ex-spies, *émigré* dissidents, an academic researcher who denounced him in death as a blackmailer, and an Italian gadfly whose name, Mario Scaramella, would become closely entwined with the story of Litvinenko's final days.

It was a period that charted a dramatic swing from the optimism of his sanctuary in a new land to self-doubt about his mission in life, his ability to feed his family and his relationship with the children he left behind in Moscow from his first marriage. Often there was a potent undertow of menace: Litvinenko's world was rarely free from peril. But it began with a remarkable display of fealty.

After his arrival in London on 1 November 2000, Litvinenko took his young son Anatoly to the Tower of London to show him the British crown, available for public inspection behind thick bulletproof glass (except, of course, for those ceremonial state occasions when it was in use by the monarch).

The crown, encrusted with gems from Britain's one-time colonies and overseas possessions – most notably the Cullinan diamond from South Africa – was the symbol of an island nation proud of its ability to project its power across oceans and to withstand aggression from beyond its shores. The tower itself, by contrast, had been known in centuries past as a place of dark deeds and treachery of a kind that must have been familiar to Litvinenko from his days in the Russian security services. But, according to his friend Vladimir Bukovsky, Litvinenko took his son there to impress upon him that the family had arrived in a secure new nation worthy of loyalty.

'This is a crown which protects us, guards us, and you should always be faithful to it,' Litvinenko said.

As the years of self-exile unfolded, he encouraged his son to see himself as a British schoolboy in his flannel trousers and school tie and dark uniform blazer. For his own protection, the boy went to classes under an assumed, English name and came to treasure his pseudonym. Litvinenko's wife Marina, by her own account, lived a very English, suburban life between home and school and husband. But, as with so many aspects of Litvinenko's story, that was only part of the truth. While his family led an English life, he moved in the crepuscular world of Russian conspiracy. And while he nurtured one small nuclear family in London, another felt excluded and forgotten in Moscow.

His estranged father was in Nalchik with part of Litvinenko's adoptive clan; his mother lived alone in Moscow. His half-brother Maxim was in Italy. But the most wrenching part of this familial tangle lay with his son Alexander and daughter Sonya from his first marriage, who had spent some brief time with him after the press conference in 1998, barely getting used to his presence in their lives before he was gone again.

It is always easy to think of people solely by reference to their headline labels – spy, defector – or to define them exclusively by the persona they choose to project. But that was never the complete picture of Litvinenko. Husband, father, traitor, whistleblower, son, spy, lover, fugitive: all offered points of triangulation to chart the man, pinpoint his strengths and failings. Litvinenko was different things to different people: a tough guy facing down organized crime gangs; a romantic cop wooing a new bride; a philanderer abandoning one woman for the bed of another; a thug beating suspects; an investigator to rival Hercule Poirot.

His former colleagues denounced him as a Judas; so did his former wife, Natalia. His half-brother Maxim had kinder words, calling him 'a person you could always ask for advice. He was very sincere, decisive, organized.'

But one person who knew him under different circumstances offered a more conflicted account of a father who never quite measured up to the expectations she had of him.

'I didn't know my father at all until I was nine,' his daughter Sonya said in an interview in the late summer of 2007 in Moscow.

'I first saw him on television during the press conference he gave. After that he first came to see me at school. That was the first time I saw him in front of me. It was a bit uncomfortable. He didn't kiss or hug me, he just said: "Hi, I'm your dad." I think he felt embarrassed. So did I.'

There seems, by his daughter's account, to have been the familiar strains and tensions tugging the heart of an errant father caught between old and new families. And, of course, Litvinenko was not always physically accessible to either of his tribes. His jailers and prosecutors saw to that.

'I guess we saw him for a little over a year,' Sonya Litvinenko said, talking about a time of attempted, or half-hearted, reconciliation after the press conference in 1998. 'Then, once again, we stopped seeing him. When he was in jail, we wrote to him, but I didn't see him until after he left Russia and moved to Britain. He didn't say anything to us before leaving.' Of course, he had not said anything about his looming departure to his second wife, Marina, either: the security of their escape depended on discretion. But there was nothing in the KGB manual to teach a man how to win back a son and daughter in a distant land, or how to persuade a lost child to love a new wife.

'I used to go to visit him in London pretty regularly,' Sonya recalled. 'In the six years he was there, I went eight times.

Alexander didn't see our father any more after he left for London. He did not get on with Marina.

'It wasn't easy to talk to my father,' his daughter acknowledged. 'He was absolutely obsessed with Russian politics. Any conversation would end up with him going on about Putin's regime, and at times I used to think that he was a little crazy. He would wind himself up to such an extent he couldn't stop, as if he was out of his mind.'

That might have been an extreme assessment, but certainly Litvinenko came across to some of his visitors as eccentric. Jos De Putter, the Dutch filmmaker who interviewed him at length in February 2004 at home in Osier Crescent, described the house as being modestly furnished – 'IKEA at best.'

As De Putter set up his camera gear for the interview in the shuttered kitchen at the rear of the house, Litvinenko disappeared briefly to change into clothes he considered more appropriate for the encounter.

'He comes back looking like your standard Russian contract killer in a black leather jacket,' De Putter said. 'Why do you wear that in your kitchen?'

At the beginning of his self-exile, Litvinenko must have seemed an oddity, even among the established *émigrés* from the Soviet era. For dissidents and free spirits like Bukovsky in the suburbs of Cambridge the KGB had represented the worst of the Kremlin's cruelties – the jailer and torturer of the Soviet empire. But Litvinenko, Bukovsky said, professed ignorance of the true nature of the KGB when he joined. Now, meeting with a man who had been the victim of the organization to which he swore loyalty, Litvinenko was overcome with a powerful sense of remorse.

Litvinenko 'felt intensely guilty in front of me that he worked for the KGB,' Bukovsky recalled. 'I finally said to him: "Sasha, stop it. That's nonsense. Look, by the time you ran away from Russia, you were not an officer of the KGB. You were a prisoner, a political prisoner, and that you can carry with pride." Do you know what he did? He said: "Yes, it's true, huh?"'

'And I have a padded jacket from jail,' Bukovsky continued. 'It's a kind of memento. He said: "Can I wear it, your padded jacket from jail?" I said, "OK" ... He felt much better. He suddenly kind of removed this stigma from himself.' Bukovsky paused for a second, and then added: 'He was a very strange fellow.'

On the first anniversary of Litvinenko's death, his friends and associates published a collection of his writings translated into English called *Allegations*. A photograph in the book showed the former KGB operative and the former Soviet dissident with their arms around each other's shoulders. Bukovsky was in shirtsleeves, with the beginnings of a half-smile on his face. Litvinenko wore the jacket from the Gulag. His hair was cropped short, his chin stubbled, his expression inscrutable.

When he arrived in London, Litvinenko had few friends and needed the imprimatur of such figures as Bukovsky. But the blessing was by no means automatic: a former FSB officer arriving out of the blue in post-Cold War London could all too easily have been sent on some secret mission by the Kremlin. Not only that, the voluble Litvinenko somehow did not fit the Identikit image of a KGB man.

Litvinenko was 'a bit too talkative, a bit too naive', Bukovsky said. 'And yet he's a lieutenant colonel in the KGB who, according to what he says, worked in one of the most secret and dangerous departments dealing with organized crime. How come?

'So we examined him for a while, but then, slowly ... You know he was a very sincere man ... He was uncomfortable with lying, you know, definitely,' Bukovsky said.

From his British redoubt, protected by the same crown that he had shown his son, Litvinenko was determined to continue the crusade against the FSB that he had launched with his news conference in 1998. Now he resumed the attack, this time choosing the events that led to the Second Chechen War, in effect assailing the very roots of Putin's political legitimacy.

In September 1999 a series of bomb attacks destroyed apartment blocks in Moscow and Volgodonsk, killing 243 people. The authorities blamed the bloodletting on Chechen terrorists, whipping up xenophobic sentiment among ethnic Russians and providing a pretext and overwhelming public support not just for the bloodiest war of a new century in Europe but also for the man who ordered it.

Ever since their humiliation in Chechnya in 1996, Russian generals had been clamouring for an opportunity to redeem their defeat with a decisive victory. When Chechen rebels launched an incursion into neighbouring Dagestan in the autumn of 1999, it seemed the moment had come.

For months, the Russian military had been planning to seal the borders of Chechnya and occupy parts of the territory regarded as pro-Russian. But, rejecting the advice of some of his predecessors, Putin – newly anointed by Boris Yeltsin as prime minister – resolved to take matters further, making the capture of Grozny, the heavily defended Chechen capital, his overriding political goal.

In late September, Russian aircraft began bombing targets in Chechnya, including the Grozny airport. Ground troops followed on 30 September. It soon became apparent that Putin was fighting far more than a military campaign in Chechnya.

In Moscow, the battle to succeed Yeltsin in elections scheduled for March 2000 was well under way, and Putin's ratings were low. He had come to the prime minister's office as a virtually unknown political figure, supported by members of Yeltsin's family but with no public credentials to lead a country the size and importance of Russia. No one expected him to even keep the job.

The war in Chechnya thus was fought on two fronts – on the killing fields of the Caucasus and in the corridors of power at the Kremlin.

Whatever Putin's military tactics, the political manoeuvres seemed set to secure victory.

On 20 October 1999 Putin scored what looked at the time like a major propaganda victory in the political battle: for ten minutes he took to the air in a Sukhoi-25 fighter plane over Chechnya. His popularity ratings, 2 per cent one month earlier, now stood at 27 per cent, closing the gap on his major rival, Yevgeni Primakov.

The fight on the ground was harder. Only on 18 January 2000 did Russians claim to have entered parts of central Grozny, and only on 6 February 2000 was Putin able to announce, 'The last stronghold of the terrorists' resistance was taken . . . So we can say that the operation for the freeing of Grozny has ended.'

For outsiders, it did not look like liberation in the classic sense of the word.

'Russian soldiers did not capture Grozny. They obliterated it,' the New York Times correspondent Michael Gordon reported from the city when it became possible for Western reporters to enter it. 'Grozny is now Chechnya's capital in name only.'

Robert Service, a British historian at Oxford University, offered this assessment: 'The invasion was unimaginably savage. There were tens of thousands of deaths and half the population of the region fled over the borders. Chechnya was reduced to a moonscape.'

But the political fight had already been won. Putin was named to succeed Yeltsin on New Year's Eve 1999. After the Chechen war, the outcome of the presidential election three months later was virtually a foregone conclusion.

The question that lingered for some Russians was why all-out war had been necessary and whether the apartment bombings that preceded it had been a cynical and bloody ploy to win public support for the invasion.

That was the thesis Litvinenko set out to prove in a book called Blowing Up Russia, written with Yuri Felshtinsky and first published in English in 2002, accusing the FSB of choreographing the apartment-block bombings.

The accusation had been around for some time, and had already been rebutted by Putin.

'We are not attacking. We are defending ourselves,' Putin insisted in the series of interviews he gave in early 2000 that were published as First Person.

'We knocked the rebels out in Dagestan, and they came back. We knocked them out again, and they came back again. We knocked them out a third time. And then, when we gave them a serious kick in the teeth, they blew up apartment houses in Moscow, Buinaksk and Volgodonsk.'

What, then, of the theory that the authorities had schemed to blow up the apartment blocks in order to make the case for war?

'What?! Blowing up our own apartment buildings? You know, that is really . . . utter nonsense. It's totally insane,' Putin said. 'No one in the Russian special services would be capable of such a crime against his own people. The very supposition is amoral. It's nothing but part of the information war against Russia.'

Blowing Up Russia was not the first or the only publication to document the allegations that the FSB had orchestrated the apartment-block bombings. Those were the same allegations as Mikhail Trepashkin had been urged to investigate by Sergei Kovalev, a human rights activist and member of the Duma.

But Litvinenko and Felshtinsky did chronicle a sequence of events that they depicted as clear evidence of FSB complicity in the bombings, centring on an episode on 22 September 1999 in the city of Ryazan, two hundred miles south of Moscow, just days before the Second Chechen War got under way in earnest.

According to their research, Alexei Kartofelnikov, a driver who lived in Ryazan, called the authorities at 9.15 that evening to say he had seen two men and a woman unloading sacks of an unidentified substance from a Zhiguli car with a Moscow licence plate into the basement of a twelve-storey apartment building at 14/16 Novosyolov Street. The police who duly arrived on the scene described seeing 'some kind of electronic device' wedged into one of the sacks – a detonator set to explode at 5.30 the following morning. Explosives experts called to Ryazan used a gas analyser to establish that the sacks contained what seemed to be some sort of 'hexogen-type explosive substance'. The Interior Ministry in Moscow confirmed those findings one day later.

Hexogen is one of the most powerful explosives, used usually for military and industrial purposes. In its pure form it is a white crystalline substance known particularly for the speed with which it reaches its peak pressure, creating enormous force to shatter anything around it.

'If there had been an explosion, the entire building would have collapsed,' Litvinenko and Felshtinsky concluded.

After Kartofelnikov's warning, the people who lived in the apartment block were evacuated, some in their nightclothes, some barefoot, hopping 'from one foot to the other in the freezing wind for several hours', as the newspaper *Trud* reported. Initially, the authorities depicted the discovery triumphantly as the thwarting of a terrorist plot. But then they changed their tune. On 25 September Nikolai Patrushev, a close Putin ally and his successor as head of the FSB, announced that the so-called terrorist plot had been nothing more than a 'training exercise' using sacks of sugar, not hexogen.

His assertion did not go unchallenged. First of all, Litvinenko and Felshtinsky observed, the whole idea of 'exercises' by the FSB did not emerge for several days, during which government officials, including Putin, said publicly that the substances found in the sacks were explosives. The FSB, moreover, made no announcement that an exercise was under way. But, they said, there was FSB involvement of a different kind: the suspected 'terrorists' had called an FSB office in Moscow for advice on their escape route. The allegation was clear enough: the FSB had planned to blow up the apartment in Ryazan, had been caught red-handed, and had used the story of 'exercises' as a cover-up.

The three apartment-block bombings that did succeed in killing hundreds of people, the authors claimed, were 'Ryazan-style exercises . . . carried through to their intended conclusion, and the lives of several hundred people were abruptly cut short or completely devastated.'

The book was completed in 2001 and published in 2002, but it achieved widespread currency only after the events of November 2006. One of its two authors did not live to see his work reach a significant audience: as in other ways, Litvinenko's celebrity was posthumous.

'We tried to be safe and to stay alive – Alexander in Britain and I in the US,' Felshtinsky wrote in a foreword to an edition dated 10 December 2006. 'I lost my co-author, six years after he landed in London. On 1 November 2006, he was poisoned and this foreword is signed only with my name.'

At the time he was co-writing, Litvinenko could have felt only frustration that his message would not be spread beyond a narrow circle of *émigrés*. The Kremlin went to extraordinary lengths to limit its distribution, seizing a shipment of 5,000 volumes on their way into Russia from Latvia. Oddly, though, a Russian news agency did report that the reason the books were confiscated was that both *Blowing Up Russia* and *Lubyanka Criminal Group* disclosed state secrets – a curious description for allegations dismissed so scathingly by Putin himself.

On 30 April 2003, the Russian authorities formally closed their investigation into the apartment-block bombings, concluding that nine Russian and foreign Islamic fighters carried out the attacks. (None of the accused seemed to be Chechens, which raised questions about why the bombings had been deemed to justify a war in Chechnya.) Five of the accused were already dead, and two others remained at large, including Achemes Gochiyayev, whom Litvinenko and Felshtinsky had sought unsuccessfully to interview in Georgia's Pankisi Gorge in 2002. The Russian prosecutors did not even try to explain the motive behind the bombings and had no discernible interest in reviving the debate.

Later, people asked whether Litvinenko's writings offered a motive for wishing him dead in the complicated and gruesome manner of November 2006.

At first glance, that hardly seemed likely. The allegations of foul play in the apartment-block bombings had been made, and dismissed, for years. As far as the Kremlin was concerned, the story was history. What point was there in breathing new life into obscure and out-of-print volumes that had drawn so little attention when they were first published? The beneficiary could never be the Kremlin – only its enemies. But there was no doubt that the accusations contained in *Blowing Up Russia* added to the catalogue of reasons to regard Litvinenko as a traitor to the Kremlin leadership and to his own former institution, the FSB.

In his six years in London, Litvinenko crossed the paths of many people with the ability, and even the motive, to do him harm. But could it also be argued that, like the hero of a classic Greek or Shakespearean tragedy, he unwittingly invited his own downfall?

No tragedy ever played out without what Aristotle called *hamartia* – the tragic error – and Litvinenko made plenty of them, primarily with the presumption that he could tilt at the Kremlin with impunity, ignoring the tradecraft of his erstwhile profession. Certainly his story aroused the twin sentiments of pity and fear required by Aristotelian theory: pity because his life contained the seed of a misfortune so enormous as to be disproportionate to any error or hubris on his part; and fear because his death aroused deep concerns that his destiny might all too easily have been shared by many others, not just opponents of the Kremlin.

Even Litvinenko's adversaries reached for Shakespearean references, if only to describe Russia's frustration with Britain over the course of events and Moscow's affront at the way the world treated it. 'Do you think I am easier to be played on than a pipe?' Sergei Lavrov, the foreign minister, said in the autumn of 2007, quoting from *Hamlet*. 'Call me what instrument you will, though you can fret me, yet you cannot play upon me.'

But tragedy implied catharsis, the cleansing of emotion, the acknowledgement of error that modern experts call closure; and it was questionable whether the opaque and deliberately obscured events that began on 1 November 2006 coaxed forth such clarity.

The final explanation may have been simpler: perhaps Litvinenko ceased to believe his own warnings; perhaps he placed too much faith in the bejewelled crown he had shown to his son as their protector; and perhaps, more prosaically, he was too ready to talk to anyone who showed the slightest interest in what he had to say.

*

The rendezvous place in late 2003 was in a familiar location – beneath the statue of Eros at Piccadilly Circus, not far from the itsu sushi bar that would provide such a prominent setting for the subsequent drama of Litvinenko's final days in London.

Possibly, in the elbowing, pulsing crowds of the city centre, the former KGB officer felt safe, surrounded by Londoners and outsiders, transients and predators. Like the opening scene of a B movie, so many narratives of encounters with him began with some person or other waiting beneath the statue and Litvinenko appearing from nowhere in the starburst of streets and thoroughfares leading north, south, east and west.

But it could surely not be wise tradecraft to make such frequent appointments at this same bustling intersection, this crossroads at London's heart. If he could observe, then he could be observed. If he could escape into the multitudes of anonymous crowds, so could his enemies. And if, as former spies like Oleg Gordievsky argued, Litvinenko's demise had all the hallmarks of what was once called KGB 'wet work', then who might have tailed Litvinenko along his well-trodden route from Piccadilly to the sushi bar on that mild November morning six years after his self-exile began?

The winged, nude statue atop the Shaftesbury Memorial Fountain in Piccadilly Circus dated from the late nineteenth century and was intended to depict Anteros, the twin of Eros and the god of selfless love. It was sometimes called the Angel of Christian Charity. Given the monument's location so close to the red-light district of Soho and the nightclubs all around it, the more usual identification with Eros – the deity favoured by passionate lovers – seemed more fitting.

In the autumn of 2003, Litvinenko's encounter under the statue was part of a story about a man from his past, the FSB operative Andrei Ponkin, once an ally who had appeared at his side in the 1998 press conference in Moscow.

Ponkin had been Litvinenko's second-in-command in the

notorious URPO unit denounced by its dissident members as little more than a death squad, part of a corrupted service. Five years on, Ponkin had made his peace with the FSB, recanting his support for Litvinenko. He was a bluff, hail-fellow kind of person with shifting loyalties and a taste for expensive suits and Mercedes cars, Litvinenko's widow said, but her husband bore him no grudges.

As Litvinenko told the journalist Andrei Soldatov, Ponkin had put out word in 2003 that he wanted to meet with Berezovsky to discuss the financing of an operation against Vladimir Putin.

Fearing a classic Soviet-era ploy, a provocation, Berezovsky seconded Litvinenko to make the preliminary contact – but only after informing the British security services of the timing and location of the encounter. When Ponkin arrived in London in September 2003 accompanied by an unidentified man said to be a lawyer, he was walking into a trap.

Litvinenko took a degree of pride in the operation, and had no hesitation in explaining it to a wider audience, including Soldatov.

'We met at Piccadilly Circus,' Soldatov said later – the prelude to so many reminiscences about Litvinenko.

It was a wet November night, with rain in the air to judge from the spotting on the camera lens when Soldatov posed Litvinenko for a photograph against the railings guarding the entrance to the underground station at Piccadilly Circus. (Again, one had to ask of Litvinenko: was this the behaviour of a man on his guard, a man who would later be accused by his foes of being an agent of the British? Or was it the behaviour of a man courting publicity, miscalculating the consequences?)

Litvinenko was smiling, relaxed, his light brown hair cut in a short, slightly curled fringe. He was wearing a navy blue nylon bomber jacket over a polo shirt in the same colour, dark trousers and brown leather shoes. The backdrop was Piccadilly Circus, looking north towards Regent Street. 'He invited me to a Chinese restaurant that he had chosen. He was very careful. He recorded our conversation,' Soldatov said.

'I asked him to explain about a strange story that two guys, one from the FSB, had called him in 2003 to propose that Litvinenko kill Putin and he asked for some financial help from Berezovsky for this. Litvinenko thought this was some kind of FSB provocation.'

There were several versions of the encounter with Ponkin. One, by Litvinenko and relayed to Soldatov, suggested that Litvinenko arranged to meet Ponkin in a hotel room bugged by MI5 operatives who then arrested the two visiting Russians and deported them. Another came from Berezovsky in a newspaper interview shortly after the encounter.

Ponkin told Litvinenko that 'there are people who are very dissatisfied with the situation, who don't like Putin, who believe that he is destroying the country, and who have made the decision to remove him,' Berezovsky said. 'But because no one trusts anyone, but all of them think that I can be trusted in this matter, these FSB officers sent Ponkin so that Litvinenko might put him in touch with me to discuss and arrange Putin's murder. I told Litvinenko to put together a statement in order to report this incident to Scotland Yard.'

Ponkin denied that the episode ever took place. And, in Soldatov's mind, the mission remained murky, not quite as clear-cut as others depicted it, the lines blurred by the overlap between private and public business.

'There were two things under discussion,' Soldatov said. 'One: plot to kill Putin. Two: the question of protecting a sports shop in Moscow. I cannot understand how two former FSB men can discuss the killing of the Russian president and then discuss the protection of a sports shop in Moscow. These guys are very strange. They have in their minds the total mixture of state interests and commercial activity and racketeering.'

But Soldatov had no doubts about what Litvinenko told him, and the British police at the time did confirm that Litvinenko had delivered a detailed affidavit about his meeting to Scotland Yard. The police also reported that two Russians were held for five days before being released on condition that they return to Moscow.

According to one report, Litvinenko had varied his tradecraft for this encounter, choosing a bench outside the Wagamama noodle bar in Leicester Square to meet Ponkin – a rare departure from the nearby statue of Eros.

But could this encounter in fact have foreshadowed events three years later, when the mechanism was the same: an emissary from Moscow, known to Litvinenko from his past in the FSB, arriving in London with a proposition cloaked as the action of a friend?

There was more than a whiff of conspiracy about these moments when shadowy Russian figures entered the chronicles of Litvinenko's self-exile and his close association with Berezovsky. But if his *émigré* contacts were sometimes mysterious, there was nothing ambivalent about Litvinenko's status back home in Moscow.

A series of court cases in Russia lasting until 2003 reconfirmed a three-and-a-half-year suspended sentence on charges of abusing the powers of his office and stealing explosives. Almost three years after he left Russia, prosecutors still sought to stiffen the sentence so as to order his arrest, formally at least, possibly to be able to issue an Interpol warrant for his detention as he travelled in Europe. In any event, the stubbornness of the judicial process suggested that someone in Moscow was not prepared to let his case drop. The only question was how the sentence should be enforced.

Alongside the courts, some of Litvinenko's former associates offered a more macabre solution, perhaps literally with a degree of gallows humour.

In 2003 a Polish journalist acquired footage made one year earlier showing a line drawing of Litvinenko's face being used at a Russian Special Forces centre for target practice.

The same drawing resurfaced at a private shooting gallery used by the Vityaz Training Centre in Balashikha near Moscow, run by Special Forces veterans. Photographs of the Litvinenko target, freckled with bullet holes, came to public view – perhaps by coincidence – in early November 2006. Television footage showed Sergei Mironov, the head of the upper house of the Russian parliament, visiting the Vityaz centre, whose director, Sergei Lysyuk, insisted he was unaware of the significance of this unmistakable image. 'The fact that it was Litvinenko, we only found out later from the press,' he said. 'We did not shoot at Litvinenko; we shot at a target.'

His words sounded callow. At the time Mironov visited Vityaz, the man depicted as a target was dying an excruciating death in a hospital in London. Clearly, Litvinenko had not slipped off Moscow's radar.

Neil Barnett, a British writer, met Litvinenko in 2003 ('in Piccadilly by the statue of Eros'). At that encounter, Litvinenko claimed that a man from the Russian Embassy in London 'was harassing him by calling unannounced at his house at night'.

Two years later, the calling card was different: a Molotov cocktail struck the wall of the house in Osier Crescent, damaging the wall and a child's scooter.

In late 2006 Mikhail Trepashkin, a former FSB agent who sat in on the whistle-blowers' 1998 news conference in Moscow and had conducted his own inquiries into the apartment-block bombings in 1999, smuggled a letter from a prison in Siberia, reminding Litvinenko of a warning he had offered four years earlier.

The tone of the letter – composed while Litvinenko lay dying – seemed both matter-of-fact and petulant, almost 'told-you-so', as if Litvinenko had only himself to blame for his predicament. Trepashkin seemed to have written the letter before he understood the true nature of Litvinenko's condition, saying he was 'sorry to hear that you have been poisoned'. But, the letter recalled, Litvinenko had been warned about the perils facing him as far back as August 2002. At that time, Trepashkin asserted, he had been approached in Moscow by Viktor Shebalin, another former officer in the URPO unit, warning him that Litvinenko's family in Russia was in mortal danger and that a hit squad had been formed to 'f*ck [sic] everybody connected with Berezovsky and Litvinenko'.

Like Andrei Ponkin, Viktor Shebalin was one of the dissident

FSB officers at the 1998 news conference, although his role within the renegade group was unclear. And, like Ponkin, he now had no love for Litvinenko. The essence of Trepashkin's warning – repeated when he was released from prison in late 2007 – seemed to be that Litvinenko's alliance with Berezovsky exposed them and their families to danger.

'Sasha was constantly threatened,' Vladimir Bukovsky said.

'I was there and he got a call from Moscow and someone said: "So you think you are safe in London: remember Trotsky." We were walking in town. His son was there. The sun was shining. It was springtime. His mobile rang and the threats came.'

But why had Litvinenko not heeded the signs?

In his six years in London, Bukovsky said, Litvinenko 'finally became completely relaxed, and that's, of course, a danger for people like him being still involved in many things'.

One of those 'things' was an on-off working relationship over several years with a man called Mario Scaramella. The association led Litvinenko into the most improbable attempts to tunnel into the secret history of the KGB in Europe. But, as with so many other liaisons, the encounters with Scaramella were far more likely to create enemies than friends.

10

A ROLODEX TO DIE FOR

The beginnings of Alexander Litvinenko's association with Mario Scaramella are opaque, but the ending is well documented: on 1 November 2006 Scaramella, an Italian academic, lawyer and self-promoting environmental security campaigner, met with Litvinenko for a late lunch at the itsu sushi bar, just down the road from the statue of Eros, and showed him an e-mail purporting to demonstrate that both their lives – along with that of an Italian senator, Paolo Guzzanti – were at risk from Russian hit squads.

It was the day Litvinenko began the slow and painful slide that ended with his death.

'I said: "Who poisoned you? Who did you have a meal with?" ' Oleg Gordievsky said a few days later, recalling a conversation with Litvinenko as he lay dying. 'He said: "I had a meal with Scaramella. He was very nervous. He was very strange, but he is always strange." '

Strange, indeed.

Under scrutiny by reporters and investigators in several countries, little in the life of Mario Scaramella turned out to be precisely the way he depicted it. His involvement in the final act of Litvinenko's story was no exception: he seemed, at first, to be a suspect, and then he was not; he claimed, at first, to have suffered the same fate as Litvinenko, but he did not; he told associates he intended to go to London from his base in Naples on 12 or 13 November 2006, but he did not.

He changed his plans and was in London on the very day that Litvinenko became mortally ill.

'It was not a coincidence,' Litvinenko's half-brother Maxim said. 'He was sent by someone.' Maxim's theory was coloured by his fondness for and loyalty to his half-brother and demanded a leap of logic in assessing what was known of the sequence of encounters on 1 November 2006. But in light of what emerged about Scaramella's other adventures, it had a certain symmetry and even plausibility.

Mario Scaramella was born on 23 April 1970 in Naples and was raised in the affluent Vomero district on a hillside above the teeming, tumbledown centre. It was a fitting city for the upbringing of a man who seemed drawn to the dark side of life. Under the harsh sun and searing heat of the Mediterranean, against the backdrop of Vesuvius, Naples was at once elegant and decayed, rich and poor – a point of transit to the elegant watering holes of Capri and Amalfi and a nest of violent, drug-fuelled crime.

It was a place where rules were bent and the law was often meaningless, where the reality of any given situation was filtered through the requirements of the person or group defining it. From the very beginning Scaramella understood the significance of connections and labels, letterheads and shadowy structures that imparted respectability and gave access to funding and more connections. From his late teens onwards he showed a skill in setting up organizations then finding supporters to give them substance. He seized on dramatic ideas and persuaded many people to take his organizations seriously. With his saturnine, baby-faced looks, he liked to hint at connections in the ambiguous, chiaroscuro world where espionage met organized crime.

He boasted of links to the Italian secret services. But in the end even he acknowledged that his ambitions and dreams outstripped his achievements.

Writing for *Slate,* the online magazine, Alexander Stille, a New

York-based author, called him 'a kind of Rosencrantz or Guildenstern of the Litvinenko tragedy, a minor character who sheds a revealing sidelight on the larger drama while also illuminating a different and very Italian tragedy. He is a type that shows up in spy stories – a teller of tall tales and half-truths; part Walter Mitty, part conman, part spy; a person who by virtue of bogus credentials and connections acquires real credentials and real connections. The Italians have a term for people like this that has no exact equivalent in English: *millantatore di credito* – someone who claims to know a lot more and to have done a lot more than he really does.'

At the age of eighteen, Scaramella emerged as the head of an organization called Nuclei Agenti di Sicurezza Civile, roughly translated as Centres of Civil Security Agents, an environmental police group with loose connections to the right-wing Movimento Sociale Italiano – once the political party of Benito Mussolini – of which an influential uncle was a representative. At that time, in the late 1980s, long before ecological concerns entered the political mainstream, the notion of an environmental version of Ghostbusters was a smart, if precocious, move: environmental protection was a broad concept, ranging from ecological matters to breaches of zoning laws. But who could argue against its virtue? Scaramella made his organization into something more substantial, participating in operations to close down illegal bars, restaurants, hotels and even a clandestine racetrack. That phase of his career ended when he was accused – and acquitted on appeal – of impersonating a police officer. He was still only twenty years old and went on to qualify as a lawyer. An early associate was Filippo Marino, an American-Italian who crisscrossed Scaramella's early career and met Litvinenko in the process.

Scaramella's next venture was the Special Research Monitoring Centre, an organization he described as a 'virtual network of scientists', which also drew in Marino, through whom he later sought to make contact with serving or former members of the CIA.

But his most enduring feat was the establishment in the mid-1990s of what he called the Environmental Crime Prevention Programme, or ECPP, whose website described it as a 'permanent intergovernmental conference' devoted to global environmental security.

Through this creation, Scaramella established ties with bona fide institutions, including NATO, the UN's Environmental Protection Agency and the International Maritime Organization. The NYU School of Law invited him for a conference in November 2000 that included a panel discussing 'the utilization of remote sensing and other technologies by governmental organizations and intergovernmental organizations'. Scaramella was identified as representing 'University of Naples II; Secretary General, Environmental Crime Prevention Program'.

One of the ECPP's more persistent campaigns revolved around his allegation that a Soviet November-class submarine had deposited some two dozen nuclear mines on the seabed in the Bay of Naples set to explode in 1973 during the Brezhnev–Nixon negotiations on limiting nuclear arsenals, when the US Sixth Fleet was operating in the area. There was in fact some basis for the allegation. In 2001 a report from the International Atomic Energy Agency in Vienna, listing accidents at sea involving nuclear materials, mentioned an incident on 10 January 1970 when an unidentified submarine supposedly sank in the Bay of Naples with the loss of nuclear torpedoes. But, the IAEA report said, the incident was 'not confirmed'. Later, Scaramella speculated that the nuclear explosives were to be detonated by an antenna hidden on the flanks of Mount Vesuvius, and in the course of a search of them, he recounted, he became involved in a mysterious shoot-out. The ECPP also received lucrative contracts from the authorities at an Italian national park to demolish illegal structures and carry out environmental clean-up works. The contracts, worth over $1 million, later came under scrutiny from police who accused Scaramella of fraud.

Throughout his career, Scaramella accumulated a remarkable CV listing teaching positions at universities such as Stanford,

Arizona, San Jose State, Greenwich (in London), Haifa and Naples. Some of those institutions said later that they had never heard of him or at least disputed the way he depicted their relationship.

Scaramella dabbled in potentially dangerous games. He told the police that shady characters with links to secret services were plotting to kill him. In October 2005 he denounced a group of Ukrainians who were allegedly transporting arms to a former KGB officer in Naples to assassinate him and an associate. When the Italian carabinieri raided a truck heading for Naples with a cargo from Ukraine, four men were arrested and spent over a year in prison. Scaramella had provided information enabling the officers to identify the vehicle, which was said in unconfirmed news reports to be carrying two hand grenades hidden in a hollowed-out Bible. The four Ukrainians were later acquitted.

Some of his contacts, including Oleg Gordievsky, the former Soviet double agent, dismissed Scaramella as an insignificant figure. 'He is just a soap bubble,' Gordievsky said in late 2006, but revised that opinion later, saying he spoke dismissively of Scaramella only because of early suspicions about the sequence of events leading to Litvinenko's death.

But Scaramella certainly became more than a soap bubble in the life of Alexander Litvinenko.

In 2003 Scaramella was appointed as a consultant to an Italian inquiry called the Mitrokhin Commission, set up in 2002. Its mission was to investigate whether archives smuggled out of Russia in 1992 by the Russian archivist Vasili Mitrokhin contained evidence of high-level KGB penetration of the Italian political elite.

The commission – and Scaramella's role in it – offered one of the most curious subplots of the whole Litvinenko affair.

In the murky world of Italian public life, some suspected that the unstated aim of the Mitrokhin Commission was to produce incriminating evidence to feed into the country's voracious political mill of rumour, allegation, occasional fact and frequent gossip.

When Scaramella sought out Litvinenko in 2003, he was trawling for proof (which he never found) of a stupendous allegation that Romano Prodi, the one-time Italian prime minister and head of the European Commission who went on to serve a second term as premier, was or had been a KGB agent.

If that accusation could be proved, the political damage to Prodi would be immeasurable, to the benefit of Silvio Berlusconi, Prodi's arch-rival, who had set up the commission during his own second term of office as prime minister. Indeed, the very notion of a European Union leader being a member of the KGB would have been a sensation to rival or even dwarf Moscow's earlier triumphs in sending its moles deep into the fabric of the Western elite.

Using the British travel and identity documents provided when he won asylum, Litvinenko went to Naples to meet with Scaramella and associates in early 2004.

From the beginning there was some doubt about the methods Scaramella used to persuade Litvinenko to testify.

'Scaramella promised my brother that he would help me get asylum,' Maxim Litvinenko recalled during a conversation on the beach in Senigallia, the Adriatic resort where he lived, in the summer of 2007. Alexander Litvinenko 'only came to Italy because Scaramella promised him that he would get my papers. There were promises, promises. We made a mistake about the people we were talking to,' Maxim said. 'They weren't as powerful as they liked people to think they were.'

Alexander Litvinenko had hinted at strains between himself and Scaramella over the way his younger half-brother had been used. 'We arranged that I would come to Italy in February 2004. Then around that time something inexplicable happened. I have a brother called Maxim who has lived in Italy for four years. A month before I was due to arrive, Maxim called me in a desperate state' to say his student visa had been revoked and he faced deportation to Russia.

'I gave the commission all the help they wanted, and Maxim was given political asylum,' Litvinenko told an Italian newspaper.

'Maxim told me Mario had gone to the police station in Rimini and spoken to the police. I'm certain the whole thing was done to convince me to cooperate.'

But Litvinenko had his own separate agenda when he agreed to cooperate with the Mitrokhin Commission, at least according to a Scaramella associate present at that first encounter in Naples in 2004. 'He seemed like a guy who was eager to be heard and say his piece,' the associate said. 'Scaramella was trying to steer people towards the issues to do with Italy. Litvinenko seemed to be interested in talking about the real power structure within the FSB. He could see Mario's need for specific information about the Italian angle, and he was trying to fit that into the story that he wanted to tell.' Each man, in other words, was seeking to manipulate the other. But Litvinenko 'was ten times the skilful manipulator Mario Scaramella could ever have been'.

One question that arose later in assessing Litvinenko's personality was whether he was paid for his appearance in Italy – a charge he rebutted angrily. Scaramella was said to have offered the former FSB officer several hundred dollars after he spent five days in debriefings in Naples. 'I felt humiliated,' Litvinenko told the Italian newspaper *La Repubblica*. 'I told him he was mistaken if he thought Colonel Litvinenko was reduced to selling his information.'

But after Litvinenko's death, the question of his ambiguous attitudes to money would colour the profiles drawn of him by friend and enemy alike. Even in his dealings in Italy, Litvinenko seemed to have dropped heavy hints that he was angling for a reward.

'It came up once or twice that it wasn't easy to make a living in London,' a participant at the Naples meeting said. 'But Scaramella said he was paying Litvinenko's expenses, travel expenses and the like.' The expenses included five days at the Hotel Britannique in the Corso Vittorio Emanuele in Naples, a slightly passé *belle époque* lodging that may have appealed to Scaramella's romantic sense of derring-do. Litvinenko had less fanciful concerns.

'He was quite wary about his personal security,' the associate said. 'He was a guy who kept vigilant care of himself. He was in excellent physical shape.'

In Litvinenko's mind there was good cause for prudence.

On 3 February 2006 Litvinenko sat down in a hotel room in Rome facing a video camera and began to talk. He was wearing blue jeans, a navy blue blazer and a sky-blue shirt, and he sat on a low sofa against a pinkish wall. On the DVD recording of his deposition it is possible to make out the outline in semi-profile of his half-brother Maxim, turned away from the camera and translating between Russian and Italian. 'Today is February 3, 2006. I am in Rome. My name is Litvinenko, Alexander V.,' Litvinenko began. 'I am a former colonel of the KGB-FSB. I am former deputy chief of a secret department responsible for political homicides of people who were problematic.'

After Litvinenko's introductory remarks, Mario Scaramella, his black hair cut short, moved in to sit next to Litvinenko. He, too, was wearing indigo blue and questioned Litvinenko in Italian, translated into Russian by Maxim. It is clear from the DVD that the session was meant to be secret. In response to a question about his readiness to go public with his testimony, for instance, Litvinenko sought a guarantee that his disclosures would remain confidential. He pointed out that the information he had given had already cost lives. 'That's why this tape must remain secret and it must only be used to carry out secret investigations,' Litvinenko said.

Much of Litvinenko's testimony concerned General Anatoly Trofimov, the former deputy head of the FSB shot dead in 2005. Trofimov's death, of course, meant that there was no one to confirm or deny Litvinenko's account of what the general had told him.

As Litvinenko planned to flee Russia, he said in the recording, Trofimov counselled him against going to several European countries, including Italy. 'I asked him why not, and he told me that in these countries, in the government, there were former KGB agents, many of whom had started working for the KGB again.

After 1996 they renewed their contacts with the KGB, so I asked Trofimov: "But is it possible that in European countries there are still KGB agents?" and Trofimov said that today the president of the EU is Romano Prodi, the man with whom we are working. Is that name enough?'

Questioned by Scaramella, Litvinenko went further. 'What Trofimov told me is that Prodi was a KGB agent, that word they tried not to use. Trofimov told me: "Prodi is our man, a man of the KGB."'

Paolo Guzzanti, the head of the Mitrokhin Commission and an Italian senator from Berlusconi's Forza Italia party, told me later that he ordered Litvinenko's testimony to be classified as secret because it contained allegations that could not be confirmed. Nonetheless, the recording leaked out, and Prodi vigorously denied Litvinenko's allegations. Indeed, Litvinenko himself acknowledged on the recording in 2006 that he had no way of confirming what he had been told. 'Apart from what Trofimov told me, I have no other proof of what I have said,' he said. Since both the participants in the conversation between Litvinenko and Trofimov were dead by the time the DVD came to light, there was no way of going back to the original sources to check out what really happened. Scaramella himself was arrested in Italy one month after Litvinenko died and spent the next half-year in prison – part of it, he said, in solitary confinement – before he was placed under house arrest. Throughout this period, according to court documents, he was under investigation for – but not formally charged with – slander, fraud and arms trafficking. He was freed on 14 February 2008, under a complicated legal arrangement, without a formal admission of guilt.

At one level, these tangled episodes from the Scaramella files would probably have been consigned to the recycle bin had it not been for the fact that Scaramella met Litvinenko just before he began to die and showed him a sheaf of e-mails.

Those messages were the result of a chain of contacts that included Scaramella, Litvinenko and one more secretive Russian with KGB connections, Yevgeny Limarev. It was Litvinenko who introduced Limarev to Scaramella, suggesting that Limarev might be in a position to provide the kind of information sought by the Mitrokhin Commission. In the end, though, according to Limarev, Scaramella became a paying client in 2004, subscribing to Limarev's services as a consultant with expert knowledge on the inner workings of the Kremlin.

That relationship, too, would have made no waves if Litvinenko had not died. But Litvinenko did die, and it was Limarev who passed on the information in the e-mails Scaramella was so keen to show to Alexander Litvinenko on 1 November 2006.

So who was this mysterious purveyor of such valuable information?

Yevgeny Limarev seemed to encourage an aura of mystery, boasting that no photograph of him existed on any publicly accessible database. Indeed his website mockingly displayed a spoof photograph of a handsome, Slavic-looking man with a high blond quiff and dark glasses – not, presumably, the real thing, but certainly the stereotype of a KGB spy in the mould portrayed by Ian Fleming in his James Bond novels. 'I tried to keep myself in shadow, live discreet life out of media for security and other personal reasons,' he said. 'Nobody so far managed to publish a single recognizable photograph of mine [sic].'

By September 2007 so much speculation about Limarev's supposed links to Soviet intelligence had begun to swirl around him that he resolved to post an autobiography on his website, rusglobus.net, stressing that he had never worked for the KGB.

Limarev described himself as the son of a Soviet diplomat and intelligence officer posted to various parts of French-speaking Africa. After attending Russian diplomatic schools in Morocco and elsewhere, he studied languages at a prestigious institute at Moscow State University, qualifying as an interpreter in four languages, two of them useful in Europe, French and English, and two further afield, Farsi and Dari, dominant in Iran and Afghanistan respectively. The authorities in Moscow, however, cancelled a plan for him to use his Dari as a military translator when Soviet troops began to withdraw from Afghanistan in 1988.

As the Soviet Union entered its death throes, Limarev said, he worked as a civilian language instructor with Russian Spetsnaz troops – Special Forces – in units known as Alfa and Vympel at a KGB training centre in the garrison town of Balashikha-2 near Moscow. (He denied that he worked at the places that used an image of Litvinenko for target practice.)

'I worked and studied mostly with Vympel commandos specialized before in sabotage and diversion operations. Now their official mission is to defend nuclear units (including those producing polonium) from terrorists,' he told me.

'I attended some special courses and entered intelligence institute of the KGB, but did not study there,' Limarev said on his website.

In a subsequent telephone conversation, Limarev said, he had passed the requisite examinations to study at the KGB academy but never enrolled. One of the main reasons, he maintained, was that his father was still a serving KGB officer and Soviet-era rules forbade the deployment of two members of the same family on intelligence missions.

Limarev's background in the general milieu of intelligence and security equipped him for what became a familiar career pattern. Like many others – Andrei Lugovoi and Dmitri Kovtun among them – Limarev moved into the new Russia as a businessman with close ties to the power centres of the former KGB and military. But, according to the autobiography posted on his website, Limarev fell foul of an organized crime gang and moved himself and his family first to Switzerland in 1993, then to France in 2000. His self-portrait made clear that he harboured political ambitions in Russia in the 1990s, supporting a rival to Vladimir Putin for the leadership of the Kremlin. But his aspirations to wealth and power unravelled, mired in allegations of complicity in the death of a business partner at a sugar refinery in the Belgorod region of Russia – accusations that he denied.

By the time he became embroiled, albeit at long range, in the climax of the Litvinenko saga, Limarev – then forty-one years old – worked as a consultant on security issues, living in near anonymity in the Haute-Savoie region of France, just across the border from Switzerland. He operated his public website and fed more private material by confidential e-mail to fee-paying clients. His speciality was to chart the manoeuvres of the influential players, the *siloviki*, brought into the corridors of power by Vladimir Putin.

In 2002 Limarev made contact with the Berezovsky circle living in London and the United States – including Litvinenko, Goldfarb and Felshtinsky. He played a role, Limarev said, as an expert witness in the legal preparations for Berezovsky's quest for asylum in Britain, offering his knowledge of the way Berezovsky's businesses had been tracked by the security services and of the security situation in Russia itself. The encounter with the Berezovsky group also promised some direct cooperation with Litvinenko.

'We decided to exchange information on the activities of the Russian mafia and former members of the secret services,' Limarev said in an interview with *Paris Match* in December 2006. 'I must have met Alexander four or five times. But we spoke often on the telephone. Litvinenko was very hard, with a thirst for action, the perfect prototype of an FSB man. As time passed, he became more and more radicalized, extreme. He was obsessed by Putin.'

Looking back on Litvinenko's last year in London, it seems as if events were hurrying him along, as if an unseen dramatic hand were building the set and assembling the characters for the denouement. Part of the problem was financial.

As Berezovsky himself acknowledged, he reduced a monthly stipend to Litvinenko worth £5,000 and Litvinenko complained to any number of people that money was tight. (Berezovsky continued to pay Anatoly's school fees and, later, displayed considerable generosity towards the widowed Marina Litvinenko.) As Marina depicted the situation, the impetus for the break with Berezovsky came from Litvinenko himself. He had improved his English and wanted to become independent of Berezovsky by entering the lucrative market in due diligence reports and insider information about Russian business.

To Litvinenko's surprise, Berezovsky raised no objections to his going his own way.

'Sasha understood that he can do things himself, he can find a job, he can speak English, he can make some contacts,' Marina recalled. 'He works with businessmen in Russia just looking for information . . . He liked to have this independence, and it's very important that you are a useful person . . . '

To some extent, that tallied with Berezovsky's version of events.

The question of Litvinenko's financial situation assumed great importance in considering the causes of his death and the motives behind it: had he become so desperate for money that he lost all sense of discipline and proportion; had he become reckless to the point that he no longer recognized the threat? Certainly, he seemed gregarious to a fault, easy to approach, even bringing relative strangers into his home in Muswell Hill. Not all of them were discreet – or sympathetic.

Immediately after Litvinenko's death, most British news reports painted a broadly favourable portrait of the former KGB officer, casting him as the victim of a sinister plot by the Kremlin. But Julia Svetlichnaya, a thirty-three-year-old Russian graduate student living in England since 1994, caused something of a stir with a less flattering portrayal.

She had spoken with Litvinenko several times during 2006 along with a fellow researcher, James Heartfield, from the University of Westminster, where they were both enrolled.

Svetlichnaya approached Litvinenko by way of Boris Berezovsky as part of research into events in Chechnya, and, she said, she found his behaviour erratic. In British newspaper reports, she described Litvinenko as 'a disillusioned exile in London, a defector who seemed unable to plan for the future, whose conversation often darted from one subject to another in bewildering fashion'. She disclosed that he sent her photographs, including one of himself in a tam-o'-shanter, clutching a Chechen sword and wearing KGB fingerless gauntlets. In another, he had posed, clean-shaven and with a boyish smile, at his home in Muswell Hill alongside Akhmed Zakayev and Anna Politkovskaya shortly before her death.

The photograph of Litvinenko wielding a double-handed sword might almost have been designed to offset the near-saintly expression of doomed resignation that he wore on his deathbed. But Svetlichnaya also told the *Observer* that Litvinenko 'was going to blackmail or sell sensitive information about all kinds of powerful people, including oligarchs, corrupt officials and sources in the Kremlin'. She repeated the allegation in an interview with CBS News, although she never identified the person Litvinenko purportedly planned to blackmail.

Svetlichnaya's description of a mercenary and unstable Litvinenko drew a chorus of outrage from the Berezovsky camp and produced allegations from Litvinenko's supporters that the Kremlin had launched a classic KGB disinformation campaign to smear Litvinenko's memory. Svetlichnaya successfully challenged the *Sunday Times* for suggesting just that, and the newspaper issued an apology.

Her account of her meetings with Litvinenko began with a familiar preface.

They 'agreed to meet at Piccadilly Circus', she told me, recalling a telephone call on 28 April 2006. 'He said he will be wearing a leather jacket. He said he will find me. I was waiting there by the sculpture, and he approached me from behind. He said he had been watching me.'

Svetlichnaya met Litvinenko four times – once in Piccadilly, once in Hyde Park, once at his home in Muswell Hill and once in the company of Zakayev at the Park Lane Hilton. In Hyde Park, she recounted, they walked round in circles so as not – according to Litvinenko – to be overheard by hostile eavesdroppers. 'He started talking about blackmail,' she said, but she seemed to suggest that extortion was not his prime goal. 'The main point was not blackmail. He did not have any money. I always paid for our coffees. He would always say: life is tough. He didn't strike me as an avaricious person at all. He needed the money.

'I'm sure he found something, but he was not a player. He was not someone who could find something. But he was getting information from somewhere.'

Litvinenko, she concluded, was 'not a dissident. He was a lost soul, paid by oligarchs.'

The point, perhaps, was what these encounters said about Litvinenko. There was no suggestion in Svetlichnaya's account of any impropriety – indeed Litvinenko introduced her to his wife at home in Osier Crescent. But there was a sense from Svetlichnaya's account – taken at its most charitable – that he was casting around for a new purpose. In an article in the *Daily Telegraph* two days after Litvinenko died, Svetlichnaya and Heartfield, her fellow academic, wrote: 'The epitaph for Alexander Litvinenko might read: "He was caught up in events bigger than he understood." '

The conclusion sounded patronizing, and some in his extended family detected a deeper restlessness.

'With time I and my father became quite close,' his daughter Sonya said in the late summer of 2007. 'We got to know each other, and he could be sweet and show moments of tenderness. Actually, by the end he wanted me to stay with him in London. I also got the impression that he missed Russia. I speak better English than he did, and I don't think he ever integrated. His only friends and acquaintances were always only Russian speakers.

'Towards the end we had the impression that he was depressed,' she said. 'I don't know why, but he complained about lack of money and once even said he was considering moving to another country. I got the impression that he was having some problems, but we didn't talk about it.'

In the discreet streets of Mayfair there are equally discreet offices where a client might seek to arrange a private army to guard an oil field or a bodyguard for a chief executive or a dossier on the corporate standing of a potential business partner. It is an area, with landmarks such as the Millennium Hotel, the American Embassy and Boris Berezovsky's office, whose well-heeled denizens dine at spots like Harry's Bar and George's to conclude their business or simply to relax, often at someone else's expense. This zone of quiet, unpublicized business stretches from the luxury hotels of Park Lane to the expensive shops of Bond Street, demarcated to the north by Oxford Street and to the south by Piccadilly. Nearby, there are showrooms and shops selling Bentleys and Rolls-Royces, Porsches, diamonds, artworks, antiques, bespoke suits, costly shoes. And it was in this milieu, among people whose trade was primarily in information, that Litvinenko saw a chance to offset the loss of income from Boris Berezovsky.

Russia was still the enigma, the puzzle. Outsiders did not venture there unguided. London became the place where people like Litvinenko might translate their insiders' knowledge of their own country into lucrative deals as consultants and advisers to Western companies looking for business in Russia. In some places at least, Litvinenko was well received.

'Litvinenko had a Rolodex and a diary to die for,' said a British security specialist who did not want his name to be published. 'He maintained links to Russia, to the FSB, among fellow dissidents. He told me: "Everything in Russia is for sale. There is no loyalty." ' The security specialist recalled Litvinenko as 'a naive, nice young man. He got very excited when he got his UK passport. He was very proud.'

But Litvinenko's knowledge was imperfect. 'He wanted to learn about Yukos, Gazprom, oil and gas. In return, he was able to help with due diligence on Russian companies and businesspeople.' But it was in that trade-off that he may well have strayed into much deeper waters than he was used to.

'Litvinenko blundered into high-stakes manoeuvres relating to Yukos and Gazprom,' the security specialist said as we sipped coffee in one of the vaulted, old-style clubs with their panelled walls and leather armchairs that dot the St James's district just south of Mayfair.

Some time around April 2006, Litvinenko embarked on a mysterious mission to Israel, travelling there to hand over a document on the Yukos affair to Leonid Nevzlin, a fugitive senior executive of the company sought by the Kremlin. 'Alexander had information on crimes committed with the Russian government's direct participation,' Nevzlin said in a statement from his office in Tel Aviv, issued after Litvinenko's death. 'He only recently gave me and my attorneys documents that shed light on the most significant aspects of the Yukos affair.'

Nevzlin did not elaborate beyond saying that he had handed this secret dossier to Scotland Yard. But it was hard to imagine that the Kremlin took kindly to further whistle-blowing by a rogue FSB operative whom it wished to forget. Indeed, in December 2006 Russia's prosecutor general said it had established a link between the Litvinenko case and its inquiries into Nevzlin and the Yukos affair. Nevzlin dismissed the allegation as ridiculous.

Far beyond his familiar tirades, Litvinenko was dabbling now in businesses worth billions whose cash flow sustained the Kremlin in many ways.

Accusations of human rights abuses, of intolerance, of belligerence and of deviousness could all too easily be dismissed by Russia's leaders as the figments of warped imaginations on a lunatic fringe far from the clogged boulevards and booming economy of Moscow.

Business was different, a central preoccupation of the former KGB men in the Kremlin who had gathered Russia's strategic energy resources to themselves and kept close tabs on the doings of a new generation of oligarchs grown rich from banking, steel and minerals. Just from observing the grisly fate of prying reporters, Russians were used to the idea that people who showed too much curiosity about the business of the elite often did not survive to tell the tale.

But there was some doubt about the nature of the information that was being peddled in London – was it such blue-chip insider knowledge as to merit a killing?

Alexei Mukhin, head of a think tank in Moscow called the Centre for Political Information, said Litvinenko and Lugovoi had apparently been offering documents that originated in his organization, passing them off as bona fide intelligence dossiers. Indeed, in June 2007 Lugovoi told the *Izvestia* newspaper: 'There are Brits who want to invest in Russia. But they are scared or just want to make sure their investments won't be pilfered. So we were offering various analytical materials in different spheres of the economy. We received money for these materials directly, and Litvinenko got 20 per cent in cash from them. That is what he told me. If they were to transfer, say, $10,000, they would transfer $8,000 and give the rest to Litvinenko.'

Months after Litvinenko's death, Lugovoi said he became suspicious of the business because it was dragging him into a relationship with the British security services and embroiling him in 'the sale of the country' to foreigners. And later he sought to disavow the entire trade, contradicting his earlier statements by saying: 'I've never said Litvinenko and I sold informational and analytical files about Russia to anyone in England.'

There was another good reason to be suspicious of dealings with the Russian *émigrés* in London.

In July 2006, little noticed by outsiders, a new law approved by the Duma in Moscow empowered the Russian secret services to strike beyond their borders in pursuit of targets regarded as terrorists or extremists. The subtext was this: no matter what happened to Russia's enemies in London or anywhere else, no one would be punished in Moscow. But still Litvinenko did not seem overly concerned.

In the closing days of October 2006, Maxim Litvinenko said, he spoke to his half-brother 'two or three days, maybe a week'. before he was poisoned. 'He said he had business deals coming up and he would try to bring me in,' Maxim recalled. 'He said he would set up his own company and they would do something in

Italy in oil, gas, metals, petroleum.'

That was the kind of promise that might be made by a man given to fantasy or hope – but not by a man expecting to die within days. On 13 October 2006, the same day that he attended a memorial service for Anna Politkovskaya at Westminster Abbey, Litvinenko had boasted to friends that he was British now – and safe: the same message that he had offered his son Anatoly six years earlier.

The acquisition of British citizenship seemed a happy, innocent time for all the family. They had taken a written examination in citizenship in July 2006 – part of newly introduced British measures to control unwanted immigration – and had studied in advance on the Internet. 'Sasha tried to prepare himself very hard,' Marina said, recalling that her husband immersed himself in mediaeval British history when in fact the real questions related to humdrum matters like the voting age.

When they took the examination, the widow said, 'Sasha started to complain it's not exactly the same, and some people complained that I helped him, and I said, "No, he is just nervous and I will calm him down." '

With the examination passed, they proceeded some time later to the formal group ceremony to pledge their oaths of citizenship from the two texts on offer – civil or religious.

'One couple was completely, like, punk,' Marina said, gesturing to denote long spikes of hair. That couple chose the civil oath of loyalty. 'We chose something religious,' she said.

After the service, Litvinenko took his son, now twelve, with him to the Politkovskaya memorial service at Westminster Abbey.

Pledging their loyalty, 'we had had this very happy ceremony, and I saw other people who were so happy to be British citizens,' Marina said.

In the closing days of October, there was another curious incident that, with hindsight, deepened the impression – no more than that – of strange omens.

When Scaramella flew to London, the rendezvous with Litvinenko was not the only appointment on his agenda. On 31 October 2006 he was set to meet with another Russian, Igor Ponomarev, Moscow's ambassador to the International Maritime Organization.

(It was a measure of its plausibility that the ECPP, Scaramella's environmental security group, had observer status with the respected IMO, a specialized agency of the United Nations, although that status did not survive the harsh scrutiny of Mario Scaramella after the death of Alexander Litvinenko. In mid-2007 the IMO formally ended its association with the ECPP, calling it 'the invention of one determined individual, who, after receiving some support, succeeded in obtaining accreditation and created a "niche" for himself in international meetings of NATO, UNEP, IAEA, and the London Convention and Protocol, as an expert in the field of prevention of environmental crimes, including investigations of reports of activities involving putative sea disposal of radioactive materials'.)

In particular, Scaramella wanted to talk about his assertion that a submarine from the former Soviet Union had deposited nuclear mines on the seabed in the Bay of Naples. There is some evidence that he had discussed this claim in the past with the IMO and was hoping to hear more details from Ponomarev.

At a meeting of the London convention against marine pollution under IMO auspices held between 30 October and 3 November 2006, moreover, Scaramella claimed to have signed an agreement to cooperate with 'the Russian Federation State Rocket Centre' as part of his inquiries into the illegal dumping of nuclear waste and other radioactive material.

But he did not see Igor Ponomarev.

On the evening of 30 October 2006, after a night at the opera, Ponomarev died at forty-one years of age of what was described as a heart attack, although at least one British tabloid said he died after complaining of a massive thirst – among other things, a symptom of radiation sickness.

In any event, his body was repatriated quickly to Moscow.

On 6 November 2006 Scaramella wrote an e-mail in poor English to Litvinenko: 'It was very strange that you were sick soon after our meeting. Mr. Igor Ponomarev I scheduled to meet in London at International Maritime Organization suddenly died for [sic] a heart attack on October 30 the day before our meeting. Such an incredible coincidence. Anyway I report to UN IMO countries our development with the state rocket center.'

It was indeed an 'incredible coincidence'.

And as 1 November approached, other coincidences began piling up.

The date was the anniversary of the Litvinenkos' arrival in London after their flight from Russia. It was the day Moscow's CSKA football team would play Arsenal at the glittery new Emirates Stadium that had replaced the club's venerable Highbury ground. Thousands of Russians would be flying in and out of London for the game; one or two more or less would not draw attention in the airport immigration queues, in the crowds of anonymous men and women heading for hotel rooms and bars and the turnstiles leading into the ground. It was the day Dmitri Kovtun, Lugovoi's associate, flew in from Hamburg – tired and faintly hungover from a late drinking session – for a business meeting with Lugovoi. It was the day Andrei Lugovoi, Vyacheslav Sokolenko and Lugovoi's family met up in the Millennium Mayfair Hotel to prepare to watch the game. A photograph showed the two men with friends and children at a steak house in Piccadilly on the way to the stadium. It was the day Mario Scaramella met Litvinenko in the itsu sushi bar to show him a sheaf of e-mailed memos from Yevgeny Limarev. It was the last day ever that Litvinenko would pass by the statue of Eros that had been his marker, his beacon, at the heart of an alien capital.

It was also the day Alexander Litvinenko began to die.

In fact, the mysteries began two days earlier, on 30 October 2006, when Mario Scaramella received the first of two confidential memos focusing on a perceived threat to him and his boss on the Mitrokhin Commission, Paolo Guzzanti.

The e-mailed memo catalogued a series of events that had raised concerns among some secretive Russians about the behaviour of Scaramella and Guzzanti – including the seizure of the four Ukrainians on their way to Naples in 2005. It suggested that Litvinenko had been lying when he told friends that he had secured British citizenship. It spoke of serving officers in the SVR, Russia's foreign intelligence service, and of a group of KGB veterans called Dignity and Honour.

'Meanwhile, above-mentioned Russian intelligence officers speak more and more about necessity to use force against PG and MS, considering their "incessant anti-Russian activities" – as well as against Berezovsky and Litvinenko,' the memo said.

The initials were those of Paolo Guzzanti and Mario Scaramella.

The e-mail referred to the head of Dignity and Honour, calling his involvement 'the most troubling and dangerous development'. It even said a Russian agent had been in position in Naples for over a month with a network of KGB agents at his disposal for what 'could be serious provocation or even assassination attempt'.

The same memo contained what might have been the most interesting nugget for Litvinenko, suggesting that Dignity and Honour agents were 'presumably involved in the assassination of Anna Politkovskaya in 2006 as well as in elaboration of other similar assassination plans in Russia and Baltic states – by order and on behalf of FSB/SVR'.

Then a second memo on 31 October identified the purported agent in Naples as a former Special Forces officer who 'specializes in preparation of subversive operations'.

'Nowadays he is about 46, with black (rarely [sic] greyish) hair, lean but muscular, of about 185 cm, is slightly lame in his right leg. Speaks well English and Portugal [sic], is master in judo.'

The memo suggested that the purported agent was on a ' "reconnaissance mission" in Napoli – preparing grounds for some action, but is quite unlikely to participate in it himself.'

Initial news reports identified the author of the e-mails as

Yevgeny Limarev. That contention dovetailed neatly with a subsequent claim by Paolo Guzzanti, Scaramella's boss, that the e-mails were sent by Limarev as part of a conspiracy to lure Litvinenko to the sushi bar, distracting his attention from his subsequent encounter at the Pine Bar.

But Limarev insisted that the e-mails related primarily to Scaramella and Guzzanti – not to Berezovsky and Litvinenko – and, more significantly, that he was not their author. They had been sent to him by a source in Russia he did not identify. Under the business arrangement between them, Limarev passed them on to Scaramella, without knowing that the Italian would show them to Litvinenko in the sushi bar.

'Information from sources within Russia was coming via me,' Limarev said. 'These two e-mails I have received, I have made some small linguistic changes and sent them on. But I'm not the source.'

Despite that, Limarev said on his website, he had been falsely accused of participation in a 'special "cover operation" of assassination of Litvinenko'.

According to Paolo Guzzanti, Scaramella called him in Rome after lunch at the itsu sushi bar and told him that Litvinenko had not taken the e-mails seriously.

'When Scaramella called me around 4.00 p.m., he said, "I feel really relieved. He read those e-mails and said they were pure shit, just something sent to scare you," ' Guzzanti said.

Twenty-two days after uttering those words, Litvinenko perished, the victim of the first act of nuclear terrorism in a Western capital.

11

POISON AND PR

The pain began in Litvinenko's stomach, a racking, wrenching convulsion that turned into uncontrollable vomiting as if his entire being were seeking to expel an alien intruder. He drank water, but his body threw it back before it could be absorbed.

Every breath became an effort, a gasp.

His heart seemed to have no strength to fight.

Then it was his bowels, reduced to liquid. When he inspected the outflow from his cramping innards, he thought he saw blood. In the early days of his sickness, after 1 November 2006, while he was still at home, he opened a window to let cool night air chill his makeshift sickroom. The family doctor – a Russian – came to examine him at home, but the merest touch of the physician's hands made him cry out in agony. After two days, it was all too much. His skin was pale, and when he needed the bathroom, he could no longer walk unassisted. But if he was laid low, if venom had found its way into his being, should he have been surprised? This, after all, was what he had been schooled to expect. This was what the KGB did.

Marina Litvinenko dosed her husband with Milk of Magnesia – a popular antacid in Britain and in Russia. She made him drink water. She checked his temperature and found it veering crazily between fever and chills. But his underlying condition merely worsened. A man who pumped iron was being reduced to a husk.

In the early hours of 3 November, he told her: 'Marina, I can't take it any more. Call an ambulance.'

'We had thought briefly that maybe it was poisoning, but no one was seriously worrying about that,' Marina Litvinenko said later. 'It was Sasha who finally started saying to me: "Marina, this is something abnormal. When I was in school at the military academy, we studied poisoning like this that was caused by a chemical weapon. This really reminds me of that." '

That must have seemed an improbable story at Litvinenko's local hospital in Barnet, north London. He was not even registered under his own name: Litvinenko had used the English pseudonym that came with his asylum for his admission to the hospital. Who would believe a story of KGB conspiracies and poisoning from a man called Edwin Carter?

For Marina, there was an extra dilemma familiar to anyone baffled by the mysteries of the National Health Service – a blend of care and bureaucracy, at once ponderous in its workings and yet a source of potential salvation for her husband. She felt frustrated as much with her own hesitancy as with the system itself. For months afterwards she was haunted by uncertainty over whether she – or the doctors – could somehow have been persuaded to do more to save Litvinenko in those early days of his illness at Barnet. And it is easy to imagine how an overworked, underfunded staff might have responded to her entreaties. A sick Russian with a strange ID and fantasies about poisoning by the Kremlin was hardly likely to elicit concern from an underfunded local hospital battling with budget cuts and shortages of beds and nurses. Marina Litvinenko was left to ponder the best course of action: to hope for the best, or complain loudly at the risk of alienating medical staff?

Months after her husband's death, that retrospective sense of frustration and failure brought tears to his widow's eyes. Starting on the night of 1 November, when her husband began to vomit uncontrollably, Marina Litvinenko remained at his side in a remarkable sustained vigil, never really believing until the very end that he was doomed, trying to balance his need for her with her son's hunger for reassurance. Her suffering traced an unchecked downward slide into despair, frustration, rage and self-recrimination as the physicians first failed to identify his illness and then misdiagnosed it.

'We told them to check for evidence of poisoning with something unusual,' she said. 'We didn't want to say who Sasha was, but we did say he had received political asylum and that maybe somebody didn't like that. They listened but they didn't do anything about it. I can't blame them, though. I blame myself: why didn't I insist, why didn't I make a fuss?'

The symptoms were getting worse. When Marina Litvinenko touched her husband's head, hair came off in her hand, falling on to the sheets and pillows. But still no one seemed to accept their deepening belief that he had been poisoned. Physicians pursued the familiar battery of tests, working by a process of elimination to arrive at whatever finding remained after all the analyses had been done and the results tabulated.

Some of the tests required X-rays, and, at the nurses' behest as they prepared their patient, Litvinenko's wife removed the Orthodox Christian cross that dated from his clandestine baptism more than four decades earlier. That single casual act of caring opened yet one more subchapter in the annals of his demise.

Friends came to visit. One of them was Akhmed Zakayev, the Chechen separatist who was the Litvinenkos' neighbour at Osier Crescent. Zakayev was a devout Muslim. Litvinenko had some-how fallen under the thrall of his friend's faith. They had spent hours together, talking about conditions in Chechnya, about the clash of faiths and identities in the northern Caucasus, about the yearning to be free from Russian control. Litvinenko may not have fought directly in Chechnya – as Zakayev had. He may not have felt the pull of the muezzin's call to prayer. But as he sickened, he began to yearn for it. When he got better, he told his wife, he would like to attend the mosque with his friend Akhmed – a vain ambition, as it turned out.

Zakayev arrived at Barnet Hospital to visit just one day after Marina removed her husband's baptismal cross. It was the moment Litvinenko chose to declare himself.

'Sasha said to Akhmed: "Look at me. I don't have my cross. How do you speak with God?" And Akhmed says a few words and Sasha repeats them, and for Akhmed it was enough,' Marina recalled.

It was left to his other friends to argue later over whether Litvinenko had truly embraced Islam in the very last days of his life.

By Tuesday 7 November 2006, physicians at Barnet concluded that Litvinenko had some kind of bacteria in his intestine that released toxins after natural protections had been destroyed by antibiotics.

But Litvinenko was not taking antibiotics.

'They tested him for AIDS and hepatitis. He started turning yellow,' Marina Litvinenko told Natalia Gevorkyan, the *Kommersant* journalist who had been one of a trio of reporters to spend time with Vladimir Putin years earlier, conducting the interviews collected and published as Putin's memoir, *First Person*.

On 13 November an official report from Barnet Hospital revealed that Litvinenko had been checked for radiation but, it concluded, there was 'no radioactive emission from patient'. The possibility of radiation poisoning, in other words, had been considered at least ten days before the toxins in Litvinenko's system claimed their victim. But the standard checks had been designed for the most common kind of radioactivity. Most detection devices are designed to pick up gamma rays – the kind of radiation emitted from uranium, for example, which penetrates matter and reaches deep into the human organism. But there are other kinds of radiation known as beta and alpha emissions, and alpha emissions – though highly toxic once inside the human body – cannot even pierce a sheet of paper or a layer of skin. The device at Barnet did not look for those. If it had, the course of

Litvinenko's decline would probably have been different, but not the outcome. Litvinenko's bone marrow had been virtually destroyed. His immune system was collapsing.

Then, unexpectedly, in all the pain, there was a brief, bright respite, a moment of strength. Litvinenko rallied sufficiently to rise from his bed and walk – a miracle. He swung his arms as if to exercise and made his way alone to the toilet to attend to himself. It was a cruel deception, a calm before the resumption of the storm, the relapse.

The pain returned. His tongue swelled to fill his mouth. His hair was all over the pillow and sheets of the hospital bed, like stuffing from an old armchair spilling from torn fabric. Medical staff shaved his head to restore some dignity to his patchy, tufted scalp. His skin became yellow, jaundiced.

The physicians did more tests. They took him to the cancer ward because he looked like the patients there after chemotherapy, only more so – hairless and sucked dry of life.

On 16 November there was another false dawn, a further distraction that seemed to offer a ray of hope. A nurse arrived at Litvinenko's bedside to announce that he had been diagnosed with poisoning by the highly toxic substance thallium, which had a long history of use in murders and had been used in insecticides and rat poisons before people realized just how dangerous it was to humans.

The nurse brought the antidote – known as Prussian blue and named for a dye first produced in 1704 for the colouring of Prussian military uniforms. In its therapeutic form, the substance had been used since the 1960s, usually supplied in a soluble capsule. For patients like Litvinenko who could not easily swallow, the capsule was broken open and the contents dissolved in water.

Even then, when it was administered to Litvinenko he complained that it hurt his throat.

Prussian blue – known by various scientific names including ferric hexacyanoferrate – worked by trapping toxins in the intestine to prevent their reabsorption into the bloodstream, reversing the effects of poisoning by ensuring that the toxic substances were excreted so that damaged organs would regenerate.

At first, the mention of thallium seemed like a breakthrough. The substance was once widely known as 'the poisoner's poison' – tasteless, odourless and with a delayed action that gave assassins time to make an escape. Agatha Christie chose thallium as the murder device in her novel *The Pale Horse*. Modern history is studded with rumours and stories of thallium being conceived by state bodies, including the CIA, as a vehicle to poison figures as illustrious as Fidel Castro. Iraq's Mukhabarat secret police had a particular liking for it, using it to lace drinks offered in friendship to prisoners as they were released from Saddam Hussein's torture chambers. Apartheid death squads in South Africa were said to have contemplated its use against Nelson Mandela during his incarceration on Robben Island. As recently as February 2007, two American women – both *émigrées* from Russia – were diagnosed with thallium poisoning during a return visit to Moscow.

Most significantly, though, the symptoms of thallium poisoning included the same hair loss as afflicted Litvinenko in November 2006.

The talk of thallium changed everything. Demonstrably, Litvinenko had been poisoned. Physicians had a diagnosis to work with. The police had a crime to investigate. As Marina Litvinenko recalled, 'Everything started with the thallium diagnosis.'

On 17 November the patient was transferred to University College Hospital, an almost new medical facility clad in jade-green glass and steel on the Euston Road, just north of the city centre, perhaps one mile from Litvinenko's more usual haunts around Piccadilly Circus.

'They took him to a different hospital,' Marina Litvinenko recalled. 'That was on Friday. The police came – it was just like an American action movie. They put him in an ambulance with flashing blue lights, I sat in the police car, and we drove from one hospital to the other as if someone was trying to kill us. And it was so strange, because three weeks earlier no one had taken any notice of anything, and now all of a sudden everybody was trying to save him.'

As Litvinenko's condition seemed to stabilize somewhat over the weekend of 17–18 November, the Berezovsky camp brought in John Henry, a renowned clinical toxicologist with a strong track record in high-profile poisoning cases. In 2004 he had achieved some renown in identifying dioxin as the poison that afflicted Viktor A. Yushchenko during the presidential elections in Ukraine. This time, on the BBC and elsewhere, he named the poison as thallium.

'It is tasteless, colourless and odourless,' he said. 'It takes about a gram to kill you.' As to whether Litvinenko would survive, he was less sure. 'He's got a prospect of recovering. He's got a prospect of dying,' he said.* But there was a flaw in the new diagnosis: Henry realized that Litvinenko was not displaying all the symptoms of thallium poisoning. As Henry shook hands with the dying man, Litvinenko's grip was still strong, whereas thallium usually produces muscle weakness.

In fact, Litvinenko's condition was far more dire than his friends suspected. Andres Virchis, a physician at Barnet Hospital, said on 19 November that apart from the loss of his hair, Litvinenko's bone marrow had failed and he was not producing any normal immune cells or white cells. Thallium poisoning, in theory, was reversible. Litvinenko had taken the known antidote. It even showed up in X-rays of his stomach. And yet Alexander Litvinenko continued his inexorable slide towards death, his organs failing one after the other until finally only a heartbeat sustained him.

Just twenty-four hours before his heart finally abandoned its hold on life, he uttered his final words to his wife: 'Oh, Marinochka, I love you so much.'

* Henry himself died just a few months later, at the age of sixty-eight, of complications related to the removal of a kidney many years earlier.

'All his organs were shot,' his father Walter recalled. 'He bit his lip through. That's how painful it was. He gnawed at his lips to deal with it. Just before his death, I walked to his bed. "Dad, my coccyx hurts so much," he complained to me. I put my hand under – the bed can be raised, but it's slow – I got my hand under to support him, and then it all flowed out and his eyes froze.'

Alexander Litvinenko died without even knowing what killed him.

When Litvinenko fell ill on 1 November 2006, there were none of the banner headlines and satellite news bulletins that were to follow as word of his decline spread around the world. The beginning of the end was slow, painful, mystifying, and largely unchronicled.

On the night he began to vomit, there had been the special chicken dinner at home, cooked by Marina to mark the sixth anniversary of their arrival in London. There had been the usual check on what turned out to be his last-ever e-mails. Even when the sickness began, no one in Osier Crescent thought for a moment that he would not recover to resume what passed for a normal life: his wife suspected nothing beyond a bad stomach. But at that moment, his vital organs were under terminal attack from an enemy too small to see.

Towards the end of his life, terse and infrequent police bulletins spoke of a 'deliberate poisoning' and an 'unexplained death'. For days on end, Scotland Yard shied away stubbornly from the M-word: 'murder'.

Yet there were indications, relatively early in the illness and from sources that the police might not routinely consult (but which the security and diplomatic services almost certainly would), that this man with his history in the KGB and FSB, this fugitive from Moscow and associate of many shadowy and dangerous people, was suffering from something far more sinister than bad sushi.

The first public sign came one week after Litvinenko's en-counters in Piccadilly and Mayfair, when a journalist from a

Russian newspaper phoned Yuri Felshtinsky, his co-author, seeking comment on reports that the former KGB operative had been poisoned. Felshtinsky called Litvinenko on 8 November 2006.

Litvinenko 'told me he had lost around 15 kilograms [over 30 pounds] of weight, that his body wasn't accepting any food or liquids,' Felshtinsky wrote. Significantly, though, 'that day, Alexander believed that he had survived the assassination attempt.' During a conversation lasting fifteen or twenty minutes and maybe longer, Felshtinsky said, 'his voice was very strong.'

On Saturday 11 November – little noticed beyond his immediate circle – Litvinenko gave an interview to the BBC Russian-language service in which he said quite clearly that he had been poisoned, but he seemed to lay the blame at the door of his Italian lunch partner, Mario Scaramella – albeit without identifying him by name.

'I was contacted by a person. He suggested a meeting,' Litvinenko said. 'The meeting happened on the first of November at one of the London restaurants. He passed me some papers where the person was named who apparently might be connected to the murder of Anna Politkovskaya. That's it. After several hours I felt sick with the symptoms of poisoning.' The papers to which he referred were the e-mail printouts from Yevgeny Limarev, which Mario Scaramella had handed over to him. As in his conversation with Felshtinsky, Litvinenko was clinging to straws, speaking of a day that would never come 'when I feel better, when I am back home'.

Litvinenko also alluded several times to a police investigation into the poisoning, when in fact the police inquiry began in earnest only many days later.

And in those relatively early days, it did not seem to occur to Litvinenko that the Russians he had met later on the same day as he lunched with Scaramella might have had a hand in his poisoning.

A version put about by Alex Goldfarb, Boris Berezovsky's close aide, who spent many of Litvinenko's final days visiting him in the hospital, suggested that Litvinenko hinted at Scaramella's involvement as a diversionary tactic to keep the real suspects off guard – another of the bluff-and-double-bluff theories that grew from the Litvinenko mystery. But even if Goldfarb's version did not reflect the reality, Litvinenko's remarks to the BBC sent a message on several levels. They told those who knew the real story that Litvinenko had survived long enough to implicate them. They told them he knew that he was the victim of foul play. And they boasted that the attempt to kill him had failed since he was already planning his recovery.

The interview on 11 November 2006 was conducted by telephone, and already his voice had weakened. But journalists in London were generally slow to seize on the story, and some remained sceptical of its news value. Among reporters with inside knowledge of the Berezovsky circle, Litvinenko was often depicted as a dreamer and romantic, obsessed by the evil machinations of Vladimir Putin. But his illness, and the growing certainty that he had been poisoned, cast this fantasist in a new light. Finally, everything Litvinenko said about the Kremlin seemed to be coming true.

Acting through the PR guru Tim Bell and Alex Goldfarb, the Berezovsky camp displayed increasing desperation to get the Litvinenko story on to the front pages. But, as one person familiar with their deliberations said later, 'We did not know how much media interest there would be in a rather obscure ex-KGB officer living in Britain.' Additionally, there was a calculation that the British would not buy into Litvinenko's condemnations of Vladimir Putin. 'The Brits wouldn't believe it, wouldn't want to believe it.'

It took eight days from the Russian-language interview with the BBC for Litvinenko's plight to become big news in Britain – eight days in which Bell worked the phones assiduously – and the first reports still pointed towards his meeting with Scaramella at the itsu sushi bar as the most likely crime scene.

'I ordered lunch, but he ate nothing,' Litvinenko told the *Sunday Times*, whose reporter interviewed him before his condition deteriorated beyond repair. The interview appeared on Sunday 19

November 2006 – eighteen days after he began to sicken and four days before he died. In the light of what emerged about the nature of his poisoning, it was a miracle that he survived long enough to become a media star. His abrupt celebrity had a nightmarish quality: his name and appearance were suddenly known around the world, but the object of this attention was invisible, sequestered incommunicado under armed police guard in the hospital. And he was dying.

'I do feel very bad,' he told the *Sunday Times,* acknowledging for the first time in public that he might not make it, that his adversaries might prevail. 'I've never felt like this before – like my life is hanging on the ropes.'

At the start, the police remained aloof.

If Litvinenko was being depicted in banner headlines as a crusader, sounding his alarms like a latter-day Joshua, no obvious crime seemed to have been committed: where, after all, was the weapon, the motive, and – until his death – the body? Only on 20 November – nineteen days after Litvinenko fell ill – did the police acknowledge that a specialist crime unit – not, initially, the counterterrorism command – had been assigned to the case. 'We are investigating a suspected deliberate poisoning of a 41-year-old man in London,' a police press release said.

The statement did not even mention Litvinenko's name. The age was wrong, too: Litvinenko was forty-three when he died.

'We are in the very early stages of our investigation and so are unable to comment on speculative reports in the media until we have confirmed details,' the police bulletin said. 'We hope to provide further information in due course. There have been no arrests in connection with this inquiry at this stage.'

In fact, according to Marina Litvinenko, the police investigation began several days earlier, on Friday 17 November, with officers arriving at Litvinenko's bedside to interrogate him for several hours at a stretch. 'He gave an interview to the investigators, and they were amazed by his courage,' she said. 'He answered questions for three or four hours, even though it was very difficult for him to speak because, as was starting to come to light, he was burning up inside.'

Marina complained that the police questioning was too stressful for her husband in his rapidly worsening condition. But, sensing that time was running out, Litvinenko himself insisted on continuing to talk to the officers from Scotland Yard, offering them a close account of his movements in the days before and on 1 November 2006. The police reticence may thus have been tactical, designed to keep any other suspects ignorant of what Litvinenko told his questioners before his illness closed over him like the dark hood of an executioner.

When she realized her husband would die, Marina said, it was as if her very being had been punctured by a sharp needle.

If the police remained tight-lipped, however, Litvinenko's handlers did not, launching one of the slickest and most effective media campaigns of the decade: the suffering of a little-known former KGB officer in a British hospital became a global news event that transfixed readers and viewers from Moscow to Washington.

A firestorm of choreographed publicity, medical assessments, speculation, accusation and news reports burst around his inert figure.

The essence of an effective campaign to mould public opinion is always to devise a simple, consistent and dramatic message. Litvinenko's story was compelling, appealing to every ingrained Western suspicion about Putin's Russia: noble defector brought low by Kremlin. It was a story that would build quickly to a climax that no one had foreseen. But it was not told in words alone. The key was the now-famous photograph of the stricken former KGB officer on his deathbed.

One moment, Litvinenko's suffering had been relayed only by word of mouth. The next, its import was magnified a thousand-fold by the photograph. With all the speed and facility of digital technology, the image sped around the world on websites, television stations, cell phones, news agency wires and newspapers. The portrait of a dying man became ubiquitous – graphic and seemingly incontrovertible evidence of Russian malevolence, of a resurgent Cold War, of a mystery full of imponderable questions and players: spies, tycoons, poisoners and conspirators. Twinned with the unsmiling images of an undemonstrative Vladimir Putin, the photograph bonded the two men for ever – autocrat and victim.

A few months later, in his fifth-floor office above London's fashionable Curzon Street, Tim Bell reminisced about his coup, sitting in shirtsleeves with an elegantly tailored pin-striped suit jacket draped over a leather chair. He smoked incessantly, leaving the windows of his eyrie open to waft away the fumes. During the conversation, he took calls from clients to advise them on all manner of public relations and presentational issues. Bell was a veteran of many campaigns, knighted in 1990 by Margaret Thatcher for advising her in three election victories, then made a life peer as Baron Bell of Belgravia in 1998, taking his title from one of London's most expensive neighbour-hoods.

'What made the whole story was the photograph,' Bell said.

It had been taken, at University College Hospital shortly before Litvinenko's death, by a little-known photographer, Natasja Weitsz. She had been commissioned by Jennifer Morgan, one of Bell's employees, for a one-off fee to shoot what she thought was supposed to be a portrait for the family. Instead, the photograph became almost literally an icon.

Weitsz seemed a curious candidate for the job of producing what would become one of the world's best-known news photo-graphs. At the time, she was twenty-nine years old, an immigrant from South Africa who had come to London seven years earlier to work off college debts and ended up staying on to acquire British citizenship.

Photography was a hobby, not a profession, and she found a job at a Snappy Snaps photographic print shop located in Shepherd's Market, a Victorian alleyway close to Bell Pottinger's headquarters in Curzon Street. In mid-November, she had been commissioned by Morgan for a corporate shoot, and Morgan judged her to be a sensitive and sympathetic person. Morgan had her cell-phone number to hand and called her on Sunday 19 November 2006, to offer another assignment: a portrait of Alexander Litvinenko on what was to become his deathbed at UCH.

Weitsz had not been following the news closely and was unaware of who Litvinenko was, although 'his name gave away the fact that he was Russian.' According to Morgan, Litvinenko himself had requested the photograph, and the publication rights would be given to his family.

Initially, the shoot was set for Monday 20 November 2006, at noon, but when Morgan and Weitsz arrived at the hospital, Litvinenko was undergoing some form of treatment to his spine, and his cries of agony rang out from his room. He was in no state to be photographed.

The two women, along with Alex Goldfarb, went to lunch and returned at 3.00 p.m. on the same day. 'He was in intensive care, the critical care unit. I had to wash my hands and wear a little apron,' Weitsz said.

When she went into the room, Litvinenko had just taken a sip of water and had sunk back into the pillows of his bed. According to Morgan, Litvinenko opened his shirt to show the medical sensors attached to his chest. 'It was: "This is what has been done to me,"' Morgan said. 'What you saw is how it was.'

Weitsz had a similar recollection.

'I was only in there for about a minute,' she said. 'I stood right by the door. I fired off six shots, and bounced flash from the ceiling. He was very weak. He had a plastic cup in his hand. He took a sip of water and leaned back. I said: "I'll be as quick as I can."'

Had she tried in that brief period to suggest how he should be posed? 'I didn't do anything to him. I wouldn't try to.'

Already, Litvinenko was coming to the end. 'He couldn't really talk or anything,' she said.

As she took the six photographs, she moved the zoom adjustment on the camera from a wide shot, displaying an array of instruments and monitors encircling his bed, to the closer, full-face portrait that became the emblem of the Litvinenko story.

Litvinenko's head was smooth and hairless. His skin was yellow as old parchment. The boyish looks and crooked smile had gone. The photograph showed him oddly resigned, his chest covered in electrocardiogram sensors. There was a faint curl of his lips: his father likened it to the enigmatic expression of the *Mona Lisa*.

Once she had taken the six photographs, Weitsz returned to the Snappy Snaps studio near Curzon Street and downloaded the images from her camera on to a computer. Then she burned the pictures on to a CD-ROM for Jennifer Morgan. Even as she was doing that, the radio playing in the studio carried a news item saying photographs of the dying Russian were about to be published. Bell Pottinger sent the photographs on to news outlets, and the images went round the world as a free handout – with no credit initially to the photographer. A more news-savvy professional would have sold the images for a small fortune, and in the days after the photograph was taken an acrimonious dispute erupted between Snappy Snaps and Bell Pottinger.

A year later, Weitsz insisted that she had not become rich from it. Indeed, she said, she struggled to come up with the year-end airfare – usually around £1,000 – to her native country. Both sides indicated to me that some kind of settlement had been reached, belatedly giving the photographer credit for her work and placing the sales of the image in the hands of a major international picture agency, Getty Images. There was a financial settlement involving Snappy Snaps, too, but neither Morgan nor Weitsz would discuss it.

The photograph had enormous impact. By the time Weitsz got home that evening, 'It was absolutely everywhere. It was even on the news in South Africa,' she said.

In no time, Litvinenko and his handlers convinced even the most sceptical observers that his fate was real.

'People were questioning how ill he was, and what the picture did was to say: here is a really ill man. He wanted the world to know,' Bell said.

In case anyone missed the point, Alex Goldfarb, who had by now become the public face of the Litvinenko saga, came up with the soundbite *du jour*. 'He looks like a ghost,' he said.

In Moscow, a parallel strand of events offered a tantalizing sub-plot. Andrei Lugovoi, the former KGB bodyguard who had worked for Boris Berezovsky and who had met Litvinenko in the Pine Bar on the day he began to sicken, was one of the very first suspects identified in British newspaper reports. But if he was a killer, he behaved like an extremely solicitous murderer – or like a master of yet one more play of bluff and double bluff in what was rapidly turning into a chronicle of deceit and disinformation.

Lugovoi made a series of telephone calls starting the day after his final face-to-face meeting with Litvinenko in the Pine Bar and continuing until after his death. From the timing of the calls, it seemed Lugovoi knew of Litvinenko's plight even before the newspaper *Novaya Gazeta* called Yuri Felshtinsky to ask for comment on 8 November.

'I called him on the seventh,' Lugovoi said. 'He was in the hospital already. His wife took the phone when I called, she gave him the receiver, and we spoke for some time. I asked about his health, and he said he had been unconscious for two days and said he thought he had probably been poisoned. I would say that when we spoke on the seventh, he was not as categorical about it as he was later.

'I called him on the thirteenth after he already made the state-ment and all these declarations regarding Italy started circulating in the press. I mean this Italian, I won't mention his name, I am not sure I remember it right.'

After Litvinenko's death on 23 November 2006, Lugovoi called Marina, ostensibly to offer condolences.

But Marina was not answering her cell phone. In the voice mail Lugovoi left, the widow told me later, he promised he would do all he could to find out what happened to Alexander Litvinenko.

'I was just shocked, actually,' Marina told me. 'Actually, I was surprised because he said, "I don't know why everybody says that I killed Sasha, but I will try to do everything just to know who did it." '

In the last few days of his life, Litvinenko slipped in and out of consciousness. Reporters huddled on the dank November pavement outside University College Hospital, awaiting snippets, bulletins from those authorized by the family to run the gauntlet of armed and uniformed police officers guarding his room in the intensive care unit.

'Finally the bastards got me,' Litvinenko told a visiting friend, the Russian filmmaker Andrei Nekrasov. The remark was duly relayed to journalists.

Late on the evening of 22 November and in the early hours of 23 November, his heart failed. He was resuscitated, but not for long. On the evening of Thursday 23 November 2006, Litvinenko finally expired. A police bulletin put the time of his death at 9.21 p.m. The cause of death was not stated.

Twenty-two days after falling ill, Alexander Litvinenko was dead, not – as his poisoners may or may not have wished – in anonymous silence and obscurity, but in a klieg-light blaze of global publicity. For his supporters, his death provided the final, grisly vindication of his indictment of Vladimir Putin. But more sceptical outsiders raised another, troubling question: had he been cynically used, even as he lay dying, for the purposes of *émigré* propaganda?

The morning after Litvinenko died – but before the British authorities publicly announced the nature of his poisoning – Alex Goldfarb stood outside University College Hospital to recite what was said to be Litvinenko's deathbed testament, the final joust in his long duel with the Kremlin.

Encircled by rolling television cameras, photographers' flash-bulbs and reporters scribbling into notebooks, Goldfarb read from a text full of bathos and melodrama:

I would like to thank many people: my doctors, nurses, and hospital staff who are doing all they can for me, the British police who are pursuing my case with rigour and professionalism and are watching over me and my family. I would like to thank the British government for taking me under their care. I am honoured to be a British citizen.

I would like to thank the British public for their messages of support and for the interest they have shown in my plight.

I thank my wife, Marina, who has stood by me. My love for her and our son knows no bounds.

But as I lie here, I can distinctly hear the beating of wings of the angel of death. I may be able to give him the slip, but I have to say my legs do not run as fast as I would like. I think, therefore, that this may be the time to say one or two things to the person responsible for my present condition.

You may succeed in silencing me, but that silence comes at a price. You have shown yourself to be as barbaric and ruthless as your most hostile critics have claimed.

You have shown yourself to have no respect for life, liberty or civilized values.

You have shown yourself to be unworthy of your office, to be unworthy of the trust of civilized men and women.

You may succeed in silencing one man, but the howl of protest from around the world will reverberate, Mr Putin, in your ears for the rest of your life. May God forgive you for what you have done, not only to me but to beloved Russia and its people.

The precise origins of the statement seemed something of a mystery: why was it in English when Litvinenko spoke so little English – and certainly not fluently enough to compose such a stirring self-eulogy? Just five weeks earlier, Litvinenko had asked for a translator at the Frontline Club. So where had he found this oratorical flourish and perfect grammar? The statement was dated 21 November 2006, two days before he finally succumbed, so why was it released only after his death? And who was its true author if Litvinenko was slipping in and out of a coma for the last days of his life, his heart failing under the strain of a massive toxic onslaught?

As Putin himself remarked, somewhat acidly, at a news conference in Helsinki on the day that Goldfarb read out the statement in London: 'As far as Litvinenko's last letter is concerned, I can say that if it did indeed turn up before his death, then why wasn't it published when he was still alive? And if the letter turned up after his death, then obviously . . . well, what more can I say? The people who did this are not the Lord God. And unfortunately, Mr Litvinenko was not Lazarus.'

There was an explanation for the timing, offered by the Berezovsky camp.

Initially, Bell said, Litvinenko's family had wished to release the statement when it was completed on 21 November. They sought Bell's advice, but he insisted that its tone was too funereal at a time when Litvinenko was still alive and might, conceivably, stage a last-minute recovery.

'I said: "Don't put it out, because it reads like something someone has written to have it read out after they have died. It reads like the last will and testament," ' Bell said. The authorship seemed more of a tangle. Litvinenko had his ideas, which he offered to Alex Goldfarb. Goldfarb put together a draft in conjunction with George Menzies, the Litvinenko family lawyer who had overseen their initial asylum application six years earlier. But whose idea was it in the first place? Had Litvinenko been pressured into making a statement that would feed directly into the vicious political and personal battle between Vladimir Putin and Boris Berezovsky? Had his agony been used as a proxy weapon in the war to discredit the Kremlin and ensure that no hint of blame for Litvinenko's destiny attached to Berezovsky himself?

'When he told me that he wanted there to be a letter and a photograph, I was appalled. I definitely didn't want him to be photographed in that state,' Marina Litvinenko said in her wide-ranging interview with Natalia Gevorkyan.

'I said, "Sasha, think about it, you'll get well, and then you'll have to see these photographs." '

'But he wanted to be photographed?' the reporter asked.

'He was certain that both a written document and a photograph were necessary. And now I understand that it was only when the photograph appeared that everyone figured out that something terrible was going on.'

'So who wrote down the text of the letter?'

'Our lawyer, who has helped us ever since we ended up in England. Sasha asked me to call him.'

When Marina Litvinenko returned to this issue in subsequent conversations, she seemed to indicate that her husband's role had been more to approve the draft of the statement than to compose it. And there was a third hand in the actual drafting – Alex Goldfarb, who had so often stood guard at the key intersections of Litvinenko's destiny.

'He asked me what his chances were. I said fifty-fifty,' Goldfarb said. 'He said he wanted to do something, blame Putin. He gave me some ideas. I went and drafted it. Then read it to him. Marina was there.'

Some of the language – such as the reference to the 'wings of the angel of death' – was 'my draft', Goldfarb said. But Marina Litvinenko insisted that her husband had agreed fully and understood what would be said – even if, at that time, it was not clear when it would be made public. 'Sasha agreed with all the words that they put on paper,' she told me. The final polishing in English was left to George Menzies.

Akhmed Zakayev said he recalled Menzies arriving at the hospital to finalize the statement on 21 November before Litvinenko became comatose. But 'he was very weak' on that day, Marina Litvinenko said, 'and even the policemen decided not to interrupt him, and when we visited him, it was his decision to make this statement.'

The date of 21 November had also been inscribed on a signed copy of the final statement in the possession of Vladimir Bukovsky.

Litvinenko's signature and his inscription of the date were both in a shaky hand. It was the autograph of a man who knew that a different kind of writing was on the wall. By that day Litvinenko must have known that time was running out. The moment had come to make his final dispositions – and that extended to matters of faith.

'One day Sasha asked: "When I am out of hospital if I can go to mosque with Akhmed" – he thought one day he'll be OK,' Marina Litvinenko said. She remembered that he persisted, asking her: 'Are you OK if I go' to the mosque? 'And I said: "Why not?" I am not formal about this, and I said: "Sasha, OK. Why not?"'

As his condition worsened, though, Litvinenko's thoughts darkened, filled with foreboding that he would not pull through, nagged by worries about where he would be buried. 'When he was very bad and very weak, he asked Akhmed to give him a promise to take his body to put it in the same place [as Zakayev] because for Sasha it was like brothership,' his widow said.

'In the last couple of years when Akhmed Zakayev started to be our neighbour, they started to be very close friends. Sasha said: "I will be very proud to be Russian to speak with Chechen, to build this relationship, even if it is small."'

The friendship was such that when Litvinenko visited Israel in 2006 and spent some time in Jerusalem, he purchased a Koran in the holy city as a gift for Zakayev.*

Zakayev offered his own account.

'He converted to Islam on 4 November, in the evening. He recited the sura in Arabic. He told his wife in my presence at the Barnet Hospital and then at UCH around the sixteenth or seventeenth. On the twenty-first he said he converted to Islam and would like to be buried in accordance with Islamic law. Then he said he would like his body to be taken to Chechnya, to the

---

* Litvinenko's father recalled that when his son came to fly out of Israel, the airport security officers had some searching questions about why an Orthodox Christian was carrying a Koran on to a plane as a gift for a Chechen Muslim known in Moscow as a terrorist.

Caucasus, and be reburied there. To convert, it was enough to say: "There is no God other than Allah, and Muhammad is his prophet." It suffices to say that one sentence to be converted to Islam. From that moment, the person is to be a Muslim.'

In the very last hours of Litvinenko's life – 'when Sasha was unconscious,' as Marina put it – Zakayev brought an alim, a Muslim scholar, to the hospital to recite Koranic verses over Litvinenko to seal his conversion to Islam.

'On the twenty-second, his heart stopped twice, and then he has not regained consciousness,' Zakayev said. 'He was in a coma, and, fulfilling his wishes as he wanted to be buried in accordance with Islamic law, on the twenty-third we invited an alim . . . to give him the last rites.'

Litvinenko's father Walter, who visited several times in the hospital, acknowledged later that his son spent his last conscious hours believing he was a Muslim. 'When we lived in Nalchik, there were Russians, Muslims, living together, and I preferred the Muslims, they were better brought up,' the father said in an interview in London shortly after the first anniversary of his son's death.

Islam was by no means unfamiliar in the elder Litvinenko's family: Walter already had a Muslim son-in-law, married to his daughter, Tatiana, in Nalchik.

'When he was in hospital, I went to make the sign of the cross. Sasha said: "Wait, I have accepted Islam." I was completely taken aback by this. It was like Sasha was on a much higher spiritual level. I said: "There is no harm in having one more Muslim in the family." '

His only concern, he half-joked, half-wept, was that his son should not embrace Communism, fascism or Satanism.

Litvinenko's half-brother Maxim also displayed little surprise at the apparent conversion. 'He was always very religious. He always wore a cross. He believed in God. He was a true believer,' he said. 'And you can give God many names. The Orthodox communicate through their priests; the Muslims directly.'

But there was no doubt, either, that his wife had humoured him in his illness, not wishing to take his conversion too seriously. 'I can't say I support it,' she said shortly after his death. 'Just a few months ago he was in Jerusalem and was amazed about the Christian culture.'

Whatever the mystery of his faith, there was a more pressing question: what, and who, had killed him?

Three hours before Litvinenko died, panic bells began to sound throughout the ministries and whispering offices of Whitehall. An emergency and secret committee of senior government, police, public health and intelligence officials was called into session under the dramatic code name COBRA (the acronym denotes the Cabinet Office Briefing Room A, where such meetings take place). At around 6.00 p.m. government scientists at the Health Protection Agency were recalled to their offices and told to prepare for a major operation to contain any public health risk and to forestall national panic. Then, while the city slept, police closed down and sealed off two of the locations Litvinenko had visited on the day he began to die – the itsu sushi bar on Piccadilly and the Pine Bar at the Millennium Hotel.

Until that point, the cause of Litvinenko's death had been a mystery. But now scientists at Britain's Atomic Weapons Establishment in Aldermaston, a closely guarded 750-acre site in Berkshire, had reached a conclusion that turned the poisoning of a former KGB officer into a matter of urgent global concern. It was a discovery that raised terrifying unknowns: if the British authorities had now identified the poison, then the questions of why and how it was used suddenly seemed infinitely more opaque and menacing.

For almost a day, the British public remained ignorant of the scientists' discovery as the authorities sought to devise a strategy to break the news. Even Litvinenko's closest family was not immediately informed.

On the final day after visiting the critically ill Litvinenko, Marina said, 'I went home, and before I could put Tolya to bed – I had just gone into the bathroom – the phone rang. It was the hospital again: "Come quickly," they said. "Tolya," I said, "are you coming with me?" He told me he wanted to come. He didn't even think about it – he just decided on the spot. When we got to the hospital, they took us into a different room than where he was. I understood immediately what had happened. The doctors told me that they had been doing everything they could, but that nothing was helping, and they told us that we could go in and say goodbye to him.'

At that point, the British authorities had unravelled the secret of the toxin that poisoned Litvinenko. But it was only at 3.00 the next morning that the police arrived at the house in Osier Crescent, with its Cross of St George banner, and told Marina Litvinenko to pack and go. That, she said, was when she discovered the cause of her husband's death.

'It was a very serious talk about why my husband died, and I saw how it was difficult for them to understand that it was real. When they asked me to leave home, they said: "Could you take your clothes?" '

The order to pack for a long absence was the first inkling she had that she was unlikely to be returning to Osier Crescent any time soon, if ever.

By the morning of Friday 24 November the corridors of power were abuzz with a rumour that had been too daunting to even entertain as Litvinenko sickened – first, it was suggested, as a result of bad sushi, then because of thallium poisoning, and now because of something in a different league altogether. A Whitehall contact called me mid-morning to tell me not to leave early for the weekend: something big was happening. 'Don't leave town,' he said.

The head of Britain's Health Protection Agency, Pat Troop, had already been summoned back urgently from a conference in Helsinki, Finland. She was desperately trying to find a flight to London to address a news conference.

Then the bombshell came.

In mid-afternoon, Troop announced that Litvinenko had been

found to have ingested polonium-210 – an extremely rare radioactive isotope. His death was 'an unprecedented event in the UK in that someone has apparently been poisoned by a type of radiation', Troop said.

Most ordinary Britons had never heard of polonium-210, and scientists were baffled about how such a rare substance could have found its way into the body of a civilian with no known links to the nuclear industry.

'To most chemists this is astonishing,' said Andrea Sella, a lecturer in inorganic chemistry at University College London. 'It is one of the rarest elements on the earth's crust and also one of the most exotic.'

But politicians had a different cause for bemusement and fear. The cause of death was radiation – the ultimate threat, the nightmare that had stalked the Cold War and its build-up of nuclear arsenals. The world's main source of polonium was Russia, and Litvinenko's death had all the makings of a Russian drama conceived in the Kremlin and played out on British soil with utter contempt for British laws and sensibilities.

The use of polonium was an implicit declaration of hostilities. But it almost went undetected.

What was not generally known on the day that Alexander Litvinenko died was that the polonium had been discovered only in one of the final urine samples taken from him. If the Ministry of Defence scientists at Aldermaston had not run the extremely unusual tests when they did, it is conceivable that the nature of the poisoning would have remained a mystery, as Litvinenko's killers surely intended it to be.

Instead, the secret was out. Polonium-210 – invisible to the eye, tasteless, utterly lethal – had been introduced into his body some time on that fateful November day that had started so innocuously on a bus in Muswell Hill.

The poison had not been detected earlier because polonium is one of those substances that emits alpha rays rather than the more usual gamma rays. No one had even thought to look for alpha rays until the scientists at the Atomic Weapons

Establishment ran their tests and began to suspect the isotope's presence. Consider, too, another quality of polonium: it has a half-life of 138 days, meaning that every four and a half months its radiation ebbed by half. If the isotope had not been found when it was found, all evidence of its presence would have slowly fizzled away.

The scientists' conclusion began to explain how Litvinenko died. Once introduced into his body – either swallowed or breathed in or entering through an open wound – the isotope tore relentlessly through his bone marrow and organs, destroying the immune system. The lethal dose measured a tiny fraction of a microgram, a mere speck, but it was far more than was needed to guarantee his death.

'Once it was in his body,' a senior health official told me at the time, 'he never had a chance.'

This was no ordinary murder. Whoever planned it had gone to extraordinary lengths to carry out a killing as bizarre as it was baffling.

Two weeks after his death, Litvinenko's family, friends and associates gathered to bury him. An autopsy had been carried out, and the body had been released for burial under several restrictions: it could not be cremated for fear of releasing radiation into the atmosphere; it could not lie in an open coffin, as is the Orthodox Christian way; and it could not be washed in the Muslim way. The heavy oak casket, sealed under close scrutiny by government inspectors, was borne aloft by straining pallbearers.

On 7 December 2006 heavy rain fell over north London with a freak ferocity – as if the heavens were punishing the land. Unusually in London, a tornado pummelled some districts, tearing off roof tiles. The roll call of mourners at the funeral in Highgate West Cemetery became a Who's Who of Litvinenko's allies and the Kremlin's foes: Boris Berezovsky, Andrei Nekrasov, Akhmed Zakayev, Vladimir Bukovsky and Alex Goldfarb among them. Walter Litvinenko, the dead man's father, attended, as did his mother, Nina, his ex-wife, Natalia, and the children from his first marriage, Sonya and Alexander. Marina Litvinenko, in wraparound dark glasses and widow's sombre clothing under a black umbrella, seemed etched by grief. The father proclaimed: 'My son was killed by those who had every reason to fear what he knew. To fear the truth he told.'

A colleague recounted strolling down Swain's Lane before the funeral and coming across Berezovsky's £300,000 Maybach car parked at the roadside, with bodyguards in attendance. As he advanced, brandishing his visiting card from the *Financial Times,* a rear window slid down and a hand emerged, took the card and withdrew as the tinted window slid closed again.

The site chosen for the burial plot seemed deliberately conspicuous, close to a junction in the overgrown paths that lead through the laurels and hollies of this dark and unkempt cemetery – first created in 1839 to cope with the funeral needs of an expanding city. Now it was maintained by a charity that fought a losing battle against roots and overgrowth and obelisks canted at crazy angles – a forbidding and spooky place where many tombstones, green with age and neglect, had fallen aslant in untended thickets of foliage. There were family crypts and fallen sculptures of angels. The cemetery's design was almost fanciful, like some kind of Victorian folly suggesting the broad horizons of Britain's imperial reach in the nineteenth century. At its highest point, just below the Church of St Michael in Highgate village, a circle of family mausoleums was demarcated by pillars that might have come from ancient Egypt. It was known as the Circle of Lebanon, and a great cedar spreads its branches over a central grassy mound. There was space for above-ground coffins and a separate area, sealed by a dungeon-like iron gate draped with tributes of tulips, curved like swans' necks over the rusted crossbars of the grille. The Columbarium, as it was called, contained the ashes of those who had been cremated. For all its obvious decline, there was an exclusivity about being buried there: Litvinenko's modest plot was said to have cost Berezovsky around £7,000.

After his burial, the Litvinenko family asked that his grave not become a place of public spectacle or pilgrimage, but the regular £5-a-head walking tours through the cemetery still passed close to his final resting place. Months later, when I took the tour, the grave was still fresh, the turned soil held in place by wooden boards and covered with polyanthus plants in bright primary colours. A photograph of Litvinenko doubled as a headstone as the earth settled over his coffin. Proud of his English heritage, Litvinenko, in death, was flanked by headstones from families with distinctly British names – Benjamin and Maria Smith, families called Hitchcock and Gillette. His grave lay opposite the family mausoleum of Sir Loftus Otway, a British general who had fought in the nineteenth-century Iberian Peninsula wars. The Otway tomb was held by some aficionados of the occult to have inspired Bram Stoker's novel *Dracula* (although others argued that another cemetery at nearby Hendon had been the model). In any event, Otway's epitaph might well have been chosen by Litvinenko's hagiographers. 'Brave and gentle, honourable, generous and true, possessed of rare and highly cultivated mental powers, he has not left earth a kinder heart or more gallant spirit,' it read. 'Gone to thy rest, brave soldier, esteemed by all, and truly loved and deeply lamented by those who knew thee best.'

On the day of the funeral, accompanied by Walter Litvinenko, Akhmed Zakayev made a highly public show of mourning at the gold-domed Regent's Park Mosque in central London before proceeding to the cemetery in Highgate. To the consternation of some at the burial, Zakayev brought with him an imam to perform Islamic rites at what was supposed to be a non-denominational service attended by Christians, Jews and Muslims. Then the funeral moved on to nearby Lauderdale House, a sixteenth-century building on Highgate Hill, where a choir sang the Christian hymn 'There Is a Green Hill Far Away'.

But the imam's intervention still rankled with some of the mourners.

Goldfarb, for one, insisted that Zakayev presented Litvinenko's family with a fait accompli. 'Marina was upset but said it was OK for them to do it,' he told me later that day. 'This will be one of the big mysteries. His Islamic friends said he did convert. He was heavily sedated at the time, but if there are people who believe he converted, let them believe it.'

Sometimes, funerals bring closure. But not this time.

Rapidly, it became clear that Litvinenko's death was part of a much bigger question, one whose answer would define the geopolitics of a generation of Russians. At first, his murder seemed to be no more than some lost chapter of the Cold War, surfacing like a forgotten fragment of a manuscript discovered among the irrelevant memorabilia of a bygone age. But it was also seen by Litvinenko's friends as a thoroughly modern killing, the emblem and harbinger of a new, perilous and cavalier assertiveness in the Kremlin, a revival of the most arrogant and brutal ways of the old KGB that, by a curious irony, had nurtured both Alexander Litvinenko and Vladimir Putin.

Incontrovertibly, a man lay dead, felled by radiation poisoning in central London. For some in the conspiratorial cliques of Londongrad, it was a death that had been inevitable from the moment Litvinenko tilted at the authorities and fled Moscow. For others it raised another question: if polonium-210 could be smuggled into London, what other obscure radioactive materials were out there? And in whose hands?

The people of Britain and the United States had frequently heard their leaders evoking the need to safeguard nuclear materials from unscrupulous agents of mayhem. That had been one of the central arguments to justify the invasion of Iraq in 2003. Yet it had happened not in the Middle East or Iran or Afghanistan but in London, in the genteel confines of Grosvenor Square.

Nuclear smuggling was not by any means unknown to the world's law enforcement agencies. Led by the United States, the effort to contain nuclear proliferation had absorbed the energies of the Western nuclear powers for years. Since the end of the Cold War, Libya and South Africa had been persuaded, or had volunteered, to rid themselves of nuclear weapons. But the attentions of policy-makers in Washington, London and elsewhere had been focused on bigger threats to the delicate nuclear balance, from the activities of the errant Pakistani nuclear scientist A. Q. Khan to the nuclear programmes of Iran and North Korea.

While Western diplomats and intelligence agencies had been transfixed by the prospect of those two nations deploying nuclear weapons, a lethal quantity of nuclear material simply slipped past their gaze to surface in an English hotel across the way from an American embassy. If there was the slightest hint of Russian state involvement in the Litvinenko affair, then the killing broke all the rules – not simply those related to taking life or abusing sovereignty, but also those concerning the written and unwritten covenants of the nuclear age: only a rogue state would play murderous games with radiation.

From that perspective, Litvinenko's death alone would have been enough to grab the headlines, but it was far from the whole story. It was, in a way, Agatha Christie in reverse: an initial appearance of clarity that dissolved into a bewildering array of versions.

12

INVISIBLE ASSASSIN

It might seem whimsical to assign the characteristics of a living being to a physical substance. But in this story – Sasha's story, as some called it – polonium became not simply a weapon of destruction but a player in its own right, an entity with a distinctive history, an identifiable personality, a sinister agent with its own dark cloak and sharp dagger.

The annals of polonium stretch from groundbreaking scientific research in the late nineteenth century to the earliest days of nuclear rivalry between East and West and on, finally, to the perils of modern terrorism and the spread of nuclear materials.

Polonium had been researched in detail as a trigger for the first atomic bombs, then largely forgotten as developments in nuclear science overtook its usefulness to the military machines of East and West. Experiments on animals – and some humans – showed that its toxicity was ferocious. Learned reports demonstrated just how easily it escaped any confines imposed on it to cause harm.

The suffering of Alexander Litvinenko, in other words, had long been anticipated in the academic journals and on the laboratory benches of American and Russian scientific institutions during the Cold War. But by 2006 that knowledge had largely been buried in dusty notebooks and forgotten files. Little wonder, then, that the physicians at Barnet and UCH were so baffled by the symptoms it caused: polonium ranked as one of the most obscure, most bizarre and yet most merciless of poisons.

If it were to be anthropomorphized, or mythologized, it would be depicted as devious, sneaky, elusive – a malign sprite, an evil genie, a djinn of destructiveness. Its sheer energy punched out atoms that could attach to a mote of dust – spreading, settling on surfaces, absorbed in lungs, on lips, invisible.

Imagine an unstoppered vial left in a room overnight with just the merest trace of polonium-210 inside. By morning the room would be speckled with contamination by one of the nastiest poisons known to science. The polonium would spill, tumble, rise on air currents, attach to surfaces and solidify, emitting alpha particles that ordinary Geiger counters could not register. Its internal energy would recoil on itself, sending not just alpha particles but clusters of atoms into the air. But only when introduced into the human body by ingestion, by inhalation or through an open wound would it begin its dreadful, lethal business.

It had another quality, too.

Once identified, polonium was a telltale, a braggart, a substance whose whereabouts were blindingly evident to those who knew what they were looking for. It leaped free from any attempt to contain it, spreading and smearing traces of its presence everywhere it had been, on tabletops, door handles, clothes, light switches, taps. The isotope drove the police investigation into Litvinenko's death – not simply as a toxin but also as a vital clue in naming the prime suspect, almost a suspect in its own right.

Its characteristics enabled law enforcement officers to track the movements of Litvinenko and his adversaries as clearly as if they had worn a spy-thriller homing device, following them from where they drank to where they slept, from where they ate to where they partied. Polonium told the police who spoke to whom and where. Polonium created the distinctively gruesome manner of Litvinenko's demise, his organs hollowed out by a barrage of harmful particles generated by its ferocious internal energy. As Peter Zimmerman, an American physicist, put it at the time, 'It was as if his internal organs received a severe sunburn and peeled.'

Most important of all, polonium offered vital clues to Litvinenko's movements on 1 November: within six hours of ingesting the isotope, he would begin to show signs of radiation sickness and would begin to contaminate objects he touched much earlier.

The British authorities, in fact, narrowed down the moment and the modality of the poisoning to the tea that Litvinenko drank in the Pine Bar of the Millennium Hotel with two Russians – Andrei Lugovoi, a former KGB bodyguard, and Dmitri Kovtun, once an officer in a reconnaissance unit of the Red Army.

As improbable as it might sound, the first confirmed act of nuclear terrorism in the West came when a former KGB officer was brought low by toxins in a teapot.

Mention poisoning in London by the KGB and the first thought of many people until the Litvinenko case was of Georgi Markov, a Bulgarian journalist, author and playwright then living there. Markov left his native land in 1969 and took refuge in Britain in the early 1970s. His speciality, both at the Bulgarian-language service of the BBC and at Radio Free Europe, was to criticize the Bulgarian Communist regime led by the dictator Todor Zhivkov.

In September 1978 Markov died mysteriously at the age of forty-nine, three days after a stranger carrying an umbrella bumped into him at a bus stop near Waterloo Bridge and then walked off, apologizing as he went.

Following Markov's death, scientists at Porton Down, the secretive British germ warfare facility, discovered that a tiny metal pellet the size of a pinhead had been injected into his thigh, presumably from the tip of the umbrella. The pellet contained the poison ricin. High-level former KGB officers, including the defector and double agent Oleg Gordievsky, later confirmed that the KGB played an important part in devising and designing the means of attack. It transpired later that a similar pellet had been fired into the back of another Bulgarian, Vladimir Kostov, in Paris, ten days earlier, but had failed to kill him.

The Markov murder became a template for KGB poisoning: it was punitive and ingenious; it required a specialist knowledge of highly toxic materials and was meant to give the poisoner time to escape. No one was ever punished for the Markov killing, and the post-Communist authorities in Sofia closed the file in 2006. Yet in 2005 the Bulgarian journalist Hristo Hristov identified the assassin as Francesco Gullino, a Dane of Italian origin who entered Britain undercover as an antiques dealer with the code name Agent Piccadilly. Hristov said the killer left London the day after the attack, travelling to Rome to meet his handler. By the time Markov died, therefore, the killer had disappeared, as his superiors intended.

Perhaps the biggest single advantage of poisoning – as opposed to any other form of assassination – is that it enables the killer to melt away long before the victim dies.

The history of poisoning suggests some other basic requirements.

The crime should remain unsolved for as long as possible – preferably indefinitely: by definition, who could tell how many other poisonings had been completely successful?

The poison should contain a sufficient dose to guarantee the required outcome but remain untraceable. But if the poison is detected, then the poisoner's handlers must have prepared a plausible story to divert blame. Those criteria become all the more significant if the poisoner chooses a radioactive toxin.

Consider, for instance, the following definition of a successful poisoning using a 'munition' based on radiation: 'The source of the munition, the fact that an attack has been made and the kind of attack should not be determinable if possible. The munition should be inconspicuous and readily transportable.'

Death by polonium matched these criteria almost exactly, but the people who formulated them were not from the KGB or its successor.

Quite the opposite, in fact.

This primer in radioactive poisoning was part of a debate within the US Army about the potential use of radioactive toxins to assassinate 'important individuals'.

The American records – still heavily censored – were released in October 2007 in response to a request under the Freedom of Information Act by the Associated Press, which called its scoop 'one of the longest-held secrets of the Cold War'.

It was unclear from the documents whether the United States ever used radiological weapons in this way. But, the Associated Press reported, there was a clear desire on the part of military planners that the US government's involvement in any such attack not be traceable – a concept known in US covert actions as 'plausible deniability'.

The quest for the perfect poisoning had long preoccupied the KGB and its political masters, too.

In 1954 Nikolai Khokhlov, a senior KGB officer, was sent to West Germany to oversee the assassination of a prominent Russian émigré and dissident, Georgi Okolovich.

Khokhlov worked for Pavel Sudoplatov, a high-ranking Stalin-era spymaster who reported directly to Lavrenty Beria – the head of the KGB's predecessor. (One of Sudoplatov's best-known operations, as claimed in his memoirs, was the assassination of Trotsky in Mexico in 1940.) Khokhlov was a highly regarded operative, known for the boldness of his wartime exploits behind enemy lines. But he was reluctant to become an assassin. Indeed, his wife, Yana, let him know quite clearly that she would leave him if he became a killer.

Nonetheless, armed with an array of James Bond-esque disguised weapons – guns that looked like cigarette cases, another gun that fired poisoned bullets – Khokhlov left for Frankfurt to seek out his victim. According to his memoirs, he went directly to his victim's apartment but, instead of killing him, told him: 'I've come to you from Moscow. The Central Committee of the Communist Party has ordered your liquidation. The murder is entrusted to my group . . . I cannot let this murder happen.'

After that display of clemency towards his victim, there was no way back to the Soviet Union.

Under pressure from both American and British intelligence

agencies, Khokhlov announced his defection publicly at a news conference in Bonn in April 1954. A day later, back in Moscow, his wife, Yana, and son, Alek, were arrested and sent into internal exile for five years, despite a promise by the CIA that they would be spirited to safety. They did not meet again for thirty-seven years, by which time Khokhlov had remarried.

Once in the West, the former spy built a reputation as a foe of the Kremlin, just as Litvinenko minted his anti-Moscow credentials in London half a century later.

And just as Litvinenko drank tea on 1 November 2006, so, too, did Khokhlov lower his guard, accepting a cup of coffee from a stranger at a conference of anti-Soviet militants in Frankfurt in 1957.

He sickened within hours. His hair fell out. The initial diagnosis was thallium poisoning, as it was for Litvinenko in Barnet Hospital in November 2006. Even some of the language used at the time of Litvinenko's final sickness found an echo in Khokhlov's account of his own illness.

'Nobody suspected that a chemical agent of delayed action was working in my system like a time bomb,' Khokhlov wrote in his memoirs, describing how he was subjected to 'vomiting attacks that nearly made me lose consciousness':

> When I examined a tuft of my hair which was sticking out as if worn by a clown, I involuntarily pressed it with my hand. The tuft remained in my palm. I reached for another lock, and, again, without feeling any pain or resistance, it was in my grasp.
>
> Nearly a week to the hour after my collapse, the doctors discovered that an incredibly rapid process of destruction was going on in my bloodstream. The blood in my veins was gradually turning to useless plasma. The saliva glands in my mouth, throat, and alimentary canal were drying up. It became difficult to eat, drink and even speak. I sank into apathy and was growing feeble. That Sunday evening, my friends later told me, I took on the aspect of a dying person.

Years later, Alex Goldfarb would say Litvinenko looked 'like a ghost'.

And yet Khokhlov, then thirty-five, somehow survived, and it was left to American physicians to announce that he had been poisoned with the radioactive variant of thallium, producing some of the symptoms shared much later by Litvinenko.

For many people, Khokhlov's case faded into obscurity – one more display of murderous intent in a forgotten underground conflict between the spies of East and West. But after Litvinenko's death, the tactics and manner of the earlier poisoning suddenly seemed ominously relevant – almost as if a script had been dusted off in Moscow and revived for a different age.

In a little-noticed coda to this whole saga, the former KGB official Stanislav Lekarev said he had worked in the 1950s at a secret KGB laboratory producing polonium.

'Polonium was used once in the case of Khokhlov,' Lekarev told SBS, a public service broadcaster in Australia in March 2007. While Khokhlov survived, 'it was proved that it was the case of Russian hands and the hands of the KGB.'*

Lekarev's testimony seemed only to deepen the suspicion that Litvinenko's death was the direct result of a conspiracy hatched in Moscow. At the very least, his story showed that secret laboratories exploring the use of arcane toxins had been in operation for decades.

Sudoplatov himself spoke of a toxicology laboratory known as LAB X, on Varsonofyevsky Lane in Moscow, and directed by Professor Grigori Moiseyevich Maironovsky.

'From 1937 to 1947, Maironovsky and his subordinates were

---

* After his defection, Khokhlov emigrated to the United States, where he earned a doctorate in psychology and survived long enough to outlive Litvinenko: he died in September 2007 at the age of eighty-five, in San Bernardino, California. To the end, he remained acutely aware of the precedents set by the attempt on his life – and the parallels with the Litvinenko case. 'The KGB decided to kill me,' he told an interviewer in 2006. 'From this moment there was a general direction to hunt Khokhlov. The message was: we will get the traitor, wherever he is in the world.'

used to carry out death sentences and secret liquidations with their poisons,' Sudoplatov wrote in his memoirs. Often, he said, poisonous injections would be administered as part of supposedly routine medical checks.

When he was arrested in 1953 as part of the post-Stalin purges, Sudoplatov himself faced charges that he 'supervised the work of the top-secret toxicological laboratory, which experimented with poisons on prisoners sentenced to death from 1942 to 1946'. He claimed that he was cleared of the charge. In his memoirs, however, he acknowledged that he had 'personal knowledge of four cases in 1946 and 1947 in which I was ordered to make the executions by Maironovsky look like natural deaths'.

Litvinenko, too, had spoken quite openly about such facilities.

In 2004 he told Scott Shane, a *New York Times* reporter, in a telephone interview that a KGB laboratory – Laboratory No. 12 – in Moscow had been taken over by the FSB and still specialized in the study of poisons.*

'The view inside our agency was that poison is just a weapon, like a pistol,' Litvinenko said in 2004. 'It's not seen that way in the West, but it was just viewed as an ordinary tool.'

But there was nothing ordinary about the procedures for the deployment of toxic weapons, he insisted during a phone-in with a Chechen radio station in the same year. 'The application of poisons by the Russian special services is strictly regulated,' he said. 'Only the head of the FSB or his first assistant can give the order to apply it. If it is a political murder, the head of the FSB, Patrushev, would have never dared to do it, not having informed President Putin.' His words seemed uncannily prescient considering the firestorm of accusation and denial that swirled around his death two years later.

---

* Sudoplatov also spoke of a 'top-secret Toxicological Laboratory number 12'. Another such laboratory, in southern Moscow, was known as FSB Research Institute No. 2 according to some published accounts, and had been used to explore the potential uses of nuclear materials, including polonium.

And if his assertion was true, it meant Litvinenko's death could only have been ordered at the highest level in Moscow.

Perhaps the most potent lesson from the Khokhlov case for Russian assassins was that a failed poisoning was the worst of all options – exposing the murderer while lionizing the victim.

That made the advance preparation of a plausible legend all the more imperative: if a poisoning attack was exposed, an alternative version of events must be immediately available for dissemination through pliant media outlets; the victim's credibility must be undermined; and the accuser's motives must be distorted to deflect attention from the real killer.

In his memoirs, Sudoplatov played down Khokhlov's role in the security apparatus, suggesting that much of the narrative of his defection and poisoning was untrue. Similarly, Russia's first response to Litvinenko's death was to cast him as an insignificant and inept figure manipulated by Western intelligence agencies.

Khokhlov, Sudoplatov said, had been 'caught and turned by the CIA, who made him famous by using him in an anti-Soviet propaganda campaign'.

But he made no secret of the Kremlin's preferences.

'Our leaders were always interested in poisons,' he said.

Events much later showed just how enduring that interest seemed to be.

In 2002 a poisoned letter was the suspected cause of death for a Chechen-based Islamic fighter known only as Khattab – a figure long sought by the Kremlin. In 2003, the newspaper *Novaya Gazeta* insisted that Yuri Shchekochikhin, a lawmaker and journalist, had been poisoned when he died after what appeared to be a severe allergic reaction.

Shchekochikhin was a deputy in the Duma and a member of a commission investigating the 1999 apartment-block bombings before the Second Chechen War that fascinated Litvinenko and his co-author Yuri Felshtinsky. Of the members of that commission, another, Sergei Yushenkov, was shot dead near his house in April 2003. Another person assisting the commission, Mikhail Trepashkin – one of those who attended Litvinenko's notorious press conference in 1998 and who later warned of plans to kill him – was arrested and imprisoned in October 2003.* The commission's investigation ground to a halt.

The list went on.

Viktor Yushchenko, the president of Ukraine, was badly disfigured by poisoning ascribed to dioxin in the run-up to the 2004 elections. The poisoning began to take effect after a late-night dinner at a dacha outside Kiev with Ukrainian officials from the country's SBU intelligence agency. The agency's director, General Ihor P. Smeshko, who had been present at the dinner, denied any connection with the poisoning.

In the same year, long before she was shot to death, Anna Politkovskaya complained of becoming ill and fainting after drinking tea on a flight from Moscow to cover a hostage crisis in a school at Beslan in the northern Caucasus. She said later she believed FSB agents on the plane had spiked her tea.

One day after Litvinenko died in 2006, Yegor Gaidar, a former Russian prime minister visiting Ireland, said he, too, had been poisoned. Alexander Lebedev, a former KGB officer in London who became a billionaire banker and a financial backer of *Novaya Gazeta,* said in an interview in early 2007 that he believed his food had been poisoned in a Moscow restaurant in 2006. He lost thirteen pounds but never identified the source of the toxin. In February 2007 Luzius Wildhaber, the former president of the European Court of Human Rights, told a Swiss newspaper, the *NZZ am Sonntag,* that he had fallen violently ill after visiting Russia and suspected foul play.

'The list is rather long,' Pavel Felgenhauer, an independent Russian analyst, said in 2004. 'And since Putin assumed power in Russia, poisoning has been one of the preferred political tools used by the Kremlin.'

The British authorities called the Litvinenko poisoning the first

---

* He was released in late 2007.

of its kind. But there were others who argued that its use would never have been contemplated without some prior experience and experimentation in Russia itself.

'An assassination attempt, especially one to be carried out overseas, would require a carefully tested poison; the amount of polonium-210 would need to be enough to kill but not to cause a major public health incident,' the British expert Norman Dombey wrote in the late summer of 2007. 'Just as the KGB developed the ricin capsule in the Markov case, the best method of administering polonium-210 would have to be studied.'

Dombey set about looking through the records of mysterious deaths in Russia – a substantial archive – to trace any hint of symptoms that could be related to radiation sickness.

His research was largely limited to public sources, but, citing a radiation expert consulted by Britain's Health Protection Agency, Dombey developed the thesis that, prior to the Litvinenko affair, 'tests would have been carried out on humans as well as animals in order to determine the efficacy of the dose.'

He settled on two names: Lecha Islamov and Roman Tsepov.

The two men came from vastly different backgrounds – one a Chechen prisoner, the other a power broker close to the Kremlin elite – but they had one thing in common: they had died after displaying symptoms similar to those associated with radiation poisoning.

Lecha Islamov was a Chechen guerrilla commander serving a nine-year prison sentence who died on 21 April 2004. He had been known in Soviet-era Moscow as a criminal and gangster, but returned to Chechnya in 1995 to join the same fight for independence that came to fixate Alexander Litvinenko. The FSB finally caught up with him, jailed him and consistently sought to 'turn' him while he was in prison. The last attempt to strike a deal was made on 12 March 2004, according to Russian press accounts, when FSB officers offered him his freedom in return for his cooperation in exposing ties between the Russian authorities and Chechen criminals.

He refused.

Just over one month later, his jailers summoned him for what was termed an 'informal chat', offering him a snack and tea (a possible variant on the Iraqi 'goodwill' drink).

On the way back to his cell, his relatives told Russian newspapers, he began to sicken. Islamov was hospitalized in Volgograd. He displayed symptoms including hair loss and massive blistering. Some accounts compared his case to that of Yuri Shchekochikhin in July 2003, whose death was frequently ascribed in Russia to thallium poisoning. Islamov was by no means the only Chechen whose death was blamed by his supporters on poisoning. Salman Raduyev and Turpal-Ali Atgeriev had both died mysteriously while in prison, but the Russian authorities insisted that Islamov died of natural causes.

The significance, according to Dombey, lay in the speed with which the symptoms showed themselves and the rapidity of his decline. The online newspaper *Vremya Novostei* said doctors had found his condition 'inexplicable'.

Roman Tsepov was a different matter. When he died in September 2004, at the age of forty-two, Tsepov was one of the best-connected people in St Petersburg. He had built a reputation as a political player, close to both the former St Petersburg mayor Anatoly Sobchak and his one-time deputy Vladimir Putin. A former commissar in the Interior Ministry forces, Tsepov founded a bodyguard and protection agency – Baltik-Eskort – in the early 1990s. Russian newspapers linked his name to a string of dubious ventures, one of them involving Putin himself.

Tsepov was also said to have been embroiled in overtures between the Kremlin and the Yukos oil company following the arrest of Mikhail Khodorkovsky.

A common strand in most accounts of Tsepov's demise was that he died after a trip to Moscow and was poisoned by some exotic substance – such as a heavy metal or a top-secret chemical poison from the classified list of Russia's chemical weapons.

His white blood cell count was severely depleted. His physicians had no idea what was wrong. He perished two weeks after falling sick. Dombey's linkage of the Islamov and Tsepov cases offered no clear motives for either killing, but it did throw down a challenge. Both deaths could have been caused by radiation toxicity, and if the poison was polonium, the issue could be resolved definitively.

Given polonium's 138-day half-life, Dombey calculated in 2007, some tiny but discernible toxic traces would remain in both bodies – 'enough to be detectable in tissue samples using alpha radiation spectrometry.

'So, in principle, it would be possible to establish whether polonium has killed others – but the Russian authorities would first have to allow the bodies to be exhumed,' Dombey wrote.

It was the kind of offer the Kremlin would have no trouble at all refusing.

For most people in London and elsewhere listening to the announcement by Pat Troop, the head of the Health Protection Agency, on 24 November 2006, polonium was a mystery.

The mere mention of radiation usually inspired memories of the major nuclear accidents of the twentieth century: Three Mile Island in 1979, Chernobyl in 1986, the Windscale fire in 1957.

Among older generations in the West, the nuclear threat evoked the images, lore and urban myths of the Cold War and its philosophy of mutually assured destruction: the mushroom cloud rising in its obscene majesty towards the stratosphere; the four-minute warning of impending attack by intercontinental ballistic missiles armed with multiple warheads; the bunkers where the elite would hope to live out the earth's despoiling while the ordinary people perished in this new holocaust of fire and sickness wrought by the power of the atom bomb.

Then there was the secondary – but nonetheless recurrent – nightmare of a more modest kind of nuclear accident, caused by crime or carelessness. One notable example was the well-documented theft of a radioactive device containing caesium chloride from an abandoned radiotherapy installation in Goiânia, Brazil, in 1987 – an episode that became the model for the human, clinical and security responses to what nuclear experts call 'orphaned' radioactive sources.

But the events of November 2006 opened a new chapter, arising not from an accident or chance contamination but from a deliberate act designed to claim human life. The only common ground with Goiânia lay in the way radioactivity released in urban areas challenged civil authorities to avert panic.

In the Litvinenko case, the delivery system was nothing so visible as the orphaned capsule of Goiânia.

Polonium-210 is a microscopic grain, too small to see, a speck beyond measure, yet so poisonous that, atom for atom, its toxicity outstrips cyanide chlorine gas by factors of billions. Dissolved in water or acid, it is completely invisible. Its sheer energy is such that it is sixty-four thousand times more radio-active than plutonium-239. One gram – almost one-thirtieth of an ounce – could theoretically poison hundreds of thousands of people. Left to its own devices, half a gram of the silvery grey pure polonium metal – a substantial amount in terms of toxicity and monetary value, but tiny in physical terms – would glow a faint blue and generate a temperature of five hundred degrees centigrade. It is soft enough to be scratched, energetic enough for one-thirtieth of an ounce of it to power a 140-watt lightbulb. It is so effervescent that simply securing it in a vial or container demands the most elaborate precautions. As a weapon of poisoning, polonium – number 84 on the periodic table – was unknown to Western law enforcement agencies, but its murderous credentials are impressive. There is no antidote fast enough to counter its effects once it has begun to wreak its damage. If its presence is suspected, positive identification might take days.

And yet, paradoxically, this substance is utterly feeble, a weakling. Its radioactivity – emitting alpha particles – travels less than an inch and, unlike the beta or gamma rays of better-known radioactive substances such as uranium-235, can be stopped by paper, or tinfoil, or human skin.

Many convoluted theories – some of them no more than the

'legends' of classic disinformation – emerged later to spin a web of speculation and uncertainty around Litvinenko's death, but one fact remained incontrovertible: a radioactive isotope that was supposed to be kept apart, in the closely guarded and supposedly secure world of nuclear materials protected by national security services and international treaty, had broken free from those confines with an ease that terrorists might only dream of.

And it had been used for a purpose that was surely never intended by those who discovered its existence.

In the first stirrings of human curiosity about a mysterious new force called radioactivity, Marie Sklodowska Curie made a fascinating discovery.

She was working in 1898 with a substance called pitchblende, a dark, glutinous mineral compound mined at St Joachimsthal near the German–Czech border. At that time pitchblende was used primarily as the source of uranium extracted by chemical processes and used in glazing ceramic dishware. The process left a brown residue discarded by the ton in the dark forests near the mines, a forgotten leftover.

In theory, the residual material should have been inert since its only known radioactive component had been removed. Marie Curie and her husband Pierre discovered, however, that this residue was far more radioactive, by a factor of four hundred, than the uranium that had been extracted from it. That could only be explained by the presence of some hitherto unknown substance sharing the newly discovered quality of radioactivity.

Working together in Paris, the couple also came to the belief that the residual pitchblende contained not one but two such elements. One of them – which they called radium F – was to have enormous consequences for the development of medical science as radiation came to be widely used in X-rays and cancer treatments.

The other was to have a more chequered and ambiguous

career, long before Pat Troop brought it to the world's attention on 24 November 2006.

In honour of her native Poland, Marie Curie called it polonium.

It was not long before it claimed its first victims.

Nobus Yamada was a Japanese scientist who worked on the preparation of polonium sources alongside Irène Joliot-Curie, the Curies' daughter.

He returned to Japan in 1925 and, soon afterwards, complained of feeling ill. He wrote to Joliot-Curie to say that following his homecoming, he had fainted and been bedridden ever since. Two years later, Yamada was dead.

In 1927 Sonia Cotelle, a thirty-year-old chemist working with polonium, also began to sicken. Joliot-Curie reported that she was 'in very bad health . . . she has stomach troubles, an extremely rapid loss of hair, etc.' – symptoms that would be replicated in Barnet Hospital, north London, in late 2006 by Alexander Litvinenko. Even then, polonium's Houdini-like qualities were beginning to emerge. 'It will be necessary to examine if, in the evaporation of strong solutions, there is not some polonium carried off in the air in a notable quantity,' Joliot-Curie wrote.

Cotelle died finally after a glass containing polonium shattered in her face. Yamada and Cotelle were 'the earliest known victims of polonium poisoning', according to the British scientist Norman Dombey.

Others followed.

Dror Sadeh, a physicist working on radioactive materials at the prestigious Weizmann Institute in Israel, died prematurely of cancer after a polonium leak was discovered at his laboratory in 1957, according to a study in 2006. An unidentified Russian died within thirteen days of exposure to polonium in an aerosol – a case reported by Russian health authorities only in 2001. Joliot-Curie herself died in 1956 of leukaemia linked to her work with polonium and other radioactive materials.

By then her mother's discovery had become a far more lethal

agent of destruction than Curie could have envisaged as she stirred her vats of pitchblende at the turn of the century. She could hardly have imagined that this elusive element she had found would play a central role in detonating the atomic bombs dropped on two Japanese cities, Hiroshima and Nagasaki, in 1945. But, like some satanic genie, polonium was present there, too.

One of the challenges facing the designers of the first atomic bombs was the means of initiating nuclear fission – a problem addressed in the 1940s by American scientists, whose solution was to harness polonium-210 to another isotope, beryllium. Once in contact with each other, the two isotopes combined to trigger the nuclear explosion.*

As a result, polonium was much in demand in the United States and the Soviet Union and was produced at the secret nuclear installations of both nations. In Russia, those facilities were located in closed nuclear cities whose laboratories would play a role in the Litvinenko killing long after the threat of nuclear warfare receded.

But, as the early nuclear bomb designers soon discovered, polonium had a crucial flaw: its effectiveness as a source of radiation fell by one-half every 138 days.

The scientific term for this rate of decay in nuclear materials is 'half-life'. And in an age when nuclear weapons proliferated and were kept in huge stockpiles in preparation for the Armageddon they might wreak, 'The half-life means you are always having to change the trigger, so you use other trigger materials,' said Nick Priest, a leading British expert.

Later, therefore, the half-life of polonium became a factor in the investigation into Litvinenko's death as scientists sought to determine the date the material that killed him was produced

---

* Until then, the only practical use for polonium had been a short-lived attempt by the Firestone Company to enhance the power of the spark plugs in cars in 1940.

and thus pinpoint the precise moment when the conspiracy began.

Polonium's declining value as a component in nuclear weapons left it with few obvious applications.

At one stage, President Eisenhower sought to promote a pro-gramme called Atoms for Peace, using polonium as a power source in satellites. But, again, its short half-life limited its useful-ness. The Soviet Union sent polonium into space as a heat source in its Lunokhod moon rovers.

Its reputation – such as it was – took another severe knock in the 1960s, when American researchers at Harvard detected polonium in tobacco smoke and depicted its radioactivity as a likely contributor to lung cancer. They also encountered some of the same exasperating refusal to be corralled that polonium dis-played in the Litvinenko affair, when its sheer volatility became an important factor for investigators.

'It crawls the walls,' said Vilma R. Hunt, who helped lead the studies at Harvard. 'It can be lost for a while and then come back.'

Much of what was known about polonium's toxicity derived from studies showing how it affected the organs, and the longevity, of a variety of animals – rats, baboons, tamarins, marmosets, guinea pigs, rabbits and mice. But there had for many years been clear indications of its potential impact on humans.

Indeed, in the mid-1990s the US Department of Energy de-classified documents relating to the contentious practice of using human beings for experiments into the effects of radiation.

Much of the attention – and the outrage – was directed at the injection of plutonium into subjects who had no idea what was being done to them. But, the declassified documents revealed, polonium was also administered to five patients at the University of Rochester medical facilities, starting in November 1944. The patients – four men and a woman – were all suffering from cancers of various kinds and were aged between the early thirties and the early forties. The tests were led by Robert M. Fink, assistant professor of radiology and biophysics at the University of Rochester. Four of the patients were injected with a polonium solution, and one drank water laced with the isotope.

The amounts were apparently far lower than those ingested by Alexander Litvinenko, and the five patients – one of whom died within days apparently because of his cancer – were all described as volunteers. (The fates of the other four remain unclear.) Nonetheless, the experiments at Rochester towards the end of the Second World War seemed to be the first recorded example of polonium being deliberately administered by one human being to another. Its volatility was never in doubt.

As early as 1949, a report prepared for the US Atomic Energy Commission cited an episode concerning a scientific researcher who carried around damaged metal foils containing polonium-210 wrapped in tissue and paper envelopes. 'This person's hands, the outside of the envelopes, the coat pocket he carried them in, his trouser pockets, and his personal effects such as keys, wallet, comb, etc., were highly contaminated,' the report said. Significantly, too, the report found that simply through the touch of a finger on lips, the contamination spread inside the body, where it did most harm.

With some understatement, the report said: 'The ingestion of minute quantities of polonium may cause serious injury' since it could produce 'some of the most serious types of radiation damage'.

In January 1961 America's National Academy of Sciences reported that polonium in larger amounts even defied attempts to contain it in solutions or as a salt. 'The intense radiation of milligram samples quickly decomposes most organic complexing agents and even the solvents,' it said. 'Crystal structures of solids are quickly destroyed or altered.' It was that intensity that explained Litvinenko's suffering – and led Scotland Yard's detectives to their conclusions about who killed him.

As it lost its central position in the technology of nuclear warfare, polonium was relegated to a far more modest role, virtually forgotten as weaponry became ever more lethal and sophisticated. The early health warnings and the perceptions of acute hazard seemed forgotten. In 2006 the isotope was even peddled in the United States as a collector's item in minuscule bonded amounts via the Internet for as little as $22.50 plus tax.

In the twenty-first century, polonium was still used in American industrial plants, mainly in anti-static devices designed to remove dust from films, lenses, textile mills, printing presses and laboratory scales. Typically, these anti-static devices would be sealed and bonded using silver and gold leaf to make them safe for human handling.

Some devices, such as an anti-static fan made by a company called NRD of Grand Island, New York, and retailing in 2006 for $225, contained as much as ten times the theoretical lethal dose for a human being, meaning that an experienced laboratory technician could, in principle, obtain enough polonium to kill someone by dismantling commercially available polonium sources. In its sales literature, NRD insisted that the polonium used in the static eliminator was 'fast, reliable, and highly effective. Based upon safe alpha technology, our ionizers are powered by their own internal energy sources, Polonium-210. This naturally occurring isotope is locked inside a solid foil of gold and silver, using NRD's patented encapsulation process, assuring you of a safe, sealed source of alpha ionization.' A diagram showed a sliver of bonded metal containing polonium-210 and silver sandwiched between paper-thin layers of gold plate, silver and nickel to make the isotope safe.

After Litvinenko's death, feverish speculation erupted on the Internet and elsewhere about the possibility of transforming industrial polonium sources into the toxins that killed him.

An attempt to use commercially available polonium was not technically inconceivable, confounding those who insisted that Russia was the only possible source of the lethal dose ingested by Litvinenko. But it would require intense laboratory work and a degree of stealth in acquiring static eliminators over the brief period of time dictated by the isotope's 138-day half-life.

Moreover, scientists in the United States and Britain said the conversion of a radioactive source into a toxin would demand an unusually high level of skill and experience.

'It's just chemistry to separate polonium-210 from static eliminators. It's technically possible,' Norman Dombey said. 'But you would probably kill yourself because, once you have amounts of it, you would breathe it in and you might ingest it. And if a fraction of a microgram is enough, that's what is likely to happen.

'Only a state authority would have access to this material,' he concluded.

That narrowed the field significantly.

The bulk of the world's legal polonium production – probably 97 per cent of it – took place in Russia under the guard of the FSB, but the exact amount is disputed.

Shortly after Litvinenko's death, Sergei Kiriyenko, the head of Rosatom, Russia's nuclear industry giant, told reporters that Russia produced eight grams of polonium a month and exported most of it to the United States. The destination for the isotope tallied with accounts by international regulators, who said the bulk of manufacturers using polonium-210 were indeed located in the United States. Of fifteen known manufacturers, according to the International Atomic Energy Agency in Vienna, two were located in Russia, one in France, one in Britain and eleven in the United States.

Initially, to outsiders at least, Kiriyenko's assessment of the Russian production level seemed to represent a tiny amount – less than three and a half ounces a year. But in polonium's case that represented an awful lot of radioactivity, far beyond the amount needed for known industrial purposes in the United States, or indeed for the purposes of assassination. At around the same time, another Russian official put the monthly production figure at 0.08 grams per month – slightly less than one gram, or one-thirtieth of an ounce, per year. But the US Nuclear Regulatory Commission set the bar even lower, saying America imported as little as a quarter of a gram a year – less than one-hundredth of an ounce – most of it going to the same company, NRD, that produced the $225 anti-static fan.

The discrepancy between the different sets of figures for polonium sales raised intriguing questions, suggesting that even the Russian authorities were not sure about how much polonium the country produced, and how much was diverted. But that did not alter the overwhelming conclusion about the origins of the polonium that killed Alexander Litvinenko.

Between 1946 and 1957 the Kremlin created ten closed nuclear cities, difficult to access and remote from other populated areas. They were not shown on maps available to ordinary travellers (although their images must have been captured by American satellites) and were known only by their postal addresses – Arzamas-16, Sverdlovsk-44, Chelyabinsk-65, Krasnoyarsk-45, and so on.

In the early days, residents were not allowed to leave the closed cities for vacation or family business, according to Oleg Bukharin, a Russian physicist who became a scientist at Princeton University and conducted extensive research on Russia's nuclear facilities.

The very existence of the closed cities was not even acknowledged formally in Russia until 1992, when they were given new names to shed their association with the Cold War. Arzamas-16, for instance, became Sarov. Chelyabinsk-65 was renamed Ozersk. But these centres of highly secret nuclear research and weapons making were still governed, ostensibly at least, according to tight security regimes (as, it should be said, are nuclear facilities in the United States and elsewhere).

The closed cities formed a world apart from the sprawling mass of the Soviet Union. The nearest railroad station to Sarov was Nizhny Novgorod, in the foothills of the Ural Mountains, a twelve-hour, 250-mile overnight train ride east from Moscow. Chelyabinsk-65, now Ozersk, lay 1,200 miles southeast of Moscow at the end of a thirty-six-hour journey by rail into the Urals. Others were even more remote, far to the east across

Siberia near Tomsk and Krasnoyarsk. The distances did not diminish the sheer scale of these Cold War installations.

The restricted zone at Arzamas-16 measured almost ninety square miles, and its perimeter was patrolled by Interior Ministry forces – one of Litvinenko's first units. The need for secrecy and security was obvious: the cities powered the Soviet nuclear machine, producing both bombs and warheads and the weapons-grade uranium and plutonium they required.

Yet the closed cities also offered their residents some perquisites that made them more attractive than life on a nuclear tinderbox might otherwise seem to be. Beyond the high razor-wire fences and guard towers, they acquired something of a reputation as places where scientists were cosseted with Western consumer goods, or simply with basic supplies like butter not available to most citizens, and offered schools, clinics, day care, public transport and homes. That, too, seemed modelled on the American example.

A Soviet intelligence document quoted by the spymaster Sudoplatov pointed out that while wartime Los Alamos was 'surrounded by a wire fence' and had a 'special security system', 'the people have good living conditions: comfortable apartments, sporting grounds, a swimming pool, a community club, etc.'

Even in the post-Soviet era, the very isolation of the closed cities from mainstream life offered an attraction for some Russians.

In the 1990s, as the nation's economy spun into inflation and chaos, the population of the ten remote settlements grew by 50,000 to 762,000. 'Many choose to come to the closed cities because of their low crime, and because of better housing, schools, healthcare, and public services,' according to Bukharin, the research scientist at Princeton.

It was in these *Dr. Strangelove* facilities, under the watchful eye of the KGB, that Soviet scientists worked on the design of ever more threatening armaments as the race with Washington accelerated, consuming billions of rubles and dollars in the scramble for nuclear supremacy.

Even when the Cold War ended, visitors required permits.

Outsiders were assigned minders. Journalists were routinely banned.

Frank von Hippel, professor of public and international affairs at Princeton's Program on Science and Global Security, recalled a visit to Sarov in 2000.

'It's not easy to get around,' he said. 'My wife was with me, and she was escorted even when she went to an elementary school. There was someone sitting in the lobby of the hotel to make sure we did not go out at night.' Some leading American scientists working on projects to encourage private enterprise at Sarov were barred from even boarding the overnight train from Moscow, von Hippel said.

In the United States, though, the problems of the closed cities after the fall of Communism sounded other alarms.

Russia's massive nuclear programme had become a costly, crumbling relic of Soviet global ambitions. The economic dislocation of the early 1990s left scientists competing for reliable, paid work. Reports from some of the closed cities in the 1990s spoke of administrations in debt, workers' wages unpaid, radioactive contamination spreading, the vaunted social services in decline and drug addiction on the increase.

Western policy-makers feared that Russia's weapons specialists would offer their insider knowledge to states clamouring for illicit nuclear technology, such as Iran, Iraq and North Korea. The closed cities fuelled the nightmare scenario of rogue states and Islamic militants acquiring prohibited materials and technology. It was far better, some Americans concluded, to keep the closed cities sealed off than to allow their products and personnel to spill on to illicit markets.

In the Litvinenko affair, attention focused on two of these cities in particular.

Sarov, the former Arzamas-16, and Ozersk, the former Chelyabinsk-65, provided the wellspring of Russian polonium-210, produced quite openly as part of Russia's catalogue of commercial radioisotopes along with products such as strontium-90 and cesium-137.

In the Cold War, the Sarov facilities hosted two major weapons projects, widely known in the Western scientific and intelligence communities by their initials – VNIIEF, the Federal Nuclear Centre–Institute of Experimental Physics, and the AVANGARD Electromechanical Plant.

VNIIEF was a centre of research and development whose scientists led the quest for new weapons designs in the military standoff with Washington.

Complementing the research, the AVANGARD plant assembled the nuclear warheads for Russia's stockpiles of bombs and long-range missiles, programmed to strike targets in Western Europe and the United States.

Arzamas-16, as Sarov was known in its secret years, was devoted, in other words, to the design and construction of the weapons that would destroy London and Paris, New York and Washington.

Chelyabinsk-65 – now Ozersk – played a different role, producing plutonium for weapons, highly enriched uranium and tritium at reactor facilities called the Mayak Production Association.

In the 1990s the functions of these two closed cities changed somewhat, but not completely.

The VNIIEF laboratories and facilities at Sarov switched over to devising safety projects for nuclear power plants, the separation of stable isotopes and other civilian tasks. As it abandoned warhead assembly – and indeed began to dismantle some of the same warheads it once built – AVANGARD's new missions included the production of polonium alongside a range of commercial non-nuclear projects.

But the Sarov facilities were not equipped for every phase of polonium production.

The initial stages of the process were undertaken at the Mayak Production Association at Ozersk. Only the final refining process took place at Sarov.

Then the polonium was dispatched in sealed glass capsules, each bonded with a fraction of a gram of the isotope, packed in cube-like containers measuring about sixteen inches on all sides.

After Litvinenko's death there had been much talk of the allegedly vast cost of polonium, but Radiy Ilkayev, the director of VNIIEF, estimated that Sarov's annual polonium output earned the producers 'a sum in the order of 10 million rubles a year', in other words, around £20,000. That estimate matched those offered by Western scientists such as Nick Priest concerning the likely cost of the polonium used in the Litvinenko killing. 'It's not very expensive,' Priest said. 'It would have been a few thousand dollars.'

Until the moment it left Sarov, Ilkayev ruled out any suggestion that polonium might be diverted. 'Our control over the technological process is very strict,' he said. In the weeks after Litvinenko's death, the chorus of such disavowals from Russian officials reached something of a climax.

But the real point was this: polonium was such a tricky element to produce, store and transport that the idea of it being somehow created in a home laboratory was improbable. The toxin that killed Litvinenko almost certainly came from Russia's closed cities.

'Polonium is very difficult to produce and handle,' said Yekaterina Shugayeva, an official at the state-owned Tekhsnabeksport company, which handled deliveries of polonium-210 to the United States. 'Such capacities exist only in Sarov, I do not think anyone else has them. Nobody else produces it, or knows how.'

Its qualities as a toxin were pretty distinctive, too.

In the spring of 2007 a group of five scientists from some of the most prestigious American and British research institutes offered an assessment that reached the following conclusion about polonium's behaviour once introduced into the human body. 'Its effectiveness as a poison relies on its chemical characteristics only to the extent that they determine its distribution and retention in organs and tissues: the alpha particles do the damage,' their report, published in the *Journal of Radiological Protection,* said.

In other words, the isotope itself is merely the vehicle by which the toxin is carried around the body, attaching in particular to red blood cells. The damage to internal organs and bone marrow comes from the ferocious bombardment of alpha particles spraying out from the polonium.

A further characteristic was described by Nick Priest at Middlesex University, who had conducted experiments on rats many years earlier. After one day, the polonium had distributed itself primarily into the gut of its experimental targets. But within four days, as the bloodstream carried the poison around the organs, the liver had come to equal the gut in its toxic content. Extrapolating from those findings to the Litvinenko case, he explained that the poison did not simply work as a one-shot: it was cumulative, spreading deeper and deeper into Litvinenko's vital organs as he sickened. In other words, the organs never had time to recover after the initial toxic dosage: the level of poisoning would simply get higher until the polonium's half-life reduced its strength, and that would take weeks, by which time the victim would have died.

But there was another tantalizing question: how could polonium, this most volatile of isotopes, be transported across international frontiers?

'My gut feeling is that great care needs to be exercised to properly handle and ship this material,' said Raymond Guilmette, a scientist at Los Alamos.

Each possible delivery system had different implications for a murder.

If the isotope was delivered in some kind of spray, for instance, it would invade through the lungs, reaching the bloodstream more quickly than if it was swallowed into the gut, and would thus spread through the vital organs and bring death more rapidly. But a spray would be an indiscriminate weapon, poisoning far more people than a single target.

Assuming, then, that it was administered in some other way, Guilmette argued that polonium would reach internal organs more rapidly if it was administered in a soluble form and thus be absorbed more easily by the bloodstream.

In the subsequent police inquiry, there was a question, too, about whether the polonium was administered by injection, as it often was in the laboratory experiments that provided much of the available data on how it functioned as a toxin. Litvinenko did not refer to an injection in any of the sickbed conversations recounted later by his wife Marina and associates such as Andrei Nekrasov and Alex Goldfarb. (The results of an autopsy, which might have shown an injection site, were kept secret on orders from Scotland Yard, but there were suggestions from knowledgeable people that the autopsy had not revealed evidence of radiation ulceration, which would have been expected at an injection site.)

So the supposition was that the poison was administered orally in a solution that spread quickly and easily to Litvinenko's vital organs.

Could there have been an antidote? Guilmette argued that some theoretical counter-treatments could work, but their efficacy had been demonstrated only under laboratory conditions in which an antidote was delivered within minutes or hours of contamination. 'The longer the delay between the contaminating event and the initiation of therapy, the more radiation dose will have already been delivered and the less effective will be the treatment in removing polonium-210 from the body.'

The scientific findings had a direct bearing on the investigation into several key aspects of Litvinenko's death. But, for a poisoner, the science also influenced the calculations required to prepare the poison: too much and the risk of collateral damage to bystanders would be greatly increased; too little and the victim might survive. Those same considerations would determine the timeline, establishing when Litvinenko was poisoned and how long he would endure.

The size of the dose could illuminate another question: how many attempts were there to poison Litvinenko? And was the polonium brought into Britain in a single vial, or would several people have brought in polonium to assemble as a lethal quantity? There was every reason to believe that once the polonium was separated from the tight international safeguards covering its legal exportation, it would begin to seep out, leaving traces on those who carried it or tried to decant it into a small container for transportation or administration. Then, if a solution containing polonium was decanted into a dropper for delivery into a teapot, there was the certain risk of further leakage and contamination on a massive scale.

To a great extent, the forensic debate centred on the dosage.

The basic measure of radioactivity is called the becquerel, defined as a level of activity in which one nucleus decays every second. A single becquerel is a tiny amount of radiation, negligible in terms of harm but useful as a basic unit of measurement.*

In the spring of 2007 the report from American and British research institutes suggested that a dose of between one and three billion becquerels, of which only 10 per cent is absorbed into the bloodstream, would be likely to kill a man weighing 70 kilograms, or around 11 stone – a man, say, like Alexander Litvinenko.

At Middlesex University, Priest calculated that the dose administered to Litvinenko was three billion becquerels, of which a full one-half entered the system.

At his home in Brighton, Norman Dombey reckoned that Litvinenko ingested around 4.8 billion becquerels – way above some American estimates of the lethal dose. But even that dose with its terrible toxicity, Dombey calculated, would weigh only thirty-millionths of a gram: Litvinenko had been killed by a toxin virtually without weight or mass.

The figures may have varied, but the scientists agreed on one conclusion: the dose Litvinenko ingested was up to sixty times higher than the amount required to kill him – a massive, terminal assault.

---

* Some scientists still prefer to use a measurement called the curie, named for the discoverers of polonium and radium. One curie, based roughly on the amount of radioactivity given off by one gram of radium, equals thirty-seven billion becquerels.

13

THE POLONIUM TRAIL

Within hours of Litvinenko's death on the night of Thursday 23 November 2006, police summoned managers from the Millennium Hotel to provide access to the Pine Bar and hand over CCTV footage from the cameras in the lobby, in the bar and on all the floors. Every single item in the bar – from the chairs to the glasses in the dishwasher – was quarantined by the police as potential evidence. Not far away, in Piccadilly, the police posted uniformed guards outside the itsu sushi bar, whose managers would say later that their eatery had been closed by an incident of 'international espionage'.

Litvinenko visited both locations on 1 November 2006. Both had now shown signs of contamination by polonium.

The clues to its whereabouts were suddenly as obvious as a flare path guiding an incoming plane, as if the isotope had left a series of nuclear signposts pointing the police and the security services along the way. And if those locations coincided exclusively with the presence of certain known travellers from Moscow, then, the police began to believe, they had a strong case for charges of murder.

When headline writers called it the polonium trail, it was hard to fault the description.

As it crackled into life, its way stations marked by official British announcements, the trail showed polonium's route through the hotel rooms and restaurants of London to its tryst at the Pine Bar, as if the isotope were some macabre stalker.

But it was not a simple path. Two other strands intertwined with it.

One tracked the movements of Andrei Lugovoi and Dmitri Kovtun – the men Litvinenko met in the Pine Bar on the day he began to sicken – well in advance of 1 November 2006, indeed far earlier than anyone initially suspected.

The other began when the police moved in to investigate. Litvinenko was already dying – and the police knew he was dying – but the public did not know, and his killers began to doubt whether the plot had succeeded.

And, to complete the circle, it was the police investigation and the gentle, persistent questioning of a mid-ranking detective inspector that provided the key to these other two strands.

Unravelling the braided narratives of the polonium trail itself, the police investigation and the known movements of the players involved was like exploring an archaeological dig – each layer had reference points at another level as well as its own discrete characteristics.

Between them the strands explained how Litvinenko came to be poisoned. The question of why came later.

Even before the general public learned that polonium had been identified as Litvinenko's killer, the police, the security services and the HPA scrambled to seal off known areas of infection and begin the hunt for the rest.

First there was the call to the Millennium Hotel's managers. Then the police guard, stationed outside the itsu sushi bar. Long before dawn on 24 November the police evacuated Marina Litvinenko and her son Anatoly from Osier Crescent. The day after Litvinenko died, the authorities sealed the pale brick town house with its forlorn English flag – much to the consternation of troubled neighbours wondering whether radioactivity would pollute their tranquillity and threaten their own and their children's well-being.

Then there were other clues, delivered in a series of rapid-fire public statements from the HPA, starting with a bald and shocking announcement on 24 November: 'Tests have established that Mr Litvinenko had a significant quantity of the radioactive isotope Polonium 210 in his body. It is not yet clear how this entered his body. Police are investigating this.'

From then on, the trail lit up like a beacon.

The hospitals where Litvinenko had been treated were screened for contamination, although routine medical precautions – the use of gloves and frequent hand-washing by the staff – had kept the contamination away from doctors and nurses.

Within days, two more locations, housing the softly lit offices of Boris Berezovsky at 7 Down Street and the security company Erinys at 25 Grosvenor Street, close to the Millennium Hotel, came into the frame.

The HPA's statements offered only street addresses and did not identify occupants of those locations by name, but the co-ordinates were enough to enable the public – and the press – to begin sticking pins into the map, showing where polonium had been found. Soon, the markers became a thicket, clustered in the pricier parts of central London.

On 29 November a bulletin from the HPA identified 58 Grosvenor Street – the location of a company called ECO3 Capital – and the five-star Sheraton Park Lane hotel on Piccadilly as places where polonium had been traced.

On that same day, the HPA announced that three British Airways planes – two at Heathrow, one still at Domodedovo airport in Moscow – were also candidates for polonium contamination. The government's COBRA committee learned of the likely contamination of the planes only when one of them was virtually on its final approach into Domodedovo.

'All of us thought we were living in the middle of a John le Carré novel,' Patricia Hewitt, who was Britain's health secretary at the time, recounted at an HPA conference in London in March 2007. 'We had visions of an international incident,' she said, reflecting the fear that always seemed to weigh more heavily in

British official thinking than the reality of nuclear terrorism in central London against an individual British citizen.

Six days after Litvinenko's death, 1,325 people had called British health authorities, desperate to discover whether they had been contaminated. British Airways added to their concerns by saying that up to 30,000 people may have travelled on the suspect Boeing 767s* before they were inspected. In the end, two of the three planes showed signs of contamination. The British Airways plane at Domodedovo flew back empty to be on the safe side. But perhaps the most significant aspect of that announcement lay in the dates of the flights between Moscow and London that the police were now investigating, some of them in late October.

For the first time, it was clear that the polonium trail started days or even weeks before 1 November and the events in the sushi bar on Piccadilly and the Pine Bar: the spoor had been laid long before Litvinenko finally succumbed.

On 30 November an HPA announcement seemed to clear one of the three British Airways planes. The plane had been searched on the ground at Heathrow as its captain and crew grew ever more impatient to take off. The HPA 'does not believe that passengers on this plane were at risk', one of the agency's bulletins said. But that was not the same as saying that no contamination had been found.

One day later, on 1 December, it emerged from the HPA that a 'person who was in direct and very close contact with Mr Litvinenko has a significant quantity of the radioactive isotope Polonium-210 in their body'.

Marina Litvinenko had been contaminated, too, but her name was not published.

Then, a further hotel was mentioned – the Ashdown Park, at Wych Cross in East Sussex, where (it was learned later) Mario Scaramella had stayed – but, according to the HPA, 'nothing of

---

* British Airways gave the planes' registrations as G-BZNA, G-BNWK and G-BNWB.

public health concern' was found. (Again, it was difficult to know the precise meaning of those words.)

The authorities acknowledged that they had even checked the Emirates Stadium, where Arsenal had played Moscow CSKA on 1 November 2006. And there, the HPA said, a tiny trace had actually been found – a miracle in a 60,400-seat stadium.*

The polonium trail itself was not the only issue. People who had been close to the trail, or had strayed across it, began to fret about their own health. How many Londoners or visitors to London indeed felt vulnerable?

By the evening of Friday 1 December 2006, that tally stood at 2,974 people worried about their well-being. Of those, 170 cases were followed up by health specialists. And, after a kind of telephone triage, 24 had been referred to a clinic to be examined 'for possible radiological exposure'.

On 4 December 2006 it emerged that two more hotels had been searched – the four-star Best Western Premier on Shaftesbury Avenue at the heart of the London theatre district, and the Parkes Hotel in upmarket Knightsbridge. Polonium traces had also been found in offices at 1 Cavendish Place, the location of a private security company called RISC Management run by former Scotland Yard detectives, whose chief executive, Keith Hunter, had once provided security services for Boris Berezovsky.

On 7 December the HPA offered a major disclosure, profoundly significant in establishing where Litvinenko had ingested a lethal amount of poison.

Seven members of the Pine Bar staff had tested positive for 'low levels of Polonium-210', the HPA reported, while 'in all of the itsu sushi staff [sic] asked to provide urine samples, we have found nothing of concern.'

In other words, suspicion now focused virtually exclusively on the events and the people in the Pine Bar on the afternoon of 1 November 2006.

---

* Police had been guided to those seats by a combination of ticket numbers and CCTV footage showing who exactly was sitting in them.

But who had administered the poison? That was the question which the British police had not so far answered, in public at least.

'Preliminary results received from seven members of staff working in the Pine Bar of the Millennium Hotel on Nov. 1 show that they appear to have been exposed to low levels of Polonium-210,' the HPA said on 7 December. 'There is no health risk in the short term and in the long term the risk is judged to be very small on the basis of initial tests. All of them are assessed to have had intakes lower than the adult family member of Mr Litvinenko for whom the tests also identified they had been exposed to Po-210.'

Yet the itsu sushi bar remained closed for months. So if it had not been contaminated to the same extent as the Pine Bar, what was its exact status? Why did it not reopen? What had happened there to justify its continued closure?

To some extent, the HPA was in a bind.

According to Pat Troop, its chief executive, the agency confronted the twin challenges of discovering whether there was in fact a public health threat while allaying public fears as ordinary citizens watched masked inspectors in radiation suits entering hotels, offices and public buildings.

No one wanted a panic.

At the time, the HPA took credit for a relatively transparent approach to both issues. But, looking back at the barrage of communiqués tracking the polonium trail, it is clear that they were sometimes more opaque than they might have been.

Most Londoners did not, in fact, panic at all, inured to alarms by their exposure to Irish and Islamic terrorism, stoic and phlegmatic by nature and easily convinced that this was not a general radiation alarm or a dirty bomb – simply a spy story relating to one rogue Russian who happened to have acquired a British passport.

'Spy Radiation: Major Alert', said a banner headline in the *Evening Standard*. Police officers were shown on television removing a metal box and tote bags of evidence from the itsu sushi bar. But the story broke on a Friday afternoon, when people in the city were more focused on the weekend and many, including revellers at another of the Millennium Hotel's two bars, seemed to shrug off the news. The Millennium's lobby, its second bar and its upmarket restaurant were teeming, and the health and safety manager, Brian Kelly, tried to play down the alarm. 'If we had a radiation problem here, do you think my restaurant and bar would be so full of people?' he said.

It took more than a nuclear spy thriller to come between Londoners and their Friday evening libations.

Some of the communiqués were in fact misleading. On 29 November 2006 the HPA statement for the day noted that 'the key public areas of the Sheraton Park Lane Hotel' had been monitored for radiation and 'we can confirm that in those areas there is no risk to public health.'

Maybe not – in the 'public areas'.

But for months later, two rooms on the eighth floor of the hotel were sealed, and reporters trying to approach them were confronted by a makeshift barrier blocking off access.

Neither did the language reflect the drama of some of the searches. At the Sheraton Park Lane, 'there was a major event scheduled that evening and a member of the royal family was expected,' Troop said. 'With about ten minutes to spare we were able to tell them it was OK to go ahead.'

Given the reflexively secretive nature of British officialdom, it seemed ironic that the 'major event' was the annual awards dinner hosted by London's Foreign Press Association. Few if any of the reporters present knew that the public areas of the hotel had just been searched for polonium. The ceremony went ahead in the presence of the Duke of Gloucester, a first cousin to the Queen, and Margaret Beckett, at that time Britain's foreign secretary. Eight floors up, officials in radiation suits checked doors and carpets for contamination.

The early HPA statements did little to signal new discoveries, preferring to elide them into previous announcements. Thus on 29 November the HPA made no particular reference to the fact that a second office in Grosvenor Street had been shown to be contaminated with traces of polonium. That information was simply included as an insert into the wording of the previous day's statement, as if it had always been the case.

Reporters learned quickly to read these guides to the unfolding polonium trail with a degree of caution, if only because the language was deliberately opaque. Did the assertion that a location presented no public health threat necessarily mean that no contamination had been found? Or did it simply mean that the amount found was not big enough to cause radiation sickness? Or that polonium had been found in a private part of a building? And who would define the threshold of a threat to the public health?

Every day, the statements rammed home the message that polonium was not hazardous to humans unless it was ingested, inhaled or entered the body through an open wound.

'Most traces of it can be eliminated through hand-washing, or washing machine or dishwasher cycles for clothes, plates etc.,' the communiqués insisted, underplaying the persistence of a radio-active substance that was still showing traces of itself weeks after the initial contamination. Indeed, in one case at least, the attempt to wash contaminated objects only succeeded in spreading the infection to the dishwasher that was supposed to clean them.

Across central London, contractors and specialists in white anti-radiation suits with hoods and masks worked in teams of two, using small detectors with a sensor area just four inches square that picked up polonium contamination at a range of less than half an inch.

The HPA sent out forty-one monitoring teams, in addition to those from the police and the Atomic Weapons Establishment. The work was painstakingly slow. The teams scanned rooms meticulously 'for hours at a time', the agency reported, 'slowly moving the monitor over the surface under examination and keeping it steady at a constant distance of about one centimetre above the surface'. The searchers checked walls, carpets, curtains, bathrooms, electrical fittings, paintings and armchairs, logging the incidence of polonium as they found it.

The team members even checked each other for infection by the elusive substance they were seeking, as if they feared it might find them first.

Some contamination, it turned out, could be wiped clear with damp tissues, which were then placed in bags for disposal. Other traces could be varnished or painted over, trapping the polonium behind a defensive skin as its half-life ticked away until it became harmless.*

As might be expected, some polonium spoor were elusive, moving in the air, where they might be inhaled.

The HPA set the threshold for contamination levels cautiously low, resolving that any pollution exceeding ten becquerels per square centimetre should be 'remediated' by wiping or painting over. Once the initial cleaning had been carried out, the HPA found, 'very little of the contamination is currently removable by day-to-day activities,' meaning that it was unlikely to break free and harm anyone. But the agency did acknowledge the high risk of scatter-gun contamination 'largely in small patches rather than being uniformly spread', which made the search for it more difficult and time-consuming.

'Soft furnishings require special attention,' the agency said in a lengthy statement on 30 November 2006 that was designed to explain what its inspectors were doing. 'For these items it is more likely that apparently fixed contamination could become available for intake particularly by children. It is recommended that if contamination is detected on soft furnishing, this contamination should be treated as potentially mobile. Either the area affected or the whole item should be removed, "bagged" and taken to safe temporary storage to await disposal.'

As the physical searches of rooms, offices, cars and even a bus continued, a parallel process sought to establish who

---

* Scientists told me that their rule of thumb for calculating an isotope's decline to 1 per cent of its original intensity was to multiply the half-life by a factor of 7.5. In polonium's case, that yielded a period of 1,035 days, or, roughly, 2.84 years.

had been contaminated by polonium – and to what extent.

Most people who called in to the health authorities to express their concern were told there was little or no likelihood of contamination. But for those who may have been exposed to higher levels, the HPA conducted urine analyses – the only definitive way of establishing the level of contamination and calculating the risk of radiation sickness.

On 9 December the HPA offered up another clue, this one relating to Mario Scaramella, who had returned to London from Naples as soon as word of Litvinenko's death emerged, either to seek publicity or to offer help in the inquiry as one of the last people to meet with him before he became ill.

Characteristically, Scaramella and his patron in Rome, Paolo Guzzanti, captured headlines with an assertion that Scaramella had been found to have ingested five times the lethal dose of polonium. Oddly, though, Scaramella displayed no symptoms of radiation poisoning and seemed in rude health. Nonetheless, he was hospitalized, and first results seemed to show that even though he had no symptoms, such as hair loss or vomiting, he had absorbed polonium. Days later, HPA officials acknowledged with some embarrassment that there had been an error in the initial calculation. In fact, the HPA said, 'Mr Scaramella has very low levels of Po-210 in his body. These would result in doses that are significantly less than that from one year's natural background radiation.' Given the expertise that the HPA displayed elsewhere in charting the polonium trail, a reversal on that scale seemed highly unusual – even suspicious.

Scaramella had been in contact with Litvinenko at around 3.00 p.m. on 1 November 2006, in the itsu sushi bar. The two men had embraced, shaken hands, shared a table. Yet Scaramella showed no sign whatsoever of unusual polonium contamination.

So did that mean that as of 3.00 p.m. Litvinenko himself was clean?

The only other known venue at which he might have become poisoned was the Pine Bar, where seven members of the staff had been found to have been contaminated. On the other hand, if

Litvinenko was already contaminated at the meeting with Scaramella, the whole sequence of events had to be seen in a different light. And if Scaramella was contaminated, it would also raise the question of whether he was part of the conspiracy or a mere bystander.

Those suspicions raised the question of what had happened at itsu to justify its closure.

The answer provided Scotland Yard with a critical piece of the jigsaw.

So far, the polonium trail seemed to have scoured its path exclusively through London and aboard British planes that had tested positive for radiation. But for investigators seeking to establish the chronology of contamination, it was equally important to identify places where polonium had not been found. Only then could they pinpoint the precise moment when Litvinenko first registered the contamination that would end his life.

On 1 November 2006, for example, the electronic Oyster card Litvinenko used to pay his bus and tube fares showed no signs of contamination in the hours before he reached the city centre to keep his appointments. Yet after Litvinenko's encounter in the Pine Bar, he left a smear of polonium on the photocopier in Boris Berezovsky's offices in Down Street, Mayfair, and on a seat in the Mercedes in which his friend Akhmed Zakayev drove him home. Those discoveries could only reinforce suspicion that the Pine Bar was the prime locus of contamination.

Then came another bombshell, far from London and the Millennium Hotel.

On 4 December, eleven days after Litvinenko died, a German police officer was leafing casually through that week's issue of *Der Spiegel* news magazine when a line in an account of the Litvinenko case seemed to jump off the page: Dmitri Kovtun, an associate and friend of Andrei Lugovoi's, had been in Hamburg just before the murderous events of 1 November 2006 in London.

'We put the name in our computers and discovered that he had a residence permit,' one officer said. Ominously, the polonium trail began to sputter into life in a thoroughly unexpected quarter.

Kovtun, then aged forty-one, was a friend of Lugovoi's from their teenage years. They trained together at a prestigious military academy in Moscow. Their fathers were senior Red Army officers. After their graduation, Lugovoi joined the Ninth Directorate of the KGB – the bodyguard section – and went on to found his own security company, the Ninth Wave. Kovtun joined an army reconnaissance unit in the closing years of the Cold War, stationed in countries then called Czechoslovakia and East Germany. When the Berlin Wall fell in 1989, Kovtun stayed on and in 1992 became a resident of Hamburg in the newly reunified Germany, ostensibly as a civilian. He met a German woman called Marina Wall in 1994, and they married in 1996. Kovtun remained in Hamburg until late 2003, setting up a business consultancy for German entrepreneurs looking for deals in Russia and trying to keep the marriage alive. Both ventures faltered, the marriage ending in divorce but not, apparently, in any great hostility. ('You and your ex-wife are still close?' I asked Kovtun later when I met him in Moscow. In English he replied: 'She is my best friend.' Slipping back into Russian he added with a wolfish smile: 'I have great experience: I have been divorced three times.'

Kovtun's company, known as I-4 because there had been four partners, proved less durable and was dissolved. After his return to Moscow, Kovtun started a new company called Global Project, a business consultancy supposedly helping outside companies invest in Russia. Lugovoi had offered to help him locate some English clients.

For several years after he returned to Moscow in December 2003, Kovtun maintained his German residency status – using his ex-wife's address – and preserved his friendship with his former wife, not to mention his ex-mother-in-law, Eleonora Wall, a psychiatrist specializing in schizophrenia. Kovtun's attempt to maintain German residency was to offer the German police a key in tracking the polonium trail in Hamburg.

When Kovtun flew into the German city on 28 October 2006,

his former mother-in-law picked him up in a navy blue BMW estate car and drove him to the Altona district, where his former wife lived in an apartment in a four-storey white building over a pub and shops on a cobbled side street. It was a Saturday, and Kovtun went shopping for a pair of trousers, travelling on the S-Bahn overhead commuter railway to and from the city centre. He returned to his ex-wife's apartment and spent the night on a sofa. The following day, his former mother-in-law picked him up and drove him to her huge, rambling former farmhouse, a red-brick building with sharply angled gables in which she lived at Haselau, sixteen miles northwest of Hamburg in the neighbouring federal state of Schleswig-Holstein. 'He always called me when he was in Hamburg,' his mother-in-law told a German reporter. 'Otherwise I would have been mad at him.'

Of their encounter in late October 2006 she said: 'We sat all evening in the kitchen, drinking and talking.'

Kovtun had other business to attend to. His German papers were up for renewal. And so on Monday morning, Wall drove Kovtun to the Foreigners' Office in Hamburg, which was in charge of issuing, or revoking, residency permits for non-Germans. He signed the requisite forms and was out of the office in less than an hour, congratulating himself that the visit had progressed so smoothly and easily. That night – 30 October 2006 – he stayed with an old Italian friend in a different part of Hamburg before returning to his former wife's apartment for his last night in the city. His flight to London early on 1 November was with the low-cost airline Germanwings. It remained unclear whether his choice of accommodation was dictated by lack of money for a hotel or by a desire to leave no trace of his whereabouts on a hotel register.

Either way, Kovtun's presence in Hamburg raised no alarms at all until the first week of December, when officers, tipped off by the article in *Der Spiegel,* called in a special radiation unit from the German Federal Police, the Bundeskriminalamt, the border police, the Bundesgrenzschutz, and the Federal Office for Radiation Protection, the Bundesamt für Strahlenschutz.

The officer who took over the case was Thomas Menzel, the head of the Hamburg police's organized crime section charged with tracking down Albanian and other gangs involved in financial fraud and drug running.

Menzel was tall and slender, a thirty-year veteran of the police force who wore his greying hair swept back and who worked out of an office at the Polizeipräsidium headquarters in a leafy suburb of north Hamburg.

He code-named the Kovtun operation 'Third Man' after the Orson Welles movie based on Graham Greene's novel set in post-Second World War Vienna, and used the signature tune from the movie – the 'Harry Lime Theme' – as a ringtone on his cell phone.

The German police began by searching the apartments where Kovtun stayed, and followed the trail from there. They did not have to wait long for results: polonium traces lit up across Hamburg. Suddenly an operation that began with an idle glance at *Der Spiegel* became a major police inquiry. Some six hundred officers were drafted on to the case, scouring stores and restaurants. White-suited inspectors with radiation detection equipment appeared outside suburban homes. The apartment building where Kovtun spent the night on his ex-wife's sofa was evacuated and her children hospitalized to be tested for radiation sickness. Detectives tracked Kovtun's movements from the moment he touched down to the moment he left. Polonium traces seemed to be everywhere.

The BMW in which Kovtun was picked up on arrival showed signs of contamination that could not have been created at a later date because the car was involved in a minor accident soon after he arrived and was immobilized to await repairs. The receipt from the store where he bought trousers also tested positive. The Federal Office for Radiation Protection said the highest trace of radiation was found on the front seat of the family car owned by Kovtun's ex-wife, particularly on the headrest. But traces had also been found in her apartment on mattresses and on a sofa. It was a token of the thoroughness of the German experts' search that they discovered polonium traces in a child's nappy. The car in which Kovtun travelled to Haselau also showed traces of polonium.

None of those episodes could prove definitively that the contamination had not happened during an earlier visit to Hamburg. (There was no record of his returning to Hamburg after the incident in the Pine Bar.)

But, according to the police account, there was one moment that could not have been replicated before or after Kovtun's visit in late October. When he went to the Foreigners' Office to renew his residency papers, he signed and handled a form that was officially date-stamped 30 October 2006. That was the only time he could have left traces of polonium on the form, and German bureaucrats had the date stamp to prove it.

The only clear break in the polonium trail seemed to be on 1 November: the Germanwings plane in which Kovtun flew to London to meet up with Lugovoi at the Millennium Hotel showed no sign of contamination, although the police said it had been cleaned several times before it was finally examined more than five weeks later at Cologne Bonn Airport on 8 December 2006.

Nonetheless, the Hamburg police drew the unambiguous conclusion that Kovtun arrived from Moscow already contaminated by polonium, or possibly even carrying it on his person.

'There is probably cause for the suspicion that he might have brought the substance with him outside his body to Hamburg, and that he may not only be a victim but a perpetrator,' Martin Köhnke, the public prosecutor, said. In a statement, the German police said Kovtun was 'considered to be a suspect'.

It was the first time that Western law enforcement officers had identified a potential suspect.

The polonium trail now stretched from Moscow to Hamburg to London, with international ramifications that went even farther.

On 12 December 2006, the HPA announced that diplomats from

forty-four countries and territories had been briefed on the potential risks to their citizens who had been guests at the Millennium Hotel, the Best Western on Shaftesbury Avenue and the Sheraton Park Lane. British scientists had been in touch with their counterparts in Germany, France and Belgium and at the IAEA's analytical laboratory in Austria.

Weeks after Litvinenko's death, the polonium continued to sputter into life with new disclosures.

In early January 2007 it emerged that the contamination at the Best Western had been more severe than first indicated. Two rooms had been sealed off from the public, and a member of staff had actually been contaminated. The levels of infection were not health-threatening in the short term, but they showed that the hunt for polonium displayed as many unexpected twists and turns as the isotope itself.

Out of the blue, a restaurant – Pescatori in Dover Street, Mayfair – was found to have been contaminated, and suspicion again fell on Lugovoi and Kovtun. The two men were now being talked about quite openly in public newspaper reports as somehow linked to Litvinenko's death, but only months later would the British authorities identify their prime suspect.

The search for polonium, meanwhile, was rapidly becoming a template for the public health response to radiological alarms – an early primer in the kinds of measures that might be needed in the event of a terrorist attack using radiation devices.

By 11 January 2007 the HPA had devised a categorization system to distinguish between contamination that carried a slight health risk and contamination that carried no health risk at all.

By categorizing the victims – the collateral damage of the attack on Litvinenko – health officials were able to determine that the bulk of those in the higher category, apart from Marina Litvinenko, were workers at the Pine Bar and guests at the Millennium Hotel who had stopped by for a drink at the same watering hole.

Of all the locations found to have been contaminated, the Pine Bar lit up with pyrotechnic brilliance. By 18 January 2007 seventeen people had been found to be in the highest category; nearly all of them traced their contamination to the Pine Bar, which remained closed for one year while it was refurbished and redesigned at a cost of over £250,000.

On 19 June 2007 I asked the HPA's spokeswoman, Katherine Lewis, for the final breakdown of those seventeen. Apart from Marina Litvinenko, she said, six members of the Pine Bar staff, two other members of the Millennium Hotel staff, six hotel guests at the Pine Bar and two members of the staff at the Sheraton Park Lane had been in the highest category. There was no mention of serious contamination among staff or guests at itsu.

Quite separately from events in London and Hamburg, the pace was quickening in Russia, too, with a parallel, but far less transparent or documented, polonium trail unfolding 1,500 miles to the east of London in Moscow.

In early December 2006 Lugovoi and Kovtun checked into a hospital in Moscow, ostensibly for radiation tests. The Russian prosecutor general, Yuri Chaika, announced that he would set up his own inquiry into the death of Litvinenko and into what was described as an attempt to murder Dmitri Kovtun. The polonium trail, which once seemed so glaringly clear in London, now crossed dark glades of disinformation in Moscow. At one point, Interfax, the Russian news agency, reported that Kovtun's condition was critical and he was in a coma – an assertion that Kovtun subsequently denied. For his part, Lugovoi initially refused to say whether he had been contaminated with polonium. But there was one event in Moscow that offered some clarity. Shortly before Litvinenko died, Lugovoi and Kovtun visited the British Embassy in Moscow to offer a deposition. At that time, their names had already come into the crosshairs of the British media, and they were keen to protest their innocence.

According to British officials, the room at the embassy where they were debriefed tested positive for radioactive contamination.

The final accounting for the polonium trail in London – and the busy highway of bureaucracy running alongside it – came from Westminster City Council, which had assumed responsibility for overseeing decontamination when the HPA signed off on managing public health issues. In mid-August 2007 Westminster Council announced that forty-seven venues, including eight aircraft, had been checked for contamination and either pronounced clear or cleaned up. The number of aircraft remained something of a puzzle. British Airways had identified three of them. A fourth plane, from the low-cost easyJet airline that flew Mario Scaramella from Naples to London, was located and cleared. But a variety of British agencies refused to discuss the other four because they were part of the police case establishing the movements of the alleged killer. The aircraft, one informant told me, were part of 'a trail going back to Moscow that could not have been laid by Litvinenko'.

There was another mystery relating to the overall numbers, ascribed later by HPA officials to communications problems between the various authorities handling the case.

According to Westminster Council, four of the forty-seven venues it located had not previously been mentioned by the HPA – a Mercedes car and a Mercedes taxi, a booth in a 'gentlemen's club' called Hey Jo in Jermyn Street near Piccadilly, and a Moroccan restaurant called Dar Marrakesh in Rupert Street, off Shaftesbury Avenue near the Best Western, where 'high levels of contamination' had been found on the handle of a hubble-bubble Shisha pipe and a cushion cover.

In this postscript, it emerged that twenty of the originally suspect locations – including Scaramella's hotel in East Sussex – had been found to be completely clear of contamination.

But the main way stations of the polonium trail – the offices of risk assessment firms and of Boris Berezovsky, the rooms of luxury and not-so-luxury hotels on Park Lane, Grosvenor Square, Knightsbridge and Shaftesbury Avenue, both hospitals where Litvinenko was treated, and his home, a restaurant, a football stadium and a third hospital where an autopsy on his body was carried out – were found to be contaminated and were subsequently cleared.

From the very start, though, there was one key element missing from the daily HPA bulletins: the suspected dates of contamination, surely not all of them on 1 November 2006.

And one overriding question persisted: how had the police known where to tell the HPA inspectors to look? The answer to that question came in the second strand of the mystery – the investigation by Scotland Yard.

On 16 November 2006, fifteen days after Alexander Litvinenko's visits to itsu and the Pine Bar, physicians at Barnet Hospital called the police, as their patient had been urging them to do.

As Marina Litvinenko recounted after her husband's death, the police responded by transferring Litvinenko at high speed and with blue lights flashing to the more sophisticated and better equipped University College Hospital, a highly rated teaching hospital that drew on the expertise of teams of specialist physicians.

But they, too, were at a loss for ideas. 'The Geiger-counter readings were negative, and we did not know what was going on,' said Geoff Bellingan, the Zimbabwean-born clinical director of UCH's critical care unit.

'At the time of admission his diagnosis was not clear,' he said. Throughout Litvinenko's time at UCH, Bellingan said, 'We were working on the logic that something had poisoned his cells, and we were working on that until he died. At that stage we found out.'

Even in Litvinenko's final hours, Bellingan went public with UCH's assessment that radiation poisoning was unlikely. 'We are now convinced that the cause of Mr Litvinenko's condition was not a heavy metal such as thallium,' he said in a public statement. 'Radiation poisoning is also unlikely.'

The assessment ran on the news bulletins on the day Litvinenko died, showing just how narrowly polonium came to eluding detection by some of the world's premier diagnostic physicians.

For its part, Scotland Yard did not advertise its involvement until 20 November 2006, one day after the interview with

Litvinenko in the *Sunday Times* ignited a media firestorm. For the first time since the Markov 'umbrella murder' in 1978, it seemed as if London had been chosen as the arena for dark and murderous deeds by shadowy services linked to the Kremlin.

Public statements from Scotland Yard were notoriously bland, and in the Litvinenko case they required the usual close examination.

A police communiqué on 20 November contained two notable errors, giving Litvinenko's age as forty-one and suggesting he had been hospitalized only since 17 November.

But it was the opening line that was most striking: 'We are investigating a suspected deliberate poisoning of a 41-year-old man in London.'

For the first time, the authorities had blamed Litvinenko's condition on the premeditated acts of other people.

'We are making a number of extensive inquiries to determine the cause of his condition, including toxicology tests, interviewing possible witnesses, including the man, and examining his movements in and around the time of the suspected poisoning; and examining CCTV footage, etc.'

The statement could be read in various ways. At one level, this was no more than a catalogue of the usual police actions in response to a case of this nature and international profile.

However unusual Litvinenko's situation was, there was nothing to suggest that Scotland Yard was conducting anything other than a predictable inquiry.

But consider the statement from the vantage point of a poisoner, and the alarm bells begin to ring. First off, the target – Alexander Litvinenko – had not died; in fact, he was well enough to be interviewed by the police. The first requirement of poisoning – kill your victim – had misfired. Litvinenko had told the police where he went and with whom. There may even have been images of those meetings. And tests were being conducted that could establish the nature and origin of the toxin. It was, quite clearly, a serious case, one step away from attempted murder. From that point of view, the Scotland Yard announcement sent the clear signal that the poisoning had been bungled and the perpetrators would soon be identified.

The statement continued:

> We await the results of the toxicology tests and we are therefore not speculating as to the possible cause of his condition at this stage. We have appointed a liaison officer to the man's family to ensure that they are kept up-to-date with developments.
>
> We are in the very early stages of our investigation and so unable to comment on speculative reports in the media until we have confirmed details.
>
> We hope to provide further information in due course. There have been no arrests in connection with this enquiry at this stage. The MPS Specialist Crime directorate, led by a detective super-intendent, is investigating the matter.

Much of this was standard, but there was a twist.

The poisoning was being investigated by a unit that often dealt with murder – but there was no body.

'What we had was a murder victim who was not yet dead and could tell you who had done it and how,' one officer said later, speaking on condition that he not be identified by name. 'Litvinenko was quite clear it was the Russians. He met with a number of people. He was always of the view that Putin was behind this, but he accepted it would be very unlikely it would be proved.'

From the earliest days of his illness, 'he knew things were wrong because he was clear he was poisoned. When he was getting ill and there was no logical explanation, he knew he had been poisoned.'

Although it was not stated explicitly at the time – certainly not in the public statement – police officers already believed that Litvinenko was beyond saving.

By the time the first police statement was issued, there had already been a conversation between David Johnston, who headed the Yard's murder teams in the Serious Crime Directorate, and Peter Clarke, the head of the counterterrorist SO15 unit. The inquiry into the expected death of a former KGB agent in the heart of London could never be a simple criminal affair.

As a result of the conversation, Clarke took overall responsibility for the investigation, reflecting Scotland Yard's assessment of the likely direction the case would take – into the tricky shoals of intelligence and espionage.

Litvinenko's death raised searching questions about the Kremlin and Putin himself; it conjured allegations of dirty tricks by Russian agents linked directly to the old KGB and the newer FSB. The British agencies MI5 and MI6, not to mention the Foreign Office and even 10 Downing Street, would never be far from the investigation. Only officers in Clarke's SO15 unit had the highest security clearances providing seamless access to the British security and intelligence services.

What Clarke did not say was that he had already begun his investigation with a close scrutiny of everything MI5 had been able to amass on Litvinenko relating to his activities before and after fleeing Russia.

Clarke asked MI5 to check on the whereabouts of all the thirty-plus known operatives of the Russian SVR foreign intelligence service based in London in the weeks leading up to Litvinenko's poisoning. More used to bugging and tailing suspected Islamic terrorists, MI5 scrambled, calling on its own counterintelligence resources – including a clandestine double agent within the SVR establishment – to track the movements of the Russian spies in late October, assembling information from agents, intercepts and surveillance teams.

Within days, a British security official said, MI5 compiled a dossier that seemed to show no direct involvement in the poisoning by the known SVR spies in Britain. That meant that if Litvinenko was right about the identity of those who ordered his death, then the plot had been hatched outside Britain and a team had flown in to carry out the hit, quite separately from the Russian *residenzy* in London.

In one sense, that conclusion came as a relief. An assassination by the known SVR operatives would have been an unequivocal act of hostility – not just towards the Russian *émigré* community but also towards British sovereignty. The exoneration of the SVR, by contrast, left open a slender possibility that Litvinenko's death was simply an act of extreme criminality rather than a display of supreme arrogance by the Kremlin.

But the MI5 report was also troubling: if the assessment of the British security services was that the SVR was not involved, then, MI5 believed, the FSB – Litvinenko's former employer – almost certainly was.

MI5's conclusion was shared by the overseas intelligence specialists at MI6, with its grand and not-secret-at-all head-quarters rising like a ziggurat on the south bank of the Thames near Vauxhall Bridge. And if the FSB was involved, someone in authority had permitted serving or former officers to draw on the resources of the Russian state to perform a hostile act on the soil of – and against a citizen of – a supposedly friendly nation.

As one intelligence source explained, it was highly unlikely that any low-ranking FSB operative would embark on a mission of this magnitude without 'running it up the tree' to the highest level in advance.

The first senior counterterrorism officer on the case was Detective Superintendent Mark Holmes, a seasoned investigator, who went on after the Litvinenko inquiry to take charge of operations directed at Islamic radicalizers in Britain. But the day-to-day work of interviewing and assembling evidence remained with officers from the Serious Crime Directorate.

One of them was Detective Inspector Brent Hyatt, an officer who had joined Scotland Yard in 1982, working first as a uni-formed policeman on the beat and then as a plainclothes investigator. Since 2002 Hyatt had been part of the Yard's murder and serious crimes unit. He had achieved some fame as an expert on so-called honour killings within Muslim immigrant families, usually of daughters whose choice of partner fell foul of the conservative precepts of their male relatives. In one of his best-known cases, dating from 2002, Hyatt unravelled the testimony of Abdalla Yones, a Kurdish refugee from Iraq who claimed Al Qaeda supporters broke into his house, killed his sixteen-year-old daughter, Heshu, and then threw him over a balcony.

In fact, following Hyatt's investigation, the man himself was convicted of killing his own daughter because she was dating an eighteen-year-old Lebanese Christian. Yones then slashed his own throat and threw himself over the balcony to escape the consequences of his actions – only to survive.

Hyatt's name was on the duty roster when Scotland Yard began its investigation, but his superiors saw him as a suitable man for the job. In the Yones case, he had proved himself to be an officer with the personal skills to handle sensitive cases and delicate family concerns.

Initially, the British detectives headed out towards Barnet Hospital, unaware that Litvinenko had moved to the more modern facilities closer to the city centre at UCH. When they arrived there, they found Litvinenko strong enough to walk around his room and admire the view out over London.

He was clearly unwell. His immune system had collapsed, his skin had yellowed and his head was completely bald. But doctors told the police that there were sicker people in the hospital than Litvinenko. Some physicians went so far as to suggest that they were not at all convinced that he had even been poisoned, in the criminal sense of the word. Some members of the hospital staff regarded the former KGB officer as a fantasist. One possible diagnosis at the time was that Litvinenko had been stricken with a form of rapid-onset leukaemia and would die a natural death.

By that time, many other possibilities – radiation sickness and thallium poisoning – had already been excluded. Poisoning was far from proved, still less the cause of it.

The police officers, in other words, found themselves investigating a murder in progress, while the doctors were looking at an abstruse but natural illness that may have been caused by some outside agent entering the body without malice aforethought.

At that stage, the use of toxins was fulfilling the task ascribed to it in the annals of murder: cloaking the identity of perpetrators long gone from the scene of the crime. Even when the doctors finally accepted that Litvinenko's illness was not the result of natural causes, they were at a loss to identify the cause of his sickness and decline. As one physician put it, 'We became increasingly convinced that he was poisoned, in the sense of being poisoned or taking something, but we were not clear how it got into him.'

Neither did the police and the physicians agree on the inevitability of Litvinenko's death.

There was a hope at that time, one doctor said, that 'if it was something short-lived we could get him through, but if it was something that was much longer lasting then we did not know'.

When the police arrived, the doctors' worst fear was that the officers themselves would pass on infections to Litvinenko. No one at that stage thought of protecting the officers, or the doctors themselves, against radiation contamination, and there was no suggestion that any of the police officers were affected by radiation. But anyone visiting Litvinenko was obliged to observe what doctors call 'universal precautions', meaning rigorous hand-washing and wearing a protective apron, gloves and sometimes face masks and eye protection.

On 17 November 2006, when the police took up the case, the question for the physicians was where to start.

'If you look at someone who's got no hair and the bone marrow is not there, and you ask someone on the street what it is, they would say it looks like chemotherapy,' one of the doctors familiar with Litvinenko's case said. That was one line of research.

Rapid-onset leukaemia was considered, but 'there came a point when that theory would not hold water at all,' the physician said.

Essentially, the doctors were 'working down a series of possibilities'. Another line of inquiry related to possible heavy metal poisoning, but that, too, led nowhere. 'At that stage, we were ruling out nothing.'

In the early days of Litvinenko's treatment at UCH, the

physicians gave police the impression that they were not keen for their patient to be interviewed. But the officers asked pointedly whether Litvinenko would definitely survive the weekend to be questioned later. No such guarantees were forthcoming – or possible – the physicians replied. So the conversations that would lay the markers for the polonium trail began that same Friday night, 17 November 2006, hour after hour of them.

As a potential witness herself, Marina Litvinenko was not permitted to remain with her husband and sat outside his room as he testified. When the questioning paused, Litvinenko's family and friends were allowed to visit.

The sense of foreboding was deepening, and the call went out to Litvinenko's relatives in Russia that he might not survive much longer.

Hyatt and a colleague set up their temporary operations centre in a room next to Litvinenko's at UCH itself in order to stay close to the former KGB agent. With the officers at his bedside, Litvinenko was in the unenviable and utterly improbable position of being the prime witness in his own murder investigation.

Through the weekend of 18 to 19 November, as the case exploded into a major international news event, Hyatt continued with the quiet, diligent questioning of Litvinenko to pinpoint the movements of the people he had met. The British detective marvelled at Litvinenko's tenacity.

Late into the night, the police officers kept up their probing. Litvinenko insisted on continuing with the interview even when he seemed to be too exhausted to go on.

At earlier times of his life, Litvinenko talked up a storm for people who did not always heed him. But this time people were listening to his every word. Finally, after all his books, his public statements, his interventions at the Frontline Club, he would make a difference, not just in the hunt for his killer but also in the world's attitude towards the Kremlin.

If the police had postponed their questioning to the following Monday instead of continuing through the weekend, it is doubtful whether Litvinenko would still have had the stamina to lay out in detail his knowledge of where and when he had met the people he did meet on and before 1 November 2006.

There were some lighter moments.

Litvinenko seemed keen to strike up a friendly relationship with the police officers, showing them his family photographs. One image depicted his wife Marina and son Anatoly, and he kept it on display at his bedside. There was a piquancy about those moments. British detectives encountered many characters and criminals in their routine inquiries, but former KGB men from Moscow did not figure too frequently. The Russian-born patient at UCH must have seemed an exotic creature indeed, with his tales of war and treachery and defection.

Litvinenko clearly sensed a rapport with Hyatt. The former operative had been joshing the British detective, saying that he needed to read Litvinenko's books to help him remember what he had been told about events in Russia. One morning, Hyatt arrived at Litvinenko's room – room 9 in the UCH critical care unit – impatient to resume his interviews. But Litvinenko told him: 'Before we start, here's my book.' He had inscribed a volume of *Blowing Up Russia* as a gift for the officer.*

As Litvinenko weakened, Hyatt and the Scotland Yard team took written notes and statements from him, impressed with the precision of his recall. His testimony was videotaped in what was called a 'dying declaration' admissible as evidence in murder trials. The case was code-named 'Operation Whimbrel' after a kind of wader bird from the curlew family. (Scotland Yard made a habit of using obscure and unlikely code names to protect its operations.)

In his conversations with the British detectives, Litvinenko told them whom he met, when and where. He offered theories about

---

* Like other police officers associated with the case, Hyatt declined to be interviewed about his days with Litvinenko, citing the familiar rules relating to the prior disclosure of evidence that might prejudice a trial. This account of the police investigation thus draws on conversations with several people who spoke only on the condition that they not be identified by name. I have honoured their requests for confidentiality.

the reason for his death. He knew when his Russian business contacts arrived in London and when they left. He gave the police a route map that guided investigators to the polonium trail.

In his imperfect English, Litvinenko made clear to Hyatt that his priority was to provide the evidence and respond to the questions put to him. He refused medication to lessen the excruciating pain of the nuclear attack on his organs.

Yet by Monday 20 November Litvinenko was finding it ever more difficult to speak. His mouth was flecked with foam. He had survived almost three days of intensive questioning, but now he was weakening. Long before Litvinenko asked his family and friends what his chances were, the police officers with him knew he was going to die. The case, meanwhile, had burgeoned into a major crime. Over the weekend, three or four officers had been involved. By Monday, sixty police officers were following leads from Litvinenko's testimony. Police also spoke separately and at length to Marina Litvinenko and perused her husband's diary, assembling a clear picture of Litvinenko crisscrossing London's West End with his contacts from Moscow in the two weeks before he became ill.

By now Litvinenko was weakening rapidly, to the point where his own organs could not keep him alive. The day before he died, he was hooked up to a mechanical ventilator feeding air into a tube inserted in his throat. His vital organs began to collapse. 'His heart was getting weaker and weaker,' said Jim Down, the on-duty intensive care consultant on 23 November. 'His blood pressure dropped inexorably to nothing.'

By the time Litvinenko became too enfeebled for further questioning, detectives had names to check against hotel registers and airline passenger manifests – the beginnings of a murder case that was still being called a suspicious death. CCTV footage taken from inside and outside buildings in Mayfair showed the movements of the suspects between offices, walking along hotel corridors, standing at the reception desk of the Millennium Hotel, heading into the bar.

According to fellow police officers, Hyatt was deeply moved by the four days he spent interviewing Litvinenko and told friends that, when Litvinenko's son Anatoly was old enough to understand, he would be happy to meet him to recount his father's steadfastness in his final days.

Months later, Hyatt told friends he had never realized 'that a human being could be quite that brave and quite that dignified' while enduring such pain.

But Litvinenko could not help the detectives identify the toxin that was killing him even as he spoke.

That discovery was left to yet one more of the unlikely co-incidences that marked the entire investigation.

One version current among police officers was that John Henry, the prominent toxicologist brought on to the case by the Berezovsky team, felt embarrassed at his erroneous announcement on 19 November 2006, identifying the toxin definitively as thallium.

Physicians at Barnet and UCH had already ruled out thallium, and Henry himself knew from the strength in Litvinenko's grip that he was not displaying all the classic symptoms of thallium poisoning. As one of the UCH physicians said, in addition, 'Litvinenko had quite a lot of things that thallium does not produce.'

As he racked his brains, Henry came to the conclusion that all the signs pointed to radiation sickness, and so he urged the police to ensure that a catheter bag containing Litvinenko's urine be sent urgently for analysis.

Police officers hurried to UCH to secure the bag before it was routinely changed by medical staff – another of the remarkable breaks in the case that enabled the police to unravel what the poisoners had envisaged as the perfect crime.

If the bag had already been emptied by the hospital staff tending Litvinenko, scientists would have had to wait longer for a sample to test. And if no one had thought to check his urine for a specific kind of radioactive toxicity, then polonium might not have been discovered at all.

The urine sample was sent for analysis by Britain's leading nuclear weapons experts at Aldermaston. But those tests could not be done overnight. And in the meantime, time was running out, for Litvinenko and the investigation alike.

Without an identification of the toxin, it would have been impossible for the police to establish a connection between the poison and those who had visited the places it had been found. A murder charge would be difficult to prove. Litvinenko's decline, in other words, would have been terminal and inexplicable, fulfilling the twin criteria of the poisoner's art.

As the detectives in the hospital gathered Litvinenko's testimony, Clarke created what was called a 'gold' group – a kind of high command – drawing in representatives from the HPA, the Atomic Weapons Establishment, the NHS and the Foreign Office. To maintain coordination with the police, scientists moved into offices on the eleventh floor of New Scotland Yard. For the first time, the police also set up a new kind of unit called a Knowledge Management Centre within Scotland Yard, to bring together the strands of the investigation and to avert the crossed signals of some earlier high-profile cases, notably the killing of Jean Charles de Menezes.

Clarke himself liaised directly with his opposite numbers at MI5.

Scotland Yard was clearly bracing itself for a major inquiry, even if the police did seem to have got off to a slow start while Litvinenko sickened in Barnet Hospital. But little of this was said in public.

Britain's laws relating to unfolding prosecutions did not – and do not – favour openness. The laws governing pre-trial disclosure were extraordinarily restrictive, exposing reporters to the risk of prison terms for contempt of court if they disclosed information deemed likely to prejudice a fair trial. The closer a suspect came to trial, the tighter the regulations became. Once a suspect was charged with an offence, information dried up completely.*

---

* Scotland Yard instructed anyone directly connected with the Litvinenko case – including the physicians who dealt with his illness, the suspects in Russia, FBI officers at the American Embassy and family members – to refrain from discussing the main aspects of the inquiry with reporters. Clarke himself declined repeated requests for an interview.

Sixteen months after Litvinenko's death, the results of an autopsy had not been released, because they were construed as evidence in the case. The counterargument, in British legal circles, was that the stranglehold on public disclosure helped guarantee a fair trial since jurors and the public could not be influenced by pre-trial publicity. The alternative, British lawyers said, was trial by television, and that was no fair trial at all. But that culture of secrecy also protected British officials confronting growing evidence that an act of nuclear terrorism had been committed on their soil. None of them wanted the news to leak out prematurely in a manner that might cause national panic.

Senior HPA officials learned in the early evening of Thursday 23 November – the night Litvinenko died – about the discovery of polonium, but suspicions about its use had begun to harden somewhat earlier after scientists at the Atomic Weapons Establishment in Aldermaston began their analyses of Litvinenko's urine samples.

The tests ran to a strict protocol. But there was one crucial defining moment, little known to the public, that related to one of polonium's more arcane characteristics.

As one knowledgeable scientist explained, polonium overwhelmingly emits alpha radiation. But every so often – roughly once for every 100,000 alpha particles – polonium also blips a single gamma ray.

It was that distinctive rogue gamma ray, picked up at Aldermaston, that hardened scientists' suspicions that they had discovered traces of polonium in Litvinenko's urine.

The scientists had stumbled upon evidence as sharp and decisive as a fingerprint – or even a visiting card – left at a crime scene.

By the early evening of 22 November 2006, the day before Litvinenko died, scientists – and the intelligence services privy to their findings – were fairly sure that the improbable, if not the impossible, had happened: London was staring at evidence of radiation poisoning in the heart of the city.

If Litvinenko had died earlier – as may have been the intention considering the dose he was given – it is debatable whether the urine samples would have been collected in time.

Of course, polonium contamination would have remained for a limited period in the tissues corroded by the poison, where the isotope is known to decay more rapidly than outside the body. But it is highly unlikely that investigators would even have looked for such an arcane toxin if Litvinenko had died an apparently simple and rapid death in Barnet Hospital before his plight became an international cause célèbre. Instead, his protracted decline was accompanied by a chorus of charges from his associates that the Kremlin had turned back the clock to the days of the Cold War.

While Litvinenko endured his final hours and days in London, slipping in and out of a coma, a parallel set of events played out in Moscow.

As their notoriety grew in London – trial by newspaper, almost – Andrei Lugovoi and Dmitri Kovtun resolved to tell their version of events to the British authorities, before Litvinenko died and before the nature of his illness was made public.

The two men contacted the British Embassy on the icy banks of the Moscow River and were initially put through to a junior diplomat with the title of press officer. He sent their request up the line of command to the ambassador, Sir Anthony Brenton, and, almost certainly, to the in-place representative of the British intelligence services.

At first, the British officials were suspicious of the Russians' avowed desire for a meeting, reluctant to be drawn into what looked like a messy and diplomatically fissile affair best left to the police. Brenton was already an unpopular figure with the Russian authorities and had been subjected to fierce harassment by a pro-Putin youth movement known as Nashi. Even before the Litvinenko case, there had been the FSB's accusations concerning British intelligence agents playing spy games with a device disguised as a rock in a Moscow park.

At the back of their minds, these ever-cautious British diplomats feared a classic provocation, Cold War style, to draw them into the case. But eventually it was agreed that Lugovoi and Kovtun should come to the embassy.

The meeting took place at 2.00 p.m. Moscow time – 11.00 a.m. London time – on 23 November, ten hours before Litvinenko's death and more than a day before Troop's announcement that he died of polonium poisoning. Publicly, all that was known about Litvinenko's condition at that time was that he was seriously ill.

At that meeting – crucially, as it turned out – Lugovoi and Kovtun gave an account of several visits to London in October 2006. They made no attempt to keep their appointment at the British Embassy a secret. Indeed, Lugovoi gave an interview to the Russian radio station Ekho Moskvy on 24 November 2006 – the day after Litvinenko's death but several hours before the British authorities announced the discovery of polonium in his body.

'We met, together with Dmitri, a lawyer was with us,' Lugovoi said. 'It was an informal meeting because there were no legal grounds. We wrote a statement.'

'So, it was a conversation?' the radio interviewer asked him.

'Right, three high-ranking embassy officials were present. We handed in our statements. They gave us papers for what they received from us. And they said, "We'll contact you some time today. We are very glad you contacted us because the interest in this case is great, especially in the media, and we cannot ignore it."'

In retrospect, their visit to the embassy seems to be something of a puzzle. If they were the guilty men, why would they have gone to the British Embassy to make their deposition? There is, in any event, no way of knowing whether they would have gone to the embassy if they had realized that the cause of Litvinenko's death would be known to the world twenty-eight hours later as radiation poisoning.

Was that perhaps why Scotland Yard delayed its disclosure of the findings at Aldermaston – even to Marina Litvinenko – simply to see who emerged to begin telling their story?

Given the le Carré-esque overtones of the case, it is easy

enough to imagine that Lugovoi and Kovtun walked into a trap set by the British intelligence services, offering their London itinerary as evidence of purported innocence when the British knew full well that those same addresses of hotels and restaurants provided the equivalent of neon-lit signposts along the forensic trail. But if that was the case, no one in the British law enforcement and intelligence communities was admitting it in public. The only glitch in this carefully constructed scenario came from Walter Litvinenko, who learned early on 24 November 2006 that his son had been poisoned by radiation.

Hours before Troop's announcement, and just after Alex Goldfarb read out Litvinenko's deathbed testament, Walter Litvinenko declared publicly that his son had been killed by a 'tiny nuclear bomb'. That upset the entire choreography for letting Londoners know that they might have been exposed to radiation. According to Goldfarb, 'The police were furious.'

It could not be denied, though, that if those who planned Litvinenko's final moments believed they had conceived the perfect crime, the lone gamma ray blipping at Aldermaston had proved their undoing. And it was equally evident that the scientists at the Atomic Weapons Establishment played a role of incalculable importance in unravelling the mystery of Litvinenko's poisoning with polonium.

There were some other considerations, too.

If this had been intended as the perfect crime, then the question arose: how do you define criminal perfection?

Is it when the perpetrator is never detected? Or when the case is never solved to the satisfaction of a jury?

Or, rather, is the perfect crime one in which a suspect is wrongfully named – and the true wrong-doer escapes in anonymity? That is perhaps the most perfect crime of all.

Depending on who you listened to, the Litvinenko case fitted several definitions of perfection, all at the same time.

In public, the police marked Litvinenko's death with little more than a one-liner.

On the night of 23 November 2006, at 11.00 p.m., a bulletin from Scotland Yard announced that 'Alexander Litvinenko died at 21.21 on Thursday 23rd November at University College Hospital.'

In its clunky language, the statement continued: 'Although formal identification has not taken place at this stage, we are satisfied that the deceased is Mr Litvinenko and the matter is being investigated as an unexplained death.'

It gave no cause for Litvinenko's demise and offered no hints as to the drama the police already knew would erupt with the announcement that polonium had been found in his body. As if to underline the delicacy of the case, police press officers called up reporters to make sure they understood the nature of the inquiry – an unexplained death, not yet a murder. That must have seemed an arcane distinction to Marina Litvinenko.

The following day, Scotland Yard offered one of its hallmark bland assessments that nonetheless contained the kernel of the subsequent investigation. But it still did not mention the M-word: 'murder'.

On 4 December a team of detectives, led by Holmes but not including Hyatt, flew to Moscow, working there until 20 December in a secure room at the British Embassy electronically shielded from Russian eavesdropping. The British officers were permitted to join Russian investigators in talking to some, but by no means all, of the witnesses they wished to interrogate. But they were not permitted to question them directly.

In London, meanwhile, on 6 December 2006, at 6.08 p.m. – almost two weeks after Litvinenko died – Scotland Yard finally announced that it was treating the case as an investigation into an 'allegation of murder'.

The language was vintage Scotland Yard. 'Detectives investigating the death of Alexander Litvinenko have reached the stage where it is felt appropriate to treat it as an allegation of murder.'

Still, Scotland Yard named no names. But the identities of the Russians who met with Alexander Litvinenko in the Pine Bar on 1 November 2006 – particularly Andrei Lugovoi and Dmitri

Kovtun – began to surface with increasing frequency in British newspapers as reporters revisited the polonium trail. And it was also becoming increasingly evident that the first markers had been laid down not on 1 November 2006 but much earlier indeed.

The timeline of the polonium trail was finally becoming clear, and it tracked the movements of two men in particular.

On 16 October 2006, Andrei Lugovoi and Dmitri Kovtun were among the passengers on board a Transaero plane flying from Moscow to London.

By Kovtun's own account, this was his first visit to the British capital, and he was keen to see the sights along with establishing new business relationships. But Lugovoi had been a frequent visitor, at least since January 2006, when he attended Boris Berezovsky's sixtieth birthday party at Blenheim Palace, seated at the same table as Alexander Litvinenko.

Litvinenko's supporters insisted that Lugovoi made the approach to Litvinenko, either seeking a business partner or as part of some longer-term conspiracy to get close to him. Lugovoi maintained that Litvinenko initiated the contact, offering his services as an in-place representative with contacts in London.

'About a year ago he called me – and that was an absolutely unexpected call. He asked whether I visit London. I go there fairly often. Only this year I was there twelve, thirteen times,' Lugovoi said. 'He suggested meeting during my next visit, which we did. He told me that he was prepared to introduce me to some British companies – due to ethical reasons I would prefer not to name them – which were interested in investing into the Russian economy and coming into Russia's market.'

The assertion was thus that it was Litvinenko who sought out Lugovoi, not vice versa, pre-empting any accusation that Lugovoi had gone out of his way to lure the former FSB officer into a trap.

Paolo Guzzanti, the Italian senator whose links to Litvinenko lay through Mario Scaramella, insisted it was the other way round. 'Lugovoi called Litvinenko from Moscow saying: "How are you? I'm in business, we were close friends, you can be my agent in London." Litvinenko was very pleased because Berezovsky was cutting his stipend,' Guzzanti said.

Both accounts agree on one central point: Litvinenko was casting around for an independent source of income. Berezovsky had reduced his financial support, and he was open to – indeed desperate for – offers of work, particularly those that played to his résumé as a former FSB officer.

In April 2006 Lugovoi was again in London – one of a dozen visits over the course of a year – and the nature of his putative business relationship with Litvinenko was becoming clear.

Along with a Russian-language translator, Lugovoi and Litvinenko met contacts at a company called RISC Management at 1 Cavendish Place, just off Regent Street near the five-star Langham Hotel. The two Russian men – both in good physical shape, lithe but not heavily muscled, Litvinenko slightly the taller of the two – took the lift up to the fifth floor with their female translator. They checked in at the reception area behind a glass wall and were escorted to a long conference table in pale wood located in a boardroom overlooking the rear of the grey-stone Langham.

The company offered an array of services in risk assessment, due diligence and security. Litvinenko's link to it lay through Boris Berezovsky's acquaintanceship with Keith Hunter, the RISC chief executive.*

The meeting with RISC in April 2006 did not go particularly well, according to a person who was there and who offered an account of its proceedings only in return for anonymity.

---

* The company was the successor to an outfit called ISC Global that had been wound up in 2005 under unusual circumstances. Its founder and chairman, Stephen Curtis, a lawyer with high-level Russian contacts, including Boris Berezovsky and the former Yukos chief, Mikhail Khodorkovsky, died in a helicopter crash. The company also became caught up in a separate imbroglio and denied reports of impropriety relating to the ways it gathered information from the British police on Moscow's efforts to extradite high-flying Russian émigrés.

The Russians wanted to explore a consultancy deal, offering first-hand, non-public information about events and personalities in Russia. They produced a document, written in Russian, that was presented as an insider briefing on key strategic issues relating to the Kremlin's energy and foreign policies. But their contacts at RISC Management were mistrustful.

One of them believed Lugovoi was using the presence of a translator as a ploy when, in fact, he understood perfectly well what was being said in English. Litvinenko came across to his interlocutors as 'a typical FSB guy, building fantasies out of conspiracy theories'. But RISC Management did check out the document from the Russians, first having excerpts translated, and then sharing it with a former American intelligence official. The assessment of this former CIA person was that parts of it seemed based on information that could not have come from a publicly available source.

Apart from the offering to British companies, the outlines of the business arrangement Litvinenko sought with Lugovoi were also taking shape.

Litvinenko would be Lugovoi's agent, scouting out opportunities among companies specializing in risk management, analysis and due diligence – in other words, private or covert intelligence gathering – on deals and the people making them. It was one step away from industrial espionage but was not illegal.

Lugovoi would supply what intelligence professionals call 'the product'. The two men would be paid amounts in five figures, but Litvinenko would take a 20 per cent fixer's fee, with the lion's share going to Lugovoi.

Litvinenko would also be cultivating the contacts and garnering expertise for his own purposes.

That may be where he miscalculated.

But there was no indication that Litvinenko was aware of a plot to kill him. He took his oath as a British citizen on 13 October. He appeared at the Frontline Club on 19 October to denounce Putin over the assassination twelve days earlier of Anna Politkovskaya. He was not behaving like a man who sensed he was a target.

Indeed, when Lugovoi and Kovtun arrived in London on 16 October 2006, Litvinenko acted as if it were, quite literally, business as usual.

As his co-author Yuri Felshtinsky told me much later, 'Alexander Litvinenko did not have suspicions that it was coming. In general he knew that if they have an opportunity to kill him, they'll kill him. He never thought it was going to happen in London.'

Felshtinsky also offered himself as a witness in the case, insisting that Lugovoi and Kovtun had been in London even earlier than Scotland Yard discovered – on 12 October. If that were proved, it would undermine Kovtun's assertion that the visit on 16 October was his first. 'On October 12 in London, I met Andrei Lugovoi with the second person,' Felshtinsky wrote in an e-mail. 'So far the reports were stating that Lugovoi was in London starting October 16. But I met him on October 12 around 10 p.m. at Piccadilly Street [sic]. He was walking with his friend.'

According to Lugovoi and Kovtun, when they arrived on 16 October 2006, they found that Lugovoi's personal assistant in Moscow had booked them into the Best Western hotel on the crowded pavements of Shaftesbury Avenue. Only one room was ready for occupation, so the two men left their bags and went on to meet Litvinenko.

The three men met on 16 October and agreed to meet again the following day. Kovtun seemed to suggest that there was something accidental about the whole series of encounters that brought the two Russians into contact with Litvinenko in mid-October.

'We came on the sixteenth and went to the hotel. We left our luggage – one room was ready and one was not – and left everything in Andrei's room, and we went to meet Litvinenko at Grosvenor Street,' Kovtun said. 'It was maybe fifty metres from Erinys. After that meeting we went to itsu, but I have learned the name of it only from the mass media.'

itsu, of course, was the sushi bar on Piccadilly that initially seemed so central to the entire case.

Before it became known that the three Russians ate there on 16 October the spotlight fell on a subsequent visit by Litvinenko on 1 November, when he met his Italian contact Mario Scaramella in the same place.

Indeed, when polonium traces were found in the sushi bar, many people initially assumed that they had been left when Scaramella met Litvinenko on 1 November 2006, to show him what was said to be an e-mailed hit list of the Kremlin's foes.

But several weeks later Scaramella insisted that the polonium trace at itsu had not been found in the area where he had met Litvinenko, and several British officials corroborated his claim.

As Kovtun told the story, the three Russians – Lugovoi, Kovtun and Litvinenko – held a hastily scheduled meeting on 16 October at the offices of the Erinys private security company at 25 Grosvenor Street, whose headquarters in London also handled the company's business in Russia.

Erinys had been founded five years earlier and specialized in guarding oil installations and offering private security consultants, risk assessment and business intelligence.*

The following day, 17 October, Lugovoi and Kovtun checked out of the Best Western on Shaftesbury Avenue, apparently seeking more luxurious accommodation, and moved into the upmarket Parkes Hotel in Beaufort Gardens – a thirty-three-room privately owned boutique hotel far more to their liking.

The hotel was located a hundred yards from Harrods, in a tree-lined cul-de-sac. Rooms cost from £200 for a single to £500 for a superior suite. Quite apart from business, the two Russians wanted to enjoy their stay in London in some style. The Parkes exuded a quiet sense of comfort and affluence. It had no restaurant or bar, but guests could tarry in an opulently furnished lounge behind heavy wooden doors. Its rooms offered minibars with arrays of upscale single-malt whiskies.

* The company's name was taken from Greek mythology, denoting the avenging goddesses also called the Furies.

'Our rooms are spacious, our suites sumptuous, and our staff will go that extra mile,' the hotel's website boasted. Indeed, in January 2007, the Parkes won an award naming it the most luxurious hotel in London on the grounds that, as the citation said, staying there was 'like staying in a wonderful private home'.

It soon acquired another distinction: the Parkes Hotel, along with the Best Western and the offices of Erinys and of RISC Management, was identified by the HPA as showing contamination by polonium.

On the same day that Lugovoi and Kovtun changed hotels – 17 October 2006 – there was a further meeting with RISC Management, at which, one source said, Lugovoi and Litvinenko were accompanied by 'a third man with striking black hair, possibly Georgian, who said nothing but had a laptop' containing what was said to be the product of 'black bag' operations in Moscow – the kinds of clandestine operations that require entering premises unlawfully to gather information.

The 'third man', according to this informant, 'did not resemble Kovtun or [Vyacheslav] Sokolenko' – the two other Russians most frequently associated with Lugovoi's journeys to London. Indeed, British press reports later locked on to the idea of a mysterious 'third man' in addition to Kovtun and Lugovoi. But when Lugovoi and Kovtun recalled their visits to London, they scoffed at the idea of this mysterious fellow traveller.

Lugovoi and Kovtun returned to Moscow soon after the meeting on 17 October, again flying on Transaero, a Moscow-based carrier that had been the first Russian airline permitted to challenge the state carrier Aeroflot in the freewheeling 1990s.*

---

* When British investigators asked to inspect the plane that had been used routinely on the Moscow–London route, including on 16 and 17 October, they were not able to do so, because a different plane was put into service on that same flight sector, according to a British scientist with close knowledge of the inquiry. Lugovoi always insisted that no polonium had been found on the flights carrying him into London.

Lugovoi's next known visit to London was around 25 October, and this time he used the Sheraton Park Lane, later identified as a point of such serious contamination that part of the eighth floor was blocked off for weeks.

There was a further meeting at Erinys, and a British business consultant who met Lugovoi during this trip complained later of becoming ill with vomiting and diarrhoea after an encounter with the visiting Russian.

It was during this visit that, according to Lugovoi, he dropped by Boris Berezovsky's offices on 27 October – but Berezovsky was later adamant, both in newspaper interviews and in encounters with Russian and British investigators, that the meeting took place four days later, on 31 October.

The date was significant. According to Berezovsky, Litvinenko had not been a regular visitor at the offices in Down Street for months since the two men went their separate ways. In order to check his memory, he brought his staff together, 'and everyone concluded it was October 31' that Lugovoi visited Berezovsky's offices. Berezovsky's point was to pin the bulk of the polonium contamination found at Down Street on Lugovoi.

'Litvinenko had not been here for weeks,' Berezovsky said during a conversation in the boardroom of his offices in late 2007.

Moreover, he insisted, those parts of the offices visited by Litvinenko on 1 November displayed 'eight hundred times less radiation' than those where Lugovoi had sat.

Whatever the date, Berezovsky insisted to me that the furniture Lugovoi sat on as the two men chatted had been so heavily contaminated by polonium that it had to be removed and destroyed. The confusion over the date did not, however, disguise the fact that the polonium trail started on 16 October and continued between 25 October and 28 October before it reached its grisly climax on 1 November.

At one point along the trail, radiation inspectors encountered perhaps the only humorous moment in the grim task they had been set in tracing the isotope's meanderings across London.

During their investigation, the police came across a credit card receipt tracing some of the Russians to a disco and dancing nightspot called Hey Jo at 91 Jermyn Street. The place was run by Dave West, a shrewd operator from the East End of London who had made money selling cheap wine to British tourists in northern France before opening his establishment between the expensive shirtmakers and men's shoe shops of Jermyn Street in 2005. Hey Jo was located in the basement, one floor below another of West's ventures – a restaurant called Abracadabra. A man wearing a harlequin costume and a clown's hat stood outside on the pavement to lure in guests, radioing ahead down a staircase decorated in bright jacquard colours of red and blue that customers were on the way.

Hey Jo was so popular among Russians that West's cell-phone voice mail was recorded in both English and Russian. The head manager, West said, was Russian, too.

According to West, he recognized both Litvinenko and Lugovoi as Hey Jo customers – despite Marina Litvinenko's disavowals of such behaviour by her husband.

'You remember the ones that come regularly. He was a regular. He used to have tea, but his colleagues drank. They always spent £200 to £500,' West said – a tidy sum for a man like Litvinenko, whose stipend was supposedly being reduced, but small beer for a 'New Russian' like Lugovoi on a roll in London.

West complained that the police had been slow to warn him that his establishment was under threat. Only in January 2007, he said, did he learn that Hey Jo may have been infected with polonium. Contamination was indeed found in the booth where the Russians had sat and on a stair rail.

Combined with the polonium traces found on a Shisha pipe at Dar Marrakesh in Rupert Street, the visit to Hey Jo seemed to betray a certain laddishness about the behaviour of the Russians. Indeed, Scotland Yard seemed to suspect that some of their contacts had nothing to do with business.

'Investigators ask some strange questions,' Kovtun said later, discussing the way British police questioned him in Moscow in December 2006. 'For example, did we say anything to Parkes Hotel personnel that we were not lucky today – something like that? Were we visiting some prostitutes at such and such address? But we haven't. Strange things.'

When the inspectors arrived at Hey Jo, they discovered a half-lit, low-ceilinged room with curtained booths of narrow velour benches ranged around a small dance floor delineated in the gloom by a strip of under-floor lighting that glowed a kind of cerise colour. But there was one particularly curious item of decoration alongside one of the benches opposite a well-stocked bar – a large representation of a phallus about two feet high and cast in polished brass.

In order to be certain about the extent of the contamination, the radiation inspectors were obliged to run their scanners over the entire area – and that included the phallus.

As one scientist put it later, 'It tested negative.'

The precise locations on the polonium trail only became known publicly when the HPA began sending out its daily communiqués following Litvinenko's death. But by cross-checking those locations against reliable accounts of the Russians' movements and appointments, the authorities were able to draw some initial conclusions.

For the first time, polonium had been demonstrably linked to places where Alexander Litvinenko had never been. But wherever the two visiting Russians went, polonium showed up, too.

The trail built an unbreakable umbilical link between Lugovoi, Kovtun and the radioactive substance that had taken on a life of its own.

On 31 October 2006 Lugovoi returned to London, this time accompanied by his wife, two daughters and an eight-year-old son.

The mission? If the Russian's account is true, it was to do a little business, give the family a shopping break in the British capital and watch Moscow CSKA play Arsenal at the newly opened Emirates Stadium. If British police suspicions were correct, though, his true intention was much more sinister.

The supposed pleasantries extended to what seemed a sociable visit with Boris Berezovsky.

'I want to stress one important thing. I trusted Lugovoi completely,' Berezovsky said later.*

The tycoon recalled the Aeroflot trial in Moscow when Lugovoi had been jailed for an alleged attempt to free Nikolai Glushkov, a Berezovsky ally, in the early years of the decade. 'And of course this enhanced my trust, my level of trust to him,' Berezovsky said.

There were other pleasantries to exchange. Lugovoi's company, the Ninth Wave, had provided security when one of Berezovsky's daughters, Liza, visited Russia a few months earlier.

'I wanted to thank him for providing the protection for my daughter,' Berezovsky said. 'We had a bottle of wine together with him, and the fact that I mentioned before, the chair he was sitting on both in my room and in the reception contained an awful lot of polonium traces.

'We discussed two issues,' Berezovsky continued. 'The first one was: I said I thanked him for helping my daughter. And the second he told me that he had a very successful business in Russia now. Its turnover was tens of millions of dollars. And he is very happy with this development in his life.'

Lugovoi had also asked Berezovsky's son-in-law Igor to arrange 'more than five and less than ten' tickets for the Arsenal-CSKA game, and Lugovoi picked them up either on 31 October or on 1 November.

---

* As part of the separate Russian inquiry, Berezovsky was questioned on 30 March 2007 at West End Central police station in London. Like the British officers who had visited Russia in December, the Russian investigator, Alexander Otvodov from the Prosecutor General's Office in Moscow, was permitted to listen while the British detectives read his translated questions from a prepared list. Berezovsky released a transcript of the session on the Internet, and part of it related to his meeting with Lugovoi just before Litvinenko began to sicken.

Arguably, that added to the improbabilities of what Lugovoi was accused of doing – or the cold cunning of his cover. How many assassins, after all, bring their families along for a vacation and then take in a football game immediately after carrying out the hit?

Lugovoi and his family checked in at the Millennium Hotel. According to a person familiar with the arrangements, they took two rooms, one on the first and one on the fourth floor, and Vyacheslav Sokolenko, Lugovoi's business associate, took one on the third. The family had reserved the rooms on the Internet but, when they arrived, discovered they had all been allocated single rooms. After Lugovoi's wife complained, they were reassigned to double rooms, according to a hotel staff member. (Lugovoi offered a different account later.)

On 1 November 2006, Kovtun, by his own account, flew in from Germany after a night's drinking and two hours' sleep in Hamburg. He did not have a pre-booked room and told reporters later that he shared with Sokolenko.

On that same morning, Alexander Litvinenko rose, as usual, in Muswell Hill, at Osier Crescent, and took the bus to town.

14

HIT MEN OR FALL GUYS?

As the events of 1 November 2006 unfolded, Andrei Lugovoi and
Dmitri Kovtun attended a meeting together at 58 Grosvenor
Street, close to the Millennium Hotel, at the offices of ECO3
Capital, an independent financial advisory firm acting on behalf
of a company for which the Russians had done some consultancy
work.

For the two Russians, the purpose of the meeting that day,
according to an ECO3 Capital executive, was to solicit a new
contract. For its part, the executive said, ECO3's client wanted
Lugovoi and Kovtun to produce the reports they had already
promised but failed to deliver. Throughout that meeting, Kovtun
said later, Lugovoi's cell phone jangled as Litvinenko called him
insistently, suggesting that they all meet up.

'Andrei told him, "If you have time, we will be at the Millennium
in one hour," ' Kovtun said. '"Let's meet at one of the bars. Call us
when you come. You should know we have no time."'

In other words, Litvinenko himself not only initiated the event
leading to his own downfall but actually insisted on it.

Litvinenko came to the Pine Bar, where the two Russians were
drinking, after meeting Scaramella at itsu.

He had just learned, according to Scaramella, that he was on a
list of people under threat because of his activities in denouncing
the operations of the former KGB in Italy. That had been part

of the message in the sheaf of e-mails Scaramella had shown him.

Yet if Litvinenko had taken the e-mail as some kind of fore-warning, he showed no suspicion when he met Lugovoi and Kovtun. The group gathered around one of the pale wooden tables that dotted the blue chevron carpet of the bar. Litvinenko drank tea poured from a pot that, he later told his wife Marina, was already on the table when he arrived. The others drank liquor. One witness said Litvinenko was flanked by Lugovoi and another Russian while four more unidentified Russians were sitting nearby in a circle around his table. All of them paid in cash.

The bar was popular with Russians, according to hotel workers, and their presence drew little particular attention.

In the Pine Bar, Vyacheslav Sokolenko, an associate of Lugovoi's and a former KGB bodyguard, was introduced briefly to Litvinenko, as was Lugovoi's eight-year-old son. To judge from the available accounts, the meeting was rushed, lasting no more than half an hour. At one point, Lugovoi, keen to move on to the Arsenal game, left Kovtun and Litvinenko together while he went upstairs, ostensibly to change out of his business clothes.

According to Norberto Andrade, the sixty-seven-year-old head waiter in the Pine Bar and one of the few witnesses who spoke out publicly, he went at one point to serve drinks at the table but found he was being obstructed in a manner that he did not under-stand, and he was unable to see what was happening at that precise moment.

'When I was delivering gin and tonic to the table, I was obstructed. I couldn't see what was happening, but it seemed very deliberate to create a distraction. It made it difficult to put the drink down,' he said.

'It was the only moment when the situation seemed unfriendly and something went on at that point.'

From the beginning, suspicion about the means of poisoning centred on the teapot. Hotel staff believed that it was targeted with a spray of some kind because polonium traces were found in many places surrounding the chair on which Litvinenko was sitting.

'I think the polonium was sprayed into the teapot. There was contamination found on the picture above where Mr Litvinenko had been sitting and all over the table, chair and floor, so it must have been a spray,' Andrade said. He was one of the Pine Bar staff found to have been contaminated with the higher levels of polonium on the HPA scale.

'When I poured the remains of the teapot into the sink, the tea looked more yellow than usual and was thicker – it looked gooey,' he recalled. 'I scooped it out of the sink and threw it into the bin. I was so lucky I didn't put my fingers into my mouth or scratch my eye as I could have got this poison inside me.'

There was another line of inquiry that led to the teapot.

According to a British scientist, a member of the hotel staff used the same pot to brew tea after it had been washed following Litvinenko's departure from the bar. That person, whose name was not made public, tested positive for almost the same level of polonium contamination as Marina Litvinenko.

The pot was not examined by the police until 28 November – almost four weeks later – and it still showed signs of contamination despite multiple washings in a dishwasher that had also become infected. After they discovered the teapot's significance, the police placed it in a lead-lined box to preserve it as evidence.

'The polonium was put in the teapot at the table in the Pine Bar,' a British source said. 'Either a capsule that dissolved and spread into the tea or via an aerosol or dropper of some kind fired into the spout. Once in, the polonium would begin to spread out and up from the teapot and stick to the porcelain.'

That explained the intensity of the contamination recorded in the Pine Bar.

'The traces were around the outside of the chair, up the wall, on the cash till, across the table,' another informant said.

Derek Conlon, the bar's resident pianist, had a particularly harrowing story. He arrived for work after the Russians had left and ordered a cup of coffee. The cup, it turned out, had been used by Litvinenko to drink his tea and, even though it had been through the dishwasher, was still contaminated.

'My jacket, my piano, my PA system, everything I sing through, was contaminated. I had people from the Health Protection Agency with Geiger counters in white suits going through my house. All the neighbours were saying, "What's going on?"' Conlon said. He was found to have one of the highest levels of contamination.

But the polonium traces were not only found in the Pine Bar. The door leading to a men's toilet showed a virtual outline of polonium traces in the shape of a man pushing the door to enter. A toilet stall, a washbasin and a hand drier also showed evidence of polonium contamination.

On the third floor, traces found in one of the rooms 'looked like an explosion', an informant said. 'The only item not replaced was the carpet underlay. It was on bedding, curtains, in the toilet, on picture rails, on the taps.' The third-floor room was shared, according to Kovtun, by him and Sokolenko, although Sokolenko insisted later that he had shown no signs of contamination by polonium.

The day continued.

Lugovoi, his family and Sokolenko went on to watch Arsenal and Moscow CSKA draw 0–0. On their way to the Emirates Stadium, they stopped off at a steak house in Piccadilly, and Lugovoi's wife, Svetlana, used Sokolenko's camera to snap a photograph of the group. The snapshot resurfaced later in a British newspaper. (Sokolenko claimed a journalist stole his camera to gain access to the image.) Apart from Sokolenko, Lugovoi and some of his family, the group included two young men, both identified by Lugovoi as family friends. Considering the police allegation about what had just happened, the photograph showed nothing more sinister than an innocuous family group.

But, for his part, Litvinenko was showing such intense signs of irradiation that 'you could see his palm print' on one of the surfaces he touched, a British informant told me.

After the encounters at the Pine Bar, Litvinenko showed up at Berezovsky's office to make photocopies of the e-mails Scaramella had received from Yevgeny Limarev, alluding in part to threats against Litvinenko and others.

'He came to my office,' Berezovsky said. 'On that day I was in a hurry because I was leaving England. He came to the copying machine. Later on, traces of polonium also were found there. He photocopied the documents which he had, and handed them to me. I didn't have time to look at them carefully. I passed them to my colleague and asked him to give them back to me when I come back from the business trip. Alexander insisted that I look at them immediately. I said that I didn't have a possibility to look at them straight away but possibly I would look at them while on the plane.'

Litvinenko then hitched his ride home with Akhmed Zakayev.

'Around 5.20 p.m., Litvinenko came to my car in order to go home,' Zakayev said in December 2006. 'He came straight from Berezovsky's office. We got into a traffic jam, but he felt fine. When we arrived home, I parked the car and he went home. He told me he would pop in at my house in about one hour and a half. That's all. He never came.'

Alexander Litvinenko had begun to die.

The polonium trail still had a couple of stages to run.

'The thing is that we met on the first of November and agreed to meet again on the second,' Lugovoi said later, referring to his plans with Litvinenko after the fatal events on 1 November. The two men still had some outstanding business – a response from RISC Management about the proposal they had made in mid-October. Lugovoi was still hoping, moreover, for a deal with Erinys.

'At 8.30 on November 2 he called me,' Lugovoi said of what he depicted as a fairly routine telephone conversation with Litvinenko. 'We were supposed to meet at 10.00 a.m. in one of the companies. He called me and said: "Andrei, you know, I suddenly got sick, something is with my stomach. I am spitting out my guts. I don't think I'll be able to make the meeting." Since we agreed not to take an interpreter, I told him: "It would be difficult for me without you. Let us postpone the meeting." So we agreed to postpone the meeting to a later date.' On 3 November 2006 the Russian visitors returned to Moscow.

On 1 December 2006 pathologists carried out an autopsy on Litvinenko's body at the Royal London Hospital in the East End. That particular hospital was chosen because it had special facilities for what were deemed to be hazardous postmortems.

Several physicians took part, all wearing double anti-radiation suits in a white plasticized material, taped at their ankles and wrists. They wore hoods with clear Perspex viewing screens, breathing filtered air from a battery-powered device on their belts. The examination room, swathed in sheets of disposable plastic, became uncomfortably hot because the ventilation was switched off to prevent contamination in the air ducts leading elsewhere in the hospital. While the examination was under way, the physicians communicated through a system of internal microphones, and a contractor checked them for radiation levels. Specialists looked on from an observation room. Litvinenko's body was still recognizable from his deathbed portrait – hairless and yellow. The physicians took tissue samples in part to establish the extent to which the polonium had decayed and thus the likely date of its production.

On 31 January 2007 Scotland Yard issued another of its cryptic statements: 'The Metropolitan Police Service has this morning handed a file to the Crown Prosecution Service regarding the investigation into the death of Alexander Litvinenko. We are not prepared to discuss the contents of the file.'

And much later, on 22 May 2007, the Crown Prosecution Service issued a statement by the Director of Public Prosecutions, Sir Ken Macdonald, in which he said: 'I have today concluded that the evidence sent to us by the police is sufficient to charge Andrei Lugovoi with the murder of Mr Litvinenko by deliberate poisoning.'

Finally the British authorities had identified the prime suspect by name.

'I have further concluded that a prosecution of this case would clearly be in the public interest,' Macdonald continued. 'In those circumstances, I have instructed Crown Prosecution Service lawyers to take immediate steps to seek the early extradition of Andrei Lugovoi from Russia to the United Kingdom so that he may be charged with murder – and be brought swiftly before a court in London to be prosecuted for this extraordinarily grave offence.'

That pronouncement, according to a spokeswoman at the Crown Prosecution Service, reflected an assessment that the police dossier on the case satisfied two key criteria: first, that there was sufficient evidence to ensure a 'viable prosecution' (though not necessarily a guilty verdict) and, second, that a prosecution would be in the public interest. In the British view, the Litvinenko case met both requirements. But one question the spokeswoman declined to address was whether the police had sought to prosecute more than one person for Litvinenko's murder.

The answer to that question came in a roundabout way exactly one year after Litvinenko died when Louise Christian, a prominent British human rights lawyer retained by the Berezovsky camp, addressed a news conference in London on 23 November 2007, called as part of the commemorations of Litvinenko's death.

'I believe that they investigated the involvement of other people, and the conclusion they reached was that there was enough evidence to charge Mr Lugovoi, but not any other person,' Christian said.

That seemed plausible enough. But then, in an almost offhand way, she dropped a bombshell that could only have come from Litvinenko's deathbed recollection of his time in the Pine Bar.

'At the time the polonium was put in' the teapot, Christian said, 'Lugovoi was alone with Mr Litvinenko, and there was not a third party present.'

If proved, that would be the most damning evidence so far to incriminate Andrei Lugovoi.

Yet no one flanking Christian at that news conference – Boris Berezovsky, Marina Litvinenko, Alex Goldfarb, Akhmed Zakayev and Walter Litvinenko – seemed to believe that Lugovoi had acted without orders from much higher in the chain of command. After accusing Lugovoi directly, Christian quickly added, 'That is not to say that Mr Lugovoi was acting alone.'

Berezovsky had a blunter assessment. 'I don't have any doubt that the Russian government is behind the death and definitely is responsible for the murder.'

Berezovsky never did give a detailed, scientific explanation for his allegation of Russian complicity – and the British authorities did not want him to either. 'Mr Berezovsky does not have to answer that question,' said a British detective present when Alexander Otvodov, a Russian investigator, interviewed Berezovsky in March 2007 in London.

The next step was for the Crown Prosecution Service to formally seek Lugovoi's extradition, sending a summary of the case and of the evidence (though not details of the prosecution case) to Moscow. Technically, Russia's constitution prohibited the extradition of its own citizens, but on 15 November 2006 – even as Litvinenko sickened – the Russian Prosecutor General's Office and the Crown Prosecution Service had signed a memorandum of understanding on legal co-operation. Article 3 said quite clearly: 'The Participants will co-operate in the sphere of extradition and in other issues of mutual legal assistance. Where appropriate, this shall include consultation and the provision of advice at the stage when such requests are being drafted.'

Russia's response came as no surprise to anyone, especially to those who had voyaged to Moscow.

Lugovoi's office was located in the business centre of the 410-room Radisson SAS Slavyanskaya, a supposed luxury hotel in white stone looking on to the frozen Moscow River and across to the crenellated spires of the Stalin-era Foreign Ministry.

The hotel was known as one of Moscow's fanciest, and in the lobby a low-slung Lamborghini sports car was on display, brand-new but without a visible price tag – an eloquent emblem of the ostentatious shows of wealth coveted by the so-called New Russians, men like Lugovoi who had made good in the Putin era. Even in the plumpest parts of central London, there did not seem to be quite so many Bentley coupés, dark-windowed Range Rovers, BMW X5s, Mercedes 600s and 7-series BMWs as in Moscow, locked in traffic, smeared in the toxic road muck of a Russian winter, parked up on the pavements outside fancy restaurants and nightclubs.

The large, broad-shouldered, shaven-headed bodyguard dispatched by Lugovoi to receive his guests seemed a sign of the times, too.

Lugovoi's visitors that day in March 2007 were told to wait in the mezzanine area, surrounded by paintings of the kind generally known as sofa art to denote where a purchaser might hang a new acquisition in relation to the living-room furniture.

Then, hurrying across the pink carpeting, came Andrei Lugovoi – a compact man of medium height and build, wearing a striped blue jacket.

His pace suggested a hurried schedule, but his office, in a side hall off the main mezzanine, seemed more modest than might be expected of a supposed millionaire businessman.

Lugovoi also seemed much more relaxed than might be expected of a suspected killer.

For me it was crucial to hear his story at first hand. The tone of the narrative until that point had been set – in the West at least – by Tim Bell, Alex Goldfarb and Boris Berezovsky. By contrast, the Russian PR effort seemed – to Western eyes – clumsy and unconvincing.

A few days earlier, a diplomat based in Moscow had spoken of parallel and mutually exclusive stories propelling the news in the East and the West. He was not wrong. If Lugovoi and

Kovtun were suspects in Britain, here in Moscow they were patriots and heroes.

Lugovoi's quarters offered few obvious personal clues about the man who occupied them. Against one wall an ornate, glass-fronted cupboard contained a handful of books and some souvenir bottles of liquor. One compartment contained the two-inch-thick indictment of the celebrated Aeroflot fraud court case in the early years of the twenty-first century that had sent Lugovoi to prison for fourteen months until charges were dropped.

In a corner of the office, a flat-screen television was tuned to Russia's own version of CNN – an English-language twenty-four-hour news outlet – though the sound was turned down. On his desk, Lugovoi had positioned for easy reading a copy of the *Guardian* from 26 January 2007, with a headline proclaiming him to be a suspect. A colour photograph of him took up a good chunk of the front page, and the headline proclaimed: 'The Suspect: UK Wants to Try Russian for Litvinenko Murder'.

Lugovoi served coffee from a large white vacuum jug carried from a smaller office by his personal assistant.*

For scheduling reasons, he said, he and Kovtun would be interviewed separately, one after the other.

'I want you to understand one thing,' Lugovoi said as he leaned comfortably into a high-backed swivel chair, switching his blue-eyed gaze among his guests to reinforce the point and twirling a pencil in his fingers as he spoke.

'Myself and Dmitri Kovtun, we consider ourselves the injured party. Intentionally or by accident we had been assaulted. The assertion made by the media – because there was no official statement to this effect – that polonium traces were found wherever we went only underscores that we had been attacked with polonium. And they are trying to present it so that we were using this polonium.'

---

* I waited to see him drink from a cup that had come from the same pot before I raised my own.

In other words, while the rest of the world believed Litvinenko had been the victim, Lugovoi and Kovtun argued precisely the opposite. For Lugovoi at least, his recollection of his supposed victim went way back.

In his early days as a private security consultant, Lugovoi explained, he had been head of security for the ORT television station controlled by Boris Berezovsky. In that same period, Litvinenko had been an aide to Berezovsky in his capacity as head of the Commonwealth of Independent States.

'We were not close to each other, but we met occasionally,' Lugovoi said of the man the British accused him of killing. 'It was when Berezovsky became a Duma deputy elected from the northern Caucasus and made him his aide. When Berezovsky went to the northern Caucasus, I accompanied him on several occasions together with the officers of his personal security service.'

'And Litvinenko?' I said.

'Litvinenko accompanied him, too. Litvinenko, other assistants, some other people . . .

'So when we flew together, three or four times, we exchanged views with Litvinenko. I don't even remember on what; it was not business, just something.'

The interview fast-forwarded to 2006 and the question of what had really brought him to London.

'All were business trips having nothing to do with Litvinenko. But we met.'

The relationship had been purely business?

'Business, and nothing personal,' Lugovoi said. 'And when we say business, it sounds too grand . . . he acted as an intermediary on several occasions in establishing contacts between myself and several British companies.'

As a security expert, Lugovoi made no attempt to disguise episodes at the Millennium Hotel that he might have suspected would show up clearly on CCTV surveillance footage now in the hands of Scotland Yard.

His account of the precise sequence of the confusion over hotel reservations differed from those offered by hotel staff.

Nonetheless – and this was perhaps the intention – Lugovoi's version suggested a family outing, with a child sharing a parent's bed and other family members in tow, that seemed at odds with the murderous purposes ascribed to his visit by Scotland Yard.

'On November 1, my two daughters were with me as well as my son. One daughter is nineteen, another is twenty, my son is eight. And my son was staying in the same room with my wife and myself. In fact we were surprised at the reception in this hotel, which was not quite typical for a hotel of this level.

'Since my son was to stay in the same room with us, I booked and was prepared to pay for a suite or a two-room suite so that my son could have a bed of his own. We were accommodated in a regular double. And three days running I was going to the front desk arguing with them and demanding another room for us. It was not provided, and our son had to share a bed with us. He is not a three-year-old; he is eight. This was the strangest thing which accompanied our visit. At the same time, when my two daughters were given a room which was too cold, they went and said it was too cool there, please give us another room. They immediately received another room, but the next night they moved back because the new room turned out to be even colder.

'Of course, cameras installed in the Millennium should have registered how I quarrelled with the reception desk people, how my daughter went to ask for me. My elder daughter studied at Cambridge for one year and two years in Toronto. People say her English is brilliant, so she explained to them everything in intelligible way. So my bad English could not be an excuse for their refusal. So, when some people say I was mixing polonium in my room with my son in bed there, it's simply crazy.'

After Lugovoi left, Kovtun arrived and sat in the same swivel chair, wearing a zipped black top and blue jeans.

He was almost cheerful about the events of October 2006.

'To see Westminster Abbey for the first time was fantastic!' he proclaimed with a big grin.

Thinking of them arriving in London, I imagined the two Russians, hurrying in from Heathrow, looking askance at the hotel that had been booked for them on Shaftesbury Avenue, keen to get on with the business at hand. But what was that business? If the emerging British narrative was halfway correct, then somewhere there was a small vial of some kind containing polonium-210, an invisible, elusive time bomb waiting to explode on an unsuspecting victim. But the Russians' account was diametrically opposed.

'As soon as we flew into London,' Kovtun said, 'literally as soon as we checked into the hotel on the sixteenth, we immediately met with Litvinenko. Literally after a half an hour we went for a meeting with him.

'While we were on the plane, Andrei told me that there was a man that was offering to meet with serious English companies, which work in the gas and oil sector. Moreover, the company that we visited was located on the same street. Grosvenor Street 58. When I came to London, I was not going to meet with the company. But such a meeting was proposed, and I thought, why not.'

Kovtun gave the impression of a person who wanted to be liked, always looking for a smile from his interlocutors, always ready with a wisecrack.

When word of polonium poisoning first emerged in London, Kovtun and Lugovoi dramatically checked into Moscow's No. 6 hospital, ostensibly to be tested for evidence of radiation sickness. Kovtun had even been seen with a bald pate that mimicked the appearance of the sick Litvinenko. Now his hair was growing back in a salt-and-pepper stubble. He had shaved it, he said, because hair follicles were particularly vulnerable to contamination, and he feared his own head might be impregnated with radiation.

In the interview Kovtun insisted that he had been 'seriously' contaminated but had survived his brush with radiation without long-term health risks.

'The most horrible thing for me in this whole story is that I could have killed the children of my former wife in Germany. That was the most frightening,' Kovtun protested with some indignation.

But, like Lugovoi's, Kovtun's strongest message was his insistence that Litvinenko was the source, witting or unwitting, of the polonium contamination blamed by the British and German authorities on himself and Lugovoi.

'All I think is that, at the moment of our meeting, Litvinenko was seriously polluted,' Kovtun said. 'This is what I think. This is why I shaved my head, because he was sitting next to me. There was a moment when Andrei went upstairs with his family to change before the soccer game. And I was standing with him in the lobby. I don't like standing so close. I was standing too close to him. He kept talking and talking.

'On the first of November, we didn't speak with Litvinenko for a long time, but he looked strange, and he was sitting next to me,' Kovtun said. 'He kept talking, he didn't close his mouth. And this is why I thought that if infection by polonium was possible through breath – and moreover we were sitting at the same table – I thought about what the consequences could be.'

But there was a gap in their narrative.

If Litvinenko was poisoned in the Pine Bar, the British accusation maintained, then he was killed by polonium slipped into a pot or cup of tea. But who ordered the tea, and who saw Litvinenko drinking it? What had transpired in the vital few minutes when Lugovoi left the Pine Bar ostensibly to change his clothes, and after he returned? Those were questions the Russians – like Scotland Yard – refused to answer.

There was a moment in the conversation when I had the impression that Kovtun in particular wanted to convey the impression that Litvinenko's behaviour was irrational, as if he were drunk or even taking drugs. But those were not accusations Kovtun wanted to make in public. What he did want to say was that, contrary to the version of events that had taken root in the West, Litvinenko was the source of the polonium – both at their meetings on 16 October 2006 and at the fateful encounter over tea at the Pine Bar on 1 November.

'So where did the tea come from?' I asked Kovtun. 'He ordered his own tea?'

'Of course I remember this, but I am not going to talk about it,' he replied.

'Was that the day you were exposed?' I asked.

'I think that was the day,' he said, seeming to confuse the dates of his first and second visits to London in mid-October and early November. If he was contaminated only on 1 November, how could he have left polonium traces on a date-stamped official German document on 30 October?

So how did the polonium get to Germany?

'I think that Alexander had a contact with polonium either purposefully or unintentionally before that,' Kovtun said. 'When we met, we shook hands with each other, then he gave us documents dealing with the Erinys company.'

Kovtun laid out what he called his theory, suggesting that Litvinenko had self-administered polonium as part of his crusade against the Kremlin.

'For example,' Kovtun said, 'the Institute of Biophysics, a well-known Moscow institute, has a large group of scientists who sometimes perform experiments on themselves. For example, thirty employees carried out the following experiment.

'For example, this group drinks different amounts of liquids with caesium in it. It is a radioactive nuclide, which leaves similar traces, but in concentrations that are not dangerous to one's health. Then they explore different ways of removing this caesium from their bodies. And every day they conduct analysis and write diagrams like this. These things are not dangerous, but with a certain approach you can declare to the world that someone has tried to poison you.

'If you, for example, confuse caesium with polonium – this is just a version – it would be easy to come to other results.'

So what was he actually accusing Litvinenko of doing?

'I just told you a story,' he said with an enigmatic smile. 'He was a strange guy. Even to me, a stranger to him at that time, he told me strange things. I did not once take seriously anything that he told me.'

Later, Kovtun mused on the curious coincidences of the polonium trail, inferring from its sequences that he and Lugovoi had been placed in harm's way. In Britain the police had drawn the opposite conclusion.

'When they began to tell the addresses where the traces of polonium were found, we realized that we visited those addresses only on the sixteenth and the seventeenth. I thought that my contact was from there, since they found it in Germany, it could only have been brought from there. And when I realized that those traces stayed for a long time, I thought that they could have only come from there. I had never had any contact with polonium, or with any radioactive substance.'

'Could it have come from Germany?' Kovtun was asked.

'It's kind of a vicious circle. And it came to Germany from London,' Kovtun insisted.

But if the Russians were telling the truth, why did Scaramella – whom Litvinenko met on 1 November – show no sign of contamination? Why was no polonium found on the Oyster card Litvinenko used on the morning he left Osier Crescent?

Sitting first with Lugovoi and then with Kovtun for almost three hours, I felt as if, like Alice, I had entered a topsy-turvy wonderland where my preconceptions were upended. There were indeed two narratives – at least – but none was more striking in that afternoon's conversation, conducted through the *New York Times* Russian interpreter Viktor Klimenko, than the assertion by both men that they were in fact the victims, if not of what Lugovoi called an 'attack', then certainly of a massive conspiracy.

London's hit men were Moscow's fall guys.

Not only that, they maintained, they were as mystified by the whole puzzle of Litvinenko's death as we were, even though there was no disputing that they had been sitting with him on the day – and possibly at the very moment – when he ingested a massive dose of polonium-210. Of the two, Lugovoi seemed the more evasive, more economical in disclosing some of the key aspects of his stay in London, more skilled in the art of diversionary digressions.

But they both seemed confident enough in suggesting that the British had got it all wrong. Their manner was almost swaggering, exuding confidence, neither contrite nor uncertain. They arrived without advisers, spin doctors or lawyers. There was no hesitation in their delivery, no dent in their projection of their own righteousness. Of course, they had known each other long enough to synchronize their versions.

What was most remarkable was the way both men had taken the chronologies and events established by the London police and turned them into a different story altogether – a technique long familiar to students of disinformation, as much in Moscow as in Washington.

In the West, Litvinenko cast himself as a whistle-blower, a thorn in the Kremlin's side who might one day be brutally expunged.

In Moscow, the entire weight of the counter-narrative by Lugovoi, Kovtun and their backers was devoted to depicting Litvinenko as a trivial player, a flake, a non-person. Several serving and retired FSB officers went out of their way to play down the importance of their former colleague, asserting that he simply did not rank high enough in the lists of the Kremlin's foes to merit assassination (the corollary presumably being that more significant foes might well be rubbed out).

'He was just a clown,' Kovtun told us. The antipathy seemed to be mutual. As he sickened, Litvinenko told his wife that 'some guy he really didn't like had turned up with Lugovoi'. As far as Litvinenko was concerned, 'he hadn't liked the man because he had said something about how he doesn't give a damn about anything in life except money.'

I recalled the cautionary words of one of the German investigators in the case: legends, he said, always beware of the legends.

15

PUTIN'S DOPPELGÄNGER

After the British authorities formally identified Andrei Lugovoi as the prime suspect in the murder of Alexander Litvinenko, matters proceeded rapidly to judicial and diplomatic stalemate. Manoeuvring to extend his leadership of Russia, Vladimir Putin dismissed Britain's call for Lugovoi's extradition as 'pure foolishness' and demanded that Britain hand over the results of Scotland Yard's investigation so that Lugovoi could be tried in Russia. Britain rejected the demand. In any event, Putin insisted, Russia's constitution prohibited the extradition of its citizens to foreign lands. The Kremlin, in other words, was in no mood to cooperate – or make gestures that could be seen as weakness or an admission of guilt.

The British response was not long coming.

Under a new administration in London led by Gordon Brown, Britain ordered the expulsion of four Russian diplomats on 16 July 2007. It was the latest in a series of expulsions over the decades that had provided a barometer of the state of relations between London and Moscow.

John Scarlett, the head of MI6 at the time of the Litvinenko affair, had himself been expelled from Moscow for spying in 1994.

The orders in 2007 were far less dramatic than those of an earlier British administration in 1971, when 105 Soviet Embassy personnel were told to leave London – the biggest mass expulsion by any Western government. Many of those told to leave Britain had been denounced by Oleg Lyalin, a KGB officer working undercover in London as a Soviet trade official. Oleg Gordievsky later described the expulsions that year as a severe setback for Soviet intelligence. In return, the Kremlin ordered eighteen British diplomats to leave Moscow.

In 2007, the British government justified the newest expulsions by going public with the broad outlines of its case against Lugovoi. The authorities offered no detailed evidence – but, nonetheless, it was an unusual move in the light of Britain's restrictive laws covering pre-trial publicity.

'It is part of the prosecution case that on the afternoon of November 1, Mr Litvinenko drank tea which he had poured, after an invitation from Mr Lugovoi, from a teapot which was later found to be heavily contaminated with polonium-210,' David Miliband, the foreign secretary, said, taking advantage of the legal privilege enjoyed by statements to the British parliament.

'There is also evidence that shows a trail of polonium-210 on aircraft in which Mr Lugovoi travelled to and from London.'

Litvinenko died 'of an acute radiation injury', Miliband added. 'The facts are therefore that a UK citizen has suffered a horrifying and lingering death; his murder put hundreds of others, residents and visitors, at risk of radiation contamination; and the UK government have [sic] a wider duty to ensure the safety of the large Russian community living in the UK.'

The signal to Moscow was not exclusively hostile. Miliband prefaced his remarks by tallying the areas in which British and Russian interests overlapped, quite separately from the Litvinenko case: international diplomacy on climate change, Iran, Kosovo, the Middle East and Sudan. Russia, he said, was a 'key international partner' in fighting terrorism, in combating the proliferation of weapons of mass destruction and in matters such as illegal migration, drugs and international crime. Tellingly, Miliband also acknowledged 'considerable benefits for the City of London' from its financial and trade relationship with Russia.

At a time when the price of oil was heading for $100 a barrel and Britain's own supplies of North Sea oil and gas had peaked, the question was whether Britain would place the long-term advantages of friendship with Russia ahead of its moral concerns about the death of Alexander Litvinenko.

Indeed, beyond words and gestures, what power did Britain have to force Russia to do anything? Britain's ability to project influence had shrunk irrevocably with the crumbling of empire and the global ascendancy of the United States. Formally, the European Union supported the demand for Lugovoi's extradition, but continental Europe, too, was heavily dependent on Russian gas supplies. And how realistic was the British demand? Russia was hardly likely to extradite one of its own citizens when Britain was not prepared to reciprocate by delivering up Boris Berezovsky and Akhmed Zakayev, as Moscow had frequently demanded.

At the time of Miliband's announcement, officials at the Foreign Office in Whitehall were not sure how Russia would reply. But in matters of expulsions and espionage, a tradition dating from the 1980s suggested that the Kremlin would generally respond to expulsions of its diplomats by sending home exactly the same number of foreign diplomats from Moscow.

Moscow's riposte came as something of a relief.

On 20 July 2007 – four days after Miliband's announcement – Russia ordered four British officials out of Moscow. On the surface, the balanced expulsions revived memories of the Cold War, but there was a sense among British diplomats that Moscow's response was not out of proportion and did not presage a breach in relations.

That certainly seemed to be the message from Vladimir Putin, who said in remarks carried on Russian state television: 'It is necessary to measure our actions with common sense, to respect the legitimate rights and interests of partners, and everything will work out in the best way . . . I am sure we will cope with this mini-crisis.'

The outcome left British officials in a self-satisfied mood, calculating that a line had been drawn, demarcating moral from commercial concerns without creating a full-blown crisis abroad or drawing criticism at home, or losing income for British businesses. The cynicism underpinning the mutual expulsions left Litvinenko's supporters seething with rage.

'In the nineteenth century the British navy would have sailed to St Petersburg and started bombarding,' Vladimir Bukovsky, the Soviet-era dissident, told an audience at the release of Litvinenko's book *Allegations* on the first anniversary of his death. 'In the twentieth century, they would have broken off relations . . . I am afraid the British government did not stand up to the test . . . They kicked out only four people. So what have they got? It's ridiculous, it's weak, and it's appeasement. We all know what appeasement leads to. We have had one world war caused by it already.'

In all of this, the United States seemed little more than a bystander, reluctant to become embroiled in a fight over Litvinenko at a time when it was involved in the much bigger dispute with the Kremlin over its plans to station an anti-missile defence system in Eastern Europe – almost Russia's backyard. But in February 2008 the US Congress did take a stand in the form of a resolution, endorsed by the Foreign Affairs Committee of the House of Representatives, expressing 'significant concerns about the potential involvement of elements of the Russian government in Mr Litvinenko's death, and about the security and proliferation of radioactive materials'.

The resolution also urged the Bush administration to press Russia 'to ensure the security of the production, storage, distribution, and export of polonium-210 as a material that may become dangerous to large numbers of people if utilized by terrorists'.

The dispute between Britain and Russia took on some more arcane characteristics.

In June 2007, in the Queen's Birthday Honours Diplomatic List, Oleg Gordievsky, the one-time double agent and Soviet defector to Britain, was honoured for 'services to the security of the United Kingdom,', becoming a Companion of the Most Distinguished Order of Saint Michael and Saint George, or CMG – a decoration less than a knighthood but relatively exclusive.

The honour seemed a deliberate snub to Russia, recalling one of the most humiliating episodes in the KGB's Cold War history. The slight was not something the Kremlin was prepared to ignore.

In November 2007, Russia awarded the Order of Friendship to George Blake, a British intelligence officer said to have betrayed the identities of possibly hundreds of British agents in the early years of the Cold War. Blake was eighty-five years old when his honour was made known – just days after the Kremlin gave its highest award posthumously to another high-value spy. George Koval, an American of Russian descent, had provided the Soviet Union critical intelligence about the Manhattan Project, which produced America's first atomic bombs. His espionage reports were held to have helped the Soviet Union build its own device in 1949.

When the honour was announced on 2 November 2007, Vladimir Putin's office said Koval was 'the only Soviet agent who infiltrated secret US nuclear facilities that produced plutonium, enriched uranium and polonium for building atomic weapons'. The citation's reference to polonium was not accidental.

The Kremlin was signalling its scorn.

The awards for the Soviet intelligence veterans once again reminded the outside world of the esteem in which Putin and his allies in the Kremlin held their alma mater – the KGB. That should have been comforting news for Andrei Lugovoi, shielded by the Kremlin from extradition and displaying a growing self-confidence in Moscow. On frequent occasions he accused Britain's security services of trying to recruit him and of conspiring to kill Litvinenko as 'an agent who got out of the secret services' control', as he put it.

Time and again, Lugovoi assailed the British security and intelligence services for their purported complicity in Litvinenko's death. He went so far as to accuse Litvinenko of being an MI6 recruiter who became too garrulous, too much of a loose cannon, boasting publicly of his links to British intelligence and embarrassing his handlers. It was the British, Lugovoi said, who paid Litvinenko's wages – £2,000 a month – and the British who hired him to trawl the Russian business and *émigré* world for informers and agents.

But was Litvinenko really a British secret agent? Or was he more a person on the restless fringes of the mainstream intelligence community, seeking a point of entry to pursue his commercial goals as a purveyor of information?

True, many of the people Litvinenko met and sought to do business with in his final months in London had roots in British law enforcement, the military and, possibly, intelligence. In the world of private security companies in which they moved – raising private armies to guard pipelines in Iraq, scouring the gossip of Moscow for snippets and nuggets of information about Putin and his entourage, seeking former FSB and KGB contacts to work for them – it would have been surprising if none of Litvinenko's contacts had links of some kind with the security and intelligence establishment.

Or, to put it another way, it would have been very surprising indeed if the British intelligence agencies were not at all interested in the activities of an entire community of secretive characters devoted to gathering commercial and political information.

But Lugovoi's accusations contradicted the recollections of some of the most senior people with knowledge of Litvinenko's defection in 2000 and of his subsequent relationship with Britain's spymasters.

In the year 2000, Litvinenko arrived in London at a moment when the nascent friendship between Tony Blair and Vladimir Putin had trickled down to their respective security and intelligence services, permitting collaboration that would have been inconceivable in the Cold War. It was not a time that looked kindly on disaffected intelligence officers from beyond what Winston Churchill had once labelled the Iron Curtain. A new era had come. Before the London–Moscow friendship chilled, fugitive spies and mischief makers were an embarrassment.

In this cruel new marketplace, Litvinenko had little to sell. He had given away what he thought was his last big secret to the Americans at their embassy in Ankara, offering details of the smuggled technology used in the Dudayev killing in Chechnya in 1996. The CIA had dismissed his offering as insignificant. The British seemed to do the same.

'Litvinenko turns up in London and puts himself around and frankly is not very interesting,' a former British intelligence officer recalled in a conversation in 2007, before Lugovoi began reciting his litany of accusations. 'Having presented himself as someone with a great knowledge, he just did not know very much. He wasn't a big deal at all. In fact he was a bit of a pain in the neck. At the time he turned up, he was not a very important player.

'Alexander Litvinenko attracted a lot of attention among Russians living outside' their own country, the former officer said. 'The irony is that the [British] intelligence agencies weren't interested. The Russians were much more interested.'

That assertion coincided with an account that Oleg Gordievsky offered in late 2007 in response to Lugovoi's increasingly shrill denunciations of Litvinenko as a British secret agent.

'I spoke with him heart to heart, brain to brain and eye to eye on many occasions, and he told me about every interesting encounter he had, so I know this was not the case,' Gordievsky said. 'He was invited to MI6 on two occasions to provide education on how the Russians worked, but he was not given any operational tasks. He was paid £800 for each of these lectures, but that is all. He believed if he impressed MI6 he would one day be able to ask them for a job which would later give him a pension. But MI6 told him they were not going to employ him any more, and this deepened his depression, as this had been his secret plan.'

Lugovoi's claims, he said, were 'utter nonsense'.

Marina Litvinenko, too, denied that her husband had been recruited as a British spy – as she might well be expected to – although she did admit that he had been paid for information about Russian organized crime syndicates and businessmen in London. 'He talked with officials at the Home Office about his former work, but he didn't know exactly who they were,' she said.

From the very beginning, MI5 and MI6 sought to forestall the inevitable accusations that they had played a part in the events that led to Litvinenko's death or used him in some way to recruit Russians transiting London.

The Russian intelligence services followed a somewhat more tangled game plan. At first, the FSB leadership – and Putin himself – dismissed Litvinenko out of hand as insignificant, a guard for truck convoys and railway transports. Then the FSB seemed to change tack, permitting his accused killer to depict him as a tool or even an active agent of the British intelligence services – a safe propaganda ploy since, as a British security official explained to me, 'They knew very well that we would never confirm or deny publicly the identity of anyone on our books.'

If Litvinenko was a secret agent during his self-exile, then he chose a remarkably public way of going about it, denouncing Putin, decrying the death of Anna Politkovskaya, seeking to penetrate a world of secretive and aggressive tycoons and politicians where vast fortunes were quickly made and fiercely guarded.

Yet when he began to die, he was treated by the British authorities as an unknown: unlike Gordievsky's dramatic rescue from Moscow in 1985 by British secret agents, no one came to pluck the ailing Litvinenko to safety.

The supreme paradox was that his death achieved far more than he looked likely to attain in life. It amplified his accusations against Putin beyond anything Litvinenko had written in his books or on dissident websites.

It transformed him into Putin's doppelgänger.

The spectral image of Litvinenko on his deathbed would haunt the Russian leader for years. The names of two former KGB lieutenant colonels – Putin and Litvinenko – would be linked in search engines, movies, photo libraries, television documentaries, books and articles for evermore.

The death of Litvinenko would come to be seen as a defining moment of the Putin presidency. Putin sought to restore

Moscow's greatness. The death of Litvinenko ensured that Russia's reputation as a land to be feared for the worst of reasons was revived for all the world to see – at least in its relationship with Britain.

In December 2007 the Russian Foreign Ministry announced that it would close two offices of the British Council – a cultural agency financed by the British government – in Yekaterinburg and St Petersburg. 'The British side has deliberately deteriorated relations with Russia,' said Sergei Lavrov, Russia's foreign minister.

Russia's hardball tactics secured plaudits from unexpected quarters. In December 2007 *Time* magazine anointed Putin as its Person of the Year, ahead of other contenders, including former Vice President Al Gore and General David Petraeus, the American commander in Baghdad.

Despite – or perhaps because of – the chill he brought to relations with the outside world, Vladimir Putin seemed on track to perpetuate his power.

On 10 December 2007 Putin announced that he would support Dmitri Medvedev – his viceroy in Davos a few months earlier – in the presidential elections scheduled for 2008. Medvedev duly let it be known that Putin would become his prime minister. The Russian constitution reserved supreme executive power for the president, but the constellation of forces taking shape in the Kremlin suggested that Putin was not done yet with reshaping his land.

If Litvinenko did not behave like a secretive spy, neither did Lugovoi display any of the reticence that might be expected of an accused murderer.

In December 2007 Lugovoi was elected a member of the Duma – a move that Russia experts judged unlikely without the high-level approval of the Kremlin. On his pre-election tours of remote reaches of Siberia as a candidate for the far-right Liberal Democratic Party, people clamoured for his autograph. He was hailed as a defender of the motherland against the perfidious British. He compared his victory to spitting in the face of the British authorities.

As a legislator, Lugovoi enjoyed immunity from prosecution, at least inside Russia; if he travelled outside Russia, the British let it be known, they would seek his arrest under an international warrant. But Lugovoi showed no concern at the British threats. In one documentary, he was filmed in a variety of roles – accepting the praises of his new political party, receiving a pair of snakeskin Texan boots as a gift at a birthday party, hunting on the Volga River with his buddy Dmitri Kovtun, blasting away somewhat ineffectively with shotguns at ducks. Was the interpretation, perhaps, that a man who could not kill a duck was hardly likely to poison a spy? Or was it more brutal: this man had no fear of getting blood on his hands, no compunction about deploying disproportionate firepower against a weak and wounded creature?

But there was a much darker side to the balancing act played out by Andrei Lugovoi.

If he was at any stage held responsible for the Kremlin's embarrassment at the course events had taken, then he was as much in the potential firing line as Litvinenko had been – not in a city such as London, where CCTV cameras and zealous detectives tracked murderers, but in a huge metropolis that was no stranger to gun law.

Lugovoi rode about town in a 7-series BMW tracked by a chase car of bodyguards: as much as he was running from British justice, he was constantly on the lookout for a rougher, Russian version of it in Moscow. Indeed, it must have crossed his mind that his own demise would bring the Litvinenko affair to a close in what Muscovites knew from experience to be a familiar and expedient manner.

While Scotland Yard did not say so in public, officers came to believe that the murder of Litvinenko was bungled. Serving and former detectives with contacts at Scotland Yard concluded that the attack on 1 November 2006 – whoever carried it out – had been preceded by at least one earlier attempt to poison Litvinenko using a lesser dose.

'The first attempt failed, so whoever did it came back and

finished the job,' one former law enforcement official told me.

That explained the polonium trail between London and Moscow and the traces found at locations linked to three different dates in October and November 2006. When the assassins' first attempts failed, these detectives believed, they – or their handlers – resolved to use a massive dose of polonium to ensure a quick and mysterious death. The killers would escape undetected. Certainly that theory was supported by the enormous traces of polonium found in the Millennium Hotel – not just in the Pine Bar but also in guest rooms and the nearby toilet.

But the plan failed for the simplest of reasons: Litvinenko thought the tea he was offered tasted odd. He took only a couple of sips. 'There was a miscalculation,' a senior detective said. 'He should have drunk it all, become ill very quickly and no one would have known what was wrong with him. The tests would not have been done.'

In this British scenario, polonium would never have been identified as the toxin. Litvinenko's death would have come more quickly and have remained undiagnosed and unsolved. It would not even be called murder. But among the restive *émigrés* of London, including Boris Berezovsky, the message would come through loud and clear: enemies of the Kremlin were vulnerable wherever they were, as the new law passed by the Duma in the summer of 2006 intended them to be. The message would resound through the ranks of the FSB: officers who decamped or defected or showed anything less than total loyalty would meet this dreadful, secret fate – an excruciating, inexplicable death. Yet there would be no way of proving murder, or establishing the identity of a perpetrator – unless someone botched the job and thereby laid a polonium trail for Scotland Yard to follow.

Without the evidence available at a trial, it was impossible for outsiders to evaluate either Lugovoi's denials or the accusations of the Crown Prosecution Service. If he was a killer, he was certainly no secret assassin.

Having gone to jail in the Aeroflot fraud case, for allegedly trying to help Berezovsky's ally Nikolai Glushkov escape, Lugovoi had become embroiled in the battle of the titans between Berezovsky and the Kremlin following Putin's ascent to the presidency in 2000. He had befriended the man he was accused of killing and had sipped wine with a tycoon who, at various times, had sponsored both of them.

He was hardly a stranger at court.

Clearly, there were elements of Lugovoi's past that might have aroused suspicion. If a man had spent fourteen months in prison, as Lugovoi said he did, then emerged to claim a business worth millions, was it possible that some kind of payoff had been made to reward him for his troubles? Or, at the very least, if Lugovoi had spent that period in jail, then surely there was adequate opportunity for someone to make clear that the price of his freedom would sooner or later be extracted in a more nefarious way than is customary in the West. Both theories had their adherents: if Lugovoi was not 'turned' in prison, then he was bought when he was released.

But, perhaps naively, Litvinenko seemed not to recognize in Lugovoi the dark qualities that the British police later ascribed to him.

'Sasha said he was maybe quite an open person,' Marina Litvinenko said. 'Lugovoi had been in prison, and that meant he had lost something in his life. And when they met each other, because Sasha has been in prison, it means they have something to share. But maybe more common between them was that Lugovoi had his business. Sasha was just looking to start something, and Lugovoi may be starting something in London.'

But there was a mystery in this relationship, too.

By the time Lugovoi began frequenting London, he was an avowed millionaire, taking the 1,500-mile British Airways flight from Moscow a dozen times in as many months, as if it were no more than a commute.

Despite his relationship with Berezovsky he had prospered in Vladimir Putin's Russia.

Yet Berezovsky and his entourage stood for everything Putin

resented and despised among the oligarchs held responsible for bringing a proud Russia to its knees in the 1990s.

Lugovoi's association with a close Berezovsky aide in London could hardly have gone unnoticed in a city honeycombed by Russian secret agents and informers. So how could Lugovoi maintain this friendship with Boris Berezovsky unless it was approved by Vladimir Putin himself or someone close to him? Certainly Lugovoi may have been the Kremlin's stalking horse in the Berezovsky camp. But some Scotland Yard detectives came to believe that he was vulnerable to pressure, undertaking a mission for his former bosses in the KGB under the threat of losing his wealth and status back home.

Among the many theories that blossomed (and were denied by Lugovoi) was this: Lugovoi spiked Litvinenko's tea, but had been told that he was administering something far less lethal or volatile than a radioactive isotope. His mission was to get alongside Litvinenko, leaving him in a position where others would be able to carry him off, interrogate him, frighten him, silence him.

A possible parallel lay in the case of Ivan Rybkin, a Russian politician supported by Berezovsky who disappeared mysteriously during the presidential election campaign in 2004, in which he was a candidate, albeit without much hope of success. Rybkin went missing for five days, claiming later that he had been lured to Ukraine under false pretences, drugged and subjected to unspecified compromising acts recorded on videotape – a longstanding KGB tactic used in the Cold War to discredit adversaries of the Kremlin.

Rybkin subsequently withdrew from the presidential race.

The single incontrovertible fact was that Lugovoi was closely linked to the presence of polonium in London.

The forensic trail led directly, almost literally, to his door. But the clumsiness of the handling of this most capricious isotope suggested that whoever scattered its confetti-like traces from Moscow to Hamburg to London had not been well briefed or was unaware of its properties.

At the same time, the technicalities of polonium production in Russia's closed cities meant that the isotope could not have been simply diverted from the commercial supply chain. Polonium was produced to order in minute amounts; its short half-life meant that it could not simply be stored for years until required; it must, therefore, have been produced on demand for a specific purpose.

If Litvinenko's supporters – and British security officials – were to be believed, only the FSB would have the power and the long-established laboratory facilities to do that. 'You have to control the whole industry to create this kind of poison,' Yuri Felshtinsky, Litvinenko's co-author, said.

That was not the only version, of course.

'Polonium is just a demonstration. It's like a visiting card left at the scene of the crime,' said Stanislav Belkovsky, a Russian Kremlinologist whom I met in Moscow in early 2007. 'Polonium was used just to show it was the secret services,' Belkovsky said. 'If the FSB were really involved, they would have used another tool.' His remarks echoed those of a former British intelligence official who told me that 'if he had been murdered professionally by the FSB, I don't think we would know he had been murdered.'

Indeed, the polonium trail went cold a long time before it produced direct evidence of high-level complicity. While Lugovoi and Kovtun both claimed to have been contaminated, there was never any suggestion of radiation inspectors prowling the corridors of the Kremlin or the Lubyanka seeking vestiges of polonium.

'It would be unlikely that some individual would undertake this without getting consent,' a British official said, 'but it would be very unlikely for anyone to go right to the top and get a written order.'

In the absence of explicit orders, this official told me, the most probable scenario would resemble that which led to the murder of Thomas à Becket, the twelfth-century English cleric killed by royal supporters after King Henry II asked: 'Will no one rid me of this troublesome priest?'

'Another variant of this is that there is an informal traitors' list,' a former State Department official told me. 'It gets circulated through a thuggish community of ex-agents with the message that if this person were to meet with some kind of accident, you would get some credit from it. That would not require high-level approval. It's people thinking: this is how they show their patriotism.'

The theory was convenient since it avoided the issue of who, specifically, approved the complicated manoeuvres required to acquire, package and transport polonium-210 as a toxin. In other words, it sidestepped the question of whether the West was dealing with a Russian leader ready to order – or at least not prevent – assassination on foreign soil.

If it was assumed that Vladimir Putin exercised control at the apex of a 'vertical' power structure, then an act with the ramifications and consequences of Litvinenko's death could surely not have been conceived without authorization or at least prior knowledge at the highest level. But if the Kremlin, as it insisted, was not involved in Litvinenko's death, what did that say about the authority of the supposedly all-powerful cabal of former KGB officers running Russia?

By denying involvement, Marina Litvinenko mused during one conversation, was the Kremlin tacitly acknowledging that it had lost control of its radioactive supply chain? 'It means you don't have any serious control of it,' she said. 'Russia pretends to be a serious country and control everything. But nobody controls Russia at all.'

Yuri Felshtinsky summed up the versions neatly. 'Either he was killed by his enemies or by his friends,' he said in early 2008.

One of those friends, of course, was Boris Berezovsky, who had his own theory about the motives for the killing. It had been designed, he said, to 'kill two rabbits' at once. One intention of the killers was to silence the troublesome Litvinenko and thwart his inquiries into the business affairs of such prominent figures as

Vladimir Putin and Roman Abramovich. But the subliminal intention was to lay the blame at Berezovsky's own door. 'I think the plan was to kill Litvinenko and create a story that I was the person who planned to kill him,' Berezovsky said in March 2008. The plan, however, faltered, he said, when polonium was identified as the toxic agent and it became evident that the Russian state controlled the production and distribution of the isotope. So how did he respond to those who accused him of killing his former aide? 'I do not pay any attention to people who try to accuse me that I am behind the death of Litvinenko,' he said, ascribing such accusations to 'political motivation created by people in the Kremlin, Putin and people around him'. Neither did he believe, Berezovsky said, that Litvinenko's death could have been an accident.

Berezovsky did, of course, have close ties to the main players – Lugovoi and Litvinenko in particular. But he also treasured his status in Britain as a political refugee, shielded from extradition to Russia. Any suspicion attaching to him in the Litvinenko case would most certainly have brought an abrupt halt to Britain's hospitality towards him. And in Russia, only jail – or worse – awaited him.

One year after Litvinenko died, the only undisputed fact known to the public was that Britain wanted Andrei Lugovoi to face a murder trial in London and he did not wish to attend it.

Scotland Yard's investigation did not extend to the question of who ordered the hit. On that issue, the blogosphere went into overdrive with its anonymous commentators spinning their webs of speculation.

One theory was that Litvinenko killed himself – either to embarrass the Kremlin or as a result of a nuclear-smuggling venture gone awry. No law enforcement officer I spoke to supported this idea, or its corollary that the polonium was part of some terrorist plot inspired by Litvinenko's sympathies for the Chechen separatist cause. It was conceivable – though unlikely – that polonium might have been sought by terrorists for one of its historic purposes as a trigger for a nuclear explosion. But that would require a high degree of scientific knowledge and the additional diversion of beryllium – the second isotope used in the triggers of early atomic weapons.

Litvinenko's association with Chechen separatists, particularly Akhmed Zakayev, nonetheless encouraged some conspiracy aficionados to suggest that he was part of a terrorist plot to smuggle radioactive materials into Britain to build a dirty bomb or a suitcase bomb.

But the arguments seemed flawed. Many British and American experts said polonium was probably the wrong choice of isotope to use in a radiological device, certainly in the amounts discussed in the Litvinenko case. In any event, it was difficult to see what political advantage could accrue from such an attack, turning British public opinion against the Chechens and jeopardizing Zakayev's protected status in Britain.

In Washington, Vahid Majidi, an assistant director in the Weapons of Mass Destruction Directorate of the FBI, acknowledged that terrorists were on the constant lookout for radioactive materials. 'We have seen intelligence traffic showing that various terrorist groups are interested in getting their hands on anything that can do harm, including those that can be ingested. They are very non-discriminatory: they are looking for anything,' he said.

He went on: 'If you look at polonium specifically, it's an expensive element to use for a terrorist activity. It just doesn't make sense to use polonium-210. It needs a good amount of capital outlay. It has to be ingested or injected.' Unlike other forms of radioactivity, 'alpha radiation can be stopped with a sheet of paper', and while 'as a poison it is incredibly effective', it would be far more difficult to deploy it as a weapon creating mass casualties.

After Litvinenko's death the International Atomic Energy Agency in Vienna let it be known that until late 2007 it had been made aware of only nineteen cases relating to the unlawful diversion, loss or theft of polonium, mostly in the United States.

But there was one episode that seemed to suggest that someone somewhere had been interested before 2006 in getting his or her hands on polonium-210.

According to the IAEA, 'The incident allegedly involved an attempt to illegally transport several containers of Po-210 to Ukraine. The material was seized.'

If there had been one attempt to smuggle polonium out of Russia, was it possible – as some bloggers and critics of Litvinenko suggested – that he himself had been trafficking the polonium that killed him?

'If the polonium was needed for murder, the motive for smuggling is clear,' a senior IAEA official said. 'If smuggling is the issue, the motive is not clear.'

Nonetheless, the use of polonium rang alarm bells among nuclear regulators and experts.

Until Litvinenko's death, the deepest fear of Western security agencies had been a 'dirty bomb' terrorist attack using conventional explosives to spray a deadly hail of radiation.

Now the perception changed dramatically.

'The assumption that has to be put aside is that the dirty bomb is the only way to do it,' the senior IAEA official said. 'There are other ways – water supplies, airflow in the subways, at the entrance to subway stations. The consequences are multifaceted and unpredictable.'

To unnerve a major city, in other words, there did not necessarily have to be a big bang.

Those ideas found a powerful echo in an article that appeared in the autumn of 2007 in a quarterly publication called *Survival* published by the respected International Institute for Strategic Studies in London.

It described the Litvinenko case as 'likely the first provable act of radiological terror.

'The Litvinenko affair . . . graphically illustrates something known for a long time: once inside the body, even a minute quantity of a radioactive material can be deadly. In light of this reminder, it is important to re-evaluate the threat posed by radiological terror.'

The authors came up with a name for this new threat, I³ – 'inhalation, ingestion and immersion attacks' – and sketched a variety of scenarios: poisoned water supplies, radioactive water sprays, inhalation of airborne particles in theatres, sports arenas, concert venues.

The dirty bomb, the authors concluded, was 'not the worst-case scenario.

'By forcing their victims to ingest or inhale radioactive material, or by immersing them in radioactivity, terrorists could do much worse in respect to public health – physical and mental – and the financial costs of an attack. Some of the most deadly I³ scenarios are among the simplest to execute. They could credibly kill hundreds and contaminate a much wider area than a dirty bomb. Moreover, and perhaps more importantly, an I³ attack would scare the public more than a dirty bomb. Academics, analysts and decision-makers can no longer afford to ignore them.'

In the twilit world of speculation the versions proliferated.

In Rome, Senator Paolo Guzzanti – a close political ally of the former prime minister Silvio Berlusconi – developed a theory that the origin of the Litvinenko case lay in the Mitrokhin Commission, which the senator himself had chaired.

Encouraged by Mario Scaramella, Litvinenko had testified in front of a video camera that he had been told Romano Prodi was a KGB agent – an allegation Prodi vigorously denied. Nonetheless, the accusation had been repeated under rules of parliamentary privilege by Gerard Batten, a British legislator at the European Parliament, on 29 December 2006. 'Since Alexander can no longer testify to this effect, as he was ready, willing and able to do,' Batten said, 'I am pleased to provide this service for him.'

In July 2007 I met Guzzanti at his cluttered offices above the Piazza delle Cinque Lune – Five Moons Square – just off Rome's cobbled Piazza Navona with its outdoor cafés, fountains and statues, pavement artists and mimes.

'The motive is the key question,' Guzzanti said. 'They killed him because he threatened the main Russian agent.' By that, he meant Prodi – a bitter adversary of Berlusconi and his Forza Italia party, which Guzzanti represented. The central idea of the Guzzanti theory was that Litvinenko was murdered to protect Prodi's cover (if anything, the episode succeeded only in spreading the allegation against him). Guzzanti also offered a different chronology – one that sought to explain what happened in the missing few hours between Litvinenko's departure from Osier Crescent and his arrival at the itsu sushi bar. 'Litvinenko was poisoned around noon at the Millennium,' Guzzanti insisted, rejecting the case laid out in Parliament a few days earlier by David Miliband, the British foreign secretary. 'In the Pine Bar in the afternoon nothing happened. It wasn't poisoned tea.'

Guzzanti's theory shared some ground with a version offered soon after Litvinenko's death by Oleg Gordievsky, who argued that Litvinenko ingested the poison before he met Mario Scaramella on the afternoon of 1 November 2006.

In January 2007 Gordievsky said he believed the poison was administered by 'a professional killer using a European Union passport. The killer left, not to Moscow, but to some other destination, using a route where there are no checks – Harwich, Cherbourg, Eurostar.' In this version, Litvinenko was 'already poisoned when he came to the sushi bar', and the episode in the sushi bar was part of the conspiracy to divert attention to Scaramella, and away from the real killers. Guzzanti's theory was only plausible if you accepted that the prime minister of Italy was an agent of the former KGB and Russia's top spy in Europe. Not everyone was prepared to make that leap, least of all Prodi and his supporters.

Guzzanti's account did overlap at some points with the views of other people. One idea common to several people interested in the case was that Lugovoi was in a strong position to befriend Litvinenko because of their common past in the Berezovsky camp and because of Litvinenko's need for a business partner in Moscow.

Nonetheless, there are critical discrepancies between Guzzanti's version and that of Scotland Yard with its emphasis on the Pine Bar as the location of the poisoning.

If Litvinenko had been poisoned at noon, then he would have begun to show symptoms of severe radiation sickness earlier in the day. His anniversary dinner at home with his wife and son would almost certainly have been pre-empted by the first symptoms of his decline.

Perhaps one of the most striking aspects of the whole affair was Litvinenko's readiness to trust Lugovoi.

On the surface, the two men had little in common, either as comrades in arms or in their relationship with the Kremlin.

They had been in different sections of the KGB. Litvinenko had patently burned his bridges, leaving former comrades seething with anger inspired by his accusations against the FSB at his news conference in November 1998. But the two men were not strangers. Lugovoi may have had high-level contacts that would interest Litvinenko. If anyone from Moscow had the credentials to get alongside Litvinenko, it was Lugovoi: not only did he have the other man's confidence, but he also had the opportunity to meet him on common ground when his guard was down. He was in a position to lull his former comrade into a false sense of security and persuade him that riches would soon come his way through their new common ventures.

With Litvinenko's links to Berezovsky fraying, Lugovoi offered a lifeline. When Litvinenko became ill, after all, his first accusations fell on Mario Scaramella, not Andrei Lugovoi.

As Yuri Felshtinsky said in one of several conversations, 'It's a great mystery to me how Litvinenko did not become suspicious' about his new business partner.

Shortly after my first visit to Moscow I travelled, closer to home, in more genteel neighbourhoods, to talk with Vladimir Bukovsky in Cambridge. His manner was warm, welcoming. Litvinenko's death had in some ways returned him to a prominence he could never have anticipated when he befriended the former KGB agent and his family, giving them entrée into the circle of dissidents with whom Bukovsky felt comfortable. Bukovsky had no doubts that

Lugovoi and Kovtun had played a role as agents of some higher, less visible power. It was even possible, he said, that they had been unwitting tools, drawn into a conspiracy whose parameters went far beyond their knowledge of them.

The role of Lugovoi, he said, 'was only to bring polonium in. And he probably didn't know what it is. He was told: just smuggle this small capsule and give it to so-and-so, there and there.

'And he suspected he might be set up. And that's very common in the KGB. So he must have become suspicious. Probably was paid good money, saying: "Look, this is what you have to give to the service." And he agreed, but was very suspicious.

'Lugovoi apparently, probably even, did not know what he was doing,' Bukovsky continued. 'He was used as the best connection to get close to Sasha because he used to be friends long ago and they still maintained relations. So it was a very good way to approach him.'

It was perhaps the most charitable of the theories about what precisely happened on 1 November 2006.

There was still the question of a specific motive.

Litvinenko had made a lot of enemies: he betrayed the FSB by holding it up to criticism as corrupt and murderous. Individual officers among his former colleagues nurtured a profound and personal sense of resentment towards him. It would be natural enough for them to seek vengeance.

The historical echo was clear from the defection of Nikolai Khokhlov in the 1950s: only when the KGB officer thought he had escaped the Kremlin's long reach did an assassin penetrate his guard, attacking him with a radioactive isotope. And the main intention was to punish a defector so as to discourage treachery in the future.

'The main motive was that Litvinenko had defected from the FSB,' Felshtinsky said in November 2007, shortly before the first anniversary of Litvinenko's death. 'If he had sat quietly in London, they would probably have left him alone. But he didn't.'

There was little doubt that the press conference in 1998 at

which Litvinenko sought to expose corruption within the FSB drew much hostility – and at a very high level. In one of several conversations, Felshtinsky told me about a lengthy meeting with General Yevgeny Khokholkov – Litvinenko's superior in the URPO unit of the FSB, who had no love for his former subordinate's whistle-blowing.

On 22 May 2000, Felshtinsky said, he went to visit Khokholkov at a restaurant he owned, 'to see if something might be done to "forget" Alexander Litvinenko' and permit him to lead a normal life in Moscow.

'We had a very long conversation – five hours. He explained to me that the answer is no. There's no way they are going to pardon him,' Felshtinsky recalled. 'He committed treason . . . He basically explained to me that Alexander Litvinenko is not going to be pardoned by the system and the system is going to punish him. He just put his hands together and said: "If I ever meet him in a dark corner, I'll kill him with my own hands." He said: "I'm joking," but he wasn't joking at all.

'They hated Alexander Litvinenko quite strongly after that press conference. It was mainly the press conference. The thing is that he went public. Internally they could discuss many things. But the press conference – and siding with Berezovsky – not only he went against the system, but he sided with Berezovsky in fighting against the system. This raised the level of his crime.'

Another theory suggested a more materialistic motive.

According to Yuri Shvets, the Washington-based former KGB operative, Litvinenko accepted – or solicited – work for a risk analysis company, compiling reports on leading figures in the Kremlin. Shvets had held the rank of major in the KGB, working undercover as a Tass correspondent linked to the KGB residency in the Soviet Embassy in Washington from 1985 to 1987. From around 1990, he made his living in the West as a consultant advising on security and intelligence matters.

In September 2006 Litvinenko sought his help, and Shvets provided an eight-page document concerning a business deal that involved a very high-ranking Kremlin insider. Litvinenko received the document on 20 September 2006 and 'within the next two weeks he gave the report to Andrei Lugovoi. I believe that triggered the entire assassination,' Shvets told the BBC.

By this account, Lugovoi himself showed the document he received from Litvinenko to the person it related to, whose identity has never been publicized.* The report's findings prompted a British company to pull out of a deal in the making with the unidentified senior Russian, who lost 'dozens of millions of dollars', Shvets said. According to this theory, Litvinenko's murder was ordered as an act of vengeance.

'Litvinenko was trying to make a name for himself using other people's documents,' a person who claimed to have seen the Shvets report told me. 'The document looked like classic KGB, giving a psychological profile of a senior Kremlin figure.' This informant also mentioned a name from the very highest and most powerful levels of those surrounding Vladimir Putin.

After Litvinenko's death, events seemed to prove that the idea of extrajudicial killing by the security services was not at all improbable. The Russian authorities even admitted it.

In August 2007 Yuri Chaika, then the prosecutor general in Russia, announced the arrest of ten people implicated in the contract killing of Anna Politkovskaya. Chaika blamed outside forces for the killing, claiming it had been carried out to discredit the Kremlin. But he said quite openly that those under arrest included a police major, three former police officers and a former FSB officer. The ten men, working with a criminal gang led by a Chechen underworld figure, had operated in two groups, first to place Politkovskaya under surveillance and then to kill her. The former FSB officer was identified by Politkovskaya's former employers at the *Novaya Gazeta* newspaper as a lieutenant colonel, Pavel A. Ryaguzov, who worked for a unit of the FSB investigating crimes by its own officers.

* Various names have emerged, all from Putin's inner circle.

Politkovskaya had reported intensely on developments in Chechnya, and after her death Litvinenko pledged to unmask her killers. As it turned out, his own destiny caught up with him before he was able to inquire into Politkovskaya's fate. But, like her, he had been fascinated by Chechnya, no longer as an FSB officer touched by the First Chechen War, but as a polemicist exposing the possible roots of the second.

Indeed some analysts insisted that Litvinenko's accusations, blaming the FSB for the apartment-block bombings that preceded the Second Chechen War, provided a compelling motive for murder – but why would the killers wait so long to exact their vengeance?

Above all, the question remained: who gave the order? To some extent that was just shorthand for asking whether Vladimir Putin, the president of an assertive new Russia, was prepared to order the murder of a man he claimed was not worth knowing.

In Western eyes, Putin had far more to lose by ordering an assassination than by continuing to ignore Litvinenko's virulent attacks on him. But as events showed so graphically, if he had foreknowledge, he did nothing to prevent the killing, and once it had happened, he did nothing to facilitate Lugovoi's extradition, remaining aloof as the accused killer paraded himself for election to the national legislature.

The British police investigation put Putin in a difficult position.

If this was merely some kind of sinister play that had got out of hand among ill-disciplined underlings, he could barely admit that his authority had been so easily flouted. If the conspiracy reached higher, into the Kremlin itself, he could not admit it without implicating himself or his associates. And, as the strongman leader of a nationalistic land, he could hardly hand over a Russian citizen to the justice of foreigners without a humiliating loss of face.*

---

* For ultra-conspiracy theorists, Britain's demand for Lugovoi's extradition created a convenient counterweight to Russia's insistence that Berezovsky be sent home. But it may stretch the fevered imagination too far to argue that Litvinenko's death was devised by the Kremlin to incriminate Lugovoi and thus give Moscow a bargaining chip in its long-running effort to secure Berezovsky's repatriation. On the other hand . . .

In the end, the simplest theory of all emerged from the polonium trail. Traces of the isotope had been found everywhere Andrei Lugovoi and Dmitri Kovtun had stayed overnight or dropped by for a conversation or a drink. The trail, moreover, showed that traces of polonium had been left at places in London on three distinct dates.

And few experts doubted that the source of the polonium lay within Russia – an assertion the Russian authorities strongly denied.

Indeed, in late 2007, Russian investigators maintained that their inquiries into the Litvinenko case had failed to establish the origin of the polonium and that they had no idea where it might have come from.

'The first phase of the investigation has shown that the polonium has no identification signs,' Alexander Bastrykin, head of the investigative committee at the Russian Prosecutor General's Office, said in a newspaper interview cited by the RIA Novosti news agency. Bastrykin did not say where Russian scientists obtained the sample for its investigations or how they had drawn their conclusion. Theoretically, the only known source available to Russia would have been in the contamination of Lugovoi and Kovtun when they went to the hospital in early December 2006. It seemed odd for a Russian official to acknowledge that the polonium was available in amounts large enough for forensic analysis. 'We are trying to determine the polonium's original source, which is very important,' Bastrykin said.

The same question had preoccupied Western investigators.

In December 2006 Mark Hibbs, a nuclear specialist living in Bonn, argued that the amount of polonium used in the killing, though quite large in terms of toxicity, was 'too small for most conventional forensic techniques used to obtain chemical signatures'.

In other words, it was unlikely that the polonium used to kill Litvinenko would be traced back to Russia with the kind of certainty required in a court of law.

But Hibbs by no means ruled out a high level of official

connivance. According to the investigators he had spoken to, he said, the amount used in the Litvinenko case was large enough 'to suggest that it was not diverted from a known civilian application by black marketeers but was removed directly from a government-supervised nuclear establishment, and that the perpetrators were to some extent familiar with the challenges of handling it'.

The quest for a motive defied easy answers.

Litvinenko had been making inquiries about the collapse of Yukos – an affair that had claimed many high-level casualties. According to Berezovsky, moreover, Litvinenko had been involved in investigating money laundering and property deals in Spain relating to an oligarch with a very senior Kremlin backer.

When people talked about Litvinenko's freelance projects, they spoke of inquiries into the affairs of people such as Roman Abramovich and Vladimir Putin. But if Litvinenko had been in a position to make some disclosure, one Russian specialist believed, he would have done so in public. 'We have first to forget the version that he was killed because he knows something, because if he had known something, he would have published it,' said Andrei Soldatov, the Moscow journalist and intelligence specialist who talked at length with Litvinenko in 2003.

There was a theory, too, that power brokers in the Kremlin among the so-called *siloviki* engineered the death of Litvinenko as part of byzantine conspiracies within the power clans that had grown up since Putin's rise to power. The intention was to force Putin into a hard-line response that would distance him from the West and make it more difficult for him to dismantle his Kremlin power base as the nation headed for the presidential elections in March 2008.

'Litvinenko was killed by one of the *siloviki* clans, not on the direct orders of Putin, Patrushev or the KGB,' said Yevgeny Limarev, the Russian security analyst living in France whose e-mails to Mario Scaramella attracted much attention on 1 November 2006.

'So somebody is interested in making things more rigid in Russia, to create a new Berlin Wall.'

But 'no one expected this to be discovered,' Marina Litvinenko said. 'And when people say: "Why not kill him like Anna Politkovskaya?" I say: "Because it's London. They'll find it immediately." CCTV cameras – it's so easy because it's open. Anna was killed by a gun in Russia. And they couldn't do it exactly the same in London, because it's different country.'

But London did not offer the protection Litvinenko expected of it.

If he had lived his latter years as a crusader seeking regime change in Russia, Alexander Litvinenko died in vain, and his death offered a cruel warning to others who might emulate him.

True, he besmirched the name of Vladimir Putin, linking it for ever to an allegation of murder. But Litvinenko's death hardened Russia's resolve to show itself as an authoritarian counterpoint to the liberal West. Perhaps his death brought him a perverse kind of status, offering a memory in perpetuity that he would never have achieved in life. But most of all, Sasha's story showed that events do not conclude with sharp edges, or the defeat of evil, or the words 'happily ever after'.

Sasha's story ended without justice.

EPILOGUE

On 23 November 2007 a knot of people in dark clothes gathered in the gated parking lot of Highgate West Cemetery below the pale stone turrets of the deconsecrated chapel at the burial ground's entrance. The weather was icy, with a blustery wind.

It was exactly one year since Alexander Litvinenko died, and this was the memorial arranged by the same close friends, family and associates who gathered in December 2006 to bury him. Walter and Marina Litvinenko arrived along with Litvinenko's son Anatoly. Marina wore Prada sunglasses and sombre clothing. Her son wore a hooded top and blue jeans. Litvinenko's mother, Nina Belyavskaya, was there, and so was Sonya, his daughter from his first marriage. Boris Berezovsky swept in, his hallmark Maybach tailed by bodyguards in a black Mercedes SUV. His third wife, Elena, arrived separately in a chauffeured Bentley. Among the denizens of Londongrad, Akhmed Zakayev and Vladimir Bukovsky attended this tribute to their fallen comrade. So did Alex Goldfarb and the filmmaker Andrei Nekrasov. Just under a year earlier, they had struggled with Litvinenko's heavy coffin. Now they had no burden beyond their memories and, for some, enduring grief.

Once assembled, the memorial party moved off on the familiar route, up steep, dark, worn steps, along a broad, overgrown pathway where the fallen leaves had become frozen, half-decomposed, on to the gravel that led to the Litvinenko tomb. There was still no headstone, and a photograph of the former KGB officer – an amateurish shot taken with a flashbulb against a background of brown wooden panelling – peered back at those who had come to praise him. As they gathered under a pale wintry sun, a robin chirped, then a cell phone. Wearing a cream beret, Nina Belyavskaya approached the tomb clutching a white plastic bag marked 'Personal laundry' and withdrew from it a candle, a cleaning cloth and red satin hearts emblazoned with Russian words in Cyrillic script meaning 'I love you and remember you'. Pointedly, like a mother silently reprimanding an errant daughter-in-law, she wiped grime from Litvinenko's photograph, lit the candle and prayed.

Sonya Litvinenko wept, her shoulders heaving below a cascade of blonde hair.

Walter Litvinenko removed his cap.

Akhmed Zakayev raised his upturned hands in Islamic prayer.

Boris Berezovsky crossed himself in the Orthodox Christian manner. His wife laid a wreath of long, slender lilies bound in thick black ribbon. Marina Litvinenko, clutching a bouquet of red and white roses, fixed her gaze on the grave flanked by its British neighbours – the Smiths, the Otways.

It was a moment to recall that in all the sound and fury, the politics, the international manoeuvring, very simple and familiar events had occurred: a woman had lost her husband; a mother had buried a son; children mourned their father.

A premature death had robbed them all.

There was much else, too. Some of those at the graveside were famous now. Marina Litvinenko and Alex Goldfarb had written a book, signed a movie deal. They had given scores of interviews across Europe and the United States. They had devised campaigns to seek justice from the European Court of Human Rights. They believed the British coroners' courts might one day force Scotland Yard to open its findings to scrutiny. They believed they knew who, ultimately, was responsible.

'It is almost certain that the Russian state or government was involved in supplying the polonium-210 used in poisoning Alexander Litvinenko,' their lawyer, Louise Christian, told a press conference in central London, just before the quiet moment in Highgate West Cemetery.

But the survivors were nowhere near a prosecution, or closure.

In some ways it had come down to a propaganda war, a long-range contest with the protagonists 1,500 miles apart, fighting not simply for justice but for advantage.

'One day we definitely will know who was responsible for this, because without this knowledge we just cannot feel we are safe,' Marina Litvinenko said. Watching them all, I had the feeling that this was but a modest army to raise against the massed battalions of the Kremlin.

But what of Andrei Lugovoi, the man accused of murdering her husband?

'I am waiting for him here in London,' Marina Litvinenko said.

ACKNOWLEDGEMENTS

My thanks are due to many people at the *New York Times,* particularly Bill Keller for supporting my desire to write this book – and giving me time to do so – Jill Abramson for her keen interest in the story and Susan Chira for her unflagging support in covering it. The staff of the London Bureau provided incisive coverage of the Litvinenko story, and in the Moscow Bureau I am particularly grateful to Viktor Klimenko and Nikolai Khalip, along with the former bureau chief Steven Lee Myers and the correspondents Chris Chivers, Michael Schwirtz and Andrew Kramer, and Mark Landler in Frankfurt.

I owe a special debt to three people who played a huge role in the research and interviews: Mark Franchetti in Moscow, Elisabetta Povoledo in Italy and Stewart Tendler in London.

At Doubleday Broadway, I was greatly helped by the editors Charles Conrad and Bill Thomas. My agent, Michael Carlisle of Inkwell Management, was – as ever – a friend, guide and inspiration.

For an understanding of Russia, I spoke with, among many others, Anthony Robinson in London and Celestine Bohlen and Alison Smale in Paris. I would also like to thank Robinson for showing me an unpublished manuscript, translated by him from the Italian and covering much ground in modern Russia. People with knowledge of security, diplomacy, intelligence and law enforcement, whose names may not be published, offered me their versions of the events of November 2006. I hope they will recognize their valuable contributions.

Most of the scientists and academics who helped me are identified in the book. In addition, Milton Leitenberg of the University of Maryland provided advice and access to his archive of published sources.

I thank all my family for putting up with my reclusiveness during the writing of the book, and most of all I thank my wife, Susan Cullinan, for her unstinting and invaluable support as researcher, editor and muse. It could not have happened without her.

NOTES AND SOURCES

PROLOGUE The reconstruction of Litvinenko's movements on 1 November 2006 is based on interviews with many people, including Marina Litvinenko and Akhmed Zakayev. The description of the route to central London was drawn from personal observation.

CHAPTER ONE: BROKEN HOMES, BROKEN EMPIRE The accounts of Litvinenko's early years and career are drawn from interviews in Moscow with his mother, Nina Belyavskaya, and his first wife, Natalia Litvinenko, and with the British novelist Gerald Seymour in England.

CHAPTER TWO: POOR MAN, RICH MAN Boris Berezovsky's remarks were made in several interviews in London and in his personal appearances. His three-volume collection of articles and interviews – *The Art of the Impossible* – was also useful. George Soros's comments are from a lengthy telephone conversation. Three books provided valuable material on Berezovsky in the 1990s – Paul Klebnikov's *Godfather of the Kremlin*, Chrystia Freeland's *Sale of the Century* and Alex Goldfarb and Marina Litvinenko's *Death of a Dissident*.

CHAPTER THREE: ACOLYTES References to Alex Goldfarb are based on several personal interviews with him and on *Soros: The Life and Times of a Messianic Billionaire* by Michael T. Kaufman. I also drew on personal interviews with Andrei Lugovoi and Lord Tim Bell. Dispatches from the Associated Press were helpful, as was the Rich List published by the *Sunday Times*.

CHAPTER FOUR: RENEGADE Interviews with Natalia Litvinenko and Marina Litvinenko offered valuable insights. The photograph of Litvinenko's second wedding was seen in *Death of a Dissident*, which also referred to the Vlad Listyev murder case.

CHAPTER FIVE: WAR STORIES Details of Litvinenko's experiences related to the Chechen wars were provided by Akhmed Zakayev in an interview, Alexander Gusak quoted by the BBC, and Martin Sixsmith in *The Litvinenko File*. Chechen war reporting here and in other chapters was drawn from accounts in the *New York Times* by Michael Gordon and Michael Specter. Personal interviews with Jos de Putter and Andrei Nekrasov offered more detail. I also drew on Litvinenko's *Lubyanka Criminal Group*. The story of the clandestine videotape is based on an account in the *Wall Street Journal* of 23 May 2007. The transcript of Litvinenko's press conference was published by the Official Kremlin International News Broadcast. Much early archival material was found by Alain Delaquérière of the *New York Times* research department.

CHAPTER SIX: FROM RUSSIA WITH STEALTH The account of the Litvinenkos' escape from Russia drew primarily on conversations with Yuri Felshtinsky, Alex Goldfarb, Marina Litvinenko and Vladimir Bukovsky. I also found details in Alex Goldfarb's foreword to *Lubyanka Criminal Group*, translated by Viktor Klimenko of the *New York Times* Moscow Bureau, and in *Death of a Dissident*.

CHAPTER SEVEN: *SILOVIKI* The account of Davos, 2007, is from personal observation, including Medvedev's media and dinner appearances. The remarks by Thomas Graham are from 'The State of U.S.–Russian Relations and the New Bush Administration'. Vladimir Putin's autobiographical comments are largely from *First Person*, a series of interviews conducted by three journalists. I also drew on published articles in the *Sunday Times*, Reuters, *The Economist* and the Trusted Sources website. The account of Anna Politkovskaya's murder is based on Michael Specter's article in the *New Yorker* of 9 January 2007. I also referred to Steven Lee Myers's reporting of the Yandarbiyev trial in the *New York Times*. *Kremlin Rising* by Peter Baker and Susan Glasser has interesting detail about the Khodorkovsky case.

CHAPTER EIGHT: GILDED EXILES Reporting for this chapter came from news reports in London, estate agents and personal interviews by myself and staff of the *New York Times* London Bureau, particularly Sarah Lyall and Heather Timmons. Simon Sebag Montefiore's *Young Stalin* offers useful historical background. Peter Clarke's remarks about terrorism in Britain came from the Colin Cramphorn Memorial Lecture, which he delivered in London on 24 April 2007.

CHAPTER NINE: CROWN PROTECTION? Sonya Litvinenko's remarks were made in an interview, as were Vladimir Bukovsky's and Andrei Soldatov's. Robert Service's comments were made in an article in the *Sunday Times*. I quoted from *Blowing Up Russia* by Yuri Felshtinsky and Alexander Litvinenko. The quotation from Sergei Lysyuk was carried by the Associated Press. Neil Barnett's article appeared in the *Spectator*. The text of Mikhail Trepashkin's letter was published in the *Chronicle of Political Persecution in Present Day Russia* (Dec. 2006).

CHAPTER TEN: A ROLODEX TO DIE FOR For details of Mario Scaramella, Elisabetta Povoledo provided reporting and archival material. The Mitrokhin Commission's classified DVD showed Litvinenko interviewed by Scaramella. Yevgeny Limarev spoke to me on several occasions, as did Maxim Litvinenko. Julia Svetlichnaya talked to me in London. Details of Scaramella's actions concerning the IMO emerged from published accounts and *Lloyd's List*.

CHAPTER ELEVEN: POISON AND PR Details of Litvinenko's illness were provided by Marina Litvinenko in interviews with me and in an interview published in Russia by Natalia Gevorkyan. Litvinenko's attitude towards Islam was covered in interviews with members of his family, Alex Goldfarb and Akhmed Zakayev. The PR aspects emerged from interviews with Tim Bell, Jennifer Morgan and Natasja Weitsz. The origins of Litvinenko's deathbed testament were covered in conversations with Alex Goldfarb, Marina Litvinenko and Akhmed Zakayev and in *Death of a Dissident*.

CHAPTER TWELVE: INVISIBLE ASSASSIN Two memoirs were invaluable: Pavel Sudoplatov's *Special Tasks* and Nikolai Khokhlov's *In the Name of Conscience*. The US Army report on radiation poisoning was obtained by the Associated Press. Norman Dombey's theories emerged in interviews after an article he published in the *London Review of Books* on 2 August 2007. Details of the discovery of polonium came from *Marie Curie: A Life* by Susan Quinn and from Curie's personal writings on radioactive substances. The fate of Dror Sadeh is chronicled in *The Bomb in the Basement* by Michael Karpin. An early study into polonium for the US Atomic Energy Commission was written by Fred A. Bryan and Louis B. Silverman. Radiy Ilkayev and Yekaterina Shugayeva spoke to various Russian media outlets. Details of Russia's closed nuclear cities are laid out in 'Conversion and Job Creation in Russia's Closed Nuclear Cities' by Oleg Bukharin, Frank von Hippel and Sharon K. Weiner, published by Princeton University in November 2000. A definitive report on polonium as a poison was written by John Harrison, Rich Leggett, David Lloyd, Alan Phipps and Bobby Scott and published in the *Journal of Radiological Protection* (March 2007). Raymond Guilmette's remarks were in an interview and in *Health Physics News*, 2 February 2007. For an understanding of the chemistry of polonium, I spoke to Michael Clark of the Health Protection Agency. James McNish of Britain's Royal Society of Chemistry also made archival material available, particularly 'The Chemistry of Polonium' by K. W. Bagnall, published in 1957.

CHAPTER THIRTEEN: THE POLONIUM TRAIL This chapter draws on public statements by the Health Protection Agency, the British police and British Airways. Pat Troop and Paolo Guzzanti spoke in interviews. Details of the police investigation and the polonium trail are based on personal reporting in London, Moscow and Hamburg. Litvinenko's time at UCH was described by Geoff Bellingan and others both to me and to

Popular Science in June 2007. The description of Hey Jo is based on personal observation. Reporting relating to Erinys and RISC Management was based largely on confidential sources.

CHAPTER FOURTEEN: HIT MEN OR FALL GUYS? The interviews with Lugovoi and Kovtun took place in Moscow on 2 March 2007. The questioning was conducted by me and by Steven Lee Myers, the *New York Times* Moscow Bureau chief, translated by Viktor Klimenko of the *New York Times* Moscow Bureau. Apart from my own conversations, staff at the Millennium Hotel spoke to the *Daily Telegraph* in July 2007, the *Los Angeles Times* on 9 December 2007, and *USA Today* in February 2008.

CHAPTER FIFTEEN: PUTIN'S DOPPELGÄNGER Litvinenko's standing with British intelligence in 2000 was described by confidential sources. The British police assessment of the events leading to Litvinenko's death was provided by sources who requested anonymity. Yuri Shvets spoke to the BBC. Mark Hibbs's analysis was published in *Nuclear Fuel*, 4 December 2006.

EPILOGUE The description of events at Highgate Cemetery is based on personal observation.

SELECT BIBLIOGRAPHY

Baker, Peter, and Susan Glasser. *Kremlin Rising*. Lisa Drew/Scribner, 2005.

Curie, Marie. *Radioactive Substances*. Dover Publications, 2002.

Felshtinsky, Yuri, ed. *The Art of the Impossible*. Vols. 1–3. Terra-USA, 2006.

———. *Verdict*. Terra-USA, 2007.

Felshtinsky, Yuri, and Alexander Litvinenko. *Blowing Up Russia*. Gibson Square, 2007.

First Person: An Astonishingly Frank Self-Portrait by Russia's President Vladimir Putin. Public Affairs/Perseus Books, 2000.

Freeland, Chrystia. *Sale of the Century*. Little, Brown, 2000.

Goldfarb, Alex, and Marina Litvinenko. *Death of a Dissident*. Simon and Schuster, 2007.

Jack, Andrew. *Inside Putin's Russia*. Granta Books, 2004.

Kaufman, Michael T. *Soros: The Life and Times of a Messianic Billionaire*. Alfred A. Knopf, 2002.

Khokhlov, Nikolai. *In the Name of Conscience*. Frederick Muller, 1960.

Klebnikov, Paul. *Godfather of the Kremlin*. Harcourt Books, 2000.

Litvinenko, Alexander. *Allegations*. Aquilion, 2007.

Montefiore, Simon Sebag. *Young Stalin*. Weidenfeld and Nicolson, 2007.

SELECT BIBLIOGRAPHY

Politkovskaya, Anna. *Putin's Russia*. Harvill Press, 2004.

Quinn, Susan. *Marie Curie: A Life*. Da Capo Press, 1995.

Service, Robert. *The History of Modern Russia from Nicholas II to Putin*. Penguin, 2003.

Shevtsova, Lilia. *Putin's Russia*. Carnegie Endowment for International Peace, 2005.

Shvets, Yuri. *Washington Station: My Life as a KGB Spy in America*. Simon and Schuster, 1994.

Sixsmith, Martin. *The Litvinenko File*. Macmillan, 2007.

Sudoplatov, Pavel. *Special Tasks: The Memoirs of an Unwanted Witness, a Soviet Spymaster*. Little, Brown, 1994.

INDEX